1st ANNUAL EDITION

2015

CRAFTER'S

MARKET

How to Sell Your Crafts and Make a Living

Kelly M. Biscopink, Editor

Fons&Porter

CINCINNATI, OHIO

fw

www.fwmedia.com

Distributed in Canada by Fraser Direct
100 Armstrong Avenue
Georgetown, ON, Canada L7G 5S4
Tel: (905) 877-4411

Distributed in the U.K. and Europe by F+W MEDIA INTERNATIONAL
Brunel House, Newton Abbot, Devon, TQ12 4PU, England
Tel: (+44) 1626 323200, Fax: (+44) 1626 323319
Email: postmaster@davidandcharles.co.uk

Distributed in Australia by Capricorn Link
P.O. Box 704, S. Windsor NSW, 2756 Australia
Tel: (02) 4577-3555

ISBN-13: 978-1-4402-3978-6
SRN: T0022

Edited by Kelly Biscopink
Designed by Hannah Bailey
Production coordinated by Greg Nock

Attention Booksellers: This is an annual directory of F+W, a Content + eCommerce Company. Return deadline for this edition is December 31, 2015.

CONTENTS

MARKET LISTINGS

© Tonia Jenny

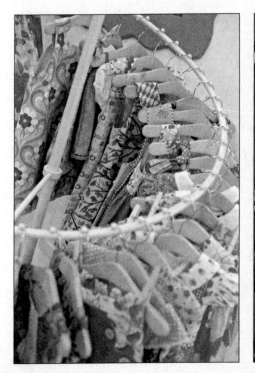

© Lindsay Wilkes

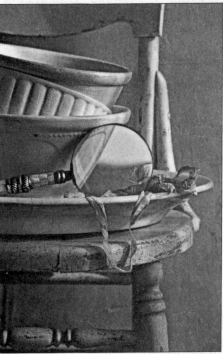

© Elizabeth Maxson

FROM THE EDITOR

"Craft" is such a little word, but it includes an enormous amount and variety of work. From traditional needlework and quilting to modern crochet and scrapbooking and everything in between, crafting is an art form, and those that do it are true artisans. Creating handmade, one-of-a-kind items is at once gratifying and inspiring, and keeps craft artisans constantly pushing toward achieving new success.

With the help of certain websites like Etsy, Ravelry, Craftsy, ArtFire and others, as well as social media, it is easier than ever for crafters to sell their handmade products from the comfort of their own home. For those crafters who want to turn their passion into their business, this book is both a starting point and a research tool. A section of articles from crafty professionals provides insight, tips and advice into business-related subjects such as branding, packaging, social media, publishing and copyright. This shrewd business advice is sprinkled with personal stories from the front lines of craft business ownership. The writers featured in this first edition of *Crafter's Market* are thrilled to help up-and-coming craft professionals start, build and grow their business, and their advice will certainly help new business owners avoid some common mistakes.

The bulk of the book is filled with listings—names, contact information, company descriptions, submission guidelines and more—from companies and events that provide avenues for building and growing a craft business. These listings are broken down into the following categories: Book Publishers, Craft Magazines, Industry Shows, Craft Communities, and Craft Fairs and Online Marketplaces. You can use these listings to expand your business into new arenas, and to discover opportunities you may not have known existed.

Happy crafting!

Kelly M. Biscopink

HOW TO USE
THIS BOOK

//

If you're picking up this book for the first time, you might not know quite how to start using it. Your first impulse might be to flip through and quickly make a mailing list, submitting your work to everyone with hopes that *someone* might like it. Resist that urge. First you have to narrow down the names in this book to those who need your particular style. That's what this book is all about. We provide the names and addresses of places to sell your handmade creations and publish how-to instructions, along with plenty of business advice. You provide the hard work, creativity, and dedication to making and selling handmade goods.

Listings
The book is divided into market sections, from craft fairs to publishers. (See the Table of Contents for a complete list.) Each section begins with an introduction containing information and advice to help you break into that specific market. Listings are the meat of this book. In a nutshell, listings are names, addresses, and contact information for avenues through which you can sell your craft and hone your business.

Articles and Interviews
In this book, you will find helpful articles and interviews with working crafters, editors and experts from the craft world. These articles give you a richer understanding of the marketplace by sharing the featured artists' personal experiences and insights. Their stories, and the lessons you can learn from other crafters' feats and follies, give you an important edge over competition.

How Crafter's Market Works

We suggest you follow the instructions in the listings and explore the different methods and avenues you can use to successfully sell your handmade goods. Whether your interest lies in publishing, craft fairs or growing your online presence, you will find instructions in the listing on how to reach out to the correct people.

Working With Listings

1. Read the entire listing to decide whether that publisher, craft fair or website is a good fit. Do not use this book simply as a mailing list of names and addresses. Reading listings carefully helps you narrow your list to select the most appropriate places to sell your work.

2. Read the description of the company in the first paragraph of the listing. Then jump to the Needs or Media heading to find out what type of artwork is preferred. Is it the type of craft you create? This is the first step to narrowing your target market. Only consider working with those places that need the kind of work you create.

3. Send appropriate submissions. It seems like common sense to research what kind of samples a listing wants before sending off just any artwork you have on hand. But believe it or not, some artists skip this step. Look under the First Contact & Terms heading to find out how to contact the market and what to send. Some companies and publishers are very

<table>
<tr><td colspan="2">**KEY TO SYMBOLS & ABBREVIATIONS**</td></tr>
<tr><td>☼</td><td>Canadian market</td></tr>
<tr><td>☽</td><td>market located outside of the U.S. and Canada</td></tr>
<tr><td>☊</td><td>market prefers to work with local artists/ designers</td></tr>
<tr><td>b&w</td><td>black & white (photo or illustration)</td></tr>
<tr><td>SASE</td><td>self-addressed, stamped envelope</td></tr>
<tr><td>SAE</td><td>self-addressed envelope</td></tr>
<tr><td>IRC</td><td>International Reply Coupon, for use when mailing to countries other than your own</td></tr>
</table>

picky about what kinds of samples they like to see; others are more flexible. Failure to follow directions in submissions may result in automatic rejection from a publisher or show.

4. Be sure to read the Tips. This is where editors and directors describe their pet peeves and give clues for how to impress them. The information within the Tips will help you get a feel for what a publisher might be like to work with or a show might be like to attend.

These steps are just the beginning. As you become accustomed to reading listings, you will think of more ways to mine this book for potential craft outlets.

Pay Attention to Copyright Information

If you are using this book to locate a publisher or find a magazine to work with, it's important to consider what rights publishing companies buy. It is preferable to work with companies that buy first or one-time rights. If you see a listing that buys "all rights," be aware you may be giving up the right to sell that particular craft in the future. See the "Copyright Basics" article in this section for more information.

Look for Specialties and Niche Markets

Read listings closely. Most describe their specialties, clients, and products within the first paragraph. If you are primarily a knitter, it probably won't be beneficial for you to apply as a vendor to International Quilt Market. If you design plushie patterns, look for a magazine that caters to sewing or general craft, not scrapbooking. Make sure your submissions and applications are targeted to maximize the potential success of your craft endeavor.

Browse the listings for new information. A publisher you thought was only interested in quilting patterns may in fact have an imprint dedicated to cross stitch.

COMPLAINT PROCEDURE

If you feel you have not been treated fairly by a company listed in *Crafter's Market*, we advise you to take the following steps:

- First, try to contact the company. Sometimes one e-mail or letter can quickly clear up the matter.
- Document all your correspondence with the company. If you write to us with a complaint, provide the details of your submission, the date of your first contact with the company, and the nature of your subsequent correspondence.
- We will enter your complaint into our files.
- The number and severity of complaints will be considered in our decision whether to delete the listing from the next edition.
- We reserve the right to not list any company for any reason.

See You Next Year

Use this book for one year. Highlight listings, make notes in the margins, fill it with Post-it notes. In November of 2015, our next edition—the *2016 Crafter's Market*—starts arriving in bookstores. By then, we'll have collected hundreds of new listings and changes in contact information. It is a career investment to buy the new edition every year. (And it's deductible! See the "How to Stay on Track and Get Paid" article in this section for information on tax deductions.)

Hang In There!

Building a professional business doesn't happen overnight. It's a gradual process. It may take two or three years to gain enough information and experience to be a true professional in your field. So if you really want to be a professional crafter, hang in there. Before long, you'll experience the exhilaration of seeing your name in print, your social media stats rise, your work pop up on Pinterest and your sales steadily increase. If you really want it and you're willing to work for it, it will happen.

FREQUENTLY ASKED QUESTIONS

1. **How do companies get listed in the book?** No company pays to be included—all listings are free. Every company has to fill out a detailed questionnaire about their art needs. All questionnaires are screened to make sure the companies meet our requirements. Each year we contact every company in the book and ask them to update their information.

2. **Why aren't other companies I know about listed in this book?** We may have sent these companies a questionnaire, but they never returned it. Or if they did return a questionnaire, we may have decided not to include them based on our requirements.

3. **I applied to a show or sent a proposal to a company that stated they were open to reviewing the type of work I do, but I have not heard from them yet. What should I do?** At the time we contacted the company, they were open to receiving such submissions. However, things can change. It's a good idea to contact any company listed in this book to check on their policy before sending them anything. Perhaps they have not had time to review your submission yet. If the listing states that they respond to queries in one month, and more than a month has passed, you can send a brief e-mail to the company to inquire about the status of your submission. Some companies receive a large volume of submissions, so you must be patient.

4. **A company says they want to publish my artwork, but first they will need a fee from me. Is this a standard business practice?** No, it is not a standard business practice. You should never have to pay to have your work reviewed or accepted for publication. If you suspect that a company may not be reputable, do some research before you submit anything or pay their fees. The exception to this rule is craft fairs and shows. Most fairs and shows have an application fee, and usually there is a fee for renting booth space. Some galleries may also require a fee for renting space to exhibit your work.

HOW TO STAY ON TRACK AND GET PAID

As you launch your craft career, be aware that you are actually starting a small business. It is crucial that you keep track of the details, or your business will not last very long. The most important rule of all is to find a system to keep your business organized and stick with it.

YOUR DAILY RECORD-KEEPING SYSTEM

Every artist needs to keep a daily record of art-making and marketing activities. Before you do anything else, visit an office supply store and pick out the items listed below (or your own variations of these items). Keep it simple so you can remember your system and use it on automatic pilot whenever you make a business transaction.

What You'll Need:

- a packet of colorful file folders or a basic Personal Information Manager on your smart phone, computer or personal digital assistant (PDA).
- a notebook or legal pads to serve as a log or journal to keep track of your daily craft-making and craft-marketing activities.
- a small pocket notebook to keep in your car to track mileage and gas expenses.

How to Start Your System

Designate a permanent location in your studio or home office for two file folders and your notebook. Label one red file folder "Expenses." Label one green file folder "Income." Write in your daily log book each and every day.

Every time you purchase anything for your business, such as envelopes or art supplies, place the receipt in your red Expenses folder. When you receive payment for a sale or other crafty job (such as writing an article for a magazine), photocopy the check or place the receipt in your green Income folder.

GETTING PAID

Read "Pricing Your Work" by Grace Dobush about determining pricing for your handmade items. Be sure to factor in the value of your time and supplies, and then add 50 percent to arrive at your retail price. This 50 percent increase will allow you to sell wholesale without taking a loss.

For standard items offered in your inventory, be sure to receive payment upfront before sending the item to its new home. Once you have sent off the merchandise, you may have a problem collecting unpaid bills. If you are taking custom orders, consider how you'd like to handle payment. Will you require full payment before starting the work, or just a deposit? Decide how and when you need to be paid for custom work, and be sure to collect the final amount due before sending the final product.

When writing for magazines or working with a publisher, you will most likely be asked to submit an invoice with the finished work. Some book deals may include a small advance prior to beginning work, and others may not. Be sure to understand the terms of a publishing contract or agreement before starting work. Pay close attention to how and when you will receive payment, and ask if you need to submit an invoice or if you will be paid automatically upon completion of the work.

Take Advantage of Tax Deductions

You have the right to deduct legitimate business expenses from your taxable income. Art supplies, studio rent, printing costs, and other business expenses are deductible against your gross craft-related income. It is imperative to seek the help of an accountant or tax preparation service in filing your return. In the event your deductions exceed profits, the loss will lower your taxable income from other sources.

To guard against taxpayers fraudulently claiming hobby expenses as business losses, the IRS requires taxpayers to demonstrate a "profit motive." As a general rule, you must show a profit for three out of five years to retain a business status. If you are audited, the burden of proof will be on you to validate your work as a business and not a hobby. The nine criteria the IRS use to distinguish a business from a hobby are:

- **the manner in which you conduct your business**
- **expertise**
- **amount of time and effort put into your work**
- **expectation of future profits**
- **success in similar ventures**
- **history of profit and losses**

- **amount of occasional profits**
- **financial status**
- **element of personal pleasure or recreation**

If the IRS rules that you sew for pure enjoyment rather than profit, they will consider you a hobbyist. Complete and accurate records will demonstrate to the IRS that you take your business seriously.

Even if you are a "hobbyist," you can deduct expenses such as supplies on a Schedule A, but you can only take craft-related deductions equal to craft-related income. If you sold two $500 quilts, you can deduct expenses such as fabric, patterns, books and seminars only up to $1,000. Itemize deductions only if your total itemized deductions exceed your standard deduction. You will not be allowed to deduct a loss from other sources of income.

Figuring Deductions

To deduct business expenses, you or your accountant will fill out a 1040 tax form (not 1040EZ) and prepare a Schedule C, which is a separate form used to calculate profit or loss from your business. The income (or loss) from Schedule C is then reported on the 1040 form. In regard to business expenses, the standard deduction does not come into play as it would for a hobbyist. The total of your business expenses need not exceed the standard deduction.

There is a shorter form called Schedule C-EZ for self-employed people in service industries. It can be applicable to those who have receipts of $25,000 or less and deductible expenses of $2,000 or less. Check with your accountant to see if you qualify.

Deductible expenses include advertising costs, brochures, business cards, professional group dues, subscriptions to trade journals and magazines, legal and professional services, leased office equipment, office supplies, business travel expenses, etc. Your accountant can give you a list of all 100-percent and 50-percent deductible expenses. Don't forget to deduct the cost of this book!

As a self-employed "sole proprietor," there is no employer regularly taking tax out of your paycheck. Your accountant will help you put money away to meet your tax obligations and may advise you to estimate your tax and file quarterly returns.

Your accountant also will be knowledgeable about another annual tax called the Social Security Self-Employment Tax. You must pay this tax if your net craft business income is $400 or more.

The fees of tax professionals are relatively low, and they are deductible. To find a good accountant, ask colleagues for recommendations, look for advertisements in trade publications, or ask your local Small Business Administration.

Report All Income to Uncle Sam

Don't be tempted to sell your work without reporting it on your income tax. You may think this saves money, but it can do real damage to your career and credibility—even if you are never audited by the IRS. Unless you report your income, the IRS will not categorize you as a professional, and you won't be able to deduct expenses. And don't think you won't get caught if you neglect to report income. If you bill any client in excess of $600 (for example, if you are consistently writing for a magazine), the IRS requires the client to provide you with a Form 1099 at the end of the year. Your client must send one copy to the IRS and a copy to you to attach to your income tax return. Likewise, if you pay a freelancer over $600 to assist with any portion of your work, you must issue a 1099 form. This procedure is one way the IRS cuts down on unreported income.

Register With the State Sales Tax Department

Most states require a 2–7 percent sales tax on artwork you sell directly from your studio or at art/craft fairs, or on work created for a client. You must register with the state sales tax department, which will issue you a sales permit or a resale number and send you appropriate forms and instructions for collecting the tax. Getting a sales permit usually involves filling out a form and paying a small fee. Reporting sales tax is a relatively simple procedure. Record all sales taxes on invoices and in your sales journal. Every three months, total the taxes collected and send it to the state sales tax department.

In most states, if you sell to a customer outside of your sales tax area, you do not have to collect sales tax. However, this may not hold true for your state. You may also need a business license or permit. Call your state tax office to find out what is required.

Save Money on Craft Supplies

As long as you have the above sales permit number, you can buy craft supplies without paying sales tax. You will probably have to fill out a tax-exempt form with your permit number at the sales desk where you buy materials. The reason you do not have to pay sales tax on craft supplies is that sales tax is only charged on the final product. However, you must then add the cost of materials into the cost of your finished product or the final work for your client. Keep all receipts in case of a tax audit. If the state discovers that you have not collected sales tax, you will be liable for tax and penalties.

Some states claim "creativity" is a non-taxable service, while others view it as a product and therefore taxable. Be certain you understand the sales tax laws to avoid being held liable for uncollected money at tax time. Contact your state auditor for sales tax information.

Save Money on Postage

When you send out postcard samples or invitations to openings, you can save big bucks by mailing in bulk. Artists should send orders via first-class mail for quicker service and better handling. Package flat work between heavy cardboard or foam core, or roll it in a cardboard tube. Include your business card or a label with your name and address on the outside of the packaging material in case the outer wrapper becomes separated from the inner packing in transit.

Protect larger works—particularly those that are matted or framed—with a strong outer surface, such as laminated cardboard, Masonite, or light plywood. Wrap the work in poly-foam, heavy cloth, or bubble wrap, and cushion it against the outer container with spacers to keep it from moving. Whenever possible, ship work before it is glassed. If the glass breaks en route, it may destroy your original image. If shipping large framed work, contact a museum in your area for more suggestions on packaging.

The U.S. Postal Service will not automatically insure your work, but you can purchase up to $5,000 worth of coverage. Artworks exceeding this value should be sent by registered mail, which can be insured for up to $25,000. Certified packages travel a little slower but are easier to track.

Consider special services offered by the post office, such as Priority Mail, Express Mail Next Day Service, and Special Delivery. For overnight delivery, check to see which air freight services are available in your area. Federal Express automatically insures packages for $100 and will ship art valued up to $500. Their 24-hour computer tracking system enables you to locate your package at any time.

The United Parcel Service automatically insures work for $100, but you can purchase additional insurance for work valued as high as $25,000 for items shipped by air (there is no limit for items sent on the ground). UPS cannot guarantee arrival dates but will track lost packages. It also offers Two-Day Blue Label Air Service within the U.S. and Next Day Service in specific ZIP code zones.

Always make a quick address check by phone before putting your package in the mail.

CAN I DEDUCT MY HOME STUDIO?

If you freelance full time from your home and devote a separate area to your business, you may qualify for a home office deduction. If eligible, you can deduct a percentage of your rent or mortgage as well as utilities and expenses like office supplies and business-related telephone calls.

The IRS does not allow deductions if the space is used for purposes other than business. A studio or office in your home must meet three criteria:

- The space must be used exclusively for your business.
- The space must be used regularly as a place of business.
- The space must be your principle place of business.

The IRS might question a home office deduction if you are employed full time elsewhere and freelance from home. If you do claim a home office, the area must be clearly divided from your living area. A desk in your bedroom will not qualify. To figure out the percentage of your home used for business, divide the total square footage of your home by the total square footage of your office. This will give you a percentage to work with when figuring deductions. If the home office is 10 percent of the square footage of your home, deduct 10 percent of expenses such as rent, heat, and air conditioning.

The total home office deduction cannot exceed the gross income you derive from its business use. You cannot take a net business loss resulting from a home office deduction. Your business must be profitable three out of five years; otherwise, you will be classified as a hobbyist and will not be entitled to this deduction.

Consult a tax advisor before attempting to take this deduction, as its interpretations frequently change.

For additional information, refer to IRS Publication 587, Business Use of Your Home, which can be downloaded at www.irs.gov or ordered by calling (800)829-3676.

COPYRIGHT BASICS

As creator of your artwork, you have certain inherent rights over your work and can control how each one of your works is used, until you sell your rights to someone else. The legal term for these rights is called *copyright*. Technically, any original artwork you produce is automatically copyrighted as soon as you put it in tangible form.

To be automatically copyrighted, your artwork must fall within these guidelines:

- **It must be your original creation.** It cannot be a copy of somebody else's work.
- **It must be "pictorial, graphic, or sculptural."** Utilitarian objects, such as lamps or toasters, are not covered, although you can copyright an illustration featured on a lamp or toaster.
- **It must be fixed in "any tangible medium, now known or later developed."** Your work, or at least a representation of a planned work, must be created in or on a medium you can see or touch, such as paper, canvas, clay, a sketch pad, or even a website. It can't just be an idea in your head. An idea cannot be copyrighted.

Copyright Lasts for Your Lifetime Plus Seventy Years

Copyright is exclusive. When you create a work, the rights automatically belong to you and nobody else but you until those rights are sold to someone else.

Works of art created on or after January 1978 are protected for your lifetime plus seventy years.

The Artist's Bundle of Rights

One of the most important things you need to know about copyright is that it is not just a singular right. It is a bundle of rights you enjoy as creator of your artwork:

- **Reproduction right.** You have the right to make copies of the original work.
- **Modification right.** You have the right to create derivative works based on the original work.
- **Distribution rights.** You have the right to sell, rent or lease copies of your work.
- **Public performance right.** You have the right to play, recite, or otherwise perform a work. (This right is more applicable to written or musical art forms than to visual art.)
- **Public display right.** You have the right to display your work in a public place. This bundle of rights can be divided up in a number of ways, so that you can sell all or part of any of those exclusive rights to one or more parties. The system of selling parts of your copyright bundle is sometimes referred to as divisible copyright. Just as a land owner can divide up his property and sell it to many different people, the artist can divide up his rights to an artwork and sell portions of those rights to different buyers.

Divisible Copyright: Divide and Conquer

Why is divisible copyright so important? Because dividing up your bundle and selling parts of it to different buyers will help you get the most payment for each of your artworks. For any one of your artworks, you can sell your entire bundle of rights at one time (not advisable!) or divide each bundle pertaining to that work into smaller portions and make more money as a result. You can grant one party the right to use your work on a greeting card and sell another party the right to print that same work on T-shirts.

Divisible Copyright Terms

Clients tend to use legal jargon to specify the rights they want to buy. The terms below are commonly used in contracts to indicate portions of your bundle of rights. Some terms are vague or general, such as "all rights." Other terms are more specific, such as "first North American rights." Make sure you know what each term means before signing a contract.

- **One-time rights.** Your client buys the right to use or publish your artwork on a one-time basis. One fee is paid for one use. Most magazine assignments fall under this category.
- **First rights.** This is almost the same as one-time rights, except that the buyer is also paying for the privilege of being the first to use your image. He may use it only once unless the other rights are negotiated. Sometimes first rights can be further broken down geographically. The buyer might ask to buy first North American rights, meaning he would have the right to be the first to publish the work in North America.
- **Exclusive rights.** This guarantees the buyer's exclusive right to use the artwork in his particular market or for a particular product. Exclusive rights are frequently negotiated by greeting card and gift companies. One company might purchase the exclusive

right to use your work as a greeting card, leaving you free to sell the exclusive rights to produce the image on a mug to another company.

- **Promotional rights.** These rights allow a publisher to use an artwork for promotion of a publication in which the artwork appears. For example, if *The New Yorker* bought promotional rights to your cartoon, they could also use it in a direct mail promotion.
- **Electronic rights.** These rights allow a buyer to place your work on electronic media such as websites. Often these rights are requested with print rights.
- **Work for hire.** Under the Copyright Act of 1976, section 101, a "work for hire" is defined as "(1) a work prepared by an employee within the scope of his or her employment; or (2) a work specially ordered or commissioned for use as a contribution to a collective work, as part of a motion picture or other audiovisual work . . . if the parties expressly agree in a written instrument signed by them that the work shall be considered a work made for hire." When the agreement is "work for hire," you surrender all rights to the image and can never resell that particular image again. If you agree to the terms, make sure the money you receive makes it well worth the arrangement.
- **All rights.** Again, be aware that this phrase means you will relinquish your entire copyright to a specific artwork. Before agreeing to the terms, make sure this is an arrangement you can live with. At the very least, arrange for the contract to expire after a specified date. Terms for all rights—including time period for usage and compensation—should be confirmed in a written agreement with the company.

Since legally your artwork is your property, when you create a project for a magazine you are, in effect, temporarily "leasing" your work to the client for publication.

Chances are you'll never hear an editor ask to lease or license your work, and he may not even realize he is leasing, not buying, your work. But most editors know that once the magazine is published, the editor has no further claims to your work and the rights revert back to you. If the editor wants to use your work a second or third time, he must ask permission and negotiate with you to determine any additional fees you want to charge. You are free to take that same work and sell it to another buyer.

However, if the editor buys "all rights," you cannot legally offer that same image to another magazine or company. If you agree to create the artwork as "work for hire," you relinquish your rights entirely.

What Licensing Agents Know

The practice of leasing parts or groups of an artist's bundle of rights is often referred to as licensing, because (legally) the artist is granting someone a "license" to use his work for a limited time for a specific reason. As licensing agents have come to realize, it is the exclusivity of the rights and the ability to divide and sell them that make them valuable. Knowing exactly what rights you own, which you can sell, and in what combinations, will help you negotiate.

Don't Sell Conflicting Rights to Different Clients

You also have to make sure the rights you sell to one client don't conflict with any of the rights sold to other clients. For example, you can't sell the exclusive right to use your image on greeting cards to two separate greeting card companies. You can sell the exclusive greeting card rights to one card company and the exclusive rights to use your artwork on mugs to a separate gift company. You should always get such agreements in writing and let both companies know your work will appear on other products.

When to Use the Copyright © and Credit Lines

A copyright notice consists of the word "Copyright" or its symbol ©, the year the work was created or first published, and the full name of the copyright owner. It should be placed where it can easily be seen, on the front or back of a piece of work.

Under today's laws, placing the copyright symbol on your work isn't absolutely necessary to claim copyright infringement and take a plagiarist to court if he steals your work. If you browse through magazines, you will often see the illustrator's name in small print near the illustration, without the Copyright ©. This is common practice in the magazine industry. Even though the © is not printed, the illustrator still owns the copyright unless the magazine purchased all rights to the work. Just make sure the editor gives you a credit line.

Usually you will not see the artist's name or credit line next to advertisements for products. Advertising agencies often purchase all rights to the work for a specified time. They usually pay the artist generously for this privilege and spell out the terms clearly in the artist's contract.

How to Register a Copyright

The process of registering your work is simple. Visit the United States Copyright Office website at www.copyright.gov to file electronically. You can still register with paper forms,

---

COPYRIGHT RESOURCES

The U.S. Copyright website (www.copyright.gov), the official site of the U.S. Copyright Office, is very helpful and will answer just about any question you can think of. Information is also available by phone at (202)707-3000. Another great site, called the Copyright Website, is located at www.benedict.com.

---

but this method requires a higher filing fee. To request paper forms, call (202)707-9100 or write to the Library of Congress, Copyright Office-COPUBS, 101 Independence Ave. SE, Washington, DC 20559-6304, Attn: Information Publications, Section LM0455 and ask for package 115 and circulars 40 and 40A. Crafters should ask for package 111 and circular 44. They will send you a package containing Form VA (for visual artists).

You can register an entire collection of your work rather than one work at a time. That way you will only have to pay one fee for an unlimited number of works. For example, if you have created a hundred works between 2012 and 2014, you can complete a copyright form to register "the collected works of Jane Smith, 2012–2014." But you will have to upload digital files or send either slides or photocopies of each of those works.

Why Register?

It seems like a lot of time and trouble to complete the forms to register copyrights for all your artworks. It may not be necessary or worth it to you to register every artwork you create. After all, a work is copyrighted the moment it's created anyway, right? The benefits of registering are basically to give you additional clout in case an infringement occurs and you decide to take the offender to court. Without a copyright registration, it probably wouldn't be economically feasible to file suit, because you'd be entitled to only your damages and the infringer's profits, which might not equal the cost of litigating the case. If the works are registered with the U.S. Copyright Office, it will be easier to prove your case and get reimbursed for your court costs.

Likewise, the big advantage of using the Copyright © also comes when and if you ever have to take an infringer to court. Since the Copyright © is the most clear warning to potential plagiarizers, it is easier to collect damages if the © is in plain sight.

Register with the U.S. Copyright Office those works you fear are likely to be plagiarized before or shortly after they have been exhibited or published. That way, if anyone uses your work without permission, you can take action.

Deal Swiftly With Plagiarists

If you suspect your work has been plagiarized and you have not already registered it with the Copyright Office, register it immediately. You have to wait until it is registered before you can take legal action against the infringer.

Before taking the matter to court, however, your first course of action might be a well-phrased letter from your lawyer telling the offender to "cease and desist" using your work, because you have a registered copyright. Such a warning (especially if printed on your lawyer's letterhead) is often enough to get the offender to stop using your work.

TIPS AND TRICKS FOR A SUCCESSFUL CRAFT BUSINESS

by Lindsay Wilkes (The Cottage Mama)

Starting a craft business can be one of the most exciting, scary, fulfilling, exhausting and rewarding experiences of your life. As creative individuals, we all dream of having a job or business that allows us to do something we are passionate about every single day. I am proof-positive that you can go from having a home-based hobby to an income-producing business if it's something you really want to do. But before you start a craft business, you need to ask yourself, "Do I want to be in business?" Having a hobby and passion is one thing, but running a true business is another. Loving your craft doesn't necessarily mean you should go into business, and it definitely doesn't guarantee success.

Successful craft businesses don't happen because of luck; they happen because of a lot of hard work. And I mean incredibly hard work. Although things sometimes seemed to happen in my business due to good timing, absolutely every step forward in my children's sewing pattern business has happened because I worked for it, put myself out there and made it happen. You can do the same.

Here are some tips and tricks for running a successful craft business. This list might seem a little long, but there are lots of things to think about and I want you to be prepared for this exciting ride.

Business Name

So you've decided that you want to turn your creative hobby into a business. So what's next? First, you need to come up with a name for your business. Search around the internet and see if any of the names you have come up with are already taken. First and foremost, you want to be able to purchase the domain name for your business (aka .com), so if that is already taken, rule out that name and move on. It's not worth the hassle of having to add in a hyphen or some other symbol into your web address. Also, consider using your name as your business. If you are looking to be recognized in your industry as an artist or creative, having your name as your business/brand can be very powerful. Whatever you decide, make sure your business name is in line with the brand that you hope to create.

Branding

Branding can make or break a business. Your brand defines how you want to be perceived by your audience or customers. Your brand is you and many other components, such as your product, logo, photography, website, writing voice and more. Creating cohesive branding is essential when starting your craft business. If you do not have graphic design skills, hire a designer to help you create your logo, website and images associated with your business. Do what you do best and hire out all the rest. It might incur a little upfront cost, but it will be well worth it. Make sure you communicate well with your designer about the vision for

Lindsay's signature style is defined by combining traditional and modern elements when creating beautiful clothing for little girls. Vintage elements, like ruffles and sashes, are combined with modern prints and color combinations to create an aesthetic all her own.

your brand to help them make your dream a reality. There are many designers online and you can find many of them on Etsy. If you are active in your industry, ask another industry friend for a recommendation. If there is a brand you admire, e-mail them and inquire about their logo or design. They will probably be flattered to hear from you. Make sure you take time to develop your branding because it's one of the most important driving forces behind a successful craft business.

Define Your Signature Style

Decide what it is about your craft or art that makes you unique. Is it the colors you use? Is it vintage inspired? Modern? Is it in the detail in your art? Whatever it is, make sure you define it. Don't start your business trying to be anybody but yourself. If you try to have a business or style like someone else's, they will always be one step ahead of you. Identify and embrace your own defined sense of style; if you're not sure what that is, take the time to figure it out before you start down this business path. You may not have found your signature style because perhaps you have not created enough to know what it is. Creating a large body of work and seeing it all together can help you see the signature style that may have been there all along. Also, look around your house at your decorating style or in your closet at the types of fabrics and colors your tend to gravitate toward. Your signature style might be staring you right in the face.

Write a Business Plan

You don't need a huge, formal business plan for your craft business, but you need to have the goals and vision for your business down on paper. You should know where you are headed and exactly how you will get there. Executing your plan will be much easier if you can see it laid out in front of you. Check in with your plan often to make sure you are staying on task to turn your dream into a reality.

Hire an Accountant

If you are going into business for yourself, you need a good accountant—one who will advise you about the best structure for your craft business. These professionals know what is going to work best for you from a tax perspective. Taxes are just a part of business and you can't avoid them. Hiring a good person is essential and will make the process easier in the long run.

Pricing Your Craft

This is a tricky topic and you need to think long and hard about your pricing. You can always increase your pricing down the road as you become more well-known in your industry, but you really can't reduce your price. If someone purchases a handmade mug from you for forty dollars but the next year see you are selling the same thing for thirty dollars, they are not going to feel warm and fuzzy about you or your business.

Consider the cost of your materials, the cost of your time, the cost of photographing and listing your product, the time and cost of shipping the product; then on top of all that, you need to make sure you make a profit. You're obviously not starting a craft business for the fun of it; let's not forget the end goal—to make money. It can be helpful to look around the internet to check out the pricing for other comparable products. Figure out what you want your profit margin to be for your craft. Add up your expenses and then add the amount that will ensure you hit your margins. If it doesn't make sense on paper, it probably doesn't make sense for you to go into business. (Read "Pricing Your Work" for more insight into pricing your items.)

Selling

There are many avenues for selling your product. You definitely want to have an online presence with your product. You could certainly start out with your own website, but I wouldn't advise that unless you are already well-known for your craft. Etsy, an online handmade marketplace, is a great place to start because it brings your target audience to one place without them even knowing who you are. Etsy charges a small fee per listing and transaction, but is a very inexpensive marketplace option. Also, Etsy allows the buyer to leave reviews about your product; good reviews help people feel more confident about purchasing from you.

At this stage of my business, I have my own stand-alone website because I drive a lot of my own product traffic and I'd prefer to avoid Etsy fees whenever possible. However, I still keep my Etsy shop active. Etsy still brings in new customers that may not have found me otherwise. There are other online selling websites as well. Some successful businesses sell their products on Facebook and Instagram, too. Consider all of your options when choosing marketplaces to sell your product. This book is a great resource for discovering new online marketplaces through which you can sell your handmade goods. (Read "Finding Success on Etsy" for more insight into selling on Etsy.)

Start a Blog

For me, blogging was an amazing platform to build my brand and was a jumping off point for my business. Blogging affords you the opportunity to connect with a wide range of like-minded individuals who share the same passion as you—whatever your craft of choice might be. On your blog you can share your expertise in your craft and talk more personally about yourself, and in return your readers will form a connection to you that will serve you well when you go into business. Blogging also builds trust. If your readers trust you as an expert in your craft, they are more likely to purchase your product. Plus, once you do go into business, you will have created a platform on which to advertise your product almost for free.

There are many different blogging platforms and advantages to each, but two of the most popular are Blogger and WordPress.

Social Media Is King

Social media is a powerful, free marketing tool that should be one of your primary advertising sources. First, think about your brand's audience and tailor your social media strategy to your audience. For me, my audience is almost all women in their early thirties or in their late fifties to early sixties. These are the two demographics that have little children in their lives (mothers and grandmothers); therefore, these are the women that typically want to purchase my children's sewing patterns. These women are very visual and their primary social media channel is Facebook, so my primary social media focus is through Facebook. If you tend to gravitate toward a younger crowd, Instagram can be a powerful tool, or you might find your target audience on Twitter. Also, don't underestimate the power of Pinterest in social media. Although you cannot directly interact with people on Pinterest, pins can definitely help drive traffic to your website. Focus on growing your own Pinterest account by pinning great visual content that is in line with your brand, so when you pin your own content it has the opportunity to go viral at a much faster rate.

The Art of Networking

Networking is a powerful business tool. In order to take your business to the next level, you need to make sure you connect to the right people. Attend industry trade shows or conferences, not only to connect with other brands in your craft industry, but also to connect with your fellow crafters. There is nothing more lonely then being in business all by yourself. Having others in the industry that you can call or e-mail when you need advice or help with something is a wonderful feeling. Also, you never know when you might want to collaborate on a project with another crafter. Having friends in your industry will take you very far.

Find a Mentor

If you can find a mentor in your industry, consider yourself a very lucky duck. If you feel uncomfortable asking for help from someone who does exactly what you do, try asking someone who does something similar to what you do. For example, when I was thinking about entering the world of children's pattern design, I had a woman who was already established in adult pattern design mentor me along the way. We were in no way direct competition with each other so she was more then happy to help me. I believe that there is enough business in this world for everyone, so if you need help from a more established industry professional, just ask. The worst they can say is "no" and I think you might be surprised how helpful the crafting and creative industry can be.

Your Business Won't Be a Success Overnight

If you think you are going to start a craft business and get rich overnight, you are in for a rude awakening. Craft businesses take time. They take years of getting your name out there, finding out what works and doesn't work, seeing what products are worth your time to create and which are not. But if you set small, incremental goals for yourself, you will be able to celebrate small successes along the way. Before you know it, those small successes will turn into big successes and your business will have grown before your eyes. Just be patient—good things take time.

Don't Compare Yourself to Others

It's not worth it. You aren't like anyone else and you can't compare your new craft business to one that has already been in business for five, ten or fifteen years. Comparison will make you feel defeated before you've even started. Remember that the established businesses you aspire toward were once where you are. Stay focused on your own business and the goals you have set. You will take baby steps, but you'll be in the big time soon enough if you work hard and work smart.

Write a Book

If you want to establish yourself as an authority in your industry, consider writing a book. Are you going to get rich from writing a craft book? Probably not. But it will be the most powerful business card you could ever have in your pocket. It will open up many teaching and speaking opportunities that you might not otherwise have unless you are published. Submit your book idea to one of the many craft book publishers listed in this book and, if your book idea falls in line with a niche the publisher is looking to fill, there is a very good chance that you will get a deal. (Read "Write and Publish a Craft Book" for more insight into writing a book.)

Teach Your Craft to Others

Not only is teaching an incredibly rewarding experience, teaching is a great way to get out from your studio and connect with others that are passionate about your craft. Teaching is in a similar realm to networking. Some of the people you meet will be fans that have been wanting to meet you and others might not know you, but there is nothing better than inspiring people to do what you love to do.

Hire Help

At some point your business will grow to a point beyond what you can handle. This is the point at which you will sink or swim. If you don't bring on help at the right time, you business can suffer; e-mails won't get answered, shipping might take longer than normal, social media will get neglected, and so on. Hire on help when you start to feel that your business is overwhelming you. Look for employees that can manage the day-to-day tasks of your business so you are free to do what you do best—your craft. If you are at the point at which you need to hire additional help, then congratulations! You are running a successful and growing craft business!

If you truly want to turn your craft into a business, you can do it. You will need to work hard, be passionate about the product or service you are creating and don't be afraid to ask for help along the way. You've got this—now go get started!

Lindsay Wilkes
Lindsay is the owner and designer of The Cottage Mama (www.thecottagemama.com), a boutique children's clothing and sewing pattern company, the writer behind the popular sewing and crafting blog, The Cottage Mama (www.thecottagemama.com/blog) and the author of *Sew Classic Clothes for Girls: 20 Girls' Dresses, Outfits and Accessories From The Cottage Mama*. She is known for her use of contemporary printed designer cotton fabric, her love of unique trims, timeless style and vintage details. Lindsay enjoys sewing, cooking, crafting and all things domestic. She resides in Chicago with her husband and three young children. Visit Lindsay at www.thecottagemama.com or www.thecottagemama.com/blog. You can also find her on Facebook, Twitter, Pinterest and Instagram as The Cottage Mama, or e-mail her directly at Lindsay@thecottagemama.com.

MAKING IT AS A CRAFTER

by Andrea Currie

Before I found the craft industry, I felt like a unicorn stuck in a boring cubical—a glittery outcast, if you will. Eventually, I sought out my own path by way of a weekly web series called *Craft-Tastic Live*. That glittery adventure coupled with my kicky little blog, HandMAKE-MyDay.com, gave me the portfolio I needed to work in television and write my own book. It sounds so easy when I summarize it like that, but my trip to the top of crafty mountain wasn't all sunshine and rainbows. In the following pages are the things I like to impart to those brave enough to step out of the mold and take the path less traveled.

Step Out of Your Comfort Zone

It's easy to meet birds of a feather, and (for the most part) flocking with your own kind can be incredibly helpful and empowering. However, staying within your comfort zone can keep you from reaching your true potential. Hanging around a different "species" may inspire you to try something new or give you the confidence to take your skills to the next level.

Andrea covered herself in glitter tattoos for the premier of her *Craft Wars* episode.

If you are in a creative rut, it may be time to step out of your comfort zone. Try a new class or attend a social gathering with people you've never met before. I find that reaching out and meeting new people gives me a fresh new perspective and usually some fun new skills to boot.

Stop Caring About What Other People Think

As a "professional" crafter, I know how hard it is to feel confident that people will take me seriously. Creative people are often looked down on as silly dreamers or children stuck in adult bodies. It's also safe to say that crafters are often seen as the least successful of the creative professionals. I have been talked down to, laughed at and mocked by various people, but it never stopped me from being me. Yes, I love to wear strange headpieces and I have an unusual relationship with glitter, but if I stopped to care about what others said about me, I wouldn't have had the time to appear on a national television program, create a successful design business and become a published author. So just remember that successful creative people don't have time to gossip or get involved in unhelpful cliques, and are therefore impervious to external destructive behaviors.

Nothing says "I love you" like a unicorn pooping our rainbow candy!

Build a Brand, Not a Product

Simply put, products are easy to imitate while brands are not. Building a single product or product line can have short-term benefits, but building a brand can open doors into a long-term, more secure future. A brand is a feeling, an ethos, a standard and a look that is attached to everything you produce, be it a product or a service. Think of your brand as your customers' best friend. You would never expect someone to become your bestie without proving that you are reliable, consistent and supportive of their needs. So in turn, you wouldn't expect someone to buy your products just because you posted your Etsy shop on Facebook, right? Spend some time building a brand that meets the needs of your target market. In return, you will receive a loyal customer base and the ability to demand more money for all of the products you create.

It doesn't matter if you sell kitten sweaters or high-end backpacks—your brand needs to fit within the lifestyle of your target market. Explore your target market more by sketching out a picture. What do they look like? What do they wear? Where do they shop? With which other brands do they most associate? Use your research to work your findings into your logos, fonts, colors, copy, packaging, values, social media presence and (of course) your products! (Read "Branding Strategies for Craft Business" for more insight into the art of branding.)

Teach, Teach, Teach

Successful Etsy sellers, designers and creative professionals all possess the same inherent power to influence and inspire. This is not to say that you must teach people how to make the products you are selling, but that teaching is a way of attracting people to your brand without having to wave a "for sale" sign in their faces. Teaching a subject or skill may not be a great fit for everyone, so here are a few other ways you can teach your way to the top of the creative mountain:

The first "He Said/She Said" crafting book.

- **Be a tastemaker:** If you always find yourself ahead of trends, consider dishing out fantastic mood boards to the inspirationally-starved masses. Pinterest is the easiest way to get started, but a blog is a better long-term strategy.
- **Be a product reviewer:** If you love to play and experiment, product reviews are a great option for you. Become an influential product reviewer and you'll have companies and customers knocking down your door for your opinions and products.
- **Be a creative group leader:** If you love teaching and learning, then you probably thrive when surrounded by other creatives. Try leading a monthly group where you teach and learn new creative techniques.

Content Is King

By now you have buckled down, found your style and identified your brand. Maybe you are even a thought leader within your space. But guess what? None of that exists unless you have the content to prove it. In other words, if it goes undocumented and isn't sent through the social media machine, it never happened. This is how the world works now, and I don't want you to go through a bunch of trouble just to have your effort go unnoticed. Here are some ways you can document all of the amazing things you do:

- **Blog:** Successful blogging is a toughie because it requires consistency and a bunch of time. I find that the best blogs are those with great photos and concise writing. When you find just the right balance, your brand is sure to get invaluable long-term exposure.
- **Social media:** Deep down you may hate it, but all successful crafters use it. To make things more complicated, everyone uses social media in very different ways. A good way to find the best combination of social media engagement is to follow the leaders in your craft genre. Maybe they use personal profiles on Facebook and a beefed up Pinterest presence. Maybe they are all about Instagram and Twitter. Follow the leader until you find a good rhythm, and don't be afraid to experiment. And be prepared to invest significant time into some social media outlets that eventually end up fizzling out.
- **Video:** Short videos are a great way to feed the content monster. Surprisingly, videos don't even have to be tutorials. Quick product demonstrations, product reviews and product roundups are easy to create and distribute. However, as with social media platforms, video platforms can quickly fall out of popularity, so be flexible and follow the trends. Right now Vine is popular. Next year, who knows? Sometimes it's best to wait and see if the new platforms are worth your time investment.

Be Grateful

Above everything, be thankful for the people that wholeheartedly support you—they may be few and far between. This is definitely not a journey you want to go on alone, so hold on tight to those willing to cheer you on through the good times and bad. I'd still be that sad little unicorn had I not scooped up an insanely brilliant husband and stumbled upon a group of crafty people who were crazy enough to believe in me. When you get to the top of your creative mountain, I'm sure you will feel the same way I do now—grateful.

Andrea Currie
Andrea is a craft personality, designer, inventor and "Champion" on TLC's *Craft Wars*. Whether she's designing innovative new craft products or demonstrating clever projects and tutorials, she always bring an intoxicating mix of artful moxie and pure glee to her work.

Andrea and her husband, Cliff, founded HandMAKEMyDay.com, a kicky creative blog where they chronicle their "he said, she said" adventures in crafting, cooking, home improvement and product development. When they aren't covered in glitter or sawdust, they are playing with their dog, Gracie, and drawing up plans for their sustainable dream home.

FINDING YOUR CRAFTY NICHE

....

by April Cobb

When you get bitten by the crafty bug, it is natural to want to turn that passion and skill into a business. Some wish to create a highly profitable business that eventually becomes less cottage and more corporate. Some aren't thinking about the money and are just excited to get their art into the hands of someone who will give it a good home. Whatever your ambitions or motives are, you can build something that is right for you and that will bring you great artistic satisfaction. Reaching that place will require a unique product, flexibility, research, and getting you and your product into the world.

I have been developing my crafty projects and designs into businesses for many years now. I have learned a few things along the way that might inspire you or simply get you started in developing a craft business. I will suggest some ideas to help you identify what sort of craft you might like to focus on and promote, if you have not yet figured out what your crafty niche is. We will explore how to sell your work, and how you can find success by putting yourself out there. Finally, I will encourage you to find ways to improve and grow once you have started your crafty business.

There are many ways to identify your best crafting skill and even more ways to build those skills into a successful business. Here I will offer a few tips and tricks to help get you started. Your journey will be different than my journey has been, but I hope to give you a gentle push in the right direction.

What Inspired You to Create?

If we are crafty, we usually figure it out pretty early in life. Sometimes it was our mothers or grandmothers who inspired us to create at an early age. Others of us were taught by friends or learned in school. Today, with the enormous number of tutorials and ideas available online, many people are exposed to and learning crafting skills online, even later in life. This little spark can grow to become a great passion that motivates us to get out of bed in the morning and that satisfies the inherent need to create throughout our lives. No doubt, I learned to create from my mother. When she wasn't cleaning or working in our family store, I always found her in front of her sewing machine or at the kitchen table with glue gun in hand. I am continuing the legacy of dragging my children from one fabric store to another, and their memories of me will be that I was always creating something. I hope that your legacy will be one of joyful crafting as well. Crafting should be fun and not stressful or overly demanding. This is important to understand as you turn your craft into a business.

Consider the memories you have of when you were introduced to arts and crafts. Often it is simply nostalgia that inspires us to craft. After years of not sewing at all, I was pregnant with my first child and felt compelled to drag out the sewing machine to sew clothing for my new baby, just as my mother had for me. Once I did, I was reminded of how fulfilling it is to create something from start to finish on my own. Whatever your story is, allow it to continue inspiring you in your crafting journey and in your craft business.

Deciding Which Craft to Pursue

For creative people, there are often many wonderful ideas whirling around in our heads. Some of us inherently know which crafts we are most drawn to and how we want to spend our "craft time" hours. But many people quickly tire of one craft and want to try new things. It is difficult to start a crafting business if you don't have a niche. With years of building brands under my belt, I have learned that you have to be known for something to be successful. If you change your focus from week to week—shifting from pot holders, to painting portraits, to making floral arrangements, to making soap—consider starting a crafting blog rather than selling one specific product. Consumers will get confused about what your ex-

April in her hometown at the Mission San Juan Capistrano during a photo shoot for her "Swallow Messenger Bag" sewing pattern cover.

pertise is. When you start a business, it is important that you figure out what your focus will be.

I know successful crafters who sell a variety of products. I share a booth at an urban farmer's market with a crafter who makes everything from moccasins and bow ties to bracelets and foam swords. But part of what makes her successful is that all of her products are geared toward children, and her brand carries an upcycled, environmentally-friendly focus. I also know successful crafters with a much more singular focus—for example, selling items that are decoupaged or items made with buttons. What I don't often see is someone who has been successful without a common theme or focus in their product offerings.

Perhaps you aren't ready to narrow down the many things you love to do into just one focus. That is okay. Explore a while longer until you feel drawn to one specific area. If you don't want to wait it out, I suggest that you just pick something and go with it. That is what I did. It may seem a little reckless, but it is more important that you get started than to be completely sure of the specific product. If you start building a business and learning about

The Macy Jayne Reversible Headbands tent where April got her big start selling crafts at the downtown farmer's market in Salt Lake City. This year, 2014 will be her ninth season.

I had been selling tote bags for a few years when I met a woman who showed me some headbands she made. They were plastic headbands, covered in glued-on fabric. She had gotten the idea from an Anthropologie headband. The headband was super comfortable and covered with cute fabric. I was smitten by these headbands! It was one of those times when I wished I had thought of it first. I couldn't copy her or Anthropologie and call it my own, but I wanted to do something similar.

It took me several months of daydreaming to finally come up with an idea of how to make a better headband, inspired by my friend's product. Using the same plastic headband, I made a removable fabric cover, which allowed the user to wash the fabric. This alone made the headband unique. I decided to use different fabric on each side of the headband cover to make it reversible. I created a headband that is comfortable, reversible and washable. Now that is unique! Soon bags became my side business and my focus came from selling a truly unique headband that was my own design. I never imagined that I could turn such a simple idea into such a big seller. I know that it all happened because my "Macy Jayne Reversible Headband" is different.

selling your crafts, you will find yourself ahead of the game. You can always change your craft later. Just start your business now.

You can start with something that you already know how to do or something that you know you can learn quickly that interests you. Start with something you can put your focus and time into and see where it takes you. Buy the supplies you need and make a few items, if you haven't already. It is important to see if you enjoy making the same thing over and over again. Find ways to vary the product and find short cuts when producing it so that you can spend less time on the parts that you don't enjoy and more time on the parts that you do.

Turning Your Craft Into a Business

The business part of turning your craft into a business is usually the scary part for many artists. We tell ourselves that it costs too much, that no one will buy our work, or that we don't have time to start a business even if we knew how. These are all legitimate barriers to getting up and running. So I suggest baby steps. Take one step at a time in turning your hobby into a business. You don't have to invest thousands of dollars or a full-time workday to make it happen. Do one thing at a time, one day at a time. Most importantly, keep taking action. Break down the tasks that you need to complete and set a goal to work toward the goal every day. Maybe setting up an Etsy shop is your first goal. Break that down into little steps and check them off your list one by one. Your first step might be coming up with a name for your business. Actively work on coming up with something you like. You can develop a logo later. Your next step might be going online and setting up the Etsy account, even though you have no products to put in the store. Day by day, one step at a time, you will get closer to completing your first goal. Before long, you will be setting more goals and completing those as well. This is one way to create a solid craft business. There are bolder, more fast-paced ways to turn your craft into a business, but if you are cautious or limited on time and money, slow and steady could be the way to go for you.

As you develop your business, it is important to identify what sets you apart from the competition. When there is a story to be told or a true uniqueness to your product, people will be more compelled to buy your product. Your uniqueness can be in your design, the sort of materials that you use to create your product, the story behind developing your product, the price of your product, or even the way your product is distributed. Come up with something that will solve a problem that competing products might have. You can use better quality or more interesting materials that customers will go out of their way to get. Books are written on this topic, but I urge you to transfer the uniquely wonderful *you* into what you are creating.

As you choose a name for your craft business, I suggest selecting a name that is broad enough to allow for product expansion down the road. My first business was called Sitting Pretty Handbags. A few years later when I added headbands to my offerings, it really complicated things. I wish I had chosen a broad and basic company name from the beginning so that I didn't have to re-brand myself completely.

As you get started, you will need to build up your inventory. This should be where most of your time is spent. As you work on your craft, ask around and do some research to find opportunities to sell your product. Are there any arts and crafts fairs in your neighborhood? Is there a local school hosting such an event? Are there any boutiques in your area that sell handmade items or will sell on consignment? Learn what you need to know about opening an online shop, building a website, or starting a blog about your product. There are so many opportunities out there—find out where the opportunities are in your area and which are most beneficial to your specific product.

Get Out There

Once you have made a list of good opportunities, set realistic goals about which selling events you can be ready for and how much product you will need to have ready by that date. If it seems feasible, apply for events and move forward. I highly recommend participating in events where you will be face-to-face with customers. This gives you a unique opportunity to get on-the-spot feedback. At my first selling events, many customers asked if I would shorten the straps for them. After several of these requests, I realized that I was probably making all the straps too long. This small problem would have taken me much longer to figure out if I weren't listening to customers on the front lines. Research and feedback are vitally important to a successful business, and selling directly to customers is a great way to learn.

I have also always benefited greatly from my crafting neighbors at events. Veteran vendors remain my lifeline in the crafting world. From these good and open people, I have learned how to build an attractive display, package my products, interact with my customers, and even price my products. These people are always helpful when I need help setting up, or pitching in when I have too many customers to handle on my own. I cannot say too much about the importance of being a good neighbor. You can scour the internet and read every book available on the crafting industry, but nothing will teach you more than getting out there and learning from the people on the ground that do it week after week or month after month. Your first few events might go terribly. You might not have any sales or your set up might get knocked over by the wind, but it is worth the disappointment if you learn from your customers and fellow vendors.

Troubleshooting

As you find and participate in more selling opportunities, whether online or in person, you might want to take a step back and reevaluate. Is your product selling? Are you packing up from events feeling that no one was interested in your product? Have your products been on Etsy for over a month with no sales? You might even be considering giving up—but don't. You might need to market your products to get them in front of the people who are looking for what you are selling. It might be the way they are packaged or displayed. Maybe the customer can't tell what your product is or how to use it. Maybe your product just isn't unique enough. Get to the bottom of the problem and make changes before you give up.

Take the time to frequently evaluate whether or not you are enjoying making the item(s) that you are selling. It wasn't long into selling my bags that I realized that spending all day behind my sewing machine replenishing my inventory was not what I had envisioned as a fun crafting career. Making a few tote bags a week was fun; making fifteen to thirty bags a week with two small children at home was insane. I knew that if I was going to move forward, I either needed to get help or I needed to find a new way of doing things.

The minute that you get help or have someone make the products for you, you are less of a crafter of your products. At the same time, you become more of a business person. You need to decide which way you want to go. If you want to be a crafter 100 percent of the time and you have more sales than you can manage, you will have to raise your prices and be satisfied with selling less. At this point, you cannot expect your business to grow—you will only be able to sell as many as you can make. If you are okay with that, then you are doing great!

However, if you do want your business to grow and to make your crafts more widely available, at some point you will need to get help. The way that I was able to remain the crafter as my business grew was to decide which parts of my business I did not enjoy and farm those out. I do not like cutting out bag pieces from fabric. I do not like any sort of bookkeeping or accounting. I would also rather design bags and sew them a couple of times than just keep making the same thing over and over again. So I hired someone to cut fabric, got a book-keeper, and eventually had portions of the totes sewn together by freelance employees. This freed up my time to design new bags, create new features on existing bags, and shop for and put together new fabric combinations.

If you are up and running and find that the whole business is a burden, step back and figure out which parts of it you do enjoy. Are you enjoying making the craft you have chosen to build your business around? If so, you know the ropes a lot better now. It is never too late to offer a new product that you might enjoy making more. Try some new things and see what your customers like. Changing up your craft can make a big difference. If other aspects of the business are frustrating, find solutions. Maybe you do not enjoy selling your product face to face to the public. If that is the case, you might find that an online shop is a much better fit for you. Work through the issues and be flexible enough to make changes to keep your business enjoyable.

Stay Connected

As the months and then the years pass, continue to get out into the public and meet people. Networking in the crafting industry is vital to finding opportunities and learning. Trends change and new opportunities arise. You will discover these by being a part of the crafting community and by meeting the people who are purchasing your products. Be a good listener and always try new things. You will be surprised how much fun you can have along the way.

Now get to work, and don't give up!

April Cobb
April is the owner of Modern Yardage, a new and unconventional, digitally-printed fabric design/ manufacturing/ retail company that is changing the way people think about and buy fabric. Before starting Modern Yardage, April worked for many years in advertising and marketing where she learned about consumer trends and identifying what sells. As a member of the sewing commu-nity, she has designed, created and sold her own products to the public, in addition to designing sewing patterns for fabric companies and designers. April is interested in creating new ways for tal-ented designers to get their work out into the world and thrives on inspiring more people to learn how to sew.

BRANDING STRATEGIES FOR CRAFT BUSINESS

....

Interview with Tula Pink

///

2015 Crafter's Market had the chance to interview Tula Pink, the popular fabric and quilt pattern designer, about her tips, tricks and personal success in branding her successful company.

Crafter's Market: When we talk about "branding," what do we mean?

Tula Pink: Branding is the personality of your business. Many people just starting out will often confuse a logo with a brand. A logo is a crucial piece of the brand, but it is just that—a piece. In a successful brand, personality is evident in every single thing that the business does, says, makes and shows. Branding is essentially the image that is projected to the consumer that clearly states who you are as a company, what you provide and the lifestyle that surrounds that image. The "brand" is communicated in the colors you choose for products and packaging, the style of your photos, the language you use in everything from blog posts and tweets to press releases and product descriptions. This can even extend to the materials that you use and the clothes that you wear to events. A good brand is a full picture and almost a being unto itself with a past, a present and a future.

Crafter's Market: In your opinion, why is a recognizable and consistent brand so important for a business?

Tula Pink: In today's marketplace, brand consistency and uniqueness is everything. Technology has created a whole new model for the entrepreneur; it has given the average person the ability to fill all of the roles of a small business themselves, from designer and photographer to marketing and sales. This change has lead to a market flooded with millions of people all competing for the attention of the consumer. The introduction of social media has made that consumer more savvy than ever and shortened their attention span significantly. Your brand must communicate who you are and what you do instantly and efficiently through consistency and recognizability.

Brand consistency builds trust with the consumer. Today's consumer is looking to buy into a lifestyle, and the products that they purchase are a reflection of themselves. For example, if you have a planet-saving, eco-friendly brand that uses only recycled materials and low-impact processes for production, and then you drive up to an event in a giant truck that gets seven miles to the gallon while throwing trash out the window dressed in polyester from head to toe towing a trailer with a farting cow in it, you will effectively betray the trust of your consumer and bankrupt your brand of any credibility that you may have built. This is an extreme example, but the point is that to create a truly successful brand, you have to live it. If it is something that you are passionate about and truly a representation of yourself, you won't even have to work at it.

Every business has competition in one form or another. You have to constantly ask yourself what makes your business special and build your brand around that difference. Being unique, even in a small way, can make all the difference. Are you quirky? Refined? Sweet? Tough? Funny? All of these things can be infused into a brand to make it unique, and this is what will make your brand stronger.

Uniqueness will get you recognized and consistency will turn your customers into believers. Once you have earned that loyalty, your customers will become your greatest asset for building a successful brand.

Crafter's Market: You are known for your representative and recognizable brand. What is the secret to your own success in brand recognition?

Tula Pink: I decided very early on that I was going to take a different path rather than imitate the people that I really admired. Basically, I didn't want to compete head to head with people who were already really successful at what they do. That would be a horrible business strategy. I have always lived in my head and was frequently asked to leave class and the dinner table as a child due to an overactive imagination. Rather than downplay my quirks, I built them into my brand, by accident at first and then with a great deal of intention.

With a name like Tula Pink, the first decision was to go with it or rebel against it completely; I chose to embrace it, but to give it a bit of an edge. My style is quirky, youthful and bold, so hot pink was a better choice than a soft romantic pink. My sense of humor is sharp, as is my logo and the sheer hotness of the color I chose to use. My design sensibilities, while bright, punchy and current, also reflect a healthy dose of adoration for the decadence of bygone eras from the endless interlocking swirls of the baroque to the extravagance of the rococo. I adore the ridiculousness in anything, and I live in a "more is more" kind of world where imagination rules over practicality. My brand, products and lifestyle carry that theme. My brand evolved as a combination of strategy and an organic reflection of the best of myself.

Every so often I stop and try to objectively evaluate how the brand has developed and whether or not it is still true to what I am trying to accomplish. It is crucial to make sure that I am communicating clearly, and social media is the ideal measuring tool. I can see in real time how my audience reacts to the things that I say and the images I show them. The Tula Pink brand shares my aesthetics, my values, my sense of humor, it has my best personality traits, my voice and (unfortunately) it also has my attitude. I am truly passionate about what I do, and I think that comes through in a genuine way—with a side dish of sarcasm, an appetizer of mild self-deprecation, all topped with a sprinkling of over-confidence.

Creating a brand that reflects yourself is a great way to infuse your own unique qualities into your business. It is a fine line to walk as well. It is easy to fool yourself into believing that, because your brand is based on yourself, the people who like your brand are your friends and want to know every little thought that pops into your head. It is important to remember that although a personal brand creates accessibility and uniqueness, it is still a business and your customers need to have faith in your ability to deliver quality and substance.

Crafter's Market: How have you seen successful branding pay off in your business?

Tula Pink: Successful branding has paid off tenfold for me in my business. My product is easily identifiable. My customers know what to expect from me and are willing to take that journey with me as I evolve. There is a trust built between my brand and the consumer. That trust has been cultivated through years of delivering quality product and a clear, consistent message. I always bring imagination and creativity to the table. I hide animals in my fabric designs and combine a traditional elegance with my own unique brand of childlike quirkiness. People are excited to see what will come next. I push myself really hard to deliver on those expectations. It is so easy to fall into the trap of thinking, "I have made it, I have tens of thousands of followers and now I can coast." Unfortunately, it just doesn't work that way. There is too much competition out there to rest on my laurels. I am only as good as my last fabric collection, and I take that to heart. I earn that following back with every new product that I design. When people buy into your brand, you have to nurture that relationship and keep it strong, which means constantly and consistently delivering on your promises.

Crafter's Market: Is there any aspect of your brand that you've adjusted during the life of your business? If so, what was it, why did you make the change, and how did you implement the change? What have the results been?

Tula Pink: My brand has certainly evolved over the years. I was lucky enough to come from a graphic design background having created hundreds of brands for the entertainment industry, mainly in music. I had some understanding of what that entailed, but designing for yourself is a whole new kind of challenge. It is much harder to identify your own brand than it is to identify someone else's. My original visual branding was very pretty, had a lot of little details, was soft and really said very little. I was giving the market what I thought it wanted, which ended up being rather generic and lacking in anything resembling my own personality. I was slowly eking my way into being noticed, but it was my product that was doing all of the work while my brand itself was weak and lazy.

It was my brother, who would eventually become my right hand in this business, who took my branding materials and put them up on a wall with all of my major competitors. It was clear instantly that mine was drowning on a visual level. It just didn't say anything. I completely overhauled the design and started really mapping out who I am and how that affects my branding. I took the brand to social media and by then had a clear message. My business began to double every year and has continued to do so.

Crafter's Market: What branding advice can you give to someone who is just starting their business?

Tula Pink: Building a brand is a tuning process; it doesn't come all at once. A strong brand is built on a solid concept. My best advice would be to open your product up to people who know you and ask them what they think the message is. Let them talk—don't explain what you think it is—and get their honest reaction. If you think you are presenting "soft and romantic" but all of your feedback says that it's "biker chic," you have a pretty serious discrepancy in what you think you are communicating and what people are actually seeing. Branding comes down to three things: Know yourself, know your audience and know your product. If you have a firm grasp on these things, then the rest will fall into place naturally.

Crafter's Market: How does branding a small business differ from branding seen in a large corporation like Coca-Cola?

Tula Pink: Branding on a large scale like Coca-Cola is really different from branding a small business—especially a craft-based business. The main difference is the target audience. A large brand needs to appeal to as many people as possible, all backgrounds, different interests and personalities. They are targeting every man, woman and child in the whole world that might ever drink a soda. The wider the audience, the more generic the branding needs to be in order to not alienate any potential consumer.

In a small, craft-related business, the target audience is very specific and extremely specialized. The community is intimate and demands a lot more of the brand in a personal way. Everybody wants to drink something, but only a select few want to make something themselves or value a handmade product. Accessibility is everything in this market. I have no idea who the CEO of Coca-Cola is but I do know the name of my favorite knitting author's dog, and the name of that dog tells me that she has a sense of humor and I like that, so I buy her books because I can relate. I also buy Coca-Cola but not because I feel a kinship to the brand, but because that's the kind of soda my parents bought. It is a very different kind of consumer decision-making process.

Crafter's Market: For someone just starting out in craft business, what is a jumping off point for developing a strategic branding plan from the beginning? What should the beginner be thinking about before launching their brand?

Tula Pink: Much of what you need to know when developing your brand can be based on three questions: Who are you? What are you selling? Who is your audience? I ask myself these three questions constantly. Get a lot of feedback and be really open to hearing what people are saying. Think clear, bold and simple. The consumer needs to know who you are in a matter of seconds or they will just move on. In today's world you are selling a lifestyle, not just a product, so whatever it is, live it to the fullest!

Crafter's Market: For someone who is diversifying or expanding their business, how can a pre-existing brand stretch/adjust to accommodate a growing business without losing its consistency?

Tula Pink: It is important to build your brand from the beginning for where you want to be, not where you are. A bold, simple but clear brand should be easily expandable. Even as you grow in a business, the brand should be able to maintain the essence of what got it there. I have seen more than one business falter because it lost it's core consumer base when it began to neglect it's original message. The bigger you get, the harder this is to maintain. As more people get involved in your business, the message can easily begin to dilute. As a small business, you work so hard to earn the trust of each new customer that keeping them on board with you is crucial to your growth. By having a firm grasp on what your branding is and constantly reinforcing that message (and teaching your employees and partners to reinforce that message), you can evolve without losing ground.

Crafter's Market: What pitfalls and mistakes should craft business owners be careful to avoid?

Tula Pink: I have seen and made many branding mistakes along the way in my business. I have learned from others and from myself many times over. It is okay to make a mistake as long as you don't make that mistake twice.

One of the biggest mistakes that I see in small craft businesses is mistaking social media as a personal platform rather than one that supports the business. Social media is perhaps the most crucial brand-building element in today's market. Entire businesses, recording artists, clothing lines and comedians have catapulted to stardom through social media and, in contrast, careers and companies have been ruined by it. The immediacy of the connection and the frequency with which you interact with your consumer can be very confusing. While it is important to be personable, accessible and honest in your brand, there is indeed a limit to what your consumer needs to know about you. Think before you post, ask yourself how this helps to reinforce confidence in your product. I may share my failures, hardships and frustrations with my family or my best friends, but not on my business platforms. My customer should never be put in a position to console me—it is my job to lift them up. They buy my product because it makes them happy, which in turn makes me happy. It's a simple, mutually beneficial relationship. So mind your media!

Crafter's Market: Can you provide any insight into what buyers and stores are looking for when it comes to brands, if anything?

Tula Pink: A small craft business is more likely to target boutique and independent shops rather than large chain stores in the beginning, but the same issues apply as you scale up. A store wants to carry a product that will sell, plain and simple. That may seem really obvious, but that is the bottom line. It is important to be aware of the retailer's needs. They may carry hundreds of different products and brands. They are not physically able to give your brand special attention. If your visual branding is clear and specific, they won't need to. It is a win for your product and a win for the retailer as well. Retailers want a brand that is supported beyond just their walls or online shop. My first job when introducing a product is to sell it to the stores, and I want my product in as many stores as possible. My job doesn't end there. Once my product has shipped and is arriving in stores, my focus switches to selling their order through to the consumer. Re-orders are the life blood of any business, big or small. I consider myself to be the retailer's partner. As a wholesale business I have already made my money once the retailers have ordered my product. If I want those retailers to carry my next product, they need to profit off of this one; each cycle of selling will build greater confidence and make the next sale that much easier for them to say "yes" to. The store will work harder for me if they know that I am working hard for them. Branding can make all the difference when a consumer is choosing between two similar products.

Crafter's Market: What are three tips you have for someone when it comes to developing a strong and recognizable craft business brand?

Tula Pink: Three tips for building a strong craft business brand is to be bold, clear and consistent. Whatever the direction you choose to base your branding on, know it inside and out. Be bold! The consumer glances at millions of products every day—sometimes you need to yell at them! You can do this through color or graphics, humor or simplicity. Clarity is key. The more you know about your own brand, the easier it is to communicate that to your consumer. And consistency is crucial. Never assume that the consumer knows what you are talking about or who you are. If you are lucky, you will have new customers every day, so you must reinforce your brand constantly. This will generate new customers and build trust with your existing customers.

Tula Pink
Tula is an American illustrator, fabric designer and author with over 300 fabric designs to her credit so far. Tula is the author of two successful books on quilting, *Quilts from the House of Tula Pink* and *Tula Pink's City Sampler: 100 Modern Quilt Blocks*. In addition to her artistic talents, Tula has developed a highly recognizable worldwide craft brand and is known specifically for her dark sense of humor, flair for hiding animals in the strangest of places (artistically, not literally) and boldly unique use of color and pattern.

CRAFTING A SOCIAL MEDIA PRESENCE

....

by Courtney Walsh

Pinterest. Facebook. Instagram. Twitter. Snapchat. Vine. YouTube. Where do we begin?

THE "DO'S" OF SOCIAL MEDIA

One thing is certain, social media is here to stay. And just when it seems we finally understand how to best use one platform, another one pops up, making it difficult to stay abreast of the best way to utilize these technological methods. Whatever platform(s) you choose to use, there are a few universal tips and tricks you can start using today to help enhance your crafty business.

1. **Identify your goals.** Yes, even with social media, it's important to have goals. As you begin, decide what kind of goals to set and write them down. Whether it's the number of followers you want to strive for or the number of views on your YouTube channel, set reasonable, attainable goals. Now, work backwards to determine a timeline on how you can best achieve these goals. For instance, if your goal is to have 500 Twitter followers, devising a strategy will keep you on target to meeting (and exceeding) that goal. Once you've reached that mark, you can create a new set of goals and begin the process again. Clear benchmarks will help keep you focused, which means you'll be more likely to be successful.

2. **Identify your audience.** Who are the people you're creating for? Whose attention do you want to capture? Where do those people hang out online and how can you get your message in front of them? Marketing is nothing more than finding groups of people and getting up in front of them. Once you know who will be most interested in what you're creating, become a part of their community. Engage in conversation. There's nothing worse than someone who posts something and disappears. People want to

connect with you, but if you're a ghost, that's impossible. By the same token, get involved in what other people in your field are doing. Encourage them. Share their work. Share your wisdom. Become a genuine member interested in genuine relationships, not just someone who shows up asking for favors. The quickest way to kill a relationship is to sell, sell, sell. Find a good balance between genuine interest in the people reading your content and sharing your own work.

3. **Make it share-worthy.** The trick to social media is in the pyramid effect. You share something. Your friends love it. They share it with their friends and on and on it goes. But in order for that to happen, you first have to create something share-worthy. Take a look at what your friends are sharing. Is it inspirational? Is it educational? Is it entertaining? How can your message achieve the same thing? Not everything you post or share needs to go viral, of course, but the more people like and share, the more likely they are to come back and the more likely you are to build your audience.

4. **Get visual.** It's true that a picture is worth a thousand words, and social media is no exception. People are far more drawn to images than they are to large blocks of text, so give them what they want! Most forms of social media allow you to share images as well as text, so adopt a "show, don't tell" policy. Your posts without photos should be few and far between (or non-existent). You're an artist. Draw your audience in with images of your process, your space or your finished work. Friends and fans love to hear how and why you do what you do.

5. **Cozy up to the (video) camera.** Photos are just one way to provide visual stimulation. Videos are even more sharable than still shots, so consider adding video to your social media feeds. Keep in mind you don't need a fancy home studio to produce share-worthy videos. Crafters and artists can utilize video in a number of ways. Create a tutorial on a technique or new product. Reveal your latest work of art. Record the entire process and speed it up to share how you created the piece. Keep in mind that if you're interested in it, odds are someone else will be, too.

A NOTE ON PHOTOS

It's important to show your work in the best possible way. That means a good camera and good photo editing software are a wise investment, as is the time it takes to learn how to use them. If your photos don't look appealing, they can actually have the opposite effect you want them to. Make sure your images are sharp and high quality. Before you spend a lot of money outfitting a private photo studio, though, check out the many online sites to help you achieve great image results without spending a lot of money.

See PicMonkey or Pixlr.com to get started.

6. **Create excellent content.** There's a saying in marketing that "content is king" and it's true. Every post should have content that is valuable to your reader. That's not to say every post needs to be the same. Some are meant to entertain, others to educate, others to connect, others to inspire. There are many facets to your social media persona, but all require a take-away for your reader. Remember, the goal is to spark conversation and build relationships with potential fans. You can't do that if you're not sharing anything interesting.

7. **Get focused.** Most social media gurus agree that social media is most successful when it's focused. For instance, if you launch a knitting blog but spend every other post talking about your hairless dogs, people probably won't come back. You don't want to pull a bait and switch with your readers. By the same token, stay focused with each medium you use. Consider a business account for each platform so you aren't "cross-contaminating" your information. If you enjoy having a public account where you can share Fluffy's latest escapades, keep it, but consider building a professional account as well. This will enable you to keep your messages separate.

8. **Be yourself.** While your fans may not care about your kids, your cat or your latest stomach bug, they do care about you. Social media is by definition social, and that means your fans want to know what you love, what you hate, what products you're using, etc. They do have an interest in your life, but in terms of how it relates to them. Decide what kind of persona you want to have and build your platform around that, but be genuine. Don't be overly negative or pessimistic. By the same token, don't be overly "sunshine and rainbows." It can read as insincere and will turn people off. Balance is the key.

9. **Be consistent.** If you start a Twitter account for your crafty persona and then tweet once a week, you're not likely to engage your followers. The key is to find the balance and stay consistent. With a blog, you set the schedule, but once it's set and you create an expectation, it's important to stick to it. Readers are more likely to come back often if there's new, valuable content, so updating regularly is crucial. However, there is such a thing as too much social media. If you're posting a new Facebook status every hour, at some point your fans may get tired of you. By the same token, hourly posts on Twitter are just fine, because Twitter moves much more quickly than Facebook. Find a balance between engaging in the conversation and being annoying.

10. **Choose wisely.** There is no rule that says you need to master or even participate in every social media platform. Let's face it, you could turn social media into a full-time job if you wanted. Decide which platforms work best for you. Do you prefer the quick-moving, micro-blogging style of Twitter? The visual snapshots of Instagram? The combination you find in Facebook? Do you create excellent videos that would lend themselves to a popular YouTube channel? Figure out where you can be the most effective, and

stick with those two or three mediums. If one proves ineffective, then you can explore another one, but you'll burn out if you try to stay engaged in each one all the time.

11. **Be patient.** Social media is an ever-growing, always changing medium and it's as fickle as its users. Any good platform will need a lot of attention and thought, and success won't happen overnight. Be patient. Pay attention to what's working and what's not, and make adjustments on a regular basis.

THE "DON'TS" OF SOCIAL MEDIA

Just like there are several universal ways you can use social media to build your creative business, there are also ways you can misuse social media and hurt your brand.

1. **Don't spam.** We've all been there. We accept someone's friend request and two minutes later, they send us a private message with instructions on how to like their page. Worse, the notifications don't stop there. They now want us to buy their e-book or tell our friends about their latest blog post. This is not okay. It's the online equivalent of telemarketing and no one appreciates it. Most likely, you'll be deleted.

2. **Don't add people to groups without their permission.** Groups and communities are a wonderful way to engage your audience, but don't add people to them without their permission.

3. **Don't use other people's platforms to promote your own work.** Chances are you know others in your field or related fields who have large followings. Whatever they do, they seem to attract large numbers and lots of interest. It's important to note that you can't compare your fledgling platform with someone else's, but it's also important not to hitch a ride on their platform. Odds are, those people worked for each follower, fan or student they have. Make sure not to link your own work on their sites, pages or various forms of social media unless they ask for it. Be willing to do your own leg work and one day people will want to hitch a ride on your platform.

4. **Don't overshare.** We've already discussed the delicate balance between being genuine and being too personal on a professional page, and while it should go without saying, it bears repeating. Don't overshare. Nobody needs to hear the messy details of your divorce or about your night on the town. If you want to be seen as a professional, you must act professionally. Keep in mind that potential editors, agents or other professionals may stumble across your page needing to hire people with your unique skill set. Don't publish anything on-line that might deter them from hiring you.

5. **Don't be negative.** The *Saturday Night Live* "Debbie Downer" sketch was funny because everyone can relate. We all have a Debbie Downer in our lives. Let's face it, you're going to have bad days. You're going to be passed over for someone you think

is less qualified. By no means is this ever something you should share through any social media channels. Constant negativity is a huge turn-off—not just for potential employers, but for your fans, friends and followers. Does that mean you should act like everything is always wonderful? Of course not. Phoniness is never advocated, but before you post how much you hate a store's customer service or how difficult your last class was thanks to one student in particular, decide if you really want to put that out there. If not, wait until you have something a bit more positive to say.

It should be noted that when it comes to social media, what works for one person might not work for you, and success is largely determined through trial and error. The trick is finding what works for you, your particular platform and your style of relating to potential readers, students or fans. Whichever platforms you choose, be wise, balanced, patient and consistent, and you'll start to see social media work for you.

Courtney Walsh
Courtney is a published author, mixed-media artist, theater director and playwright. Her debut novel, *A Sweethaven Summer*, hit the *New York Times* and *USA Today* bestseller lists. It was followed by the release of *A Sweethaven Homecoming* and *A Sweethaven Christmas*. She has also written two papercrafting books, *Scrapbooking Your Faith* and *The Busy Scrapper*. She blogs at www.courtneywalsh.typepad.com or you can find her online at www.courtneywalshwrites.com.

FINDING SUCCESS ON ETSY

by Kristen Robinson

Etsy truly offers an amazing opportunity to the artist and crafter looking to sell their work in a platform that spans the entire world. I can think of no better place that supports creatively-oriented independent businesses and encourages the creative side in all of us.

It is so exciting to think that, from start to finish, you have the ability to create and launch an Etsy store within hours. In the following pages, I have outlined the ins and outs of starting an Etsy store, but it is very important to educate yourself on all of Etsy's selling and buying policies before getting started. These policies can be found in the help section of the Etsy website.

GETTING STARTED

Congratulate yourself! You have chosen to take your crafting to an entirely new level—one that is not only rewarding but also inspiring and satisfying. Now that you stepped onto this path, the very first thing you will need to ascertain is which items and products you are going to offer in your Etsy store. Resist the temptation to run right to the login screen and create a shop name. While the initial direction for your shop might seem like an easy decision to make, it is one you must consider carefully. The items you choose to sell must fit into the guidelines that Etsy has laid out while also representing you.

As I mentioned, there are guidelines that Etsy asks each seller to follow, and I suggest that you review these prior to choosing your stock and opening your shop. Etsy has put these guidelines in place to protect both the seller and the buyer; for the most part, they are common sense and very straightforward. Understanding and adhering to these policies will help ensure your success on Etsy.

First and foremost, everything on Etsy must be made by hand, be vintage or serve as a supply to create an end craft product (such as crepe paper, ribbon or resin solder). In general and in Etsy terms, "vintage" is defined as an item that is at least twenty years old. Be sure to review the list of prohibited items that may fall into this category.

As the adage goes, honesty is the best policy. The items you sell represent you; therefore, they absolutely must be authentic. You must hold the copyright to items listed as handmade, meaning that the idea and the creation must be yours! This holds true for items that you create while taking classes or that were made from a kit; unless you have been given permission by the instructor or designer, the creation is not con-

When naming your shop and designing your banner and avatar, keep the aesthetic of your products in mind. The look of your branding should not vary wildly from the look of your product. If your products tend to be made in cool, neutral colors, a wild and bright brand aesthetic may not make sense to your buyer.

sidered to be the intellectual property of the seller. Once you have ensured that your products fall within the parameters of Etsy's rules, it's time to have a bit of fun.

When choosing items to sell, it is important to narrow your view a bit, especially in the beginning. (Read "Finding Your Crafty Niche" for more insight on selecting your focus.) Shoppers have an endless bounty of choices when it comes to online commerce. Your items will be competing with thousands of other similar products that are found online, and in craft markets, galleries and even department stores. The great news is this—your competition does not necessarily have your audience and it definitely does not have your creative voice.

Think about something you create really well and enjoy making. Once you have narrowed this down, start brainstorming ways to reinvent this item. How many different colors can you add? Can you change the shape or style? Can it be personalized? Buyers love to purchase one-of-a-kind items that others will gush over, so always offer some special pieces. If you truly want to push that one-of-a-kind item over the edge, think about ways you can personalize the item; this is always—and I do mean *always*—an eye catcher to the buyer.

Naming Your Shop

Choosing the name of your shop might seem like the first thing you should tackle, but you may find that your original idea evolves after putting together an inventory. Think about your shop name very, very carefully. Once you choose your name during the sign up process, it becomes a permanent link to you. While changing the name is not impossible, it is a bit of a process and includes redirect links that your shoppers might find a bit frustrating.

Just as you did when you created your inventory, don't get wrapped up in the process and create undo stress. Putting a little forethought and time into this part of the process will eliminate challenges in the future. Consider spelling, memorability and product representation, and research if there are other shops with similar names before naming your shop.

Begin by creating a list of names you really like. (I like working on a dry erase board.) In some cases, your shop name might just be your own name; for example, my Etsy shop is named "Kristen Robinson." When I set up my store, there were not a lot of tips and tricks available for choosing a name, and I felt that using my name made it easy to find. Now that the population of Etsy has exploded, it is helpful to have a unique shop name—one that separates you from others and tempts buyers to stop by for a visit.

Once you have brainstormed a list of names, think a little bit about the future. Will this venture evolve into a blog or website? If you have even a small inkling that it might, perform a quick search to confirm the name is not taken—you might be surprised at how many others had the same brilliant idea. If you do find that the perfect name is available, not only on Etsy but on the web, I encourage you to scoop it up.

Try to steer clear of pigeonholing yourself by narrowing your topic. For example, "Susie's Jewels" might sound perfect to you right now, but as you move forward you might find yourself venturing into other arenas. Also, keep in mind that your shop name will be crunched together without spaces, so use upper case when appropriate. For example, "JanesBaubles" is much easier to read than "janesbaubles."

The banner shown here for Spool + Sparrow features a beautiful photo of a favorite product, as well as the name of the shop in a simple, representative font.

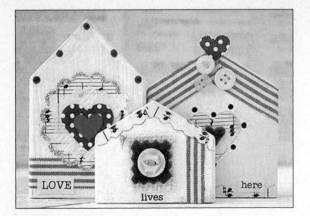

Clean and simple styling allows the group of houses to be the star of the photo.

While your shop name is a true reflection of you, there are definite pitfalls to avoid when deciding on the name. Steer clear of naming your shop after your e-mail address (especially if it includes numbers). Avoid words that have more than one spelling, and perhaps the granddaddy of them all—don't choose a name composed of so many letters it takes a dictionary to remember them all.

Creating a Banner

Your banner is an image that runs across the top of your Etsy shop. In conjunction with your shop name, your banner will not only help brand your shop but will give buyers their first impression of who you are and what wares you sell. Your banner needs to be eye catching and attractive but also relevant. If you are not savvy with photo editing software, do not panic. There are a plethora of sellers who create personal banners. There are also many online forums and blogs on banner etiquette and how-to's.

Take a bit of time to look at stores that sell a similar product. Take notes on what you find appealing about their banners; this will help you generate ideas while making sure your banner is original. As with anything, there are a vast array of opinions and thoughts on the ideal shop banner. In truth, the most important thing is to make sure it represents you and your product. If you work in creams and whites, it might confuse your buyer if your banner is composed of neon pink and bright blue. Ensure the message is clear and concise; if you sell pottery, make sure the banner doesn't imply you are a graphic artist.

Without delving into the technical aspects too much, it is important to note that your store banner cannot be more than 2MB with a pixel measurement of 760×100. Keep this in mind when gathering graphics and choosing a font; in some cases, these graphic elements will appear unattractive if not formatted correctly.

While we are talking about banners, this is also a good time to touch on your avatar. Your avatar is a small image that is used in forums, in conversations, and on item pages and other places on Etsy. This avatar represents you as well as your product. As with the banner, there are a few different opinions on what type of image is best to use. Because of my publishing and teaching presence, I use a photo of myself, which allows for instant recognition. However, if you are primarily delving into the selling arena, consider choosing a photo of your best and favorite piece. Keep in mind the avatar is a small icon, so the photo needs to be simple and perfectly photographed.

Shop Profile

A shop profile ties together everything you have done thus far. Prospective buyers want to know who you are! This is your opportunity to connect with the buyer and start building a relationship. Your profile is the place to describe the focus of your shop, talk about what you specialize in and to whom you cater. Invite your potential buyer into your story—talk about the things that attract you, inspire you and ignite your creativity. Add a few lines about your creative discovery: When did it happen? Who influenced you? What or who encouraged you to move forward with your goals?

Allow yourself to be as open as you feel comfortable. Be real and give details without giving it all away. Be sure to mention any positive press and awards as these credits only reinforce your abilities. On the same note, there is no need to list everything here; your buyers are not interested in achievements that are irrelevant to your store.

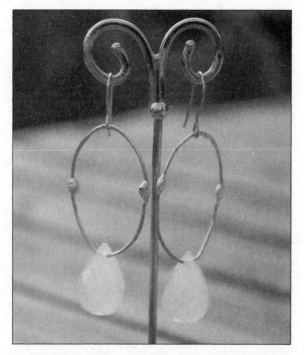

Describe your items using clear and descriptive words. For example, these beautifully photographed earrings could be described using words like "teardrop," "earrings," "aqua," and "gold."

Photographing Your Items

Prior to listing your items, you will need to photograph them. For many, this is one arena that can be challenging and a bit confusing. The good news is this—you do not need a fancy or expensive camera to shoot great photos. With the infusion of amazing camera apps, a smart phone can often do the trick, as photos meant for internet use need to be 72dpi (minimum). Along the same line, a serviceable little camera can be purchased for under two hundred dollars.

Prior to shooting your photos, do a little research. Think about your favorite magazine or the shopping you do online.

What attracts you? There are always a few key elements that are necessary. First, your photos must be clear—buyers are not interested in fuzzy photos. Next, the styling is critical. When items are shot amongst a sea of props, it is often impossible to discern what is actually for sale. Props should enhance, not detract or distract. Peruse the aisles of your favorite store and take notes. What attracts you? What distracts you?

Your photos should show how or where the item might be used, and should indicate the size of the object. If you are marketing jewelry or clothing, placing the item on a person or a dress form allows the viewer to see how the piece will drape and form to a body. If shooting artwork, take a few shots on different colored backgrounds, always remembering simpler is better. If a group of items is being sold together, be sure to include a shot that shows all the items for sale in the group.

Perhaps the most important thing to remember when taking photos is unity. Throughout your shop, style your photos in the same way and with the same color scheme. Remember that simplicity is often the key to highlighting an item while maintaining a comfortable, inviting feeling. (Read "Photo Head" for more insight into photographing and styling your work.)

Listing Your Items

I am a firm believer in listing as many items as you have to sell at once. However, if time is limited, list in batches; a full page of images translates into better online positioning. Once you have chosen the items to list, it is time to work on descriptions and tags.

When describing your item, the most pertinent information should come first. This holds true for two reasons: It creates good positioning and advertising in search engines, and it allows the buyer to engage with the item more rapidly. When describing your item, infuse your unique voice. Speak about the piece as if you

Standout packaging can add value to your product, but it also adds weight. Be sure to factor additional packaging weight in when calculating shipping costs.

were talking to a friend, highlighting the wonderful features as well as the unique attributes the item possesses. Keep things short and sweet. I had a marketing professor in college that repeatedly reminded us to write as if we were talking in bullet points. Be specific, honest and brief.

After inputing your description, you will need to move on to shop sections. In this arena I am a big believer in "less is more." The more concise the information, the easier it is to navigate. It is important to avoid being vague; stay as clear and concise as possible.

A big part of listing an item is tagging it. This process occurs after you have created your description. When tagging your item, think about for whom the item is intended. Does the item have a prevalent color? How would you categorize it—jewelry, pottery, clothing? What style is it? Avoid complicated verbiage that you don't typically use when speaking, and stay true to the item. If an item is blue say "blue," not "sea blue" or "sky blue."

After tagging occurs, move on to materials. As with all parts of your shop, be honest. Do not list "vintage chain" in the materials unless you are absolutely positive that the piece is vintage. I think you get the idea.

Pricing

Pricing is perhaps one of the top conversations that arise time and time again. After eight years of selling on Etsy, I still consult my peers to make sure I am in line with current pricing. When we create something, we tend to discount its true value. But when things are priced lower than the buyer perceives they should be, the items do not sell. Of course, the same will hold true for items that are priced higher than they should be.

It is important to price your items based on the market. Do a little research, check out how other crafters and artisans are pricing their items, and use this as a guideline. The next step is to determine what your hourly rate is going to be. Once you have these two numbers it is time to create your actual price. A very simple industry formula is: materials + labor. This sum equates to the wholesale price. Once you have this sum, multiply it by two; this is the retail price. Utilizing this formula will insure continuity for your current and future buyers. (Read "Pricing Your Work" for more insight into pricing your items.)

Shipping

Shipping is one area that you must get right immediately; if computed incorrectly, shipping can cost you a lot of money. Take the time to research carriers—from the postal service to shipping services. Choose methods that are affordable and offer tracking and insurance options.

Keep in mind that packaging definitely adds another layer of specialty to purchases. Be sure to take special packaging into account when computing your shipping charges. If your item weighs one pound and your wrapping weighs eight ounces, your shipping weight is no longer one pound. If you sell multiple items that are the same size and shape, create a shipping profile for them in Etsy; this is a huge time saver when shipping future purchases. Don't forget to take the time to keep up with rate changes your preferred carrier might impose. While shipping can be a bit confusing in the beginning, it does get easier.

Marketing and Promoting

Marketing and promoting your shop is one thing that you will require consistent work. The ability to promote your shop correctly comes down to positioning oneself in a competitive manner. It is important for you to hone in on the things that make you different from your competition and promote that aspect of your business.

First and foremost, you need to know your customer. What matters to them? What fills their needs and desires? Do your shoppers connect with you on a personal level, on an artistic level, or both? Next, take a good look at the competition you have. What items do they offer? How are they pricing their wares? Next, focus on your value. What is it that makes your product valuable in the marketplace? Do you have amazing antique elements in your work that are hard to find? Perhaps you provide one-of-a-kind items rarely found? Maybe it is as simple as providing daily shipping.

Of course there are things you can and should do on a regular basis that will market your shop all on its own. Great photos equate to more buyers looking at your shop and ultimately more sales. Be true to your brand. Everything you have should reflect your personal style and the voice of your shop. If you are selling items that are not handmade, focus on selling things you believe in. Etsy is not the place to sell just to sell.

The last two areas that come in to play are search engine optimization and social media. I will be the first one to admit I am not on top of my social media 100 percent of the time. However, when I am on top of my social media, sales happen and interest is sparked. The great thing about social media is it does not even have to be connected to an item you are listing or selling; often a quick check-in on social media will be the perfect reminder to a potential buyer to stop by and take a look at your shop.

Search engine optimization, otherwise known as SEO, is one of the most fascinating facets of marketing. When you have good words attached to your products, your search engine ranking goes up and people find you more readily with simple keyword searches. This is where those shop stats really come into play. Review this on a regular basis and change things up a bit if need be. Keep records of your successes as well as those areas in which you may need to work on or rethink. If your keywords are not working to boost your searchability, change things up a bit; replace those words and your sales will often reflect the difference.

MAINTAINING YOUR SHOP

Now that your shop is up and running, the hardest part is out of the way but the work is not over. It is of the utmost importance to keep your shop sufficiently stocked. Oftentimes shoppers may stop by to check out one item and leave with a cartful. Thumbnails of your inventory will appear on each page, providing more selling opportunities to present themselves when your shelves are stocked.

Clean house every once in a while. Perhaps you have a few items that you really want to move quickly. Offer a special coupon in relationship to these goods. Celebrate a "just because" day with a 10% coupon for select items, or offer a holiday code to boost sales. This is a simple add-on that takes just a few minutes to achieve through Etsy.

Keep up great customer service and communication, and your buyers are sure to come back time and time again. Offer new items based on those that have been popular, and consider offering lines of goods that go together.

Above all, treat your Etsy store as if it were a brick and mortar store. Check in with it daily. Follow up on questions and communicate with buyers in a timely fashion. Keep records of all your shipments and ensure they arrive as they should. Periodically review your goals and shift them as needed.

I encourage you to take a good look around Etsy prior to starting up your shop. Have all of your information ready and a banner created before diving in, because once you start the process you will not want to pause. I wish you a bounty of joy and success in your new venture!

Kristen Robinson

Kristen is the author of *Tales of Adornment: Techniques for Creating Romantic Resin Jewelry, Making Etched Metal Jewelry* and *Explore Mixed Media Collage*, as well as the DVD *Romantic Bezels: Mixed-Media Jewelry From Found Objects*. Kristen is the designer of the Rue Romantique collection and is an on-staff artist for an array of industry publications. To learn more about her art and life, visit www.kristenrobinson.net.

DESIGN TIPS AND TRICKS FOR YOUR CRAFTY BIZ

by Courtney Kyle

Do you ever wish your blog, website or craft packaging just looked a little better? You pour your heart into your business, but what does the appearance of your business say to outsiders? Is it clean and chic? Modern and simplistic? What if it appears busy or messy? You don't want that! This article is full of helpful information to help you stay on the right track when designing and promoting your business across all media—from booths at craft fairs to your blog and social media sites.

In this article you will find basic design principles, tips, resources and advice to keep in mind anytime you are creating a visual representation of or for your business.

THE BASICS

- **Balance:** Visual balance is an effective principle for conveying tension and/or mood. Symmetrical balance conveys a sense of formality and permanence while asymmetrical balance tends to convey a more lively and appealing mood. Balance is important because you want your audience to experience ease when navigating your design whether it's on your blog or a brochure you've created.
- **Hierarchy:** Hierarchy is the sizing and organization of information in a way that makes it easy to follow. It leads the reader through by order of each element's significance. Hierarchy is especially useful in blog posts, where the headline should be most prominent, followed by subheads, paragraph text, pull quotes, etc.
- **Alignment:** Look at the nearest magazine or newspaper. Notice how almost every page has some sense of organization? You may have never noticed it, but designers use grids to keep the content in magazines, newspapers and books organized and aligned. You

might consider using a grid when creating designs for your business. Use it to organize your information so that the reader can easily navigate your material.

- **Repetition and consistency:** Think of a symbol, color or font that a large brand would use. Do you notice how across all media, certain elements remain the same within a brand? Repetition and consistency are perhaps the most important design elements to remember when branding your business. When developing an image for your business, it's important to really assess which elements you want to use. Be comfortable with that decision because you'll need to stick to it in order to maintain a consistent image. Consistency equals brand recognition. While you may not be creating a large company, you still need to maintain an image that is easily recognizable by your followers. Changing it on a whim may cause confusion and lead to former customers missing you in a lineup because they didn't recognize your style. If you do decide that you are no longer happy with the look of your business, take your time and focus on the changes you need to make so that you'll be happy with the end result. Plan to push out the new brand look to your blog, social media accounts, etc., all at once.
- **Similarity and contrast:** Similarity is useful when you wish to create a sense of unity between objects, images, typography or areas of information. Use contrast to help important elements stand out. If you create a graphic or type out a blog post, ask yourself if there's something that needs to be emphasized. If so, address it by increasing size, adding color or picking a complementary font.
- **White space:** Do you ever find yourself guilty of overwriting or over-illustrating? It's okay, it happens to the best of us. But in any design—whether it's your latest blog post or a flier you're making to promote a giveaway—be sure to maintain generous margins and space betweens images and text as well as between lines of text. Avoid cramming information together and be sure to provide plenty of white space. This gives the eyes a break and helps to separate areas of information.
- **Mood:** Consider the mood of your brand. Is it fun and free? Fancy and formal? Rugged and outdoorsy? Let your design reflect the mood of your brand.

Design Tips

- **Focus on simplicity.** Less is more, and the more simplistic your logo, site navigation and graphic design is, the easier it'll be for your followers to recognize, follow and navigate your brand.
- **Keep your color palette simple.** Think about using one or two colors; then add in a neutral tone like gray or off-white.
- **Be wary of clip-art.** If it looks like something that emerged from a 1990s-era word processor, back away. Look for graphics that are clean, well drawn and relevant to your idea.

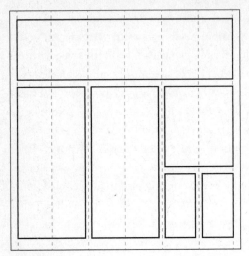

Alignment

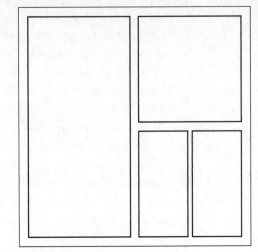

Balance (asymmetrical)

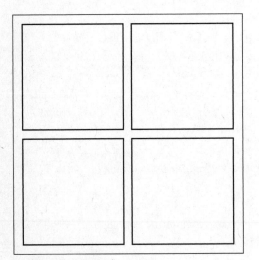

Balance (symmetrical)

Headline 1
Headline 2
Subhead
Paragraph

- Bulleted List
- Item 1

Pull Quote

Credit

Hierarchy

Mood

Repetition

Similarity and contrast

White space

- **Think about your audience.** If you're selling heirloom embroidery designs, don't use a grungy font for your logo.
- **Don't change your logo every month.** You'll seem indecisive.
- **Don't use fonts that are hard to read.**

Photography Tips

- **Check the resolution of your photography.** Whether you are using a photo on your blog or in print, make sure the resolution is 300ppi for print and 72ppi for web. If you're not sure, size the image as you plan on using it. Does it look pixelated or fuzzy? If so, try to find a better quality image.
- **If you're pulling images from the web to use in a blog post, be sure you click through and find the largest version of the image you'd like to use.** Saving images from thumbnails will only save that specific image size for you. Try following through to the original source to get the best quality image. And as always, be sure to get permission from and credit the original author.
- **Be consistent with your photographic style.** Like most crafty business owners, you'll likely have to produce your own photos to showcase your work. Play around with lighting and backdrops and see what works for you. Once you develop a style, stick to it. Your photography represents your brand as much as your logo, color scheme and typographic choices.

Typography Tips

- **When selecting fonts for your brand, use the principle of contrast to select two that complement each other.** Fonts that are too similar will look like a mistake.
- **Legibility is important because you want your readers to understand what your product is all about.** Avoid fonts that are hard to read like ornamental fonts or small scripts.

Studio Court logo

Resources

Just because you're a hands-on crafter doesn't mean you have to create every last thing by hand. Utilize online tools to help you spread information and design interesting graphics. Here is a sampling of useful tools you might use for your crafty business.

- **www.befunky.com**—BeFunky is a great photo editor if you're looking for basic photo editing and collage making. My favorite use for BeFunky is the collage tool. Its simple drag and drop functionality makes creating a new collage a breeze. And if you're not satisfied with the layout of your collage, you can switch between different collages without having to reinsert your photos. It's even got collage templates for creating Facebook covers and pins on Pinterest.
- **www.picmonkey.com**—Go the extra mile with PicMonkey. PicMonkey is more than a photo editing app. It gives you easy-to-use tools to perform basic edits such as exposure, crop, sharpen and resizing. It also provides a great selection of effects, beauty touch-ups, text and graphic overlays, fun frames, interesting textures and theme packages. I was personally impressed by the beauty touch-ups and the high quality graphics. Unfortunately, many of the great features on PicMonkey do require an upgrade to a "Royale" subscription, but thirty-three dollars per year isn't bad for a tool that does it all.
- **pinstamatic.com**—Get the most out of Pinterest by generating new content for your followers. Pinstamatic makes it easy to share things like quotes, websites, music, Twitter profiles and more.
- **thegraphicsfairy.com**—The Graphics Fairy is a website that is chock full of beautiful antique graphics, do-it-yourself projects and more. I visit this site often for inspiration and to look for vintage graphics that might complement a current project. There are thousands of images available for use in your own designs and projects.
- **www.dreamstime.com**—Dreamstime is a stock photography site that offers both free and paid stock photography. It provides a huge stock of free images to choose from for penny-pinchers like me.

The Takeaway

Consistency is the name of the game. If you take away one thing from this article, remember to be consistent. Consistency is the key to maintaining an easily recognizable brand across all media. Whether you're promoting your work on Twitter, Facebook, Etsy or a printed flyer, maintain a defined style for your brand.

For instance, the logo for my business, Studio Court, is a simplistic black and white circle logo. I use that logo on my Twitter, Facebook, Google+, Instagram and any other page or app I use. I may do something fun with it every once in a while, like turn it green on St. Patrick's Day, but my logo stays the same no matter where it's used. Likewise, the way I showcase my work is consistent whether it's on my Behance profile or the portfolio page on my website.

You don't have to be afraid of eventually re-branding. With time comes change and sometimes change is not only good, but needed. Maybe you've been chugging along with a semi-inconsistent look or maybe you've done a great job maintaining a specific style but you're ready for a change. Just don't change it up too often.

If you do decide to make a change, put some time into it. Develop a mood board, play with colors, write down some keywords to describe the impression you want your business to make. After you've put some quality planning into it—and you know you can live with your new style for a while—then you're ready to commit to your new look.

Consistency won't just help you maintain your brand, it'll make your job easier as a crafty business owner. You won't waste time trying to decide on which font to use or what color looks best. With all of the details in place, you can focus your attention on growing your business.

Courtney Kyle
Courtney believes in a world where everyone can live the life they dream by engaging in their passions! She is a graphic designer with a love of art, science and gardening. As an avid DIYer, Courtney spends most of her free-time getting her hands dirty on a variety of projects. Courtney is the owner and creative director of Studio Court, a company specializing in editorial design. She co-created and designed *Stitch Craft Create* magazine (www.stitchcraftcreate.com) and has designed several books and magazines for national and international craft publishers.

PHTO HEAD

by Elizabeth Maxson

We all live a life of illusion. We are trained to not only accept it, but also expect it. We accept that cover models are photoshopped and fluffy clouds are often added to landscapes. Pinterest, Instagram, Facebook and blogs are tools from which we cherry pick what we wish to share with others. It is very easy to leave out the messy side of life, while our retouched images conform to what we want others to see. This generation's version of "keeping up with the Joneses" is accomplished via social media—seeing how many "friends" or "likes" or "followers" we can amass compared to our peers. Painting a lifestyle of ourselves is simply retouching what we don't like and enhancing what we wish. We live in a culture that is longing for creative or unique lifestyles—a culture that is created through illusions. And those illusions begin with images.

The Importance of a Photo

Advertisers have known for decades that consumers may not necessarily want to buy a particular product, but they are more than happy to part with their dollars for the chance to buy a lifestyle. The 1970s ad campaign for Coca-Cola was about living a life "in perfect harmony" while drinking their product. The ad conveyed that it was those in happy, multi-cultural relationships and the free-spirited who drank Coke. Coca-Cola's successful lifestyle advertising led to more products following suit. Show an ad of a rugged cowboy on a horse with the sunset at his back, and we know it is the Marlboro Man before we ever see an image of a cigarette. An image of a slim, pretty woman in business attire with her hand firmly planted on her jutted hip is no doubt a Virginia Slims ad. Persuading consumers to purchase a product is sometimes more about what owning the product means than the product itself. Buying a product isn't just about the product being better, more efficient or even necessary.

We are taught that if we own a certain product, we have the good taste (such as those trendy individuals in the ad) to choose that particular product over another. The 1980s continued this lifestyle advertising with the little green alligator representing the yuppy Izod, Brooke Shields wearing her Calvins, and healthy, active people taking the "Nestea Iced Tea plunge." Just mention The Gap, Ralph Lauren, Tommy Hilfiger or Banana Republic, and what comes to mind is a group of thin, trendy, attractive friends that are sailing, horseback riding or just enjoying their care-free life—all while wearing trendy clothing, of course. "Just do it," and suddenly wearing Nike athletic shoes means we are serious about being physically fit.

The new millennium brought a new medium of advertising—social networking. Blogs, websites, Facebook, YouTube, Instagram, and Twitter made their way into consumers' homes. Companies now had the opportunity to capitalize on personalizing the products' lifestyle with their customers. Consumers may now interact with the products' sponsors the blog author or respond to a celebrity's tweet. As social media's popularity grows, getting consumers to notice, follow and become loyal to a product is more challenging. With so many social media outlets, how does one get their product to stand out?

The old saying, "A picture is worth a thousand words," is not only true, but the picture should also leave the consumer wanting more. As digital photography and photo editing software become more consumer-friendly, the competition to stand out is greater than ever before. While there are many good photography websites that offer wonderful shooting tips, expert equipment reviews and advice on how to sell your products online, I would like to share a few photography topics from my own professional experience that most photography websites do not address.

Elizabeth came across this abandoned home and just had to shoot it. No styling or props needed! This shot captures a moment in time in a way that speaks to our souls while honoring the soul of the home.

Shooting on Location

Most of us don't live in a fabulous urban, brick loft with giant windows and tall ceilings or in the lush Tuscan countryside. However, our limited location is not a reason to shoot sterile and boring product shots. To successfully sell a product, I strongly feel that an "environmental shot" must be a part of the selling equation.

Environmental shots are different from "establishment" shots. An environment shot is purposely created and styled to enhance the subject, while an establishment shot is a reference image that places the subject in its environment. Take a look at any Anthropology print ad; you'll find beautiful sets, scenery, and creatively styled images—all interweaving very specific clothing into the created environment. Similarly, Restoration Hardware catalogs have a complete aura and distinct lifestyle of their own. Anthropologie and Restoration Hardware provide their consumers with, not just a catalog filled with products, specs and ordering information, but the opportunity to be like them—to live a signature lifestyle (for a price, of course).

In the early 1990s, Martha Stewart very subtly (and successfully) began using this lifestyle type of photography. Her magazine was one of the first to photograph everyday objects, such as an egg, as art. Her images are creatively simple, right to the point, beautifully styled and leave the reader wanting more. Only *Martha Stewart Living* magazine could photograph a pair of hands holding dirty, freshly-picked red potatoes, and print it as a full-page color image with no copy. Her secret? Her images are of very common objects, shot in intriguing ways. Since Martha Stewart's magazine's success, there have been numerous magazines who followed, hoping to emulate her style of imagery. While many of her images were shot in wonderful locations, many could have been shot anywhere—on a sidewalk, over a kitchen table, on a porch floor or on a sunny window sill.

Taking time to find a unique location is well worth the effort. Research similar products to find out how they are photographed (both on the internet and in print), and then set out to shoot something different and unique. Researching products similar to yours is a great way to see how others are shooting and to discover what is working and what isn't. Your goal is to find your own style, your own look, your signature lifestyle.

There are a number of factors to consider when choosing a site. First, the basics: What does your shoot entail? Multiple locations? Indoors? Outdoors? Particular theme or look? The deadline? Budget to rent space? How much time do you need to shoot? One-day shoot? A week shoot? Do you need props? Hire models, actors? Rent equipment? How far away is the location and how much time to drive there? Those are just the very basics.

Once you find what you believe to be the perfect location, you need to examine the location even closer. Can you legally use this location? Are permits needed? Is this a public or private area? Is parking convenient, or will you have to unload elsewhere and dolly your equipment to your location? Are you allowed to fully set up, which may entail nailing into walls, moving furniture, hanging drapes or removing items? What about electrical power? Is there a way to light your set, use your computer

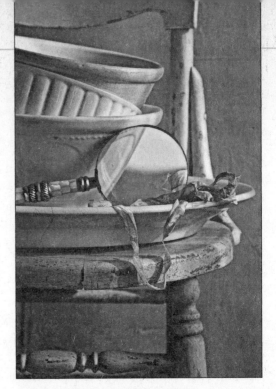

A chair and wall provide a simple but effective background for these everyday objects.

SHOOTING ORDINARY OBJECTS

When faced with shooting an ordinary object, thinking outside the box is also an opportunity to manipulate light, location or circumstances to your advantage. When I need to shoot simple and very common objects such as fruit, I try to find ways to challenge my skills. These apples were shot right on my living room table with late afternoon light. I never used a flash, and I just tested and retested different camera settings until I got a look and style that I found appealing. The key is not to give up too soon. Keep playing and clicking until you see something that speaks to you.

Elizabeth says, "This image was purposely styled for my own chapter in the cookbook, *Pie*Ography*. I shot this image with editing in mind. I left room at the top and bottom of the image for text, or to be cropped. I also slightly over-fried the pies on purpose, knowing that I needed the crusts to really show up well in the image. While food looks fantastic in an image, many times, it can be very inedible!"

or fan, or charge your batteries? Are there bathroom facilities? Will weather interfere with your shoot? How secure is the location? I shoot in many abandon buildings and these factors always come into play. Heat, cold, electricity, bathroom, parking, safety—all these things factor into a shoot.

There is also liability to consider. Liability insurance is good to have to protect you, the property and any equipment you are borrowing or renting. Accidents happen, and there could be legal issues when shooting on someone else's property. There are numerous professional liability insurance plans available; professional photographers' websites offer detailed information on the subject.

Lastly, there are location test shots to take. Take lots and lots of test shots at different times of the day. This will help you factor in shadows, lighting challenges, window glares and unwanted reflections. If time permits, before settling on a location try to shoot on cloudy days, sunny days and rainy days. This can make a huge difference. What you might have thought to be a perfect location can suddenly be a dud when you discover that after a heavy rainstorm, a huge pool of water settles nicely on the floor in the exact area where you had planned to shoot. (This was a personal experience that taught me not to settle too quickly if weather conditions are a major factor.)

Elizabeth waited all afternoon to take this shot, until the light hit the grill just perfectly. A great subject can almost always be greater with a little patience.

Always keep a log of potential places as you drive around. A simple snap on your phone with a note of the location is a great resource. One final great location tip that will save you loads of time and gas is to use Google Maps. I spend hours using the street view, traveling all over city roads looking around and taking notes, while always aware that what I am viewing may no longer be there or be really hard to find. But I have found many grand locations by using Google instead of gas.

Remember, location is just an illusion. It is up to us, the photographers, to create the world our lens will communicate to our viewers. Don't be in a rush to click the camera. Slow down and really search for the perfect location to launch the illusion that enhances your craft and creates interest for the consumer. Once you've found the perfect site, your job turns into joy, the project into play and the camera into creative communication.

Shooting at Home

We often have mini studios right at our doorstep waiting to be discovered. A chair is the perfect make-shift mini studio in waiting. Tossing a cloth over its back creates a backdrop, or the chair itself can become the backdrop for the product. Floors make wonderful backgrounds—wood, tile, marble, cement, a funky rug and chippy paint are just a few examples of what a floor may offer. I know some photographers who take textured wallpaper and hang it up on a wall as the background, and then roll it out onto a tabletop or dresser that is pushed up against the wall. You can do this with a white window shade as well to get a clean, crisp look. There are numerous "home studio" photography kits that are a great help, but they can get expensive. Attics, garages, basements with windows, small porches, side-

On the left is the full cover shot for *Quilts from the House of Tula Pink*. Lots of negative space and room to overlay text allowed the graphic designer room to play with the image when designing the final cover for the book (shown on the right).

walks, park benches, steps, the hood of a car, a small mirror on a table and even fireplaces all make great mini studios. Home mini studios are great because everything you need is near, weather is not such a strong factor, and of course, it is just plain easier and faster. However, taking the time to find a new location (even if it is only on your front porch) and getting practice shooting in different environments is a sure way to discover what type of approach best suits your products and your personal style.

Styling and Staging

While living in Germany, I worked with a small dinner theater group. My first job as a prop girl was to hunt, shop and build props for large, elaborate productions on very puny budgets. Little did I know that my eye for detail was in training for using props of another kind in my future. Years after that prop job, I staged countless vignettes and windows for my own store, styled design homes for open houses, and of course, used props in various photo shoots.

Shooting with props is an exciting challenge that all photographers face. We photographers hunger for a way to define our style and express our own creativity once we get behind our lens. How we use and what we choose for props allows us to stamp our unique style in every single image we shoot.

For me, just about anything is a prop. A prop can be anything from a piece of furniture, to a button; a scrap of paper on the floor, a water droplet, wind, nature found on location, a person in the background, a torn fabric blowing in the breeze, sunlight (or lack thereof) and even negative space is a prop. I think of props as anything I can use in the moment to manipulate my photograph to convey a meaning, message, feeling or style. I believe a good photograph should either tell a story or invite the viewer to invent one. And it is very rare that a good story is told without delicious details.

Of course, it is the product that needs to stand out in the image... or is it? Often, we are lured in by advertisers simply because an image is so moving that we don't know (or care) what is being advertised at first glance. For example, a refreshing image of white towels and cotton nightgowns gently blowing on a clothesline near a big oak tree with a white wicker basket filled with wet clothes is an advertisement for handmade, organic fabric softener. While the extra detail shots of the product (with text) give all the information the consumer needs to know about the product and how to order it, it's the environmental image that shows the simplistic, pure lifestyle that the company is offering for sale.

However you choose to style your product shots, I advise you to keep all similar products flowing with similar shooting styles. Let's say you are selling custom greeting cards. Keeping the size of the images and backgrounds the same for each card group will be easier for the consumer to follow along and will look more professional. Different categories may be shot in groups, each with its own feel. For instance, all birthday cards might be shot on old barn wood, anniversary cards on a paint-chipped door, and all seasonal cards on old canvas. The cards have categories, and each category has its own background. The background is the "prop" for the cards, just like the clothesline with hanging clothes is the prop for the softener.

Never pass up an opportunity to creatively highlight your craft, be it with simple lighting, a fun background or a completely styled environmental shot.

Editorial Shooting

We artisans not only want to sell our products, we want to get our product in front of the public eye. Short of paying for very expensive advertising in magazines, there is another way to get magazine coverage. Submit your work to the editors! The keys to getting your work published are finding a publication that features work in your field, providing spectacular images of your work and being an expert on any product you submit.

There is a particular aspect of shooting that I learned over time, after I was published—shooting editorially. When I first began shooting for magazines many years ago, I studied only the basics (that is all I knew to do) such as how the magazine shot its images, or how a photo was styled. In those early years, paying attention to how the cords were hidden in room shots or how fresh fruit or flowers seemed to always be present was all my limited experience knew to study. I did my research and studied which magazines seemed to like the detail shots or the "action" crafting shots and so on, but my eye wasn't trained to see other factors yet.

It wasn't until after seeing my images laid out with graphics and text in the actual magazine that I began to study my photography with a more critical eye. I didn't study how to make my images prettier, but I paid more attention to the layout orientations and possible "negative space" the editors were using in the magazine. I also paid more attention to the gutter of the magazine (the center of the magazine where the pages meet) and started to study the size of each individual publication. All of these things took time to work into my shooting naturally without look contrived. As a result, I have had more than one editor compliment me on how my attention to shooting editorially makes her job easier. Studying the magazines you wish to be in is a great way to approach your photo shoot.

While products may be shot differently for the internet, shoot as if your images were for the magazines you researched. Look at all the crafting magazines and study their covers. Try to shoot a "cover shot" whenever possible. Know the size of the cover and adjust accordingly. The image needs to be much larger than the actual cover so the editors may crop as needed for the title and text. The original image that I took for Tula Pink's first book, *Quilts from the House of Tula Pink* (Krause Publications, 2012), is much larger than its final cover. Don't be afraid of negative space; editors appreciate having negative space to layout text. And if they don't want to use that negative space, they have plenty of room to crop the image as needed. If you can find a creative way to shoot your images that allows editors room for text, you will save them many headaches.

Inquire with the publication about what type of format they prefer and remember that you can never shoot too large. It is easy to make an image smaller, but it can't get bigger. Take time to really study all types of magazines—be it cooking, craft, interior, gardening or whatever you are interested in—and take note how that particular magazine uses graphics and text and typically does the layout. By adding this extra editorial element in your shooting style, editors will take note. Purposeful shooting is what makes a beautiful shot a published shot.

Shooting for Online Platforms

When shooting for any social media and online site, spend a few minutes reading the image requirements (or limitations) for each platform. Keeping images within the suggested guidelines will allow your audience to upload them more quickly and with fewer interruptions. If the color of your product is very important, remember that computer screens most often do not show true colors. Screens can be calibrated for your photography needs, but what you see on your screen may be different on someone else's screen. Using exact text to communicate the true color is important. This isn't the time to be a creative wordsmith. For example, if your product is a true "red," you might consider saying "fire engine red" in the product description to help the consumer know the real color, instead of a cutesy name such as "Little Red Riding Hood." Also, remember to shoot your product with different angles, allowing your customer to truly understand what your product looks like. If size is important, placing a common object next to the product will help the consumer understand what he or she is ordering. A coin, a pencil, a dollar bill, or even a straight ruler is always helpful in showing the actual size of the item for sale. If possible, show the product being used in at least one stylized shot. Selling custom ceramic dinner plates? Show a beautifully set table which highlights the plates, in addition to the standard detail product shots. Be aware of any glares or reflections, as computer screens will highlight the glare more than the product. The most important tip for shooting products for the internet is to use a tripod! Very clear, sharp and precise focus makes a big difference, especially if you offer a magnification tool for your customer to zoom in to see your product up close.

Making and selling your own crafts is a competitive and rewarding process. The more you develop your own unique style (with both your products and photos), the more your customers are going to want to see from you. Having customers that not only want what you have to offer, but eagerly anticipate what's to come, is a really great (and profitable) position in which to be!

Elizabeth Maxson

Elizabeth's work has been featured in *Where Women Cook: Celebrate!, Quilts from the House of Tula Pink, Tula Pink's City Sampler, Pie*ography, Where Women Quilt, Romantic Homes Magazine, Where Women Cook* and many other publications. Be it home décor magazines, features in national publications, contributing editorials, crafting books, cookbooks and home décor books, Elizabeth's work is in demand for the distinctive, creative and personal quality that she brings to every project. Elizabeth's visionary ability to photograph her subject using natural light makes each image completely original. Her styling method invites the reader to imagine and to inquire, and her writing evokes a personal conversation between two good friends.

   To learn more about Elizabeth Maxson and her professional services, visit her website www.elizabethshumblehouse.com.

INDIE CRAFT SHOWS

by Grace Dobush

*Excerpted from Crafty Superstar

For the modern crafter, the old high school gymnasium craft show will not suffice. Luckily, in the last decade, the number of indie craft shows has boomed.

How do you know if the show you're applying for is "indie"? If there's a DJ, a cash bar or a live crafting competition, it's probably indie. If the average age of shoppers is under forty, it's probably indie. If there are items for sale that would make your grandmother gasp, it's definitely indie. Unlike old-fashioned craft shows, indie craft shows draw makers of all sorts—from snarky cross-stitchers and mod clothing upcyclers to geniuses with laser cutters and experimental letterpressers.

Indie craft shows exist in most every part of North America, and you don't have to be in a big metropolitan area—even mid-sized cities have them. If there aren't any indie craft shows in your area, consider starting one of your own! It takes some work, but you can do it on the cheap and help cultivate a craft community in your own town.

Getting In

Most of the big indie craft shows are juried, which means the organizers (and perhaps a jury of local craft experts) decide who makes the cut based on an application you submit. The competition is stiff—some shows have acceptance rates rivaling those of Ivy League colleges.

Consider these things before you start applying to every show that looks cool: your prior craft show experience, how much stock you'd have by the show date and, most importantly, whether you can afford it. The monster shows can cost upwards of $200 a day to display, but small, local shows are often very affordable.

Application

Organizers have a lot of things to consider when deciding who sells at their fair. Is there a good balance of different kinds of crafts? (Jewelry is notoriously over-represented in most application pools, for example.) Is a crafter doing something really unique? Some shows set aside a certain number of tables for newbies each year or focus on local talent.

If you're new to the craft show scene, consider sharing a table with a friend. It can boost your chances of getting in because it's less of a risk for organizers to have two new crafters share a table. Plus, it boosts the overall diversity of the show. If you sell Shrinky Dinks earrings and your friend sells wallets woven from grocery bags, go in on an application together!

If you really want to get into a show, the most important thing is to follow application instructions to a T, be on time and send photos that really do justice to your work. Also make sure to read the application FAQ before e-mailing the show organizers—most of the time, all the answers you need will be on their website.

Rejection

Got turned down by your dream show? Don't get discouraged. Some big shows get more than four times the number of applications they can accept. That means the judging committee has to reject some damn good crafters. Kristen Rask, who runs the store Schmancy in Seattle and works with the Urban Craft Uprising show there, has one common explanation for rejections: "People don't follow directions!" she says. "If you have 500 applicants or more, organizers get nitpicky."

So if the show organizers ask for attached photos, don't send a link. If you have to pay the table fee or an application fee when you apply, don't let yourself forget! (Table fees are generally returned to non-accepted crafters after the decisions have been made public; application fees are not returned. Whether there's a nonrefundable fee varies from show to show.)

If you do get the dreaded "thanks but no thanks" e-mail, be gracious and resist the urge to reply. Rask has received some awkward post-rejection messages. "Sometimes people send e-mails saying, 'I'm really disappointed. This is the second year I've been rejected.' I feel bad, but that's no way to make me want to take you as a vendor!"

I've had some awkward encounters with crafters rejected from our show in Cincinnati. Crafty Supermarket gets more than 200 applications for just 50 or 90 spots, so we have to be very picky about who we accept, and we often have to reject really great makers just to let new people have a chance. People who e-mail us post-rejection trying to get us to change our minds stand out—in a bad way.

Take heart in the fact that even big-time crafters and craft show organizers are rejected sometimes. Even though I run a show, I've heard plenty of nos, too. Understanding that there's a lot of competition and not taking the rejection personally is really important. Just keep perfecting your crafts and try again!

Getting Prepped

Getting that first congratulatory e-mail from the craft show organizer is an exhilarating feeling. And now the real work starts!

Travel Arrangements

Aside from tons of your crafts, a table display and other odds and ends, you also have to figure out your travel and lodging arrangements if it's not a local show. Often the organizers will send info on affordable lodging—some even try to match up crafters with local hosts or hotel roommates. It's a good idea to reach out to your Facebook friends to see if any relatives or college buddies live in the area you're visiting. Check the list of crafters selling at the show to see if any live near you, and send them a friendly e-mail to see if they're interested in carpooling. If you've got to go it alone, check sites like Priceline (www.priceline.com) and KAYAK (www.kayak.com) for airfare and hotel deals.

Planning for the Show

The show organizers will send you basic information, such as when you should arrive on the day of the show to set up, anything special you need to bring (such as a tent if you'll be

Off the Beaten Path (offthebeatenpath.etsy.com) of Dayton, Ohio, uses vintage fixtures to create a vertical display that keeps shoppers looking. *Photo by Grace Dobush for Crafty Supermarket.*

outside), and whether you need a local vendor's permit at the show. (But don't assume that if they don't say anything you're in the clear on sales tax. Check the state's department of taxation or revenue for all the rules.) Organizers are generally amazing, multitasking angels, but don't expect them to be able to hold your hand the entire time. Scour the show's website and devour all the vendor information you can find. You'll find that most FAQs are answered before you even ask. Not all shows offer electricity or Wi-Fi access—if you need it, be sure to note that in your application.

If you're bringing a friend along, enlist them well ahead of time. Having some extra hands is really helpful, and make sure you compensate them for their time, whether it's in grub, hugs or real cash.

Table Displays

First impressions are everything at a craft show. If you've been to indie craft shows (if you haven't, you need to!), you know that the most popular sellers have the most eye-catching, pretty or unusual table displays. It doesn't take big bucks to make a great setup—all you need is a good imagination and a little planning.

Practice your setup on the kitchen table before you unveil it at a show. Ask a friend to give you feedback, and take pictures so you can replicate the layout on the day of the show.

It's key to think vertically. A table with everything laid out flat doesn't catch anyone's eye from across the room. Use shelves, boxes or stands to create height. Some sellers use room dividers or other completely vertical displays for their wares rather than a table.

Assuming you're working with the common 8-foot folding table, the cornerstone of your display is the table covering. (Nobody wants to see all that scratched-up Masonite.) It should match your biz's look. Is your style utilitarian? Try plain kraft paper or corrugated cardboard. Is your style retro and hip? Go with a patterned bedsheet or curtains. Do you want to surprise visitors with something unusual? Get some Astroturf or bubble wrap!

Go through your closets and kitchen with new eyes. What could you use for a display? Borrow your roommate's coat rack, clean off the dish rack, or use a stack of cool-looking books as props. Anne Holman displays her silver jewelry in white ceramic dishes. She uses a shallow white bowl filled with red lentils to show off her rings and flat sushi trays for her necklaces.

If you're lucky enough to live near an IKEA, spend a day scouring the Swedish superstore for cheap items you could repurpose to fit your needs. Thrift stores are also full of things you can turn into killer table displays.

Day of Show

Rise and shine! Today's the big day, and as much as it might suck to be hauling your stuff around at 6 a.m., it's best to be on time or even early. After you get set up, you'll have time to relax, grab a bagel and meet your crafty neighbors.

If you're smart, you'll have gotten everything together the night before the show and checked off everything on your list. I always make a grocery store trip and a bank run the day before a show to get snacks, drinks and change. (Get snacks that are easy to put down when a customer arrives—go for tidy bite-size things like crackers, grapes or granola bars.) Also do a quick inventory check the night before the show or before the doors open to make a record of how much stuff you brought with you.

You'll have your table setup down to a science by this point, so when you arrive at the show, you'll be able to check in and get started right away. Look for an organizer or volunteer when you arrive to get registered and find your table.

Introduce yourself to your crafty neighbors! I've met a lot of awesome people—and new friends—at indie craft shows. If nothing else, your tablemates will be the folks you turn to when you gotta make a restroom run. Most next-door neighbors are happy to watch your table for a sec if you offer to do the same.

One of the big upsides of traveling for shows is that you can build up your brand in other cities where people might not know your stuff. So, be sure everyone leaves your table with a sticker or business card with your name and URL on it.

Before you know it, the doors will open and you'll be flooded with curious customers! Say hello to everyone who stops by your table, even if you doubt they'll buy anything. One great way to engage potential buyers is to share something about your technique. The most important thing is to stay friendly, even if your feet are killing you and you've been running all day on just a veggie dog. Standing behind your table makes you much more approachable than if you're sitting slouched with your arms crossed. Resist the temptation to work on your knitting when business is slow. Nothing says "I don't want to be here" more than a crafter paying more attention to her needles than her potential customers.

If you've got to collect sales tax, have a cheat sheet by your cash box for easy calculating. Having a calculator is handy, but why do the same multiplication dozens of times? Make sure everybody who buys from you signs up for your mailing list, which should be prominently displayed on your table on a clipboard with a functioning pen. Know where the nearest ATM is to be able to help cash-strapped shoppers. Some crafters don't take checks, but I generally do and haven't been burned yet. Ask to see the buyer's ID, and ask her to write her phone number on the check just in case. If you accept credit cards, always check the expiration date and for a signature on the back. To accept credit cards, all you need is a smart

Indie craft events can be anything from a small trunk show to a big crafty gala. Crafty Supermarket's holiday 2013 show drew more than ninety vendors and 4,000 shoppers to Cincinnati. *Photo by Kevin Necessary for Crafty Supermarket.*

phone and a Square (www.squareup.com) or PayPal Here app (www.paypal.com/here) and sign up for a free account.

Though you might feel like you're running yourself ragged, take time to enjoy the ambiance. Have you ever been surrounded by so many incredible, creative people in your life? This is enough to get me charged up and dancing behind my table even when I'm dog-tired. If you're lucky, the show will have a DJ to keep you pumped the whole day.

The Postmortem

And that's a wrap! You've made it through the show, hopefully with a lot of sales, some new friends and a new appreciation for salespeople.

Watch other crafters to see when they start tearing down their tables—most will begin collecting their things right at closing time. Leaving a craft show early is considered very bad etiquette, especially if you just peace out without saying anything to the organizer. The organizers will likely close the doors at the exact time the show's slated to end, but there could be a few last-minute shoppers making the rounds.

I find it really helpful to take inventory of my stock after the show to see what sold best and figure out if I broke even. Keeping track helps me be better prepared for my next show, and I can craft to meet demand. Make some general notes about your experience, too: Were the crowds good? Were the organizers organized? Would you want to do the show again? Once you've sold at a few different shows, you might re-evaluate your sales strategy, too.

Be sure to thank the organizers and let them know how your day went. If that means pointing out some shortcomings, do it diplomatically. Being courteous goes a long way, says Kristen Rask. "One woman was really rude at the end of the show, so we reconsidered when she applied the next year," Rask says. You don't have to kiss up to everyone, she adds. "But if you're gracious, you'll be remembered."

DIY Craft Shows

No show? If you live hundreds of miles from the nearest indie craft show or simply see room for a new kind of scene, start your own! It can't be done fast, but it can be done with a little money and a lot of elbow grease.

My friend Alisha Budkie and I decided to start our own craft show in Cincinnati to coincide with the release of my book *Crafty Superstar* in 2009. Now Chris Salley Davis and I run Crafty Supermarket, which attracts thousands of shoppers and dozens of top-notch crafters to the Queen City twice a year. We had a lot of great advice from other craft show organizers to work with, but every city and event is different. Take my advice for starting a show and adapt it for your needs!

1. **Pick a name.** Don't pick one that's already taken, and don't play off an established show's name, like "Crafty Texarkana Bastards" or "Renegade Craft Show 2: Electric

Boogaloo." As soon as you've decided a name, go ahead and buy the corresponding domain name. Something as simple as having a blog devoted to the show will give you some credibility and help people who search for your show. Set up a Facebook page and Twitter account while you're at it, and set up a show-specific e-mail address, such as yourshowname@gmail.com.

2. **Find a venue.** Consider your needs and what can you afford. If it's your first show, it's best not to assume you'll have one hundred vendors and thousands of shoppers. Go for something as affordable as possible for your first time. Ask around at coffee shops, bars, parks, churches, art galleries, fairgrounds, community centers and the like to see if anyone can offer you ample space for your event at a price you can afford.

    Other things I consider when considering a venue are ample parking and proximity to public transportation. Our first Crafty Supermarket was in the back room of a bar that opened early for our show. The price was definitely right, and the venue was on the main drag of a hip neighborhood. We had twenty vendors at fifteen tables—totally manageable—but then 1,000 shoppers showed up over six hours. Holy crap! Now our big holiday shows take place in Cincinnati's Music Hall Ballroom and can accommodate ninety crafters and as many as 5,000 shoppers. The price is higher, but it's well worth it for the space.

3. **Organize the business side.** Set up a checking account or PayPal account separate from your own finances for the show, and check to see if you need any city permits or insurance. If you're organizing a small show by yourself, processing the finances as personal income probably makes sense. But if you've got multiple people involved or will be handling lots of money, it's worth exploring setting up an LLC. This will involve a small-business lawyer and a few hundred dollars in fees—check out your state's business portal for instructions specific to your area.

    Figure out your costs (including space rental, table rentals, permits, supplies, payment for you!) to determine how much you need to charge per vendor space. (If you plan on soliciting sponsors, figure that into the equation as well.) The most common table size for craft shows is 8' × 2½' (2.5m × 0.75m), and a booth or standard outdoor tent space is 10' × 10' (3m × 3m). Make sure you allow at least 3' (1m) behind each table for the vendors to sit and stand, and keep your aisles wide enough to accommodate foot traffic (and don't forget about strollers and wheelchairs!).

    Some shows charge a small, nonrefundable application fee to help defray costs. Vendor fees for indie craft shows can range from $20 to $400; this is determined by the region, the show size and the show's reputation. If it's your first show, you generally shouldn't charge more than $150 for a table.

4. **Determine a date.** Saturdays are usually ideal. If you're planning to have your show outdoors, setting your date between May and September is best. Holiday shows gar-

ner a lot of traffic, so consider an indoor date in November or December. Setting the date four to six months in advance will help avoid conflicts with other shows and give you enough time to advertise and get vendors.

5. **Enlist crafters.** Post information about your show in the related forums in craft community websites and alert your local Craft Mafia and Etsy Teams. You can create your vendor list by invitation only, do a juried show, or just accept everyone until every space is filled.

   I don't recommend the last option—it can get crazy, and it's hard to maintain quality. Doing an invite-only show works well for small trunk shows; if you know you'll only have 10 tables, why slog through 300 applications?

   Doing a juried show is hard work for the organizers, but it ensures that your show lives up to your dreams. Back in the day, craft show applications involved photocopies, mailers and money orders. Today it's much easier to keep track of applications and process payments online. Crafty Supermarket uses Wufoo (www.wufoo.com), which lets you build simple, elegant forms and even connects to your PayPal account to collect payments. Set specific deadlines for the application and when you'll notify crafters as to their status. It's a great idea to see how other craft shows do it and follow their lead!

6. **Find sponsors.** Make the show a community affair. Find sponsors to help defray the financial burden, and sell ads in your program or on banner space at the show. Create a few levels of sponsorship (for example, $50 for a small ad in the program or $200 for a banner on-site or $1,000 for a mega sponsor package) to give your potential backers options. Look locally, but also approach national businesses that serve the craft community.

7. **Find helpers.** Enlist a friend to be the DJ for the day—it helps keep the energy up! I highly recommend getting volunteers or assistants to help with the show. They can help set up tables, keep trash cans from overflowing, give crafters breaks, answer questions from visitors and manage traffic. At Crafty Supermarket, the organizers usually have tables of their own, but some shows' ringleaders choose not to. In either scenario, volunteers are an absolute godsend. Reward them with a bag of donated goodies!

8. **Advertise and promote the show.** Reach out to local newspapers, blogs, websites, TV and radio stations and magazines. Send personal invites to movers and shakers in your local scene. Establish partnerships with other arts organizations to spread the word via social media and blogs.

   Set up a Facebook event so you can invite all of your friends and vendors, and they can invite all of their friends. Post a vendor list on your website when you determine the show's lineup. Enlist the crafters to help promote the show, too. "Give everyone involved easy tools to help you promote it," says Olivera Bratich, owner of Wholly

Craft in Columbus, Ohio. "Like buttons for their blogs, hashtags to use on Twitter and regular updates about the content of the event."

9. **Create a program.** This could be a simple photocopied flier or a saddle-stitched multipage deal. It should include a directory of crafters with their names, websites and hometowns, information about you and the show, and ads from any sponsors you have.

  When you create your table layout, **"Keep maneuverability in mind when making your vendor maps," Bratich says.** "Customers will need enough space to move through aisles and turns comfortably, and some of them are likely to have wheelchairs or strollers." It's also important to space out crafters who make similar things and think about the flow of the event.

10. **Get set up.** Before the show, make signage and banners for the venue so passersby are drawn into the show on the day of. At least a week before, let the vendors know when to arrive, where to park, where food is available, lodging suggestions and directions. If possible, arrange the tables and chairs at the venue the night before the show. On the day of, arrive before the crafters to make sure everything's in line for a great day. Arranging for breakfast and coffee for your vendors is a nice touch, too; you might be able to find a local business willing to spot you some grub in exchange for a sponsorship.

11. **Open the doors! It's going to be a long day, but it'll be so worth it.** Always arrive early, and wear comfortable shoes. If you have a table at the show yourself, enlist a helper for the day. Remember to take photos of the event, and having a DJ (or at least an iPod) will keep things hopping. Make some time to meet all of your vendors, and enjoy your position as a crafty ambassador.

Grace Dobush
Grace is a freelance journalist and creative entrepreneur in Cincinnati. Her *Crafty Superstar Ultimate Business Guide* was released in 2012, and she's the co-organizer of Crafty Supermarket, one of the Midwest's biggest indie craft shows. She has spoken at conferences around the world about DIY business and entrepreneurship, and she's written for *Wired*, *Cincinnati Magazine*, *HOW*, *Roll Call* and other publications.

WHOLESALE AND CONSIGNMENT SALES

by Jodie Rackley

Often times, people have great products but are afraid to take the leap into wholesale. Some mistakenly think that the only way to make this jump is to invest thousands of dollars for wholesale websites that promise a rush of customers or attend huge wholesale trade shows. However, any craft business no matter the size can take the leap into wholesaling without a lot of upfront costs by utilizing resources widely available on the internet and effectively marketing their products.

Wholesale helped me to establish my business and grow a stable monthly income that allowed me to quit my day job and work on my business full time. You cannot rely on Etsy sales, craft show income, or wholesaling alone to build your business. If your goal is to grow your business into a full-time venture, it is important to have multiple streams of income so you are never relying on just one stream to support your business. Generating new wholesale accounts and giving great service to your existing ones is an important part of building monthly income on which you can rely.

I began to sell my products through wholesale and consignment within two months of starting my business. I was not yet generating regular sales on Etsy.com, but I had a great response to my products through social media. I knew there was a market out there for my products. I contacted several stores and was able to place my products in gift shops that catered to the handmade market. I found that there was a market for my products, that my goods sold quickly in person, that stores reordered frequently, and that my online sales increased in states and cities where my products were being sold in person. Despite having slow online sales the first year, all of this encouraged me to keep building and working on my goal of making my craft my full-time occupation.

DEVELOPING YOUR PRODUCT LINE

Here are a few questions to answer that will help you in developing your own line of products for wholesale:

- What is your favorite craft?
- Who are your products for?
- Name five of your favorite things to make.
- What age group are your items made for?
- Can your products be part of a special niche audience (e.g., green crafts, eco friendly, bridal, children, geek craft, technology lovers, teens)?
- What are some of your favorite colors that you'd like to use in your items?
- Do you use any special materials or techniques for your products?
- Describe your style in ten words or less.
- What is the motto or tag line for your business?
- Name five words to describe your products: (e.g., happy, colorful, boho, rich).

Developing Your Product Line

One of the most important things to consider when you start to wholesale is your product line. Your product line is a run of consistently made goods that all go together in a cohesive way and have a similar aesthetic. Sometimes it is difficult to think of your creative outlet as a product, but doing so will help you focus on creating a better collection to present to stores. Presenting your crafted goods as a collection of products will give a look of professionalism to your items and eventually your wholesale catalog. You do not need to have a lot of items in a product line, but your products will work best if they go together in a cohesive way or solve a similar need or function.

As crafters, most of us have more than one medium that we like to work in, so it can be difficult to narrow our focus. Find what you do best and, even more importantly, what you most enjoy making, and perfect your products. Make your products the best that they can be using the highest quality materials in your budget. Choose an overall theme for your products so that they all fit into a similar style or aesthetic.

- **Love a bohemian look and want to develop a jewelry line? Think all things 1970s—hippie chic, feathers, Navajo, leather—in rich bold colors.**
- **Love the idea of pretty, feminine goods that are part of special events? Consider opening a shop that caters to brides on their big day.** Create a jewelry shop that contains all sorts of bridal themed accessories, hair pieces or boutonnières. Or consider a shop that sells nothing but beautiful signage, table wares or ring bearer pillows.

- **Want to make goods for children? Decide whether you'd like your goods to be functional, cater to moms on the go or be playful.** Maybe you want to develop a line of diaper bags and pacifier clips, or plush toys and blankets.

These are all examples of how to develop your line around a similar aesthetic and with items that go together on a theme. The more you narrow your focus, the easier it will be to market your products, think of new goods to add to your line, find specific boutiques to carry your work, and have a beautiful shop to promote.

Since most craft business are essentially micro businesses (in comparison to large manufacturers), it's always good to think of a niche market for your items. This market can be a very specific to a very broad group of people, but will have a specific interest or commonality that draws them to your product. This thought process works great for quirky shops with unique items. Decide on the type of person who will want and love your products and always keep that person in mind.

Lastly, don't be afraid to embrace your own style and place your own artistic mark on your items. Don't try to do what someone else does or make products to look like someone else's just because they have had some success. Your business will have more success by adhering to its own personal style, rather than following someone else's style. That's not to say you can't have similar types of items—lots of people sell plushies, wall hangings, prints

"Owl Smart Phone Cozies" by Lova Revolutionary

or tea towels. But embracing a style that is all your own will make your product stand out in a new way!

Packaging

With wholesaling, you will be sending your products out to be directly sold by another store or company. As a result, packaging is an important feature of your product. You will need to have some sort of hang tag, sticker or product packaging for your items. This helps you brand your items when they are out in the world and being marketed by someone else. One easy way to do it is to order some hang tags or mini business cards to use as your tags. You might also want to make your own. (I'm all about DIY, especially when you are just getting started with your business!) Get a nice paper punch and order a custom stamp with your shop name and address, and stamp your own tags. Design your own tags and print them onto cardstock to use as hang tags.

Try to develop packaging that will not conceal your item too much, but will give the customer in the store information should they want to find you online. With mobile technology being so frequently used these days you may also consider adding your own QR code to your packaging to be read by smart phones. Packaging also helps your customers find you on the web so be sure to include your web address. Stores rarely have a problem with your web address being on your packaging, but try to design something that can be easily modified in case a shop objects.

Building Your Wholesale Catalog

Having a wholesale catalog is a nice way to present items to your potential wholesale customers. You can have a printed version or a simple PDF file to e-mail to your clients. Don't worry about having a lot of items to start; when I first began I had less than ten different items in my wholesale catalog. It really does not matter how many items you carry as long as it is cost effective for you to create those products. Aim to have five to ten different items to start with and continue to build your catalog as you add more items to your line.

It is also helpful to think about variations in the line. For example, if you make handbags, can you make a similar style that can also become a shoulder bag, clutch or tote but have the same look to the main body of the bag? This is a good way to offer more items without having to design completely different items. Be sure to list each style of the bag in your catalog. Maybe you sell bath and body goods and only make soap, lotion and lip balm, but you offer each product in many different scents. List these options in your catalog and let the wholesale client choose the specific scents on each item they order.

When developing your catalog, consider what choices you want your buyer to have. You might allow your wholesaler to choose the specifics of the product variations, as in cases like the different bag styles. Or you might simply offer varieties of items instead of having your wholesale customer choose the specifics. For example, if you can make the same item in many different colors, perhaps just offer that product as an "assorted item."

Keep your catalog basic, easy to look at and organized. You should view your catalog as an extension of your branding, so be sure to use your logo, fonts and colors from your existing website when developing your catalog. Keep the following in mind when creating your wholesale catalog and linesheet:

1. **Include a cover page with your logo and perhaps a picture of one your favorite items.**
2. **Include photos of your items with small captions (or even brief descriptions) of what the item is, what it is made of, the size, and your retail/wholesale price.** Number each item with an item/catalog number that will correspond with the linesheet.
3. **Organize your catalog by the types of items that you offer.**
4. **Optional:** After you've shown all the photos of your items with brief descriptions, you may want to include longer descriptions that characterize your items in more detail or provide other necessary information such as color options, fabric options, etc.
5. **Toward the back of your catalog, include your personal information.** Include a short artist bio or brief description of your business. List other stores that carry your work with their locations. Mention any notable press, awards or accomplishments for your line. Include a photo of yourself, your workspace or studio (if it's photo-worthy), or your logo.
6. **Include all of your contact information such as name, address, e-mail, phone number, website and all of your social media information for your potential client to check out.**
7. **Create a linesheet—a brief spreadsheet or grid that a client can use to build their order while looking through your catalog.** It should include the item number, name of item, quantity, wholesale price, retail price and a section for notes.
8. **Include a section on your shop policies and wholesale terms.** This all is up to you. Do you want to have minimum dollar amount for orders or reorders? Do you want payment upfront or will you accept Net 30 and bill your customers? Do you have specific shipping terms; do you offer flat rates? List all of that type of information in your policies.

So now you're wondering how you're going to actually make a catalog since you're not a graphic designer in your spare time. You can make a simple and free catalog using any desktop publishing software such as Microsoft Word or Google Docs. If you have your own website, consider having a password-protected wholesale section for your customers to go. If you have an existing Etsy shop, you may also apply to be a part of the new Etsy wholesale section.

How to Find Shops

Find shops that cater to your market! If you sell girly items in pastel colors that fall into the shabby chic aesthetic, look for boutiques and shops that carry similar merchandise. If you make handmade gold jewelry, you may want to try high-end boutiques that sell independently designed clothing and accessories. If you sell fun and funky items, look for quirky gift shops and places in college towns that cater to a younger clientele. You get the idea! Begin with shops in your area but do not be afraid to look for shops in other cities as well, especially major cities where there is generally a bigger market for just about any type of product. When I began wholesaling, I knew I'd have an easier time selling in big cities where people already had an interest in handmade goods and that already had shops that exclusively sold handmade goods; I contacted those shops first instead of starting locally. Depending on your area, this may be a better strategy when you are first starting out.

Try to find shops that already carry handmade product lines. Search the internet with terms like "handmade gallery" and "indie craft boutique." You may also try searching on Facebook because most small businesses now have fan pages. Yelp.com is another good source; this site allows you to narrow down your searches by major cities and search for gift shops and art galleries. Review the various shops' websites and online reviews so you can find a good fit for your work. Customer comments are always a good place to look and usually describe what types of items each store carries. The most sneaky way, however, is to find other crafters that already wholesale to a similar demographic and visit their websites. Chances are you will find a huge list of stores that are carrying their works and links to their websites. Check out each shop individually and e-mail those that are a good fit for your work.

Tweet Bird Ornaments" by Lova Revolutionary

How to Approach Shops

The best way to approach shops now that you've gotten a catalog together, virtually pounded the pavement, and found some stores you'd like to get in touch with is to simply e-mail them.

I know, it sounds too simple, right? But it's true. Some of the best advice I have ever gotten is to *not* ask for appointments and *not* to travel up and down the highway scouting shops. Simply e-mail your potential wholesale client with a brief and thoughtful message. Address the store owner by name, if you know it. State in a short paragraph who you are, what you make, your interest in their shop carrying your handmade products, and maybe a bit of notable press (blogs your work has been featured on or other stores that carry your work).

Felt and vintage fabric hand-stitched, "Rag Teddy Bear Plush Toys" by Lova Revolutionary

You have to put some work in to start getting accounts. E-mail as many stores as you can; you might e-mail one hundred shops and only get twenty responses. Don't take it personally! Not everyone is ordering goods at the same time, some shops might be stocked up, maybe they think your goods will fit in a different season, or maybe they're simply not interested. However, you may get a response and an order back the very same day! Sometimes you may get a response and order a year later! Shop owners receive a lot of product pitches and a lot of catalogs, so don't get discouraged. If there is a particular shop that you are dying to have your work in, don't be afraid to follow up if you haven't heard back after several months. But for the most part, just wait and see what happens.

Shop owners generally order early for the holiday and summer seasons, so start sending catalogs in August or September for holiday orders and in March or April for summer orders.

What About Consignment?

One alternative to wholesale is to sell your goods on consignment. Often, shop owners will ask if you would consider a consignment contract instead of wholesale, especially if you are just starting out. Some handmade galleries *only* accept goods on consignment. Keep in mind that consignment and wholesale work differently. With wholesale, you are generally paid in full for the goods a client orders upfront and it is up to them to pay shipping, market and sell the goods, and set the retail price. With a consignment model, the buyer and seller negotiate which percentage of the retail price the store will receive for each item sold, and you will get paid (generally) on a monthly basis for the goods that were sold within that month. With consignment, you are not paid upfront for any of the goods that you send. You are only paid when your goods have sold. You are also responsible for shipping costs to send in goods to refill stock.

Working with retail shops on a consignment basis is a great way to start out and test the market with your products. You might find that certain items sell better in stores than online, and vice versa. Generally, the seller receives the same amount of money for their goods in wholesale and consignment models—usually 50 percent of the retail price. Many consignment shops will also offer a 60/40 split, meaning you get 60 percent of the retail price and the shop takes 40 percent for selling your goods in their shop.

Unlike most wholesale accounts, consignment accounts will have a contract that they supply outlining what percentages they take, how your goods will be handled, a limit on how long they will keep unsold goods in the shop, and different types of liability protections (for example, what happens in case of theft). The contract will contain a linesheet that you complete and send to the store along with the goods you are sending them to sell. The linesheet will ask for an item number, quantities of each type of item, a description and your basic information. For consignment, it's also helpful to include hang tags on all of your items; if you do not have professional hang tags that reflect your line's branding, simply include a generic hang tag that has your item number on it to correspond with what you have listed on your linesheet. This will help ensure that your items stay organized and that you get credit for your sales. Do not leave it up to the store to tag all of your items.

Do not sell on consignment without a contract, and make sure the shop is reputable. Often, the shop will have a list of artists and Etsy shops they work with listed on their website. Do your research and ask around!

Payment from consignment stores can vary from store to store, but generally you will get paid every month in the form of a check or through your PayPal account. The store owner will usually list out all of the goods that you've sold and might ask you to restock.

Selling on consignment is great when you are starting out since you can get your work into stores pretty easily; the shop owners don't have to pay for goods upfront, so they are more willing to take a gamble on you and your product. Selling on consignment is also a great way to test what sells in the traditional retail environment. If you're just starting out in wholesale and have no shops yet, consignment is a good way to begin building your roster of accounts.

One downside to consignment sales is that you may get a lower dollar amount in return for your goods since you are not getting paid all at once. You may send out one hundred dollars of goods but only make twenty dollars in April, forty dollars in May, and ten dollars in June instead of making all one hundred dollars at once as you would with a wholesale order.

Pricing Your Goods for Wholesale

There are many different formulas out there for pricing your goods for market. Pricing depends on many different factors, like what sort of wage you'd like to pay yourself, your cost of materials and other expenses, and also factoring in if you'd like to sell on a wholesale basis. If you'd like to sell wholesale, make sure that you are paying yourself an hourly wage for creating the piece, while covering your expenses, and still making a profit at 50 percent off of your retail price. You might find you need to adjust your pricing as you go along, but always make sure that you are getting paid for your time in order to make wholesaling worthwhile for your craft business.

Expanding Your Wholesale Business

So far, we have discussed a DIY and cost-effective approach to wholesale, but there are other ways to expand your wholesale business once you are established and have the capital to do so. One way is to attend wholesale trade shows to reach many potential wholesale customers all at once. These types of shows usually happen once or twice a year and are open to shop owners and retailers only—not to the general public. Trade shows are specifically for shop owners and retail buyers to come and browse a large variety of goods and to place orders for their shops. Wholesale trade shows are great for gaining new clients, getting your work seen by many buyers, and communicating face to face with potential clients within the course of a few days. You are also in direct contact with shops that are ready to place orders. The downside is that these shows are costly to attend. Generally, you must apply for the show and be accepted in order to exhibit. Once accepted, the booth fee is usually a few thousand dollars for a weekend-long show. The American Made Show and the NY International Gift Fair are two examples of a wholesale trade show.

Another way to expand your existing wholesale business is to hire a sales representative. A sales rep works to find new shops, galleries and opportunities for you to sell your work, and introduces your line to those new venues. Generally, sales reps take a percentage of each wholesale order that you receive as compensation for their services; there are often other fees involved as well. Sales reps also need to have materials in order to support their efforts, such as catalogs, samples, and a website.

Branching out into wholesale and consignment sales is an excellent way to expand your craft business and to diversify your income. Having multiple streams of income is vital to the success of your handmade business so you are never relying on just one stream of income at any given time. Having your goods in brick and mortar stores also helps to expand your customer base since each store will bring a slightly different clientele in contact with your products. Building your wholesale business will supply you with a steadier stream of income in order to eventually grow your business into a full-time occupation.

Jodie Rackley
Jodie is the designer and stitcher of Lova Revolutionary, a cute and colorful, handstitched eco felt gift line of whimsical décor, accessories and plush. She stitches every day in her home studio in Fredericksburg, Virginia. In 2011, Jodie released her first craft book, *Happy Stitch: 30 Felt and Fabric Projects for Everyday*. Her work has been featured on notable sites such as Etsy.com, Apartment Therapy and Martha Stewart, and she has been a featured artist for Kunin Eco Felt at the Craft and Hobby Association Trade Show. She is currently working on a new line of hand embroidery and felt craft patterns for her Etsy shop (http://lovahandmade.etsy.com).

PRICING YOUR WORK

by Grace Dobush

*Excerpted from Crafty Superstar

Since most of us start making crafts as a hobby, sometimes it's hard to think about our passion for macramé, letterpress or weldigami as a business. (And I'm not even going to start in on the whole left-brain/right-brain thing.) But if you want to be taken seriously—and you do if you want to get paid—you have to put down the knitting needles and do some homework.

Customer Perceptions

Pricing is a terrifically tricky area. When you're first starting out it's tempting to charge just what you spent on materials, but don't sell yourself short. Charging for the time you spent making each item might make your sticker price seem high, but a person who makes things by hand can't expect to compete with big-box stores' prices. Most people are so far removed from the manufacturing process that they have no idea of what making something really costs.

One thing's for sure: If you price your work too low, customers will wonder if it is

Service with a smile is essential when you're manning the booth at a craft show. *Photo by Kevin Necessary for Crafty Supermarket.*

cheap, and that's no good. In crafting, pricing your work low isn't going to increase demand. Honestly, at an indie craft show you'll see more people buying $5 letterpress cards than flimsy cards that cost 50 cents. Generally, the misers who complain about high prices at shows don't appreciate the hard work it takes to make something by hand. Pay them no mind—they weren't gonna buy from you anyway.

Lauren Bacon, the co-author of *The Boss of You*, a business guide for women, likes to say that handmade goods' high prices aren't high—they're just the real price. "The organic local food industry is a good example of this. Local artisan cheese is so much more expensive than imported cheese," she says. "The cool thing about indie economies is that you get to talk to the people who made it and ask them yourself why it costs what it does. All of those things have real, concrete value."

When you're selling at craft fairs or through Etsy, you can start a dialogue with your customers about pricing and why you charge what you do. "Instead of being afraid, look at the crafters who are established and are charging what they're worth. Ask them how they set their prices, if for no other reason than moral support," Bacon says. "If you're going to a big craft show where a lot of people's prices are lower than yours, practice your answers about why your prices are so high. Have fun with it—make a little FAQ and put it on your table, even. Explain that you use sustainable materials, or that your stitching is time-intensive and impeccable and longlasting. Engaging with your customers is what gives your product value, because they care about the item, but they also care about their relationship with you."

There are always going to be people whose bottom line is price. They're not your target market, and that's a hard thing for people who love their work to let go. "You'll make compromises and excuses to keep doing what you love," Bacon says. "But look at yourself as an employee and ask, 'Is it reasonable to be paying myself seven dollars an hour for this?'"

LAUREN BACON ON . . . OVERCOMING PRICING FEAR

"A lot of us work from a place of fear that no one's going to pay us what we're worth. When you're running your own business, you should come up with a list of reasons why you are worth that much. Figure out exactly what your costs are, calculate a price and have a friend tell you what they think, because you're probably still undercharging.

"One of the reasons we targeted our book *The Boss of You* at women is that that's something women have a hard time with, saying, 'Sorry, I'm really expensive, and you probably can't afford me.' And I think for men there's a culture where it's cool, and other guys respect you, but other women tend to look at you like, 'Well, you're a little big for your britches,' because women are educated to value modesty really highly."

Setting Your Prices

Crafters who sell their products go about setting their prices in different ways. For instance, Jessica Manack of Miss Chief Productions has a simple method to price her items. "When I'm creating a product, the first thing I do after I make a prototype is look all over the internet to see where I can get the materials to make it," she says. "The materials I find partly determine whether I go ahead with making it. I went ahead with the magnet tins I make because of the tins I found." She calculated their price based on how many she could make in an hour.

She did an experiment to see if her prices were too low. She saw a business selling 1-inch magnets for five dollars each, which she usually sells for a dollar each. "I thought I would try listing some on eBay," she says. "I first tried this on Thanksgiving weekend and sold thirty-three sets for $430." Considering she usually sells sets of nine magnets for seven dollars, that's not shabby! "Everything I have listed has sold, and some people have gone to my Etsy shop after buying stuff on eBay and bought more things. Most of the buyers are from the U.S., but I have also had some from Australia, South Korea and other places."

Manack thinks part of the increased selling price is because of the bidding war aspect—"People hate losing a contest!"—but it's also likely that her goods were underpriced to begin with. "What is something worth?" she asks. "Whatever someone is willing to pay for it."

Samantha Lopez of Knotstudio based her prices on the cost of precious metals and the time-intensive process required to make her jewelry. "I knew coming into this that in the long run it'd be much harder to raise prices than to lower them if they were too high," she says. "I first did a lot of research on the stores that would potentially carry my line and the prices of work they carried. Based on that, I saw that my niche in this case was going to be the rather high-end luxury goods market." Lopez adjusts her prices occasionally, mostly to follow the metal market. "It's important to keep in mind that, although lowering the prices may attract new customers, established clients may feel they were ripped off and take their business elsewhere. Lately, because of the economy, I've decided to keep my smaller silver

SIMPLE PRICING FORMULA		
	Example	Example
Material cost:	$10	$2
Labor cost:	$30 (2 hours at $15/hour)	$5 (20 minutes at $15/hour)
Markup: ×2	×2	×2
Wholesale price:	$80	$14
Retail price: ×2	$160	$28

pieces and offer the larger, more expensive ones only in gold—not only as a luxury but also an investment, as gold tends to hold its value." Her retail prices are simply double the whole-sale prices, which is a standard practice.

Speaking of wholesale, if you even have a single thought of selling wholesale, Bacon advises considering that when setting your retail prices. "Let's say the break-even price you find for your product is fifty dollars. When you're a product-based business, you have to think about wholesale price as well as retail. Because there will be a time when some store comes and asks you what your wholesale prices are, and they're going to expect a big dis-count from your retail price—usually 50 percent. So if you're selling an item for sixty dollars and somebody wants to buy it wholesale for thirty dollars, you're losing money."

However you decide to set your prices, it's important to consider all your costs when figuring out your prices as well as how you will sell items (e.g., in sets or individually)—an hourly rate to pay yourself, the cost of materials, administrative stuff, and taxes. And don't forget extra things like listing fees, transaction fees and shipping materials and charges.

Let's get down to the nitty-gritty of all those extra costs for a minute. Pretend you're selling a card on Etsy for two dollars. It's made from upcycled materials (read: free) and took you fifteen minutes to make. You charge 50 cents for shipping, and you accept payments via PayPal. When it sells, you just made a profit of $2.50, right?

Wrong. Etsy charges 20 cents per listing, plus 3.5 percent of the sale price—so that's 27 cents gone. Then, PayPal charges 30 cents per transaction, plus 2.9 percent of the money received—that's another 37 cents. Assuming you already have an envelope, you still gotta buy a stamp, another forty-nine cents. So your buyer sent you $2.50, but in reality, you've only made $1.37 from the sale. And since it took you 15 minutes to make the card (and not including the time you spent to list the item and go to the post office), your average hourly wage is a measly $5.48. Those little charges add up.

CINNAMON COOPER ON PRICING

My time is worth money. I've worked for years to learn how to improve the quality of my bags. I spend time seeking out sweatshop-free materials, and I make sure that the ma-terials I use will withstand wear and tear. I try to make bags that are attractive as well as functional, and that effort deserves to be compensated. However, when I price out my bags and come up with a final price of what a bag is worth, I think about whether I would save my money for a month to purchase the bag. If I wouldn't, I don't make it again. I want people to feel like they're getting something valuable, but my bags are far from the luxury pricing models.

Pricing Strategies for Creative Types

When you're running a creative business, even if it's not your sole source of income, the basis of all pricing is your hourly rate. When you're running a small business, you touch every item you sell or service you offer. Your hard work is what creates the value in your products, so it's super important to never discount yourself.

Thinking about how your creative business fits in your annual income, you might decide, based on your needs and your town's cost of living, you're cool with $15 an hour. But if you're living in an expensive place or trying to cover all the costs an employer would usually cover (like health insurance, taxes and a retirement account), your hourly rate might be much higher. (If you offer a professional service, research the going rates of other professionals in your area. For certain types of creative businesses, flat fees for projects make more sense financially.)

When you've determined the hourly rate you want, that's the basis for everything you sell. For a physical product, your price must include your cost of labor (your hourly rate times how many hours it takes), your material cost, overhead and markup.

Overhead is making sure all of your business costs are covered. Let's say, over the course of a year, you have $5,000 in overhead, including business licenses, accountant fees, craft show application fees, website hosting, equipment costs, software licenses and the like. Divide it out over the year (assuming you base it on a forty-hour workweek), and it comes out to $2.40 per hour.

Markup is your profit. If you want your business to grow, markup is what supports you and protects you. Retail theft, loss and breakage are very real risks for a creative business. Or if your business is service-based, there's the chance a deadbeat customer will stiff you. Applying markup to all of your products ensures bad luck won't put you out of business. Markup is usually 1.5 or 2 times your product's material, labor and overhead costs. And that puts you at your wholesale price. Double that again to get your retail price.

More than likely, the price you come up with for your goods will be more than their imported counterparts. And this is when you have to start having honest conversations with people about why your goods are priced like they are. Keep the conversation positive, and don't apologize for your prices. Sometimes customers can be rude, but resist any urge you have to get hostile.

This is the time for you to highlight what makes your goods valuable and different from mass-produced versions. When they buy from you, they're supporting a locally-owned business, a small business, a real person standing in front of them. If you source your supplies locally, ethically or in an environmentally sound manner, that's also worth mentioning.

Why Discounts Are Deadly

"$22 for $35 worth of letterpress cards!" "Handmade jewelry for 45% off!" "BOGO screen-printed onesies!" I get so mad when I encounter crafters selling their wares at ridiculous discounts. And recently a spate of handmade discounting schemes has popped up, making me fear the Walmartization of handmade has begun.

Modern shoppers are primed to react to discounts. (If you're into social history, I highly recommend Ellen Ruppel Shell's book *Cheap: The High Cost of Discount Culture*.) But discounts are largely a phenomenon of the era of mass production—it pains me to see handmade items' prices slashed like outlet mall jeans. Will discounts boost your Etsy sales? Maybe. But I think they'll do crafters much more harm than good in the long run, for these three reasons.

1. **Discounts make you undervalue your time.**

   Crafters are already notorious at underselling themselves. Too often, we simply price our goods at what we consider the going rate, rather than taking into consideration the cost of materials plus the cost of our time and any overhead we have. I fully believe in making a living wage, and I believe every crafter should do the same. More than likely, you're already selling your work for too little. If you discount it any further, you could even be losing money.

   When dozens of people are selling similar things on Etsy, you may think you have to lower your prices to compete. But I think some people are more likely to save up $55 to buy a pair of steampunk owl earrings that they really love than spend $5 on a pair that's marked down from $10. And those customers are the ones you want.

2. **Discounts don't draw the kind of customers you want to have a long-term relationship with.**

   You might think a buck's a buck, but fair-weather shoppers who only buy when an item is cheap aren't the kind of customers you can count on. Discounts don't create repeat customers—they only create buyers who expect more sales.

   If you consistently offer discounts on your handmade items, what incentive does a shopper have to ever pay full price? We need to focus on educating buyers of handmade items as to why our products are priced how they are and why they're worth it. Creating personal connections with customers is what handmade is all about.

   If you're struggling to make sales, maybe you don't have a solid idea of who your audience is yet. Do your products appeal more to college students or empty-nest moms? Spendthrift yuppies or up-and-coming country folks? When you know who your customers are, you can figure out how to best reach them, and what prices they'll pay. Discounts won't do that for you.

3. **Discounts cheapen your work.**

   Let's face it: Most handmade goods are luxuries. They're lovely nonessentials that people buy because they want to—no matter whether it's because they want to support a small business, to consume more ethically or simply to have beautiful things. When you're a craftsperson, being the cheapest isn't going to help your business. Making quality products—and pricing accordingly—will.

   Think about it this way—do you want to be a discount store shampoo brand, selling economy-size bottles of shampoo for $2 with a 25-cent-off coupon? Creative business people are better off following the lead of Aveda, making and selling high-quality, beautiful products that attract a clientele that doesn't need a discount incentive to be convinced to buy from you.

   If your customers are sensitive to price, make sure that your pricing strategy can handle the discounts you want to offer. (But you surely see that raising your prices in order to offer discounts is just silly.) One thing I really don't advise is offering free shipping—this is just taking money out of your own pocket. You can't avoid the cost of shipping or do anything to change it. (And free shipping is one big reason why many new companies fail.)

   If you feel the need to offer some kind of incentive to your customers—and certainly some customers are more price averse than others—consider offering a freebie with a purchase. This could be a pinback button, a notecard, a mini-size sample or something else that's attractive to your audience.

Always remember: You are worth it!

Grace Dobush

Grace is a freelance journalist and creative entrepreneur in Cincinnati. Her *Crafty Superstar Ultimate Business Guide* was released in 2012, and she's the co-organizer of Crafty Supermarket, one of the Midwest's biggest indie craft shows. She has spoken at conferences around the world about DIY business and entrepreneurship, and she's written for *Wired, Cincinnati Magazine, HOW, Roll Call* and other publications.

PUBLISHING A DIY MAGAZINE ARTICLE

....

by Shannon E. Miller

Having a project published in a magazine, in a crowd-sourced book or on a popular blog is considered by many crafters to be a major milestone—and rightly so. It is an admirable achievement that boasts a number of intrinsic rewards, from payment and new customers to general press exposure and validation of your talent. Plus, it's downright exciting to see your name in print! Furthermore, getting press can be a stepping stone to more projects down the road. Having published work under your belt can be a strong selling point for crafters wishing to author their own book later on, or for gaining new commissioned clients. If you're trying to build a name for yourself in the industry, a little name recognition goes a long way.

Start With Research

So, where do you start? First, make a long list of publications and/or publishing companies you'd like to approach. Don't just sit at home and list off magazines you already know; head to a local bookstore and peruse the newsstands for titles that fit your type of work. Look at the credits page inside magazines that appeal to you for their website address. (You may also want to take note of the magazine's publishing company as well, in case the individual title doesn't have much information on their site; this is sometimes the case.) Then, visit their websites to search for submission information or writer's guidelines. Usually, if this information is available, it will be found in the "about," "contact" or "FAQ" sections, or in a footer link (scroll to the very bottom of the page where websites sometimes display additional links that can't be found in the top menu). Also possible, though less common, is to find submission guidelines in a magazine's media kit or advertising information.

If submission information is openly available, you've hit the jackpot; read it carefully, and bookmark it for later. If not, as is often the case, you may be able to find a contact e-mail address for pitches, submissions or general editorial inquiries. If you can track down an editor's or editorial department e-mail address, even better; or, if you know an editor, you might have luck by copying them on your submission. Use these contacts to request helpful information as to whether they accept submissions from new contributors, if they are willing to provide submission guidelines, or if they can share their upcoming editorial calendar. You might hear back directly from a magazine representative, but if not, don't fret. You can still submit! However, know that unsolicited queries are not usually answered unless accepted.

This book provides a wealth of information about magazine submissions, too, including contact information. Make notes as you research the different magazines and discover more about various publishers.

EDITORIAL SCHEDULES

A note about editorial schedules: It's important to be aware that magazines usually work up to a year in advance of their release dates, meaning that you should not expect to submit Christmas projects to a publication in autumn; on the contrary, you'll notice that most holiday editions begin to go on sale in the fall. It is more likely that these Christmas issues were prepared in the summertime, and projects were accepted from contributors even earlier in the year!

Submissions

If you are able to get your hands on submission guidelines, read them carefully, and be sure to follow the instructions. These guidelines are set a certain way for a reason, and following directions as closely as possible is extremely helpful to editorial staff. Usually, you will be asked to provide a brief and concise outline of your project, a snapshot or sketch, full contact info and links to any previous work that can be seen online (such as a blog or an Etsy shop). If you do not have the submission guidelines for a particular publication, this is generally a good guide for what to offer. And it is most likely a good idea to postpone snail mail for the time being; note that in today's electronic age, submissions are almost always accepted via e-mail only, and physical work is rarely requested to be shipped before acceptance.

Let's examine the general pieces of a submission in an effort to help you put your best foot forward. First is the project itself. It is important to any editor that the work displayed in their publication matches up to a particular look and feel. Ask yourself honestly whether or not you can see your project among the others in this magazine; does it have the same sense of style and complexity? If not, you may want to rethink either your project or whether this is the right place for you to try and get published. For instance, a contemporary crafts magazine is not very likely to publish a primitive quilt; likewise, a traditional knitting magazine is probably not going to accept a bright and funky, freestyle-knitted crop top.

Next, consider that editors want to publish work that provides something unique and/ or valuable to the reader. Has your project been done before, or is the technique so commonplace that there is nothing special about your submission? If so, what can you do to make it stand out from the crowd or to give the reader something they can't get elsewhere? For example, contemporary quilt designers are wonderful at discovering creative ways to reinvent traditional quilt blocks and techniques. And while a girl's A-line dress is cute, it's not terribly unique; but perhaps you can share an interesting hem technique, or provide an original appliqué design. Make sure that whatever you're offering as a how-to article gives customers a reason to buy the magazine in question; find a focus, and drive it home in your submission query.

When writing your submission query, present yourself as a professional by using clear, complete sentences and good grammar to communicate your message. It is important to remember that if you want to be taken seriously that you present yourself as such! Also take into consideration that editors are very busy and often juggle many projects at the same time while fielding tons of e-mail every day. Don't make them think too hard when they come across your submission; be direct in your proposal without adding unnecessary storytelling or superfluous sentiment. It's one thing to say that you love the magazine and briefly share your inspiration for your project; however, it's another to ooze admiration and write multiple paragraphs detailing how your project came to be. Keep it to a handful of sentences at most. If your e-mail looks like a term paper, it will likely not get read, and your point will be lost in the shuffle.

This carries over to any visuals you share as well. Photos of your submission don't have to be professionally done, but they should be clear, bright and simple. Today's simple point-and-shoot cameras and even smart phones have the capability to snap a perfectly adequate image for submission purposes if you take the necessary steps. Natural light, a solid white or neutral-colored background and the removal of any extra "junk" from the shot will work wonders. (Read "Photo Head" for more insight into photographing your crafts.) Afterwards, review your photos with an objective eye. Are your pictures clear, not blurry? Is the color relatively true-to-life? Are there unnecessary props or other items in the shot? Is the image confusing in any way? It is also helpful to include a few detail shots, such as a close-up of any particularly interesting focal points or features, beautifully-executed workmanship and/or alternative angles. However, keep it to an absolute maximum of five shots; two or three are likely sufficient for submission review purposes. If the editor wants to see more, they will contact you.

In wrapping up your proposal e-mail, it is to your benefit to share links to any relative online presence you have, such as your craft blog, a Flickr set of past images, an online portfolio or active social media accounts where you share your crafts regularly. This gives publication staff the opportunity to click through and see more of what you're about, getting a better sense of your personality and style than would typically be offered in a short submission query. And depending on what the editor is looking for, it may also be beneficial to mention that you are happy to recreate a similar project suited to their specific needs. For instance, if your blue project is lovely but doesn't exactly fill a gap in an upcoming "red" issue, simply offering to rework as needed could be what gets your article accepted in the long run.

Lastly, don't neglect to include complete contact information, so that if your article is accepted, there is no question about how to reach you. E-mail, phone, website and physical address should all be listed for convenience (which, depending on the production process of the individual magazine, are also helpful facts to have up front for getting the ball rolling on a contract for the article, should it be accepted for publication).

The Waiting Game

After hitting "send" on your submission e-mail, the painful waiting game begins. You may receive an auto-response or a short note acknowledging receipt of your submission, but it's rare that you'll hear anything firm too quickly. In fact, you may not hear back at all if your proposal has been rejected; unfortunately, due to the sheer volume of submissions that most editorial departments receive, it would be extremely time consuming to respond individually. Don't take it personally! In the meantime, make sure you're pushing new, quality content to any of the websites or social media accounts you shared in your e-mail, as this is the first thing anyone who clicks through will see.

So, how long should you wait before assuming you can take your work elsewhere? Generally speaking, between two weeks and month is a good amount of time to allow. You might note in your submission that if you don't hear anything by X/X/X date, you will assume it has not been accepted and pitch the article elsewhere. However, there is one exception to this; if you happen to know the closing date on submissions for a particular issue, it would be smart to allow the editorial staff up to a month after this date to contact you. It is possible that they will review all submissions in one pool before accepting any to be sure that they're choosing the best, most balanced content for the issue at hand.

As far as checking back in on your submission, unless otherwise stated on the publication's guidelines, it is fair to check back after a few weeks. A good way of doing so is to forward your original e-mail (they are not likely to remember who you are or what you sent), noting that you recently submitted XYZ project, hope it was received safely and that you are happy to answer any questions, once again closing with full contact information. After that, it reflects best on you as a professional to let it go if you don't hear back. It is frustrating, of course, but again, editors' schedules are extremely hectic, and they interact with many people and projects on a day-to-day basis. If you appear to be needy and demand answers or a status report, you are probably less likely to have future submissions accepted.

If your submission is accepted, a representative of the editorial staff will get in touch with you and provide instructions for next steps, usually involving details of publication, a contract and instructions on how, when and where to send your article text and project for photography. Congratulations—you're on your way to being published!

If your submission is not accepted, don't sweat it. If you truly believe that you have presented yourself professionally and submitted a well-executed, unique, meaty article that suits the publication's needs (and be honest with yourself), remember that there are dozens of other reasons for rejection, such as:

- **The project simply doesn't fit editorial needs at the time or in the foreseeable future.**
- **The current and upcoming editorial contents are booked solid.**
- **A similar article was published very recently, or has already been commissioned for an upcoming issue.**
- **A similar article was published a while ago, but performed poorly with readers.**
- **Submissions are not being accepted at all at the time, or the publication does not typically work with freelancers.**

What next? Submit again! Create new submissions for this publication, and/or try a new publication. Then submit some more. Send out multiple submissions at one time (always in separate e-mails—remember, keep it simple for the editors). Eventually, as long as you continue pushing out quality work, you'll get a nibble. That nibble can turn into a bite, and one-time publishing can lead to more. Most importantly, remember that as long as you work with a magazine, you should maintain the same level of professionalism and confidence. This will encourage the editor to continue working with you, as well as help to protect your reputation as a solid, responsible contributor with whom they love to work.

Good luck!

Shannon E. Miller
Shannon is an editor and designer who lives in Huntsville, Alabama, with her husband and their two young children. The former founding editor of *Stitch Craft Create* magazine, Shannon has also served as an art director and on the editorial staff for *Sew Beautiful* magazine, as well as other crafts publications. Her book *Paperplay* is available September 2014 from KP Craft. Shannon blogs at www.craftyinalabama.com and is active on Twitter, Instagram and Pinterest under the username @shannonemiller.

CRAFTING A BOOK PROPOSAL

by Tonia Jenny

So, you want to publish a craft book? Let's get started!

WHY WRITE A CRAFT BOOK?

Let me guess: For months or even years now, your friends, family, coworkers and others have been telling you your projects and ideas belong in a book, right? Or, you're so incredibly passionate about your craft and you're dying to share your knowledge with as many people as possible, so a book seems like the natural answer. These are both good reasons to give thought to publishing a book, and there are other good reasons as well.

A book is a wonderful way to leave your mark in the world. It's a great marketing tool that can act as a calling card to get you through new doors that might otherwise have been closed to you. A book can give you credibility. And while it's rare for the money earned from the sales of a book to be a primary source of income, it really can be a wonderful supplement. (If nothing else, book sales can go a long way to further support the purchases needed to continue crafting.)

There are some questions, though, that you might want to ask yourself before you dive into developing a top-notch, how-to craft book proposal.

- **Are you passionate about sharing what you know with others, or do you tend to guard your best technique secrets in fear of competition?** A craft book's primary purpose is to allow others to learn and grow in the same way that you have found your groove, and it can be rewarding helping others on their journeys.
- **Does your craft have enough breadth to justify an entire book, or is it more suitable for an in-depth magazine article (another great option)?** Most craft books run at

least 128 pages, so consider whether or not you have enough projects and techniques to fill those pages.

- **Do you have the time to dedicate to writing a book?** It can take many hours to not only create the projects to fill the book, but to write all of the instruction as well. Consider what this production might look like to you in terms of fitting it into your current life. It can take forty to one hundred hours to develop the projects and another hundred or so hours to do the writing.
- **How capable are you of promoting and selling your book once it's published?** If this last question isn't as important to you, you might want to consider self-publishing because it's going to be critical to the publisher to whom you pitch your book idea. It's becoming more and more imperative that a potential author have a strong platform and a system in place to promote the book at the get-go.

Become Informed

Having answered the previous questions and being confident a book proposal is something you'd like to develop, where's the best place to start? With a little research.

- **What current books exist on the market that are similar to your idea? (There may be more than you realize.)** Look at your favorite craft books, or at ones that you find you like at the bookstore, and check to see what the imprints are, as well as the publishers. Knowing which publishers publish which type of books can help point you in a direction when it comes to contacting a publisher. (This book is a great starting place to research and narrow down publishers that may be good fits with the type of book you are proposing.)

Publishing a craft book can be a difficult and time-consuming, but extremely rewarding, experience. Carefully decide how your book will stand out from the crowd before proposing your idea.

- **If no books like yours exist, which come the closest? Also, if none exist, what might be the reasons?**

Many first-time authors are certain that they are the first person to present their creative idea, but this is not often the case. There's usually a lot of room in the boat for more than one book on a topic; just be certain about what else is out there so that you can be clear about how your book is different and needed. The acquisitions editor for the publisher is going to do this research, so be prepared.

When an acquisitions editor, the person tasked with bringing new book ideas to the publisher, considers the potential of a book proposal, she looks for what is called "evidence of need." You can give your idea a boost by doing some of this fact finding yourself. Look for quantitative data that suggests there are many crafters out there who would gladly buy your book. This data can include the number of sold-out workshops you teach on the topic each year (and the number of students per average class), communities for the category and number of members, pop culture statistics, availability of supplies, and so forth.

An acquisitions editor ultimately has to sell your idea to her publisher, and this process begins with you selling your idea to her. The bigger the case you can build for your book (with legitimate info—remember, this isn't your editor's first trip around this block), the better chance your proposal will have.

Building Your Proposal

When you've finished your research and are confident you still have a promising book idea, it's time to build your proposal. A quality book proposal doesn't necessarily take a ton of time to put together, but the love and thought you put into it will be apparent to your editor, and will give her a clear understanding of what it is you are envisioning. It will also help you work through the concept of the book and better prepare you for what will be ahead, should your proposal be accepted.

(All that said, some acquisition editors are open to receiving a pre-proposal query to see if the direction you're thinking has merit and is worth your time to develop a more detailed proposal. I, for one, am totally open to this type of query and am happy to either tell the potential author I'd like to learn more about her idea and to please send me a full proposal or that her idea isn't quite the right fit for our publishing plan at this time. I can't speak for all editors, but it might not hurt to ask.)

Once you've determined the publisher (and imprint) you'd love to see your book published by, a good place to start is with the publisher's website to see if they offer a list of author submission guidelines to tell you exactly what the acquisitions editor would like to receive from you. This is also a great place to discover who to contact with your proposal.

So how do you go about actually putting together a proposal? First, be certain you are sure about the focus of the book. For example, rather than simply knowing you want to write a book about beaded jewelry, try to narrow it down just a little bit more by figuring out what your list of beading projects might have in common. Is there an aesthetic theme (Bohemian, romantic, nature-inspired, etc.)? Or, can all of the projects be completed in an afternoon, making them perfect for last-minute gifts? Here are some questions to ask your-self as you solidify your unique book concept. (Read "Write and Publish a Craft Book" to find one author's answers to these questions.)

- **Who is the audience for your book, and what is their skill level?** (Note: As a general rule, books aimed at a beginner or beginner/intermediate skill level will sell more copies than books focused on more advanced skills.)
- **What does your list of projects look like, and is there a common theme that ties them together?** For books with simple and fast projects, you might need twenty-five or more projects in the book; for a book with complicated sewing patterns, maybe only ten. Look at similar books to get an idea of how many projects you might need to include.
- **How does the book work?** In what form will the instruction be delivered? Will you easily be able to communicate the steps to create your projects? Sometimes writing out the instructions for a sample project can be very helpful to you and the editor.
- **What makes your book special and different?** What will the readers find in your book that they can't get in other books? This doesn't mean it has to be startlingly new, but what features would it have that would set it apart from other books?

With your solidified concept nailed down, see if you can formulate a rough outline of how your book might be laid out. Think of this as the Table of Contents. Look at the TOCs in some of your favorite books as examples and then modify your techniques, projects and ideas into something that looks similar. If new techniques are explored in each project, be sure to list the techniques the reader can expect to learn with each project. If there are several projects in one chapter that use the same techniques, list the techniques after the name of the chapter.

After you've created the outline, write a short description of the book (one hundred words or less) explaining the book's purpose and how the reader will benefit from the book.

Generally speaking, this is typically enough written information to give the acquisitions editor a quick look at your book. Like so many people these days, editors are being asked to do more and more in the same amount of time, so understand the importance of making your proposal as easy for the editor to review as possible. A nice, universal way to present all of this information is in a Microsoft Word document.

The most important part of your proposal includes photographs of project samples. It's usually not imperative that you provide brand-new samples to reflect the projects in your outline, but what you submit should be safely considered very similar.

I can't stress enough the importance of providing attractive, high-quality projects (and high-quality images of the projects) with your proposal—at least six is nice. The projects themselves are the heart of your book, and to not put your absolute best work forward sends

Take great photographs of your work to submit with your proposal. Be sure to showcase details that set your work apart, or elements that will be strongly featured in the book.

a clear message you aren't really that devoted to publishing a great book.

Please don't refer an editor to your blog or Flickr page to see "the type of work" that you do, as the sole example to support your proposal. Including a link to your blog or website can be incredibly helpful, and is great to include at the end of your bio because the editor is going to want to know you have an online presence. Just be certain it's not the only example of your work. Make the time to take attractive sample photos that show the editor you are qualified to produce high-quality projects. Save the images in a resolution and file size that is easy to e-mail (72dpi, no larger than 8 × 10 inches, for example).

Finally, don't forget to include a short bio explaining what qualifies you to write this book, as well as your contact information. (You'd be surprised how many people forget to put their name and contact info in their submission document.)

When putting your proposal package together, feel free to create a fancy PDF that showcases your book description, outline, photos of your work, bio and contact info, but understand this certainly isn't a requirement. And, in fact, if an editor decides to move forward and pitch your proposal to her publisher for approval, she may ask you to resend the info in a Microsoft Word document to aid her in putting together her own document.

Most editors prefer communication via e-mail rather than snail mail (and we love it when you actually address us by name). This holds true for your proposal as well as any pre-proposal queries. When you have your proposal complete, e-mail everything to your targeted acquisitions editor, including a clear subject line such as "Wire jewelry proposal for your review."

Follow Up

So you've hit "send" and your proposal is officially on it's way to the acquisitions editor. Now what? Waiting for a response can feel like torture. At the same time, you don't want to be a pest. So how long is an acceptable amount of time to wait for a reply from the editor? I recommend waiting at least a week. (Hard, I know!) Believe it or not, what feels like long and anxious months for you is actually a week whirling by at warp speed for the editor, and sometimes returning e-mail is lower on the priority list as actual books are being created. Most editors prefer to wait until they have the time to review your proposal with the attention it deserves before replying, so try to remain patient. Don't assume that no reply automatically means the editor is not interested.

Give the editor a kind nudge after a week and see what happens, but keep in mind, the time frame can continue to require patience on your part. When you do hear back, be prepared to answer more in-depth questions if need be. Also be prepared for rejection. But understand that there are many factors that go into the decision to publish a book, and those decisions need not be a reflection of you or your work. Sometimes, your idea and the publisher are simply not a good fit. When I need to turn down a proposal, and I have appreciated the time and effort that went into creating it, I'll suggest the artist give other publishers a try, as we are often looking to fill different needs.

If you decide that proposing a book seems like a great opportunity for you to share a bit of yourself with others, then by all means, give it your all and put your best effort into each aspect of it. A published book is only one way of sharing what you know. It's a wonderful way, and a rewarding process to go through. But you are much more than a book, so keep your passion for creating alive and share yourself with the world in whatever way makes the most sense for you at the time. Stay true to your authentic voice because the world needs you just as you are—whether you publish a book or not!

Tonia Jenny
Tonia is passionate about helping other people recognize their gifts and talents. She is the acquisitions editor and senior content developer for North Light Mixed Media. A mixed-media artist and jewelry designer herself, Tonia has authored three North Light books: *Duct Tape Discovery Workshop*, *Plexi Class* and *Frame It!* When she's not busy making art, cooking, stitching, reading or exploring new ways of looking at the world, you can find her on her bicycle or on Instagram.

WRITE AND PUBLISH A CRAFT BOOK

....

by Margot Potter

Wondering how to write and publish a craft book? You're not alone. Here's what I've learned in the process of writing and publishing seven craft books of my own.

The Proposal

Your journey starts by creating a proposal to present to the publisher for review. A book proposal starts with a series of big ideas. I like to have about three or four general concepts or topics to present to my publisher and we narrow it down to something they think has potential. If you don't already have a publisher, you'll need to fully develop an idea into a presentation or a pitch. You can then send it in to the publisher via the contact e-mail you can usually find on their website. This is referred to as a "blind query" and is how I sold my first book.

Start by doing some research. See what kinds of books are currently on the market and what books are selling well. Visit the craft and book stores to see what's on the shelves and visit Amazon.com to see what's ranking high in sales. Try to glean a sense of overall trend based on the publications in your discipline and what's hot in the related blogs and on sites like Etsy, Pinterest and craftgawker. Now think about what you can add to the conversation. What kind of a book isn't there on the topics that are trending? What audience isn't being reached that might be receptive to the message? Keep in mind that publishing is a

WORKING WITH EDITORS

My most sage advice is: Don't annoy the editor. As a former editor I can attest to the fact that I stopped working with people who annoyed me, no matter how talented they were. Be savvy, not flaky. You're not a biscuit.

> **SELLING YOUR PROPOSAL**
>
> Generally, publishers want to know:
>
> 1. What makes your book unique? Why should someone buy it?
> 2. Who is your target audience and why do you think they'd want this book?
> 3. What sort of audience have you personally cultivated? Do you have an online presence? What are your blog stats, social networking site fans/followers, website stats?
> 4. What makes you an expert in this particular medium or field? Have you been published and if so, where and how often? Why should they work with you?

business. Things are tough these days for publisher which means they can't take the sort of calculated risks they could a few years back. Try to be on point in terms of what is trending and what is emerging so that your title is relevant, marketable and enticing to the sales team. Do your research because if you can't convince them that your idea has merit, they're not going to buy it. If your initial idea isn't gelling with the trends, keep reworking it until you're satisfied that it's relevant.

Do your research to find a publisher that reflects your style. Go to their website to see what they want for a query, and do exactly what they ask of you. Nothing annoys editors more than people who can't follow basic directions.

Making a how-to book is all about picking a target reader and giving them information they can genuinely use in a format that is clear, concise and hopefully entertaining. If it's too pedantic, it won't stand out on the shelves. No one likes to read stereo instructions or boring how-to books. Find an angle that is unique, but not so far from center that the publishers are going to be afraid to take a risk on it. I have noticed that best-selling craft books seem to be focused on a niche, like wire, knots, collage, journaling or metal work.

Unlike a novel, you do not need to write the entire craft book before you propose it. An acquisitions editor will want to work with you to develop a concept they believe will sell. Start with a concept, a tentative title, an introduction and a chapter breakdown. This helps organize and fine tune the book concept in your mind before diving in. Try to come up with a clever title that also clearly states what the book is about. Don't get too attached to your title because the publisher may change it. Next, plan what is going in the front material, the focus of each chapter, the number of projects based on their complexity and the standard how-to book length and the number of variations. Create compelling samples that show a cross section of what the book is going to be about. Visualize the book and the layout and try to give a strong sense of what you have in mind upfront. You will also need to create a chapter header and a sample set of instructions. The publisher needs to have a sense of your personality and the vibe or voice of your book. Most publishers have detailed information about what they want in a proposal on their websites.

Every publishing house has a team of people that regularly review book proposals. Once you've gotten the approval from editorial and worked with an acquisitions editor on creating a presentation of your idea, the acquisitions editor will present it to this publishing board. They meet on a regular basis to review concepts. A lot of the decisions revolve around the opinions of the sales team. Why? Because they're the ones in the front lines meeting the buyers. If they don't think your idea will sell, they're not going to approve it. Even though it's a tough pill to swallow when your brilliant concept gets rejected, it would be a far more bitter pill to work on the book and watch it tank after publication. (Read "Crafting a Book Proposal" for more insight into writing a winning proposal.)

Acceptance and Contract

If the stars align, the acquisitions editor gets behind your idea, the publishing board approves it and your title sells, you will be assigned an editor. Be nice to your editor. Don't have an attitude. Your editor is your lifeline and only connection to the publisher. If you upset them, you're going to find it tough to get anyone to listen to your ideas. The editor is probably not going to be the person who sold your book to the publishing board. You don't get to choose them. When you send out your proposal, wave a magic wand over it and say a few magic words in the hopes that you get an editor who understands you and will get behind you as you navigate the wilderness of creating and publishing your book.

If you can get an agent to take you on as a client, it's usually well worth the fees they'll charge to get you in the front door and negotiate a great deal for you. If you can't get an agent, you're on your own. Once you've sold your book, you'll be presented with a contract. Read every single word and go over all of the math with a calculator. Make sure you understand what it all means. Set up a time to meet with the contracts person over the phone to talk about the contract in detail. Ask for specific clarification of anything you don't understand. You can negotiate a better deal, but you have to ask for what you want. Ask to remove anything you don't like; they may say no, but you should ask anyway. Ask for more money, ask for fewer restrictions or ask for more free promotional copies. Pay attention to what rights you are signing away and if you don't want to, for example, give the television and movie rights away, ask to remove that clause. Be willing to walk away if the deal doesn't feel right. Even if you feel desperate, do not negotiate from a place of desperation. The publisher liked your idea enough to buy it, so you should be paid well for it. Everything is negotiable. You may not get everything you want, but you will have to ask to get it. Ask, and ask with conviction. This is not the time to be shy or timid.

Writing the Book

Once you've signed the contract, the work begins. You need to take this seriously. Meet your deadlines, do quality work, focus on the tasks at hand. I recommend that you make a detailed game plan. Figure out how much time you have, how much work you need to do—and then double it because things will always take longer than you expected. Once you've signed your contract, been assigned to an editor and created a solid plan, it's time to start making a craft book.

If you want to write a craft book, you'll need to find out how to take your ideas and make them real. You'll have deadlines (sometimes insanely short ones) and you will have to meet them. Deadlines are not arbitrary. Deadlines revolve around the entire team who is, in fact, waiting patiently to take your finished pieces and make a book. If you miss a deadline, someone else will have to make up for it down the line, which is not fair to anyone on the team.

Be critical of your designs; rework and improve them. Remember that the work you put into print follows you around for years to come. Make sure that your instructions are clear. Share them with non-crafters for input. Sometimes things we take for granted as obvious are actually complicated and confusing to the beginner. Make sure your materials lists are meticulously constructed; nothing frustrates a reader more than bad bead counts, missed stitch counts or incorrect measurements. You want them to have a great experience with your book. A great user experience helps with word-of-mouth advertising, particularly in the age of the internet. It also helps if you make more books, because readers will be much more likely to buy your new titles if they had a positive experience with the first one. It's always better to make a lifelong fan than a single sale.

If the photographs of your work are being taken by the publisher, be sure to send detailed instructions of how the pieces should look. I take my own sample photos to show the professional photographer how my pieces should be worn and displayed. It's usually too expensive for the publisher to re-shoot designs, so it's important to get it right the first time; sample shots help prevent confusion and mishaps. You probably won't have much say in the design of the book or the way your pieces are photographed unless you are able to negotiate that in your contract. Still, sending photographs and instructions helps guide things in a direction that should hopefully make you and the publisher happy. Many publishers will fly you somewhere to shoot the step-by-step photos. This is a great time to meet the editorial team and share your vision of the book with the book designer. The designer will plan the look and layout of the book with your editor. A book designer can make or break your book, so be nice and forge a collaboration!

When you're working on a craft book, you have to be willing to dive in and make glorious messes. When making a book, a lot of wire ends up in snarled bundles under my desk, beads are broken, head pins mangled and I reject many designs that don't quite have what it takes to be "book-worthy." If

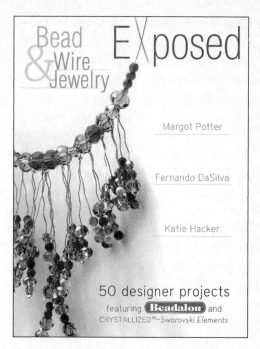

The cover of *Bead & Wire Jewelry: Exposed*

your book is just like every other book on the subject, how on earth will it sell? It's important as you're working on the text to remember that a distinct voice reflects your distinct personality; the reader will feel welcome to stick around and explore if you aren't lecturing them.

After you've submitted your project and text, the photographs have been taken and layout decided, you will get a manuscript to review. It's your job to make sure there aren't any mistakes in the instructions and materials lists. Take your time—check and re-check. You'll get several reviews during the process, but be sure to take advantage of every chance to brush things up and make the book shine.

Promoting Your Book

Once you turn in the final manuscript, the fun begins. You should start promoting your book before it goes to print. The publisher will support you, but the bulk of the promotion is up to you. Once the book is "born," your job is to teach it to walk and then help it to run. If not, your book is not likely to succeed. Like every aspect of this process, it ultimately falls on you to make promotion happen. Resting on one's laurels, even if you've had a few successes, is never a good plan. I work each and every day to build my brand, promote awareness and to generate buzz about my books. If you don't like hard work and you don't want to put the time in to make your book a success, I suggest you refrain from taking the journey.

There is nothing worse that pouring your heart and soul into something and then watching it shrivel up and die. You and only you can make the party a success, so make sure you get those invitations in the virtual mail through a targeted marketing campaign. Gather e-mail addresses on your website, engage fans on your social platforms, offer giveaways and contests leading up to and after publication. Ask the publisher if you can share some teaser projects to help drum up some excitement.

Make sure Amazon has the "Look Inside" feature activated, join Amazon Associates to get a referral fee, offer free books to colleagues to give away on their blogs, promote the book through Facebook and blog freebies and sneak peeks. Generate buzz and excitement! Have review copies sent to prominent people in your industry. If someone reviews your book positively, post a link to the review in your blog and on your social networking sites. The more you create threads that lead back to your book, the more people will be likely to find it. The more people who find it, the more copies you sell, and the more money you and the publisher can make.

Writing and publishing a craft book is a big undertaking but one that is rich with rewards. It all starts with that first step—a great idea. Like anything worth doing, it will be a considerable amount of work, but there is nothing quite like seeing your name in print in your favorite craft store.

SAMPLE PROPOSAL QUESTIONNAIRE

Sample Questionnaire for *Bead and Wire Jewelry Exposed* by Margot Potter, Katie Hacker and Fernando DaSilva

1. What is your book about? What subject matter, approaches to the subject matter, and point of view will it include?

Exposed will take beaders to the next level with a fabulous collection of dynamic, how-to make jewelry projects. With a "secrets revealed" approach, three masters of jewelry design share boutique-style projects that readers can make in an evening. The text will include sidebar "dossiers" that reveal the inspiration, tips and story behind the creation of the design. Techniques will focus on ways to move beyond beads on a string into dynamic designs that expose the beading wire or other components that are typically hidden in jewelry designs. It's a how-to book with a focus on beaded jewelry and unique approaches to design. It will reveal hidden design secrets so the reader can see the why and how behind a "fabulous" jewelry piece. These unique designs will take them far beyond the obvious or the mundane, helping them to explore the world of designer-style jewelry using the materials and elements of the beading world.

2. Who is the book intended for?

Exposed is for people who are looking for fresh ideas in beading. The projects will be accessible for beginners but will also offer inspiration and techniques for advanced beaders. *Exposed* readers love the drama of wearing crystals and jewelry that looks complicated but is actually quite easy to make. People who love fashion, glamour and wearing beautiful jewelry will find the designs appealing, enticing and simple to recreate. The designs will be focused toward people who want to express their individuality and personality with their jewelry, making a personal statement. The demographic will primarily be women in their 30s and up but will contain a fresh design approach look that will be desirable to the younger woman as well.

3. How does the book work? How will it teach the reader? In what form will the instruction be delivered (e.g., with step-by-step demonstrations, projects or exercises for the reader to do, close-up details, case studies, artist profiles, before-after or good-bad comparisons)?

Exposed will include an introduction section showcasing beading techniques the reader will need to complete the projects in the book, plus identification and explanation of beads, tools and stringing materials that are used in the book. The projects will be step-by-step demonstrations, some with variations. Each project will have a romance descriptor written in a film noir style that captures the essence of the design with a fun spy-themed vibe. The reader will be learning new techniques and perhaps more importantly, a new way to approach their work. The book will reveal all the techniques, tools, tips and possible variations in a secret agent file style. A story, an inspiration, movie tiles and iconic historical figures and fictional characters will guide the reader to a top secret beading world. All these factors will work together to retain the reader's attention so each chapter will lift their spirits high and capture their attention.

4. What makes your book special and different? What will the readers find in your book that they can't get in other books? This doesn't mean it has to be startlingly new, but what features would it have that would set it apart from other books?

With beading's huge rise in popularity, there is an explosion of beginner beading books on the market. Those books tend to focus on mainstream designs that are all variations of "beads on a string." Many beginners are entering the fold with more savvy than in the past and they're hungry for the fresh, new techniques that we're going to teach them in *Exposed*. Women are looking for designs that are wearable, designs they can work into their day-to-day wardrobes and designs that will garner compliments. People are ready to take their beading to the next level and they're interested in the "why" behind the design. There are no other books on the market with a focus on exposing wire and other usually hidden materials. Having two of the most recognizable manufacturers in the jewelry-making industry supplying product and endorsing the title should also make it a stand out on the book shelves. The book will work using a Brechtian theatrical model—we will open the curtains and show the backstage to the audience. This means that all of the traditional and non-traditional techniques, materials and tips will be literally "exposed." The language will be clear, honest and genuine so the readers can easily grasp the intent of the authors.

5. What qualifies you to write this book? Tell us your background and the experiences and accomplishments in your field that qualify you to be the author of a successful book.

Margot Potter, Katie Hacker and Fernando DaSilva are each accomplished designers in their own right. Margot and Katie are both well-established authors and experts in the craft and jewelry making worlds, with an established fan base in the U.S. and abroad. Katie appears as the beading expert on the PBS show *Beads, Baubles and Jewels*, has a regular magazine column and has sold over half a million books! Fernando is a celebrated designer in the jewelry world and is making his mark in the world of couture and high fashion in Dallas and now in Philadelphia. Margot has three successful jewelry-focused titles under her belt, is working on a fourth, does design work, consulting and teaching for companies such as Swarovski® and Beadalon®, appears regularly on QVC as a jewelry expert and has a very popular award winning blog, The Impatient Blogger.

As the Beadalon Design team, they've developed innovative ways to create stand out jewelry using widely available materials. They are masters of many jewelry-making techniques and they are unusually competent at creating exciting fresh modern and "DaaLi-Cius™" jewelry projects, enjoyable copy and clearly written instructions.

Margot Potter
Margot has written seven popular books on jewelry making including *The Impatient Beader* series for F+W Media. As a freelance designer, writer and blogger, she has worked for most of the biggest companies in the DIY jewelry making and craft industries. She's also a television and video host with over eleven years on live, unscripted television. Visit Margot at her fashion blog DIY Doyenne and her metal stamping blog icanmake: Metal Stamped Jewelry.

INDUSTRY SHOWS

///

Attending an industry trade show can be an eye-opening experience. For the craft industry, there are niche trade shows that take place multiple times a year in various parts of the country, each with potentially hundreds of top-name exhibitors. Attend one of these shows and you'll see just how popular sewing, quilting, scrapbooking, jewelry making, needlearts and craft in general continue to be. This section includes listings of major industry shows in different niches of the craft industry, as well as some that are not craft specific but still may be good places to exhibit your handmade goods.

Simply attending one of these shows and walking the floor as a new business owner can be helpful. You'll be able to see the wide variety of items produced in your industry, and identify major competitors or those that you might want to work with down the line. You will certainly have the chance to network within your chosen craft with your peers and those who inspire you. All trade shows have different restrictions on who can attend the show. Most are open only to buyers or industry professionals, not the general public, so be sure to find out if you are eligible to attend a show before showing up. You may be required to submit your business identification number, wholesale receipts, tax information or other paperwork showing that you are indeed a professional in the industry.

A major step for any professional crafter is to exhibit at an industry show. Doing so can be expensive and time consuming, but the benefits are great. Exhibiting as a vendor at one of these shows puts you in contact with retailers from around the world who are at the show specifically to place wholesale orders and stock their store. Depending on the items you sell, exhibiting at one of the major trade shows could provide you with a major increase in sales. If you are interested in exhibiting at a trade show in your industry niche, be sure to do your research. There will most likely be a lengthy application process to complete. You will also want to know how large your booth is so you can dress it well. Many booths are decorated to the gills at these events to draw in potential buyers. Make sure you are able to put your best foot forward if you choose to exhibit. Also, think through your sales process for these types of events. You'll need order sheets, sales slips, receipts, the ability to take payment information, etc. Read Jodie Rackley's article "Wholesale and Consignment Sales" for more information on trade shows and the wholesale process. Also, reach out to someone who's "been there, done that" before you exhibit for the first time. They will be able to provide you with invaluable insight as you gear up for your first show.

KEY TO SYMBOLS & ABBREVIATIONS

✪	Canadian market
⊘	market located outside of the U.S. and Canada
⌂	market prefers to work with local artists/ designers
b&w	black & white (photo or illustration)
SASE	self-addressed, stamped envelope
SAE	self-addressed envelope
IRC	International Reply Coupon, for use when mailing to countries other than your own

ALASKA WHOLESALE GIFT & FOOD SHOW

Alaska Genesis Productions, P.O. Box 200846, Anchorage AK 99520. (907)929-2822. E-mail: info@alaskagiftshow.com. Website: www.alaskagiftshow.com. Annual wholesale/cash & carry show held in January. Indoors. Open to trade only. Accepts handmade craft merchants, pattern, magazine, book publishers and other mediums. Number exhibitors: see website. Number attendees: see website. Admission: see website. Apply online. Deadline for entry: see website. Application fee: none. Space fee: varies. Exhibition space: 10×10. For more information, e-mail, visit website, or call.

○ ALBERTA GIFT FAIR

42 Voyager Court S., Toronto, ON M9W5M7, Canada. (416)679-0170. Fax: (800)611-6100. E-mail: alberta@cangift.org. Website: www.albertagiftfair.org. Annual wholesale show held in spring/fall. Indoors. Open to trade only. Accepts handmade craft merchants, gifts, collectibles and other mediums. Number exhibitors: 800. Number attendees: 16,000. Admission: see website. Apply online. Deadline for entry: see website. Application fee: none. Space fee: varies. Exhibition space: 10×10. For more information, e-mail, visit website, or call.

AMERICAN BEAD & JEWELRY SHOWS

P.O. Box 490803, Atlanta GA 30349. (770)739-0057. Fax: (866)311-7774. E-mail: info@americangemexpo.com. Website: www.americanbeadshows.com. Annual wholesale show held multiple times per year. Indoors. Open to public. Accepts handmade craft merchants, beads, jewelry, gems, gifts, body products and more. Number exhibitors: see website. Number attendees: varies. Admission: see website. Apply online. Deadline for entry: varies by date. Application fee: none. Space fee: varies. Exhibition space: varies. For more information, e-mail, visit website or call.

AMERICAN CRAFT RETAILER EXPO—LAS VEGAS

P.O. Box 4597, Mooresville NC 28117-4597. (888)427-2381. E-mail: service@wholesalecrafts.com. Website: www.acrelasvegas.com. Currently boasting 1,200 artists and 16,000 retailer members, Wholesalecrafts.com is the only successful online trade show of its kind. See website for details.

AMERICAN CRAFT RETAILER EXPO— ORLANDO

P.O. Box 4597, Mooresville NC 28117-4597. Website: www.wholesalecrafts.com. Currently boasting 1,200 artists and 16,000 retailer members, Wholesalecrafts.com is the only successful online trade show of its kind. See website for details.

AMERICAN MADE SHOW

(410)889-2933 ext. 227. E-mail: jenm@rosengrp.com. Website: www.americanmadeshow.com. Contact: Jen Menkhaus, exhibits manager. Estab. 1983. Annual wholesale show held in winter. Indoors. Open to trade only. Accepts handcrafted artist-made goods. Awards/prizes: Merit Awards. Number exhibitors: 800. Number attendees: 4,500. Admission: see website. Apply online. Deadline for entry: see website. Application fee: none. Space fee: varies. Exhibition space: 6×10; 10×10. For more information, e-mail, visit website, or call.

ATLANTA INTERNATIONAL GIFT & HOME FURNISHINGS

Website: www.americasmart.com. "We know your time is money, so we strive to make your experience at AmericasMart productive and profitable. As the leading international source for consumer goods, AmericasMart remains unmatched in convenience, amenities and professionalism. Experience AmericasMart for yourself and make it your business advantage. We've got an edge over our national competitors: nation's largest single product collection. By design, the airport connects to rapid rail that takes you directly to the heart of downtown, where AmericasMart is located." See website for more information.

THE ATLANTIC CRAFT TRADE SHOW (ACTS)

(902)492-2773. Fax: (902)429-9059. E-mail: acts@craftalliance.ca. Website: www.actshow.ca/EN/. Estab. 1977. Annual wholesale show held in February. Indoors. Open to trade only. Accepts handmade craft merchants, giftware. Juried. Number exhibitors: see website. Number attendees: see website. Admission: see website. Apply online. Deadline for entry: see website. Application fee: none. Space fee: see website. Exhibition space: see website. For more information, e-mail, visit website, or call.

BEAD & BUTTON SHOW

Website: www.beadandbuttonshow.com. Over 300 vendors will be selling one-of-a-kind finished jewelry plus precious gems, pearls, art beads, gold and silver, beading supplies and books. The show will also feature a juried exhibit of inspiring bead art and over 700 bead and jewelry classes. See website for more information.

BEAD FEST

(513)531-2690. Fax: (610)232-5754. E-mail: mkralle@interweave.com. Website: www.beadfest.com. Contact: Morgan Kralle, event planner. Estab. 2001. Annual cash & carry show held in spring/summer. Indoors. Open to public. Accepts handmade craft merchants, pattern, magazine, book publishers and other mediums. Awards/prizes: Bead Show Winner. Number exhibitors: 150. Number attendees: 3,000-5,000. Admission: $8 for expo; workshop prices vary. Apply online. Deadline for entry: see website. Application fee: none. Space fee: $850-995. Exhibition space: 10×10. For more information, e-mail, visit website, call or check social media.

BILOXI WHOLESALE GIFT SHOW

Website: www.wmigiftshows.com. "Buyers attending the Biloxi Wholesale Gift Show will experience over 300 booths with manufacturers from 22 states and a huge selection of new and trendy merchandise including holiday, home décor, tabletop, garden accessories, souvenirs, gourmet, jewelry, apparel, floral, gift wrap and much more." See website for more information.

BOSTON GIFT SHOW

(800)318-2238. Fax: (678)285-7469. E-mail: info@urbanexpositions.com. Website: www.bostongiftshow.com. Contact: Erica Davidson, show director. Cash & carry/wholesale show held annually in March. Indoors. Open to trade only; must show business ID

to enter. Accepts handmade craft merchants, pattern, magazine, book publishers, functional & decorative accessories, fashion. Juried. Number exhibitors: 500. Number attendees: 4,000. Admission: no fee, open to trade only. Apply online. Deadline for entry: August. Application fee: none. Space fee: $1,690. Exhibition space: 10×10. For more information, e-mail, visit website, or call.

❥ BRITISH CRAFT TRADE FAIR

E-mail: info@bctf.co.uk. Website: www.bctf.co.uk. "BCTF is a three-day event that takes place in April each year at the scenic Great Yorkshire Showground in beautiful Harrogate, Yorkshire. The fair is strictly trade-only and showcases work from exclusively British and Irish makers. BCTF differs from other trade fairs in that no mass-manufactured products or products made overseas are allowed. Visitors can be confident, therefore, that they will be presented with a selection of the best handmade British giftware available from more than 500 talented makers." See website for more information.

BUYER'S CASH & CARRY—MADISON

E-mail: mktsqr@epix.net. Website: www.marketsquareshows.com. Select from a large variety of unusual gift items, handcrafted furniture, gourmet food products, jewelry, as well as handcrafted quality reproductions. All for immediate inventory needs. See website for more information.

BUYER'S CASH & CARRY—MARLBOROUGH

E-mail: mktsqr@epix.net. Website: www.marketsquareshows.com. Select from a large variety of unusual gift items, handcrafted furniture, gourmet food products, jewelry, as well as handcrafted quality reproductions. All for immediate inventory needs. See website for details.

BUYER'S CASH & CARRY—VALLEY FORGE

E-mail: mktsqr@epix.net. Website: www.marketsquareshows.com. Hand-pick holiday collectibles, folk art, handcrafted furniture, and speciality foods. All available for immediate inventory needs. See website for more information.

☼ BY HAND

Website: www.byhand.ca. "By Hand, Canada's Artisan Gift Show is Canada's premier wholesale marketplace that allows buyers the opportunity to discover the very best in Canadian handmade products. Buyers who visit By Hand will see the finest in handmade glass, ceramics, mixed media, fashion, jewellery, leather, art, wood, metal, raku, home décor, stone, pottery, photography, sculpture, toys and more. At By Hand you will find new and exciting product designs that will delight your customers and separate you from your competition. By Hand is a juried show where you will meet the designers and makers of the products and come to understand the joy and passion artisans have for their work." See website for more information.

CALIFORNIA GIFT SHOW

Website: www.californiagiftshow.com. See website for more information and to apply.

CHICAGO GIFT MARKET

Website: www.chicagogiftmarket.com. Annual wholesale show that takes place 4 times a year. See website for more information and to apply.

COLUMBUS MARKETPLACE

Website: www.thecolumbusmarketplace.com. "The Columbus MarketPlace is a permanent wholesale market center offering the newest and finest lines of gifts, collectibles, home furnishings, accessories, housewares, stationery and floral items. This array of trend-setting merchandise is displayed in permanent showrooms in an easy-to-shop single floor layout." See website for more information.

☺ CRAFT

Website: www.craft-london.com. "Covering basketry, blacksmithing, book art, ceramics, enamelling, fashion accessories, furniture, glass, interiors, non-precious and precious jewellery, knitwear, leather, lettering, metal work, wood, millinery, mosaic, paper, printmaking, product design, sculptural, recycled, stone carving, textiles, traditional and more, CRAFT fills a gap in the UK market for a high-quality, juried trade event which enables over 100 leading makers and artisans to meet a substantial audience of international retailers, galleries, museums, professional buyers and collectors within a dedicated trade event in London."

CRAFT AND HOBBY ASSOCIATION CONFERENCE & TRADE SHOW

E-mail: nschwartz@craftandhobby.org. Website: www.craftandhobby.org. See website for more information.

CRAFT HOBBY & STITCH INTERNATIONAL

Website: www.chsi.co.uk. "Craft Hobby + Stitch International is Europe's number 1 trade show for the creative craft sector and provides suppliers of creative art, craft, needlecraft and hobby products with a fantastic platform to showcase their products to a worldwide audience."

DALLAS TEMP SHOW

Website: www.dallasmarketcenter.com. See website for more information.

DALLAS TOTAL HOME & GIFT SHOW

Website: www.dallasmarketcenter.com. "The Dallas Total Home & Gift Market is the premier product destination offering more than 20,000 gift and home décor lines within a convenient, easy-to-shop marketplace."

GALVESTON GIFT & RESORT MERCHANDISE SHOW

(800)318-2238. Fax: (678)285-7469. E-mail: info@urbanexpositions.com. Website: www.galvestongiftshow.com. Contact: Christina Bell, show director. Wholesale show held annually in October. Indoors. Open to trade only. Accepts handmade craft merchants and pattern, magazine, book publishers. Number exhibitors: see website. Number attendees: see website. Admission: none. Apply online. Deadline for entry: see website. Application fee: none. Space fee: $645. Exhibition space: 10×10. For more information, e-mail cbell@urban-expo.com.

GEM AND LAPIDARY WHOLESALERS SHOW

Website: www.glwshows.com. G&LW trade shows are produced in many major trade centers across the United States for the convenience of retail dealers.

HAWAII MARKET MERCHANDISE EXPO

Website: www.douglastradeshows.com. Featured products are: jewelry, gift, apparel, fashion accessories, leather goods, art and collectibles in addition to products manufactured in Hawaii. The expos are designed specifically to serve Hawaii's business buyers and sellers. The expos are not open to the public. The cash & carry format of immediate release of merchandise encourages thousands of business owners, managers and professional trade buyers to purchase hundreds of products for use or re-sale in their businesses.

INTERNATIONAL QUILT MARKET

Website: www.quilts.com. See website for more information.

LAS VEGAS MARKET

Website: www.beadfest.com. "Las Vegas Market is the most comprehensive furniture, home décor and gift market in the U.S., presenting a unique cross-section of 2,000+ resources in an unrivaled market destination. With two markets each year, retailers and designers can shop a broad assortment of product from thousands of manufacturers of furniture, mattress, lighting, decorative accessories, floor coverings, home textiles, tabletop, general gift and more delivering the most complete, cross-category wholesale tradeshow for the furniture, home décor and gift industries in the U.S."

LAS VEGAS SOUVENIR & RESORT GIFT SHOW

(800)318-2238. Fax: (678)285-7469. E-mail: info@urbanexpositions.com. Website: www.lvsouvenirshow.com. Contact: Lisa Glosson, show director. Wholesale show held annually in September. Indoors. Open to trade only. Accepts hand made craft merchants, pattern, magazine, book publishers. Number

exhibitors: see website. Number attendees: see website. Admission: none. Apply online. Deadline for entry: see website. Application fee: none. Space fee: $1,950. Exhibition space: 10×10. For more information, e-mail lglosson@urban-expo.com.

LOUISVILLE GIFT SHOW

(513)861-1139. Fax: (513)861-1557. E-mail: lpharris42@hotmail.com. Website: www.stlouisgiftshow.com. Contact: Larry Harris, president. Estab. 1960s. Wholesale show (some cash & carry and order writing) held semi-annually in February & August. Indoors. Not open to public. Accepts hand made craft merchants, pattern, magazine, book publishers, USA made, imports. Number exhibitors: 70. Number attendees: 800. Admission: none. Apply online. Deadline for entry: open until filled. Application fee: none. Space fee: $525 (10×8); $625 (10×10). Exhibition space: 10×8; 10×10. For more information, e-mail or visit website.

○ MAKE IT!—EDMONTON

Website: makeitproductions.com/edmonton. Held twice a year in Spring/Fall. "Shop for one-of-a-kind handmade items from over 140 of Canada's hottest urban artisans, designers & crafters. Make It is the ultimate upbeat shopping experience! There will be something for everyone from fashion, accessories, art, jewelry, baby items, home decor and stuff for the guys."

○ MAKE IT!—VANCOUVER

Website: makeitproductions.com/vancouver. held annually in Fall. "Shop for one-of-a-kind handmade items from over 250 of Canada's hottest urban artisans, designers & crafters. Make It is the ultimate upbeat shopping experience! There will be something for everyone from fashion, accessories, art, jewelry, baby items, home decor and stuff for the guys."

MINNEAPOLIS MART GIFT HOME & ACCESSORY SHOW

(952)932-7200; (800)626-1298. Fax: (952)932-0847. E-mail: mart@mplsmart.com. Website: www.mplsmart.com. Annual wholesale show held 4 times a year (see website for dates). Indoors. Open to trade only. Accepts home decor, accessories and appareal merchandise. Number exhibitors: see website. Number attendees: see website. Admission: see website. Apply online. Deadline for entry: see website. Application fee: see website. Space fee: varies. Exhibition space: varies. For more information, e-mail, visit website, or call.

MJSA EXPO
(508)316-2132; (800)444-6572. Fax: (508)316-1429. E-mail: corrie.silvia@mjsa.org. Website: www.mjsa. org. Contact: Corrie Silvia Berry. Annual wholesale show held in Spring (check website for dates). Indoors. Open to trade only. Accepts jewelry machinery, supplies, components, services, and finished product. Number exhibitors: see website. Number attendees: see website. Admission: see website. Apply online. Deadline for entry: see website. Application fee: none. Space fee: varies. Exhibition space: varies. For more information, e-mail, visit website, or call.

NAMTA ART MATERIALS WORLD
(704)892-6244. E-mail: rmunisteri@namta.org. Website: www.namta.org. Contact: Rick Munisteri, director of meetings. Annual conference & wholesale show held in spring. Indoors. Open to trade only. Accepts art & craft materials. Number exhibitors: see website. Number attendees: see website. Admission: see website. Apply online. Deadline for entry: see website. Application fee: see website. Space fee: varies. Exhibition space: 10×10. For more information, e-mail, visit website, or call.

THE NATIONAL NEEDLEARTS ASSOCIATION TRADESHOW
(800)889-8662; (740)455-6773. E-mail: info@tnna. org. Website: www.tnna.org. Annual wholesale show held winter, spring, fall. Indoors. Open to trade only. Accepts needle arts. Number exhibitors: see website. Number attendees: see website. Admission: see website. Apply online. Deadline for entry: see website. Application fee: none. Space fee: varies. Exhibition space: see website. For more information, e-mail, visit website, or call.

THE NEW YORK INTERNATIONAL GIFT FAIR
(914)421-3395. E-mail: paula_bertolotti@glmshows. com. Website: www.nynow.com. Contact: Paula Bertolotti. Estab. 2001. Annual wholesale market held twice a year. Indoors. Open to trade only. Accepts home, lifestyle and gift vendors. Number exhibitors: 2,800. Number attendees: 35,000. Admission: see website. Apply online. Deadline for entry: see website. Application fee: none. Space fee: varies. Exhibition space: varies. For more information, e-mail, visit website, or call.

NORTHEAST MARKET CENTER
(800)435-2775. E-mail: info@northeastmarketcenter.com. Website: www.northeastmarketcenter.com. Wholesale marketplace open several times a year. Indoors. Open to trade only. Accepts gifts, decorative accessories. Number exhibitors: see website. Number attendees: see website. Admission: see website. Apply online. Deadline for entry: see website. Application fee: see website. Space fee: varies. Exhibition space: see website. For more information, e-mail, visit website, or call.

OASIS GIFT SHOWS
(602)952-2050; (800)424-9519. Fax: (602)445-6936. E-mail: kevin@kktevents.com; kristi@kktevents.com. Website: wwwoasis.org. Estab. 1976. Bi-annual wholesale show held in January & September. Indoors. Open to public. Accepts giftware. Number exhibitors: see website. Number attendees: 3,000-5,000. Admission: see website. Apply online. Deadline for entry: see website. Application fee: see website. Space fee: varies. Exhibition space: 10×10. For more information, e-mail, visit website, or call.

OCEAN CITY RESORT & GIFT EXPO
(800)318-2238. Fax: (678)285-7469. E-mail: info@urbanexpositions.com. Website: www. oceancitygiftshow.com. Contact: Russ Turner, show director. Wholesale show held annually in October/November. Indoors. Open to trade only. Accepts handmade craft merchants, and pattern, magazine, book publishers. Number exhibitors: 200. Number attendees: see website. Admission: none. Apply on-

line. Deadline for entry: see website. Application fee: none. Space fee: $890. Exhibition space: 10×10. For more information, e-mail rturner@urban-expo.com.

OFFINGER'S MARKETPLACES

(888)878-GIFT (4438). Fax: (740)452-2552. E-mail: OffingersMarketplaces@Offinger.com; gfleming@offinger.com. Website: www.offingersmarketplaces.com. Estab. 1930. Annual wholesale show held 4 times a year (see website for dates). Indoors. Open to trade only. Accepts handmade craft merchants, giftware, home decor and other mediums. Number exhibitors: see website. Number attendees: see website. Admission: see website. Apply online. Deadline for entry: see website. Application fee: see website. Space fee: varies. Exhibition space: 12 ×10; 24 ×20. For more information, e-mail, visit website, or call.

ORLANDO GIFT SHOW

(800)318-2238. E-mail: kcunningham@urban-expo.com. Website: www.orlandogiftshow.com. Contact: Kristi Cunningham, show coordinator. Annual wholesale and cash & carry show held in summer. Indoors. Open to trade only. Accepts handmade craft merchants, general giftware, home and garden accents, gourmet gifts, party and paper goods, tabletop, holiday/seasonal, collectibles, stationery, souvenir/resort merchandise, bed, bath, and linen and other mediums. Number exhibitors: see website. Number attendees: see website. Admission: see website. Apply online. Deadline for entry: see website. Application fee: none. Space fee: varies. Exhibition space: 10×10. For more information, e-mail, visit website, or call.

THE PHILADELPHIA GIFT SHOW

(800)318-2238. Fax: (678)285-7469. E-mail: manderson@urban-expo.com. Website: www.philadelphiagiftshow.com. Contact: Marilyn Anderson, show director. Estab. 1996. Wholesale show held semi-annually in January & July. Indoors. Open to trade only. Accepts pattern, magazine, and book publishers. Number exhibitors: see website. Number attendees: see website. Admission: none. Apply online. Deadline for entry: see website. Application fee: none. Space fee: $1,750. Exhibition space: 10×10. For more information, e-mail manderson@urban-expo.com.

PIEDMONT CRAFTSMEN'S FAIR

(336)725-1516. E-mail: craftsfair@piedmontcraftsmen.org. Website: www.piedmontcraftsmen.org/programs/crafts-fair. Contact: Deborah Britton, fair coordinator. Estab. 1963. Annual showcase held in the fall. Indoors. Open to public. Accepts clay, wood, glass, fibers, leather, metal, photography, printmaking, and mixed media. Number exhibitors: see website. Number attendees: see website. Admission: $7 adults; $6 students/seniors; children 12 & under free; weekend pass $11. Apply online. Deadline for entry: see website. Application fee: none. Space fee: varies. Exhibition space: see website. For more information, e-mail, visit website, or call.

QUEBEC GIFT FAIR

(416)679-0170; (800)611-6100. Fax: (416)385-1851; (877)373-7555. E-mail: quebec@cangift.org. Website: quebecgiftfair.org. Annual wholesale show held in spring/fall. Indoors. Open to trade only. Accepts giftware merchants. Awards/prizes: Best Booth Awards. Number exhibitors: see website. Number attendees: see website. Admission: see website. Apply online. Deadline for entry: see website. Application fee: none. Space fee: varies. Exhibition space: varies. For more information, e-mail, visit website, or call.

THE SEATTLE GIFT SHOW

(800)318-2238. Fax: (678)285-7469. Website: www.seattlegiftshow.com. Contact: Lisa Glosson, show director. Cash & carry/wholesale show held semi-annually in January & August. Indoors. Open to trade only. Accepts handmade craft merchants, and pattern, magazine, book publishers. Number exhibitors: see website. Number attendees: see website. Admission: no fee for retail buyers; $30 guest fee. Apply online. Deadline for entry: see website. Application fee: none. Space fee: see website. Exhibition space: 10×10. For more information, e-mail lglosson@urban-expo.com.

STITCHES EXPOS

(800)237-7099. Fax: (605)338-2994. E-mail: stitchesregistration@xrx-inc.com. Website: www. knittinguniverse.com/STITCHES/. Annual conference and market held 4 times a year. Indoors. Open to public. Accepts fiber. Number exhibitors: see website. Number attendees: see website. Admission: $10/1-day pass; $15/2-day; $20/3-day pass. Apply online. Deadline for entry: see website. Application fee: none. Space fee: see website. Exhibition space: see website. For more information, e-mail, visit website, or call.

ST. LOUIS GIFT SHOW

(513)861-1139. Fax: (513)861-1557. E-mail: lpharris42@hotmail.com. Website: www.stlouis giftshow.com. Contact: Larry Harris, president. Estab. 1970s. Wholesale show (some cash & carry and order writing) held semi-annually in January & August. Indoors. Not open to public. Accepts handmade craft merchants, pattern, magazine, book publishers, USA made, imports. Number exhibitors: 80. Number attendees: 800. Admission: none. Apply online. Deadline for entry: open until filled. Application fee: none. Space fee: $525 (10×8); $625 (10×10). Exhibition space: 10×8; 10×10. For more information exhibitors should visit website.

TORONTO GIFT FAIR

(416)679-0170; (800)611-6100. Fax: (416)679-0175; (800)496-2966. E-mail: toronto@cangift.org. Website: torontogiftfair.org. Annual wholesale show held in spring/fall. Indoors. Open to trade only. Accepts innovative tabletop, housewares, gourmet food, garden accessories, collectibles, handmade, stationery, home decor, bath, bed and linen products. Number exhibitors: 900. Number attendees: 26,000. Admission: see website. Apply online. Deadline for entry: see website. Application fee: none. Space fee: see website. Exhibition space: see website. For more information, e-mail, visit website, or call.

WHOLESALECRAFTS.COM

(888)427-2381. E-mail: ACREinfo@wholesalecrafts. com. Website: www.wholesalecrafts.com. Estab. 1998. Annual wholesale show held 3 times a year. Indoors. Open to trade only. Accepts handmade craft merchants. Number exhibitors: see website. Number attendees: see website. Admission: see website. Apply online. Deadline for entry: see website. Application fee: none. Space fee: see website. Exhibition space: see website. For more information, e-mail, visit website, or call.

WINTER SEATTLE MARKET WEEK: GIFT & HOME ACCESSORIES SHOW

(206)767-6800; (800)433-1014. Fax: (206)767-5449. E-mail: info@pacmarket.com. Website: www. pacificmarketcenter.com. Annual wholesale show held twice a year. Indoors. Number exhibitors: see website. Number attendees: see website. Admission: see website. Apply online. Deadline for entry: see website. Application fee: none. Space fee: see website. Exhibition space: see website. For more information, e-mail, visit website, or call.

SHOWS AND FAIRS

///

What better way to sell your handmade wares than to attend a craft or art fair? Craft fairs are found in most cities throughout the year. Some are specifically geared toward holiday handmades, while others are indie shows that trend a bit cooler. From traditional to modern, yarn to paper, and quilting to woodworking, crafts of all kinds can find a home at a craft fair. The listings in the following pages are for craft and art fairs that might be a good fit for you and your artisan product.

Peruse the listings in the following pages to find the fairs that are most interesting to you. Perhaps there's a show that takes place just a few miles away from your home, or perhaps there's a show dedicated to your style of craft. After selling at a few fairs, you will learn even more about which type of show is best suited to your craft, attracts your demographic and is most valuable for you to attend. Be sure to read Grace Dobush's article "Indie Craft Shows." Her advice, while specific to indie shows, contains a wealth of information and tips for selling at any show.

Each listing includes the basic information about the show, but visiting the show will always give you a better sense of the market, and if your wares fit in that particular venue. Over time, you'll develop an instinct for knowing what market will work for your business. Selling in person at craft shows is not only a way to make money, but it provides invaluable first-hand contact with your customer. That first-hand feedback is key to developing your brand and your business. Are certain colors more popular? Do you need to expand the sizes you have on offer? Do attendees at different markets want different things, and how can that help you develop your focus? Check out April Cobb's article "Finding Your Crafty Niche" for some insights on what it's like selling in person, and what you can learn that will influence your business.

Attending craft shows can also be a way of marketing your online store. Many exhibitors note that, while they may see only a handful of sales at a particular show, they'll often see a spike in orders through their online shop from that area. That being the case, make a point to advertise your online shop. Print your website name on your packaging, of course, and have business cards and brochures available.

Whether you focus on in-person selling at craft fairs or online through sites like Etsy.com, you will find benefits to both. Meeting your customers face-to-face is invaluable for building lifelong customers, and creating a beautiful online shop allows you to craft a story through photos that your customers will want to come back to time and again.

As you become a regular exhibitor at craft shows, you'll develop a schedule, your booth's look and feel, a set plan for handling payment, and a routine for setting up and breaking down. If this is your first time out, check out the regional craft show index in order to focus on shows nearby. Over time, you can consider expanding your reach to markets in other regions.

KEY TO SYMBOLS & ABBREVIATIONS

◔	Canadian market
◉	market located outside of the U.S. and Canada
⌂	market prefers to work with local artists/ designers
b&w	black & white (photo or illustration)
SASE	self-addressed, stamped envelope
SAE	self-addressed envelope
IRC	International Reply Coupon, for use when mailing to countries other than your own

6TH STREET FAIR

Bellevue Downtown Association, 400 108th Ave., NE, Suite 110, Bellevue WA 98004. (425)453-1223. Website: www.bellevuedowntown.org. Art & crafts fair held annually in July. Outdoors. Accepts sculpture, jewelry, home décor, wood, glass, fabrics and more. Free to public. Apply online.

ADDITIONAL INFORMATION Deadline for entry: see website. Application fee: see website. Space fee: see website. Exhibition space: 10×10. For more information, crafters should call or visit website.

57TH STREET ART FAIR

1507 E. 53rd St., PMB 296, Chicago IL 60615. (773)234-3247. E-mail: info@57thstartfair.org. Website: www.57thstreetfair.org. Estab. 1948. Fine art & craft show held annually in June. Outdoors. Accepts painting, sculpture, photography, glass, jewelry, leather, wood, ceramics, fiber, printmaking. Juried. Free to public. Apply via Zapplication.org.

ADDITIONAL INFORMATION Deadline for entry: January 15. Application fee: $35. Space fee: $300. Exhibition space: 10×10. For more information, crafters should e-mail, visit or website.

AFFORDABLE ARTS FESTIVAL

P.O. Box 1634, Boulder CO 80306. (303)330-8237. E-mail: jdphotos@earthlink.net. Website: www.affordableartsfestival.com. Contact: Jim DeLutes, director. Fine art & craft show held annually in August. Outdoors. Accepts painting, jewelry, glass, sculpture, photography, wood, fiber, pottery, mixed media, drawing, pastels and more. Juried. Admission: $5. Apply via Zapplication.org.

ADDITIONAL INFORMATION Deadline for entry: see website. Application fee: $25. Space fee: $195. Exhibition space: 10×15. For more information, crafters should e-mail, call or visit website.

AIKEN'S MAKIN'

121 Richland Ave., E, Aiken SC 29801. (803)649-1200 ext. 224. Fax: (803)641-4174. E-mail: dphillips@aikenchamber.net. Website: www.aikensmakin.net. Contact: Diane Phillips, director. Estab. 1976. Annual arts & crafts show held in September the Friday & Saturday after Labor Day. Outdoors. Accepts handmade crafts, photography, art, needle crafts, pottery, wood. Juried. Exhibitors: 205. Number of attendees: 30,000. Free to public. See website for application.

ADDITIONAL INFORMATION Deadline for entry: February 28. Space fee: $200-$225. Exhibition space: 13×10. For more information, e-mail, call or see website or Facebook page.

TIPS "Follow instruction. Include good quality photos and all items requested."

ALASKA-JUNEAU PUBLIC MARKET

907-586-1166. Fax: 907-586-1166. E-mail: metcom@gci.net. Website: www.juneaupublicmarket.com. Contact: Peter Metcalfe, owner/manager. Estab. 1983. Seasonal/holiday show held annually Thanksgiving weekend (November). Indoors. Accepts handmade crafts. Exhibitors: 175. Number of attendees: 10,000 (all 3 days). Admission: $7 for weekend pass. Apply via website.

ADDITIONAL INFORMATION Deadline for entry: July 31. Space fee: $125-$980. Exhibition space: 8×8. Average sales: $5,00. For more information, see website.

TIPS "Basic salesmanship: look the customer in the eye and draw them in."

ALEXANDRIA KING STREET ART FESTIVAL

270 Central Blvd., Suite 107B, Jupiter FL 33458. (561)746-6615. Fax: (561)746-6528. E-mail: info@artfestival.com. Website: www.artfestival.com. "At this community festival, art enthusiasts discover spectacular paintings, life-size sculptures, jewelry, photography, ceramics and more, offering extraordinary art for every taste. More than $15 million in art will be on display, providing visitors with the opportunity to purchase one-of-a-kind wares and meet the artists behind the work, hearing firsthand what inspires them. Plus, visitors can delight in interactive art activities and The Art League's much-loved Ice Cream Bowl Fundraiser." See website for more information.

ALLEY ART FESTIVAL

E-mail: downtownauroran@gmail.com. Website: www.facebook.com/pages/Alley-Art-Festival/107654222593659; www.downtownauroran.

wordpress.com/alley-art-festival/. Art & craft show held annually in August. Outdoors. Apply via e-mail. **ADDITIONAL INFORMATION** Deadline for entry: see website. Application fee: see website. Space fee: see website. Exhibition space: see website. For more information, crafters should e-mail or visit website.

☺ AMAGANSETT FINE ARTS FESTIVAL

David Oleski Events, 977 Broad Run Rd., West Chester PA 19380. (610)864-3500. E-mail: davidoleski@gmail.com. Website: www.amagansettfinearts.com. "The cutting edge of individual artistic expression and the communities of the Hamptons go hand in hand, and this festival will provide a rare opportunity for the public to meet these talented visonaries in an up close and personal experience for one remarkable weekend." See website for more information.

AMERICAN FINE CRAFT SHOW NYC

P.O. Box 480, Slate Hill NY 10973. (845)355-2400; (845)661-1221. Fax: (845)355-2444. E-mail: show. director@americanartmarketing.com. Website: www. americanfinecraftshownyc.com. Contact: Richard Rothbard, director. Fine art & craft show held annually in October. Indoors. Accepts handmade crafts, basketry, ceramics, decorative fiber, furniture, glass, jewelry, leather, metal, mixed media, paper, wearable art, wood. Juried. Apply online. **ADDITIONAL INFORMATION** Deadline for entry: April 30. Application fee: $35. Space fee: $200. Exhibition space: varies. For more information, crafters should e-mail or visit website.

AMERICAN FOLK ART FESTIVAL

(707)246-2460. E-mail: gavitee@aol.com. Website: www.americanfolkartfestival.com. Contact: Susan Bartolucci. Arts & crafts show held annually in September. Indoors. Accepts handmade crafts, one-of-a-kind folk art, Americana & folk art antiques. Admission: $10. Apply online. **ADDITIONAL INFORMATION** Deadline for entry: see website. Application fee: see website. Space fee: see website. Exhibition space: see website. For more information, crafters should e-mail or visit website. **TIPS** "We are looking for outside of the norm, so feel free to experiment."

ANDERSON ORCHARD APPLE FESTIVAL & CRAFT FAIR

369 E. Greencastle Rd., Mooresville, IN 46158. (317)831-4181. E-mail: erin@andersonorchard.com.. Website: www.andersonorchards.com/apple_festival. php. Contact: Erin. Arts & crafts show held annually in September. Indoors & outdoors. Accepts handmade crafts and other items. Apply online. **ADDITIONAL INFORMATION** Deadline for entry: see website. Application fee: none. Space fee: $100. Exhibition space: varies. For more information, crafters should e-mail, visit website or call.

THE ANNA MARIA ISLAND ARTS & CRAFTS FESTIVAL

270 Central Blvd., Suite 107B, Jupiter FL 33458. (561)746-6615. Fax: (561)746-6528. E-mail: info@ArtFestival.com. Website: www.artfestival.com. "The show will be held on Historic Bridge Street. Anna Marie Island is bounded on the west by the Gulf of Mexico, the south by Longboat Key and Pass. This quaint island resort will be home to our street festival on Bridge Street. The show offers a variety of handmade crafts available for browsing and purchase by the nation's finest crafters."

ANNUAL BOCA FEST

270 Central Blvd., Suite 107B, Jupiter FL 33458. (561)746-6615. Fax: (561)746-6528. E-mail: info@artfestival.com. Website: www.artfestival.com. "Boca Fest is the longest running show presented by Howard Alan Events and has become considered Boca's #1 event to attend. Over two decades since it's inception, this esteemed community art festival continues to highlight the talents of more than 150 exhibitors displaying a wide range of works from life-size sculptures to photography, paintings, and jewelry. The festival offers many opportunities to appreciate—and purchase—art during this weekend of visual inspiration. This phenomenal art festival brings together an affluent customer base with an exceptional eye for great art, the aesthetic beauty of Boca Raton, and an abundant mix of fine art." See website for more information.

ANNUAL DOWNTOWN HYATTSVILLE ART FESTIVAL

(301)683-8267. Website: www.hyattsvilleartsfestival.com. Contact: Stuart Eisenberg, executive director. "See over 70 exhibiting and performing artists, enjoy live entertainment and eat some great food on the happening streets of Hyattsville, in the Gateway Arts District of Prince George's County." See website for more information.

ANNUAL SHADYSIDE—THE ART FESTIVAL ON WALNUT ST.

270 Central Blvd., Suite 107B, Jupiter FL 33458. (561)746-6615. Fax: (561)746-6528. E-mail: info@artfestival.com. Website: www.artfestival.com. "The annual Shadyside—The Art Festival on Walnut Street, which started out as a neighborhood street fair, is now regarded as one of the top shows in Pittsburgh. Shadyside features boutiques, shops and galleries mingled with national retailers in a neighborhood of tree-lined streets, historic homes, hip events, and distinctive restaurants." See website for more information.

ANNUAL SIESTA FIESTA

270 Central Blvd., Suite 107B, Jupiter FL 33458. (561)746-6615. Fax: (561)746-6528. E-mail: info@artfestival.com. Website: www.artfestival.com. "Hosted in an exquisite venue seated along the beautifully lush Ocean Boulevard and Beach Road, you can stroll along the beach as you take in art from 250 of the nation's most talented artists & crafters out there. Showcasing an extensive collection of work ranging from life-size sculptures, spectacular paintings, one-of-a-kind jewels, photography, ceramics and much, much more, this show truly has something for anyone. Complete with an additional green market, this spectacular show also features plants, orchids, body products, and tasty dips." See website for more information.

ANNUAL ST. ARMANDS CIRCLE FESTIVAL

270 Central Blvd., Suite 107B, Jupiter FL 33458. (561)746-6615. Fax: (561)746-6528. E-mail: info@artfestival.com. Website: www.artfestival.com. "Year after year, the Annual St. Armands Circle Art Festival makes the list of *Sunshine Artist Magazine*'s top art shows in the country. For two days, festival-goers will enjoy works from the nation's best talent, and long-time festival favorites, along with the newest names on the contemporary art scene. Come see some of America's best artists displaying one-of-a-kind jewelry, pottery, paintings, and much much more. Festival patrons and art collectors alike can meet and visit with their favorite artists—having the opportunity to view and purchase original art." See website for more information.

ARLINGTON FESTIVAL OF THE ARTS

270 Central Blvd., Suite 107B, Jupiter FL 33458. (561)746-6615. Fax: (561)746-6528. E-mail: info@artfestival.com. Website: www.artfestival.com. "Enjoy a weekend of true visual inspiration, as over 100 artists will showcase their works including glass, mixed media, paintings, jewelry, and pottery; providing all sorts of opportunities to appreciate—and purchase—art. The show is located on North Highland Street, which runs over Clarendon Blvd & Wilson Blvd" in Arlington VA. See website for more information.

ART & APPLES FESTIVAL

407 Pine St., Rochester MI 48307. (248)651-4110. Fax: (248)651-4757. E-mail: festivals@pccart.org. E-mail: lbates@pccart.org. Website: www.artandapples.com. Contact: Laura Bates, festival director. Estab. 1965. Fine arts & crafts show held annually in September. Outdoors. Accepts handmade crafts and fine art. Juried. Exhibitors: 290. Number of attendees: 125,000. Admission: $5. Apply online.

ADDITIONAL INFORMATION Deadline for entry: see website. Application fee: see website. Space fee: see website. Exhibition space: see website. For more information, crafters should e-mail, visit website.

ART & CRAFT MARKETPLACE AT THE COLUMBUS OKTOBERFEST

4275 Fulton Rd., NW, Canton OH 44718. (330)493-4130. Fax: (330)493-7607. E-mail: shows@huffspromo.com. Website: www.huffspromo.com. Estab. 1965. Arts & crafts show held annually in September. Outoors (covered). Accepts handmade crafts and other items. Juried. Exhibitors: varies. Number of attendees: 30,000. Free to public. Apply online.

ADDITIONAL INFORMATION Deadline for entry: see website. Application fee: none. Space fee: $190 (single); $380 (double). Exhibition space: 10×14. For more information, crafters should e-mail, visit website or call.

ART & CRAFT SHOWCASE AT THE AKRON HOME & FLOWER SHOW

4275 Fulton Rd., NW, Canton OH 44718. (330)493-4130. Fax: (330)493-7607. E-mail: shows@huffs promo.com. Website: www.huffspromo.com. Estab. 1965. Arts & crafts show held annually in February. Indoors. Accepts handmade crafts. Juried. Exhibitors: varies. Number of attendees: 30,000. Free to public. Apply online.

ADDITIONAL INFORMATION Deadline for entry: see website. Application fee: none; $100 space deposit required at time of application. Space fee: $395. Exhibition space: 8×12. For more information, crafters should e-mail, visit website or call.

ART A FAIR

P.O. Box 547, Laguna Beach CA 92652. (949)494-4514. E-mail: mjcahill@att.net. Website: www.art-a-fair. com. Estab. 1967. Arts & crafts show held annually in June-August. Outoors. Accepts handmade crafts, painting, sculpture, ceramics, jewelry, printmaking, photography, master crafts, digital art. Juried. Exhibitors: 125. Number of attendees: see website. Admission: $7.50 adults; $4.50 seniors; children 12 & under free. Apply online.

ADDITIONAL INFORMATION Deadline for entry: see website. Application fee: $40 (per medium). Space fee: $200 + $35 membership fee. Exhibition space: see website. For more information, crafters should e-mail, visit website or call.

ART AT THE GLEN

P.O. Box 550, Highland Park IL 60035. (847)926-4300. Fax: (847)926-4330. E-mail: info@amdurproductions. com. Website: www.amdurproductions.com. Arts & crafts show held annually in August. Outoors. Accepts handmade crafts, ceramics, fiber, furniture, glass, jewelry, metal, mixed media, paintings, drawings, photography and wood. Juried. Exhibitors: 185. Number of attendees: 50,000. Free to public. Apply online.

ADDITIONAL INFORMATION Deadline for entry: see website. Application fee: $35. Space fee: $525. Exhibition space: see website. For more information, crafters should e-mail, visit website or call.

ART BIRMINGHAM

118 N. Fourth Ave., Ann Arbor MI 48104. (734)662-3382. Fax: (734)662-0339. Website: www.theguild. org. Estab. 1981. Arts & crafts show held annually in May. Outoors. Accepts handmade crafts painting, ceramics, photography, jewelry, glass, wood, sculpture, mixed media, fiber, metal and more. Juried. Exhibitors: 150. Number of attendees: see website. Free to public. Apply online.

ADDITIONAL INFORMATION Deadline for entry: see website. Application fee: see website. Space fee: see website. Exhibition space: see website. For more information, crafters should visit website or call.

ART & CRAFT MARKETPLACE AT THE COLUMBUS OKTOBERFEST

4275 Fulton Rd., NW, Canton OH 44718. (330)493-4130. Fax: (330)493-7607. E-mail: shows@huffspromo.com. Website: www.huffspromo.com. Estab. 1965. Arts & crafts show held annually in September. Outoors (covered). Accepts handmade crafts and other items. Juried. Exhibitors: varies. Number of attendees: 30,000. Free to public. Apply online.

ADDITIONAL INFORMATION Deadline for entry: see website. Application fee: none. Space fee: $190 (single); $380 (double). Exhibition space: 10×14. For more information, crafters should e-mail, visit website or call.

ART FAIR AT LAUMEIER

(314)615-5278. E-mail: artfair@laumeier.org. Website: www.laumeir.org. Contact: Marie Oberkirsch, special events manager. Estab. 1987. Arts & crafts show held annually in May during Mother's Day weekend. Outdoors. Accepts fine handmade crafts, ceramics, fiber/textiles, glass, jewelry, mixed media, printmaking/drawing, painting, photography, sculpture, wood. Juried. Awards/prizes: $10,000 in cash awards. Number of exhibitors: 150. Number of attendees: 15,000. Admission: $10 adults 12+; $5 children 6-11; children under 5 free. Apply online at Zapplication.org.

ADDITIONAL INFORMATION Deadline for entry: January 10. Application fee: $35. Space fee: $350-$525. Exhibition space: 10×10. Average sales: $5,000. For more information, see website.

ART FAIR AT QUEENY PARK

GSLAA-Vic Barr, 1668 Rishon Hill Dr., St. Louis MO 63146. (314)997-1181. Website: www.gslaa.org. Arts & crafts show held annually in August. Indoors. Accepts handmade crafts, clay, digital (computer) art, drawing/print, fiber (basketry, paper, wearable, woven), glass, jewelry, 2D/3D mixed media, oil/acrylic, photography, sculpture, water media, wood. Juried. Exhibitors: 140. Number of attendees: see website. Free to public. Apply online.

ADDITIONAL INFORMATION Deadline for entry: see website. Application fee: $25; $50 for late application. Space fee: $225. Exhibition space: 10×8. For more information, crafters should visit website or call.

ART FAIR JACKSON HOLE

Art Association of Jackson Hole, P.O. Box 1248, Jackson WY 83001. (307)733-8792. Fax: (307)733-6694. E-mail: artistinfo@jhartfair.org. Website: www.jhartfair.org. Contact: Amy Fradley, Art Fair Director Estab. 1965. Arts & crafts show held annually in July & August. Outoors. Accepts handmade crafts, ceramic, drawing, fiber, furniture, glass, graphics & printmaking, jewelry, leather, metalwork, 2D/3D mixed media, painting, photography, sculpture, toys & games, wearable fiber, wood. Juried. Exhibitors: 135. Number of attendees: 30,000. Free for art association members; $5 per day for non-members. Apply via Zapplication.org.

ADDITIONAL INFORMATION Deadline for entry: see website. Application fee: $35. Space fee: varies. Exhibition space: varies. For more information, crafters should e-mail, visit website or call.

ART FAIR OFF THE SQUARE

P.O. Box 1791, Madison WI 53701-1791. E-mail: wiartcraft@gmail.com. Website: www.artcraftwis. org/AFOS.html. Estab. 1965. Arts & crafts show held annually in July. Outoors. Accepts handmade crafts ceramics, art glass, painting, fiber, sculpture, jewelry, graphics, papermaking, photography, wood and more. Juried. Awards/prizes: Best of Category. Exhibitors: 140. Number of attendees: see website. Free to public. Apply via Zapplication.org.

ADDITIONAL INFORMATION Deadline for entry: see website. Application fee: $25. Space fee: $300. Exhibition space: 10×10. For more information, crafters should e-mail, visit website or call.

ART FAIR ON THE SQUARE

227 State St., Madison WI 53703. (608)257-0158, ext 229. E-mail: artfair@mmoca.org. Website: www.mmoca.org. Contact: Annik Dupaty. Estab. 1958. Arts & crafts show held annually in July. Outoors. Accepts handmade crafts, ceramics, fiber, leather, furniture, jewelry, glass, digital art, metal, sculpture, 2D/3D mixed media, painting, photography, printmaking/graphics/drawing, wood. Juried. Awards/prizes: Best of Show; Invitational Award. Exhibitors: varies. Number of attendees: 150,000+. Free to public. Apply via Zapplication.org.

ADDITIONAL INFORMATION Deadline for entry: see website. Application fee: $35. Space fee: $495 (single); $1,050 (double). Exhibition space: 10×10 (single); 10×10 (double). For more information, crafters should e-mail, visit website or call.

ART FEST BY THE SEA

270 Central Blvd., Suite 107B, Jupiter FL 33458. (561)746-6615. Fax: (561)746-6528. E-mail: info@ArtFestival.com. Website: www.artfestival.com/Festivals/Art_Fest_by_the_Sea_Jupiter_Juno_Beach_Florida_March.ASPX. Estab. 1988. Arts & crafts show held annually in March. Outdoors. Accepts handmade crafts and other items. Juried. Exhibitors: varies. Number of attendees: see website. Admission: see website. Apply via Zapplication.org.

ADDITIONAL INFORMATION Deadline for entry: see website. Application fee: see website. Space fee: see website. Exhibition space: see website. For more information, crafters should e-mail, visit website or call.

ARTFEST FORT MYERS

1375 Jackson St., Suite 401, Fort Myers FL 33901. (239)768-3602. E-mail: info@artfestfortmyers.com. Website: www.artfestformyers.com. Fine arts & crafts fair held annually in February. Outdoors. Accepts handmade crafts, ceramics, digital, drawing/graphics, fiber, glass, jewelry, metal, 2D/3D mixed media, painting, photography, printmaking, sculpture, wearables, and wood. Juried. Awards/prizes: $5,000 in cash. Exhibitors: 200. Number of attendees: 85,000. Free to public. Apply online.

ADDITIONAL INFORMATION Deadline for entry: September 15. Application fee: $35. Space fee: $460.50. Exhibition space: 10×10. For more information, crafters should e-mail, visit website or call.

ART FESTIVAL OF HENDERSON

P.O. Box 95050, Henderson NV 89009-5050. (702)267-2171. Website: www.hendersonlive.com/special-events/art-festival-of-henderson#New_Artist. Arts & crafts show held annually in May. Outdoors. Accepts handmade crafts, paintings, pottery, jewelry, photography and much more. Juried. Exhibitors: varies. Number of attendees: 25,000. Free to public. Apply online.

ADDITIONAL INFORMATION Deadline for entry: see website. Application fee: see website. Space fee: see website. Exhibition space: see website. For more information, crafters should visit website or call.

ARTFEST MIDWEST—"THE OTHER SHOW"

Stookey Companies, P.O. Box 31083, Des Moines IA 50310. (515)278-6200. Fax: (515)276-7513. E-mail: suestookey@att.net. Website: www.artfestmidwest.com. Fine arts & crafts fair held annually in June. Indoors & outdoors. Accepts handmade crafts, ceramic, fiber, drawing, glass, jewelry, metal, 2D/3D mixed media, painting, photography, wood. Juried. Awards/prizes: announced after jury. Exhibitors: 240. Number of attendees: 30,000. Free to public. Apply via Zapplication.org.

ADDITIONAL INFORMATION Deadline for entry: March. Application fee: $30. Space fee: varies. Exhibition space: varies. For more information, crafters should e-mail, visit website or call.

ARTIGRAS FINE ARTS FESTIVAL

5520 PGA Blvd., Suite 200, Palm Beach Gardens FL 33418. (561)748-3946. Fax: (561)745-7519. E-mail: info@artigras.org; artists@artigras.org. Website: www.artigras.org. Estab. 1985. Fine arts & crafts fair held annually in February. Outdoors. Accepts handmade crafts, ceramics, fiber (wearable and non-wearable), digital art, drawing & printmaking, glass, jewelry, metal, mixed media, painting, photography, sculpture, and wood. Juried. Awards/prizes: $17,000 in cash awards and ribbons. Exhibitors: 300. Number of attendees: 85,000. Admission: $8 advance; $10 at gate; children 12 & under free. Apply online.

ADDITIONAL INFORMATION Deadline for entry: September. Application fee: $40. Space fee: $450 +tax (single); $900+ tax (double). Exhibition space: 12×12 (single); 12×24 (double). For more information, crafters should e-mail, visit website or call.

ART IN BLOOM—CATIGNY PARK

EM Events, LLC, P.O. Box 4332, Naperville IL 60567. (630)536-8416. E-mail: emelloy@emevents.com. Website: www.cantigny.org/calendar/signature-events/art-in-bloom. Fine arts & crafts show held annually in June. Outdoors. Accepts handmade crafts ceramics, drawing, fiber non-functional, fiber wearable, paper non-functional, furniture, glass, jewelry, acrylic, oil, watercolor, pastel, sculpture, wood, mixed media, collage, photography, and printmaking. Juried. Exhibitors: 80. Number of attendees: 8,000. Free to public. Apply online.

ADDITIONAL INFORMATION Deadline for entry: see website. Application fee: $10. Space fee: $285. Exhibition space: 10×10. For more information, crafters should e-mail, visit website or call.

ART IN THE BARN—BARRINGTON

Advocate Good Shepherd Hospital, Art in the Barn Artist Committee, 450 W. Highway 22, Barrington IL 60010. (847)842-4496. E-mail: artinthebarn@comcast.net. Website: www.artinthebarn-barrington.com. Estab. 1974. Fine arts & crafts show held annually in September. Indoors & outdoors. Accepts handmade crafts, ceramics, painting, jewelry, glass, sculpture, fiber, drawing, photography, digital media, printmaking, scratchboard, mixed media, wood. Juried. Awards/prizes: Best of Show; Best of Medium; Purchase Awards. Exhibitors: 185. Number of attendees: 8,500. Admission: $5; children 12 & under free. Apply online.

ADDITIONAL INFORMATION Deadline for entry: see website. Application fee: $20. Space fee: $100 (indoors); $85 (outdoors). Exhibition space: varies. For more information, crafters should e-mail, visit website or call.

ART IN THE BARN FITCHBURG

5927 Adams Rd., Fitchburg WI 53575. (608)835-0454. Website: www.site.artinthebarnwi.org. "Art in the Barn is dedicated to bringing quality visual and performing arts for people of all ages, in a serene and natural rural setting for life enriching experiences and pure enjoyment. Art in the Barn is a series of performances featuring local, national and international performers and visual artists. The series takes place in an 1870s restored barn in a rural setting outside of Madison, Wisconsin."

ART IN THE GARDENS

9400 Boerner Dr., Hales Corners WI 53130. (414)525-5656. Fax: (414)525-5668. E-mail: jschmitz@fbbg.org. Website: www.boernerbotanicalgardens.org. Contact: Jennifer Schmitz, gift shop manager. Estab. 2009. Arts & crafts show held annually in May. Indoors & outdoors. Accepts handmade crafts, photography, painting. Juried. Number of exhibitors: 40. Number of attendees: 1,000. Free to public. Apply online.
ADDITIONAL INFORMATION Deadline for entry: April 3. Application fee: $5 before February 3; $10 after February 3. Space fee: $75. Exhibition space: 8×8 inside; 10×10 outside. Average sales: $500-$2,000. For more information, e-mail or visit website.
TIPS "We look for quality and variety."

ART IN THE PARK (ELMHURST)

Website: www.rglmarketingforthearts.com/elmhurst-art-in-the-park. Estab. 1996. Fine arts & crafts show held annually in May. Outdoors. Accepts handmade crafts and other items. Juried. Exhibitors: varies. Number of attendees: 10,000. Free to public. Apply online.
ADDITIONAL INFORMATION Deadline for entry: see website. Application fee: see website. Space fee: see website. Exhibition space: see website. For more information, crafters should visit website.

ART IN THE PARK (KEARNY)

Kearney Artist Guild, P.O. Box 1368, Kearney NE 68848-1368. (308)708-0510. E-mail: artinthepark-kearney@charter.net. Website: www.kearneyartistsguild.com. Estab. 1971. Fine arts & crafts show held annually in July. Outdoors. Accepts handmade crafts, ceramics, drawing, fiber, mixed media, glass, jewelry, painting, photography, sculpture. Juried. Exhibitors: 90. Number of attendees: varies. Free to public. Apply online.
ADDITIONAL INFORMATION Deadline for entry: early June. Application fee: $10. Space fee: varies. Exhibition space: varies. For more information, crafters should e-mail, visit website or call.

ART IN THE PARK (PLYMOUTH)

P.O. Box 702490, Plymouth MI 48170. (734)454-1314. Fax: (734)454-3670. E-mail: info@artinthepark.com. Website: www.artinthepark.com. Estab. 1979. Arts & crafts show held annually in July. Outdoors. Accepts handmade crafts, paintings, sculpture, ceramics, jewelry, fiber, fine glass, woodwork, mixed media, photography, and folk art. Juried. Exhibitors: 400. Number of attendees: 300,000. Free to public. Apply online.
ADDITIONAL INFORMATION Deadline for entry: see website. Application fee: $20. Space fee: $580. Exhibition space: 10×10. For more information, crafters should e-mail, visit website or call.

ART IN THE PEARL FINE ARTS & CRAFTS FESTIVAL

P.O. Box 5906, Portland OR 97228-5906. (503)722-9017. E-mail: info@artinthepearl.com. Website: www.artinthepearl.com. Estab. 1996. Arts & crafts show held annually Labor Day weekend. Outdoors. Accepts handmade crafts, ceramics, fiber, glass, drawings, computer generated media, 2D/3D mixed media, jewelry, metal, painting, photography, printmaking, sculpture, wood. Juried. Awards/prizes: Best in Show. Exhibitors: 100. Number of attendees: varies. Free to public. Apply online.
ADDITIONAL INFORMATION Deadline for entry: February. Application fee: $35. Space fee: varies. Exhibition space: varies. For more information, crafters should e-mail, visit website or call.

ART IN THE VILLAGE (CLEVELAND)

270 Central Blvd., Suite 107B, Jupiter FL 33458. (561)746-6615. Fax: (561)746-6528. E-mail: info@Art Festival.com. Website: www.artfestival.com. "Don't miss out on this great opportunity to visit this one-of-a-kind event. More than 150 artists on display featuring mediums such as paintings, jewelry, photography, sculptures, ceramics and much more. This show will contain a segregated craft market place."

ART IN THE WILDS

Art in the Wilds, Attn: Marilyn Blackmore, 214 Chemical Works Rd., Kane PA 16735. (814)837-7167. E-mail: mab@penn.com. Website: www.art-inthewilds.org. Estab. 2006. Arts & crafts show held annually in September. Outdoors. Accepts handmade crafts, drawing/pastels, metal, glass, clay/porcelain, photography, print making/graphics, mixed media, fabric/fiber, wood, leather, and jewelry. Juried. Awards/prizes: Best of Show; Excellence Award. Exhibitors: varies. Number of attendees: varies. Free to public. Apply online.

ADDITIONAL INFORMATION Deadline for entry: see website. Application fee: $20. Space fee: varies. Exhibition space: varies. For more information, crafters should e-mail, visit website or call.

ART IN YOUR EYE FESTIVAL

4 ½ W Wilson St., Batavia IL 60510. (630)761.3528. E-mail: info@artinyoureye.com. Website: www.artinyoureye.com. Estab. 2004. Fine arts & crafts show held annually in September. Outdoors. Accepts handmade crafts and other items. Juried. Awards/prizes: over $4,000 in cash. Exhibitors: varies. Number of attendees: varies. Free to public. Apply online.

ADDITIONAL INFORMATION Deadline for entry: see website. Application fee: $20. Space fee: $285. Exhibition space: see website. For more information, crafters should e-mail, visit website or call.

ARTISPHERE

16 Augusta St., Greenville SC 29601. (864)271-9398. E-mail: kerry@greenvillearts.com. Website: www.artisphere.us. Estab. 2004. Fine arts & crafts fair held annually in May. Outdoors. Accepts handmade crafts, ceramic, digital art, fiber, drawing, furniture, glass, jewelry, metal, 2D/3D mixed media, painting, photography, printmaking, sculpture, wood. Juried. Awards/prizes: Best in Show, 2nd place, 3rd place, 4 merit awards, Mayor's Choice Award. Exhibitors: 130. Number of attendees: varies. Free to public. Apply via Zapplication.org.

ADDITIONAL INFORMATION Deadline for entry: early January. Application fee: $30. Space fee: $350. Exhibition space: 12×12. For more information, crafters should e-mail, visit website or call.

ART MARKET SAN FRANCISCO

109 S. 5th St., Suite 407, Brooklyn NY 11249. (212)518-6912. Fax: (212)518-7142. E-mail: info@art-mrkt.com. Website: www.artmarketsf.com. Estab. 2011. "Since 2011, Art Market Productions has produced a different type of art fair that focuses on creating the highest quality fair experience by connecting collectors with dealers in the most optimal settings and contexts. Art Market Productions is dedicated to improving the art world by creating platforms and expanding networks of connection."

ART ON THE CHATTAHOOCHEE

(678)277-0920. E-mail: brian.r.bentley@gwinnettcounty.com. Website: www.gwinnettcounty.com. "Art on the Chattahoochee is a delightful, fine art event at a unique venue along the Chattahoochee River in Jones Bridge Park. The event brings together outstanding artists throughout North Georgia in a fine art market highlighting their talent. The event also features a shaded Food Court area, a fun, interactive Kid's Craft Corner, as well as all the park amenities!"

ART ON THE MALL

The Office of Alumni Relations, Mail Stop 301, The University of Toledo, 2801 W. Bancroft St., Toledo OH 43606-3390. (419)530-2586. E-mail: artonthemall@utoledo.edu. Website: www.toledoalumni.org. Art & craft show held annually in July. Outdoors. Accepts handmade crafts, ceramics, fiber, glass, jewelry, mixed media, photography, wood. Juried. Awards/prizes: Best of Show, 1st Place, 2nd Place, 3rd Place, Purchase Award. Number exhibitors: see website. Number attendees: 12,000. Free to public. Apply online.

ADDITIONAL INFORMATION Deadline for entry: late April. Application fee: $25. Space fee: $100. Exhibition space: 10×10. For more information, crafters should call, e-mail or visit website.

ART ON THE SQUARE

P.O. Box 23561, Belleville IL 62223. (800)677-9255; (618)233-6769. E-mail: artonthesquarecompetition@ gmail.com. Website: www.artonthesquare.com. Estab. 2002. Fine arts & crafts show held annually in May. Outdoors. Accepts handmade crafts, photography, glass, jewelry, clay, sculpture, fine craft, mixed media, wood and digital art. Juried. Awards/prizes: over $30,000 in cash. Exhibitors: 105. Number of attendees: varies. Free to public. Apply online.
ADDITIONAL INFORMATION Deadline for entry: see website. Application fee: see website. Space fee: see website. Exhibition space: see website. For more information, crafters should e-mail, visit website or call.

ART RAPIDS!

P.O. Box 301, Elk Rapids MI 49629. (231)264-6660. E-mail: art@mullalys128.com. Website: www.artrapids.org. Contact: Barb Mullaly. Arts & crafts fair held annually last Saturday in June. Outdoors. Accepts handmade crafts, ceramic, drawing, fiber, glass, jewelry, painting, photography, printmaking, sculpture, wood, metal, paper, or mixed media. Juried. Awards/prizes: Best of Show, Honorable Mention, People's Choice. Exhibitors: 70. Number of attendees: 4,000. Free to public. Apply online.
ADDITIONAL INFORMATION Deadline for entry: early April. Application fee: $20. Space fee: varies. Exhibition space: 10×10. For more information, crafters should e-mail, visit website or call.

ARTS, BEATS & EATS

301 W. 4th St., Suite LL-150, Royal Oak MI 48067. (208)792-2726. Fax: (208)792-2850. E-mail: lisa@ artsbeatseats.com. Website: www.artsbeatseats.com. Contact: Lisa Konikow, art director. Estab. 1997. Fine arts & crafts fair held annually in September. Outdoors. Accepts handmade crafts, ceramic, digital art, fiber, drawing, glass, jewelry, metal, 2D/3D mixed media, painting, photography, printmaking, wood. Juried. Awards/prizes: $7,500 in cash awards. Exhibi-tors: 145. Number of attendees: 400,000. Free to public. Apply online.
ADDITIONAL INFORMATION Deadline for entry: March. Application fee: $25. Space fee: $490. Exhibition space: 10×10. For more information, crafters should e-mail, visit website or call.

ARTSFEST

P.O. Box 99, 13480 Dowell Road, Dowell MD 20629. (410)326-4640. Fax: (410)326-4887. E-mail: info@ annmariegarden.org. Website: www.annmariegarden.org. Estab. 1984. Fine arts & crafts fair held annually in September. Indoors & outdoors. Accepts handmade crafts, ceramic, digital art, fiber, drawing, furniture, glass, jewelry, metal, 2D/3D mixed media, painting, photography, printmaking, wood. Juried. Awards/prizes: Best of Show, Best Demonstration, Wooded Path Award, Best New Artsfest Artist Award. Exhibitors: 170. Number of attendees: varies. Admission: $6 adults; children 11 & under free; members free. Apply online.
ADDITIONAL INFORMATION Deadline for entry: March. Application fee: $25. Space fee: varies. Exhibition space: varies. For more information, crafters should e-mail, visit website or call.

ARTSPLASH

Sioux City Art Center, 225 Nebraska Street, Sioux City IA 51101-1712. (712)279-6272 ext. 232. Fax: (712)255-2921. E-mail: ewebber@sioux-city.org. Website: www.siouxcityartcenter.org/artsplash. Contact: Erin Webber-Dreeszen, development coordinator. Fine arts & crafts fair held annually in August. Outdoors. Accepts handmade crafts and other items. Juried. Exhibitors: see website. Number of attendees: see website. Free to public. Apply online.
ADDITIONAL INFORMATION Deadline for entry: see website. Application fee: see website. Space fee: see website. Exhibition space: see website. For more information, crafters should e-mail, visit website or call.

ARTSPLOSURE—THE RALEIGH ART FESTIVAL

313 W. Blount St., Suite 200B, Raleigh NC 27601. (919)832-8699. Fax: (919)832-0890. E-mail: info@artsplosure.org. Website: www.artsplosure.org. Contact: Sarah Wolfe, art market coordinator. Estab. 1979. Arts & craft show held annually 3rd weekend of May. Outdoors. Accepts handmade crafts, 2D/3D, glass, jewelry, ceramics, wood, metal, fiber, photography, painting. Juried. Awards/prizes: $3,500 in cash. Exhibitors: 175. Number of attendees: 75,000. Free to public. Apply via Zapplication.org.

ADDITIONAL INFORMATION Deadline for entry: January 16. Application fee: $22 (early registration); $32 (regular registration). Space fee: $240 (single); $480 (double). Exhibition space: 12×12 (single); 12×24 (double). For more information, crafters should e-mail.

TIPS "We use entrythingy.com for processing applications. The site will be updated for 2015 by October."

ARTSQUEST FINE ARTS FESTIVAL

Cultural Arts Alliance of Walton County, Bayou Arts Center, 105 Hogtown Bayou Lane, Santa Rosa Beach FL 32459. (850)622-5970. E-mail: info@culturalartsalliance.com. Website: www.artsquestflorida.com. Estab. 1988. Fine arts & crafts fair held anually in May. Outdoors. Accepts handmade crafts, ceramic, digital art, fiber, drawing, glass, jewelry, metal, 2D/3D mixed media, painting, photography, printmaking, sculpture, wood. Juried. Awards/prizes: Best in Show, Awards of Excellence and Awards of Merit. Exhibitors: 125. Number of attendees: varies. Free to public. Apply online.

ADDITIONAL INFORMATION Deadline for entry: February. Application fee: $40. Space fee: $300. Exhibition space: 10×10. For more information, crafters should e-mail, visit website or call.

ART STAR CRAFT BAZAAR

E-mail: info@artstarphilly.com. Website: www.artstarcraftbazaar.com. Estab. 2003. Arts & crafts fair held annually in May. Outdoors. Accepts handmade crafts, fabric, clay, glass, wood, paper, paintings/drawings, sculpture and more. Juried. Exhibitors: varies. Number of attendees: varies. Free to public. Apply online.

ADDITIONAL INFORMATION Deadline for entry: see website. Application fee: see website. Space fee: see website. Exhibition space: see website. For more information, crafters should e-mail or visit website.

ARTSTREET

130 E Walnut St., Suite 509, Green Bay WI 54115. (920)435-5220. Fax: (920)435-2787. E-mail: info@mosaicartsinc.org. Website: www.mosaicartsinc.org/artstreet. Estab. 1981. Fine arts & crafts fair held annually in August. Outdoors. Accepts handmade crafts and other mediums. Juried. Awards/prizes: $5,000 in cash awards. Exhibitors: 200. Number of attendees: 80,000. Free to public. Apply online.

ADDITIONAL INFORMATION Deadline for entry: March. Application fee: $35. Space fee: $225. Exhibition space: 10×10. For more information, crafters should e-mail, visit website or call.

ART UNDER THE ELMS

415 Main St., Lewiston ID 83501. (208)792-2726. Fax: (208)792-2850. E-mail: defitzgerald@lcsc.edu. Website: www.lcsc.edu/ce/aue/. Contact: Debi Fitzgerald, director. Estab. 1984. Fine arts & crafts fair held annually in April. Outdoors. Accepts handmade crafts, ceramic, digital art, fiber, drawing, furniture, glass, jewelry, metal, 2D/3D mixed media, painting, photography, pre-packaged food, printmaking, wood. Juried. Awards/prizes: announced after jury. Exhibitors: 100. Number of attendees: varies. Free to public. Apply online.

ADDITIONAL INFORMATION Deadline for entry: early January. Application fee: $20. Space fee: varies. Exhibition space: 10×10. For more information, crafters should e-mail, visit website or call.

ARVADA CENTER FOR THE ARTS HOLIDAY CRAFT FAIR

(720)763-9013. E-mail: misty@eventsetc.net. Website: www.arvadacenter.org/galleries/special-events/call-for-entries. Estab. 1979. Fine arts & crafts fair held annually in November. Indoors. Accepts handmade crafts and other mediums. Juried. Exhibitors: see website. Number of attendees: varies. Free to public. Apply online.

ADDITIONAL INFORMATION Deadline for entry: August. Application fee: $35. Space fee: varies. Exhibition space: varies. For more information, crafters should e-mail, visit website or call.

ATLANTA ARTS FESTIVAL

P.O. Box 724694, Atlanta GA 31139. (770)941-9660. Fax: (866)519-2918. E-mail: info@atlantaartsfestival. com. Website: www.atlantaartsfestival.com. Estab. 2006. Fine arts & crafts fair held annually in September. Outdoors. Accepts handmade crafts, ceramic, digital art, fiber, drawing, glass, jewelry, metal, 2D/3D mixed media, painting, photography, printmaking, wood. Juried. Awards/prizes: Best in Category, Best in Show. Exhibitors: 200. Number of attendees: varies. Free to public. Apply online.

ADDITIONAL INFORMATION Deadline for entry: April. Application fee: $25. Space fee: varies. Exhibition space: 10×10. For more information, crafters should e-mail, visit website or call.

ATLANTA FINE CRAFT SHOW

American Craft Council Shows, 155 Water St., 4th Floor, Unit 5, Brooklyn NY 11201. (800)836-3470. Fax: (612)355-2330. E-mail: shows@craftcouncil.org. Website: www.craftcouncil.org. Art & craft show held annually in March. Indoors. Accepts handmade crafts, ceramics, fiber, metal and other mediums. Juried. Awards/prizes: Awards of Excellence. Number exhibitors: 250. Number attendees: varies. Free to public. Apply online.

ADDITIONAL INFORMATION Deadline for entry: August. Application fee: $30 + $10 handling/processing fee for each set of images. Space fee: varies. Exhibition space: varies. For more information, crafters should e-mail, call or visit website.

ATOMIC HOLIDAY BAZAAR

801 N. Tamiami Trail, Sarasota FL 34236. E-mail: atomicholidaybazaar@gmail.com. Website: www. atomicholidaybazaar.com. Contact: Adrien Lucas, event producer. Estab. 2006. Arts & crafts show held annually the 1st or 2nd weekend of December. Indoors. Accepts handmade crafts, vintage clothing, kitsch, vintage jewelry, art, paper products, body products & makeup, homemade canned goods, fine

jewelry, silversmiths, shoe cobblers, T-shirt screen printing, artists and plushie makers. Exhibitors: 150. Number of attendees: 1,000. Admission: $5 adults; 12 & under free. Apply via website.

ADDITIONAL INFORMATION Deadline for entry: mid September. Space fee: $90 table; $280 booth. Exhibition space: 8×3 (table); 12×8 (booth). For more information, e-mail or visit website.

TIPS "First and foremost this show is all about handmade items made with your two hands or your hands using tools. Supplies are necessary to build our objects of desire, however, products will be scrutinized for lack of revision, upcycling, repurposing, etc., so get creative! Atomic encourages vintage clothing, kitsch, vintage jewelry, art, paper products, body products & makeup, canned yummy goods, fine jewelry, silversmiths, shoe cobblers, T-shirt screen printing, artists and plushie makers. Hopefully that helps you out a bit!"

AUSTIN CRAFT RIOT

E-mail: austincraftriot@gmail.com. Website: www. austincraftriot.com. Estab. 2011. Arts & crafts show held annually in August. Indoors. Accepts handmade crafts and vintage items. Exhibitors: see website. Number of attendees: varies. Admission: $2 adults; children free. Apply online.

ADDITIONAL INFORMATION Deadline for entry: June. Application fee: $25. Space fee: varies. Exhibition space: 8×8. For more information, crafters should e-mail or visit website.

AUTUMN CRAFTS FESTIVAL AT LINCOLN CENTER FOR THE PERFORMING ARTS

American Concern for Artistry and Craftsmanship, P.O. Box 650, Montclair NJ 07042. (973)746-0091. Fax: (973)509-7739. E-mail: acacinfo@gmail.com. Website: www.craftsatlincoln.org. Fine art & craft show held annually in October. Outdoors. Accepts handmade crafts. Juried. Number exhibitors: 250. Number attendees: varies. Free to public. Apply online or via Zapplication.org.

ADDITIONAL INFORMATION Deadline for entry: June. Application fee: none. Space fee: varies. Exhibition space: varies. For more information, crafters should call, e-mail or visit website.

AUTUMN FESTIVAL: AN ARTS & CRAFTS AFFAIR

P.O. Box 655, Antioch IL 60002. (402)331-2889. E-mail: hpifestivals@cox.net. Website: www.hpi festivals.com. Estab. 1985. Fine arts & crafts fair held annually in November. Indoors. Accepts handmade crafts and other mediums. Juried. Exhibitors: 500. Number of attendees: 60,000. Admission: $9 adults; $8 seniors; children 10 & under free. Apply online.

ADDITIONAL INFORMATION Deadline for entry: see website. Application fee: none. Space fee: see website. Exhibition space: 10×10. For more information, crafters should e-mail, visit website or call.

AVANT-GARDE ART & CRAFT SHOWS

Rebecca Adele Events, Solon OH 44139. (440)227-8794. E-mail: becki@ag-shows.com. Website: www.avantgardeshows.com. "The Avant-Garde Art & Craft Shows are based around Ohio year-round. They feature an eclectic selection of the area's most talented handmade artisans & crafters." See website for more information.

BALTIMORE FINE CRAFT SHOW

American Craft Council Shows, 155 Water St., 4th Floor, Unit 5, Brooklyn NY 11201. (800)836-3470. Fax: (612)355-2330. E-mail: shows@craftcouncil.org. Website: www.craftcouncil.org. Art & craft show held annually in February. Indoors. Accepts handmade crafts, ceramics, fiber, metal and other mediums. Juried. Awards/prizes: Awards of Excellence. Number exhibitors: 300. Number attendees: varies. Free to public. Apply online.

ADDITIONAL INFORMATION Deadline for entry: August. Application fee: $30 + $10 handling/processing fee for each set of images. Space fee: varies. Exhibition space: varies. For more information, crafters should e-mail, call or visit website.

BARRINGTON ART FESTIVAL

Amdur Productions, P.O. Box 550, Highland Park IL 60035. (847)926-4300. Fax: (847)926-4330. E-mail: info@amdurproductions.com. Website: www.am durproductions.com. Estab. 2009. Fine arts & crafts fair held annually in May. Outdoors. Accepts handmade crafts, ceramics, fiber, glass, jewelry, metal, pho-

tography, watercolors and wood. Juried. Awards/prizes: announced at awards party. Exhibitors: 125. Number of attendees: 122,000. Free to public. Apply online.

ADDITIONAL INFORMATION Deadline for entry: early January. Application fee: $25. Space fee: $415. Exhibition space: see website. For more information, crafters should e-mail, visit website or call.

BARTLETT FESTIVAL OF THE ART

118 W. Bartlett Ave., Suite 2, Bartlett IL 60103. (630)372-4152. E-mail: art@artsinbartlett.org. Website: www.artsinbartlett.org. Estab. 2002. Fine arts & crafts fair held annually in June. Outdoors. Accepts handmade crafts, paintings, photography, fiber, sculpture, glass, jewelry, wood and more. Juried. Exhibitors: see website. Number of attendees: 3,000. Free to public. Apply online.

ADDITIONAL INFORMATION Deadline for entry: April. Application fee: see website. Space fee: $150. Exhibition space: 10×10. For more information, crafters should e-mail, visit website or call.

BASS RIVER ARTS AND CRAFTS FESTIVAL

38 Charles St., Rochester NH 03867. (603)332-2616. E-mail: info@castleberryfairs.com. Website: www.castleberryfairs.com. Contact: Terry & Chris Mullen. Fine arts & crafts fair held annually in July. Outdoors. Accepts handmade craftsand other mediums. Juried. Exhibitors: see website. Number of attendees: varies. Free to public. Apply online.

ADDITIONAL INFORMATION Deadline for entry: see website. Application fee: see website. Space fee: $225. Exhibition space: 10×10. For more information, crafters should e-mail, visit website or call.

BAYOU CITY ART FESTIVAL

(713)521-0133. E-mail: info@bayoucityartfest ival.com. Website: www.artcolonyassociation.org/bayou-city-art-festival-memorial-park. Fine arts & crafts fair held annually in March. Outdoors. Accepts handmade crafts, ceramic, digital art, fiber, drawing, furniture, glass, jewelry, metal, 2D/3D mixed media, painting, photography, printmaking, sculpture, wood. Juried. Awards/prizes: Best of Show, 2nd Place, 3rd Place, Best Booth, Award of Excellence. Exhibitors: see website. Number of attendees: varies. Admission: $15 adults; $3 children 4-12; children 3 & under free. Apply online.

ADDITIONAL INFORMATION Deadline for entry: November. Application fee: see website. Space fee: varies. Exhibition space: varies. For more information, crafters should e-mail, visit website or call.

SAN FRANCISCO BAZAAR

E-mail: sf_info@bazaarbizarre.org. Website: www.sanfranciscobazaar.org. Estab. 2001. "Each year San Francisco Bazaar features hundreds of juried artists and designers. Shoppers can expect to find the crème de la crème of indie goods: handbags, pottery, letterpress stationary, silk-screened t-shirts, baby clothes, zines, posters, body products and more!"

BEAVER CREEK ART FESTIVAL

270 Central Blvd., Suite 107B, Jupiter FL 33458. (561)746-6615. Fax: (561)746-6528. E-mail: info@artfestival.com. Website: www.artfestival.com. Fine arts & crafts fair held annually in August. Outdoors. Accepts handmade crafts, clay, digital, fiber, glass, jewelry, mixed media, painting, photography, printmaking/drawing, sculpture, wood. Juried. Awards/prizes: announced after jury. Exhibitors: 150. Number of attendees: varies. Free to public. Apply online.

ADDITIONAL INFORMATION Deadline for entry: early July. Application fee: $35. Space fee: varies. Exhibition space: varies. For more information, crafters should e-mail, visit website or call.

BELLEVUE ARTS MUSEUM ARTSFAIR

E-mail: meredithl@bellevuearts.org. Website: www.bellevuearts.org. "For more than 60 years, BAM ARTSfair has been celebrating the connection between our community and the world of art, craft, and design. Devoted to bringing some of the nation's most talented artists to our region, the fair features thousands of original artworks, including painting, sculpture, fashion, and jewelry. With over 300 exhibiting artists, both emerging and well-known, BAM ARTSfair is one the region's largest gatherings and a unique opportunity to acquire art directly from the makers. Also join us for live music, artist demonstrations, community art projects, KIDSfair, and compli-

mentary admission to BAM. See more at: www.belle vuearts.org/fair/index.html#sthash.2lzYtAjm.dpuf."

BELLEVUE FESTIVAL OF THE ARTS

Craft Cooperative of the Northwest, 1916 Pike Place, Suite 146, Seattle WA 98101-1013. (206)363-2048. E-mail: info@bellevuefest.org. Website: www.bellevuefest.org. Contact: Ann Sutherland, fair coordinator. Fine arts & crafts fair held annually in June. Outdoors. Accepts handmade crafts, and other mediums. Juried. Exhibitors: 200. Number of attendees: 75,000. Free to public. Apply online.

ADDITIONAL INFORMATION Deadline for entry: February. Application fee: $40. Space fee: varies. Exhibition space: varies. For more information, crafters should e-mail, visit website or call.

BELL ROCK PLAZA ART & CRAFT SHOW

P.O. Box 20039, Sedona AZ 86341. (928)284-9627. E-mail: ohdarnitall@yahoo.com. Website: www.bellrockartshows.com. Contact: Donna Campbell. Fine arts & crafts fair held annually several times a year. Outdoors. Accepts handmade crafts and other mediums. Juried. Exhibitors: see website. Number of attendees: varies. Free to public. Apply online.

ADDITIONAL INFORMATION Deadline for entry: varies per show. Application fee: see website. Space fee: $125. Exhibition space: 10×10. For more information, crafters should e-mail, visit website or call.

BERKELEY ARTS FESTIVAL

E-mail: fabarts@silcon.com. Website: www.berkeleyartsfestival.com. Month long arts festival in Berkeley. See website for details.

BERKSHIRE CRAFTS FAIR

E-mail: paulgib@mapinternet.com. Website: www.berkshirecraftsfair.org. Contact: Paul Gibbons. Estab. 1974. Fine arts & crafts fair held annually in August. Indoors. Accepts handmade crafts, jewelry, furniture, ceramics, textiles, glassware, woodwork, and more. Juried. Exhibitors: 90. Number of attendees: varies. Admission: $7; children 12 & under free. Apply online.

ADDITIONAL INFORMATION Deadline for entry: April. Application fee: $25. Space fee: $450. Exhibition space: 10×6. For more information, crafters should e-mail or visit website.

BERKSHIRES ARTS FESTIVAL

P.O. Box 480, Slate Hill NY 10973. (845)355-2400. Fax: (845)355-2444. E-mail: show.director@americanart marketing.com. Website: www.berkshiresartsfestival. com. Estab. 1984. Fine arts & crafts fair held annually in July. Indoors & outdoors. Accepts handmade crafts, ceramic, digital art, fiber, drawing, encaustic, furniture, glass, jewelry, metal, 2D/3D mixed media, painting, photography, sculpture, wood. Juried. Exhibitors: see website. Number of attendees: varies. Admission: $13 adults; $11 seniors; $5 students; $14 weekend pass; children 10 & under free. Apply online.
ADDITIONAL INFORMATION Deadline for entry: early January. Application fee: $35. Space fee: varies. Exhibition space: varies. For more information, crafters should e-mail, visit website or call.

BEST OF THE NORTHWEST FALL ART & FINE CRAFT SHOW

Northwest Art Alliance, Suite 103, 7777 62nd Ave., NE, Seattle WA 98115. (206)525-5926. E-mail: info@ nwartalliance.com. Website: www.nwartalliance. com. Fine art & craft show held annually in October & November. Indoors. Accepts handmade crafts, ceramics, paintings, jewelry, glass, photography, wearable art and other mediums. Juried. Number exhibitors: 110. Number attendees: varies. Admission: $5 online; $6 at door; children 12 & under free. Apply via Zapplication.org.
ADDITIONAL INFORMATION Deadline for entry: May. Application fee: $35. Space fee: varies. Exhibition space: varies. For more information, crafters should call, e-mail or visit website.

BEST OF THE NORTHWEST SPRING ART & FINE CRAFT SHOW

Northwest Art Alliance, Suite 103, 7777 62nd Ave., NE, Seattle WA 98115. (206)525-5926. E-mail: info@ nwartalliance.com. Website: www.nwartalliance. com. Fine art & craft show held annually in March. Indoors. Accepts handmade crafts, ceramics, paintings, jewelry, glass, photography, wearable art and other mediums. Juried. Number exhibitors: 110. Number attendees: varies. Admission: $5 online; $6 at door; children 12 & under free. Apply via Zapplication.org.
ADDITIONAL INFORMATION Deadline for entry: January. Application fee: $35. Space fee: varies. Exhibition space: varies. For more information, crafters should call, e-mail or visit website.

THE BIG CRAFTY

E-mail: crafty@thebigcrafty.com. Website: www.the bigcrafty.com. "The Big Crafty revives the tradition of the community bazaar, a lively celebration of handmade commerce, featuring local food, beer, music, and fine wares from a juried group of select indie artists and crafters. Our free and fun for all ages events are held twice annually in the heart of beautiful Asheville, NC." See website for more information.

THE BIG HEAP VINTAGE & HANDMADE FESTIVAL

P.O. Box 4373, Cave Creek AZ 85327. (480)329-6118. E-mail: info@thievesmarketvintageflea.com. Website: www.thebigheap.com. "The Big Heap Vintage & Handmade Festival, a juried event featuring the most exciting vintage furniture and decor, fashion, adornment, and hand-wrought and hand-rendered items in the West. Our focus is beyond avoiding tetanus and lead poisoning, our focus is on style. The Big Heap will support you with the raw elements to make your own unique statement in your home, your garden and in the way you express yourself. We are not a flea market, not an antique show and we sure as he_ _ aren't a craft show. Come see us. Gon' be good." See website for more information.

THE BIG ONE ART & CRAFT FAIRS

P.O. Box 1276, 101 22nd St. SW, Minot ND 58701. (701)837-6059. Fax: (701)839-0874. E-mail: info@the-bigone.biz. Website: www.thebigone.biz. "THE BIG ONE Art & Craft Fair consists of four shows in North Dakota with over 350 different exhibitors showcasing their handmade items to thousands of consumers. Items you will see at each show are handcrafted wood furniture and decorative pieces; photography; pottery; jewelry; variety of floral arrangements to accommodate all tastes; flavorful foods including baked goods, soups, dips, jams, jellies, breads, salsa, spices, candies, and wonderful desserts; creative and comfortable clothing pieces for all ages; handmade soaps and lotions made from various natural resources; unlimited baby items from blankets to bibs and everything in between; handwoven rugs; homesewn quilts and blankets; wind chimes; 3-D photography and artwork; and handmade toys." See website for more information.

BIRMINGHAM HOLLYDAZZLE CRAFT AND GIFT MARKET

E-mail: hollydazzlemarket@gmail.com. Website: www.hollydazzlemarket.com. Holiday arts and craft show in Birmingham. See website for details.

BIRMINGHAM WOMEN'S SHOW

Southern Shows, Inc., P.O. Box 36859, Charlotte NC 28236. (800)849.0248 ext. 107. E-mail: banderson@southernshows.com. Website: www.southernshows.com. Contact: Beth Anderson, show manager. Exhibitor fair held annually in October. Indoors. Accepts handmade craftsand other items. Exhibitors: see website. Number of attendees: varies. Admission: $10 adults; $5 youth; children 6 & under free. Apply online.

ADDITIONAL INFORMATION Deadline for entry: see website. Application fee: see website. Space fee: varies. Exhibition space: varies. For more information, crafters should e-mail, visit website or call.

BITCHCRAFT TRADING POST

E-mail: btchcrafttradingpost@gmail.com. Website: www.bitchcrafttradingpost.com. "Bitchcraft Trading Post is a vintage & art collective event. We host a variety of vendors who sell handmade goods, vintage items, jewelry, artwork, records, food, beverages & more." See website for more information.

BLACK SWAMP ARTS FESTIVAL

Art Under the Elms, 415 Main St., Lewiston ID 83501. E-mail: info@blackswamparts.com. Estab. 1992. Fine arts & crafts fair held annually in September. Outdoors. Accepts handmade crafts and other mediums.

Juried. Awards/prizes: Best of Show, Best 2D, Best 3D, 2nd Place, 3rd Place, Honorable Mention, Community Purchase Award. Exhibitors: 112. Number of attendees: varies. Free to public. Apply online.

ADDITIONAL INFORMATION Deadline for entry: April. Application fee: $35. Space fee: $275 (single); $550 (double). Exhibition space: 10×10 (single); 10×10 (double). For more information, crafters should e-mail, visit website.

BLISSFEST MUSIC FESTIVAL

(231)348-7047. E-mail: jennifer@blissfest.org. Website: www.blissfest.org. Contact: Jennifer Ferguson. "The arts & craft fair is open to amateur and professional artists and craftspeople who create their own works of arts/crafts. Our goal is to provide opportunities for these creators and innovators of traditional and contemporary arts and crafts to present their respective talents in a festival atmosphere of music and dance that affirms and honors our shared cultural heritage and diversity." See website for more information and to apply.

BLUEGRASS FESTIVAL & ARTIST MARKET

922 Main St., Stone Mountain GA 30083. (404)873-1222. E-mail: lisa@affps.com. Website: www.stonemountainvillage.com/ssim.html. Contact: Lisa Windle, festival director. Estab. 2011. Arts & crafts show held annually late March. Outdoors. Accepts handmade crafts, painting, photography, sculpture, leather, metal, glass, jewelry. Juried by a panel. Awards/prizes: ribbons. Number of exhibitors: 150. Number of attendees: 7,500. Free to public. Apply online at Zapplication.org.

ADDITIONAL INFORMATION Deadline for entry: February 14. Application fee: $25. Space fee: $200. Exhibition space: 10×10. For more information, see website.

BOCA RATON MUSEUM OF ART OUTDOOR JURIED ART FESTIVAL

501 Plaza Real, Mizner Park, Boca Raton FL 33432. (561)392-2500. Fax: (561)391-6410. E-mail: info@bocamuseum.org. Website: www.bocamuseum.org. Estab. 1986. Fine arts & crafts fair held annually in February. Outdoors. Accepts handmade crafts and

other mediums. Juried. Awards/prizes: Best in Show, Merit Awards. Exhibitors: 200. Number of attendees: varies. Free to public. Apply online.

ADDITIONAL INFORMATION Deadline for entry: see website. Application fee: see website. Space fee: see website. Exhibition space: see website. For more information, crafters should e-mail, visit website or call.

BONITA SPRINGS NATIONAL ART FESTIVAL

P.O. Box 367465, Bonita Springs FL 34136-7465. (239)992-1213. Fax: (239)495-3999. E-mail: artfest@artinusa.com. Website: www.artinusa.com/bonita. Contact: Barry Witt, director. Fine arts & crafts fair held annually 3 times a year. Outdoors. Accepts handmade crafts, Paintings, glass, jewelry, clay works, photography, sculpture, wood and more. Juried. Awards/prizes: Best of Show, Best 2D, Best 3D, Distinction Award. Exhibitors: see website. Number of attendees: varies. Free to public. Apply online.

ADDITIONAL INFORMATION Deadline for entry: early January. Application fee: $30. Space fee: $400. Exhibition space: 10×12. For more information, crafters should e-mail, visit website or call.

BOSTON HANDMADE HOLIDAY GALLERY

P.O. Box 300514, Boston MA 02130. E-mail: bostonhandmade@gmail.com. Website: www.bostonhandmade.org. Contact: Jessica Burko. "Boston Handmade is staging a triumphant return to the holiday season with our Holiday Gallery of limited edition and one-of-a-kind items. A wide variety of items created in a range of media will be available for holiday gift giving from Black Friday through Christmas Eve, Tuesdays through Saturdays, 11am to 7pm, including hand crafted jewelry, clothing, accessories, home goods, art, photography, holiday décor, and toys. The Boston Handmade Holiday Gallery promotes local independent businesses and individuals creating handmade works in small studio environments."

ADDITIONAL INFORMATION Deadline for entry: early January. Application fee: $20. Space fee: varies. Exhibition space: 10×10. For more information, crafters should e-mail, visit website or call.

BOSTON MILLS ARTFEST

Website: www.bmbw.com. Estab. 1971. Fine arts & crafts fair held annually in June & July. Outdoors. Accepts handmade crafts, ceramic, digital art, fiber, drawing, furniture, glass, jewelry, metal, 2D/3D mixed media, painting, photography, printmaking, wood. Juried. Awards/prizes: First in Category, Award of Excellence. Exhibitors: see website. Number of attendees: varies. Free to public. Apply online.

ADDITIONAL INFORMATION Deadline for entry: see website. Application fee: see website. Space fee: see website. Exhibition space: see website. For more information, crafters should e-mail, visit website or call.

BOULDER MOUNTAIN HANDMADE

E-mail: annkcarr@gmail.com. Website: www.bouldermountainfire.org/bouldermountainhandmade. Estab. 1973. "Boulder Mountain Handmade is a fine art, craft and baked goods tradition since 1973. We invite you to sip complimentary cider, chat with the artists and browse unique creations in all price ranges."

BRECKENRIDGE MAIN STREET ART FESTIVAL

P.O. Box 3578, Breckenridge CO 80424. (970)547-9326. E-mail: info@mountainartfestivals.com. Website: www.mountainartfestivals.com. Estab. 2001. Fine arts & crafts fair held annually in July. Outdoors. Accepts handmade crafts and other mediums. Juried. Exhibitors: 120. Number of attendees: varies. Free to public. Apply online.

ADDITIONAL INFORMATION Deadline for entry: April. Application fee: $35. Space fee: $500. Exhibition space: 10×10. For more information, crafters should e-mail, visit website or call.

BROAD RIPPLE ART FAIR

Indianapolis Art Center, Marilyn K. Glick School of Art, 820 E. 67th St., Indianapolis IN 46220. (317)255-2464. Website: www.indplsartcenter.org/events/braf. Estab. 1971. Fine arts & crafts fair held annually in May. Outdoors. Accepts handmade crafts and other mediums. Juried. Exhibitors: 225. Number of attendees: varies. Admission: $13 adult presale; $15 adult day of; $3 children. Apply online.

ADDITIONAL INFORMATION Deadline for entry: see website. Application fee: see website. Space fee: varies. Exhibition space: see website. For more information, crafters should visit website or call.

BROOKINGS SUMMER ARTS FESTIVAL

P.O. Box 4, Brookings SD 57006. (605)692-2787. E-mail: generalinfo@bsaf.com; artbooths@bsaf.com. Website: www.bsaf.com. Estab. 1972. Fine arts & crafts fair held annually in April. Outdoors. Accepts handmade crafts and other mediums. Juried. Exhibitors: 200. Number of attendees: 75,000. Free to public. Apply online.

ADDITIONAL INFORMATION Deadline for entry: March. Application fee: $25. Space fee: $200. Exhibition space: 12×12. For more information, crafters should e-mail, visit website or call.

BROOKSIDE ART ANNUAL

Brookside Business Association, 6814 Troost Ave., Kansas City MO 64131-1509. (816)523-5553. Fax: (816)333-1022. E-mail: brooksideartannualkc@gmail.com. Website: www.brooksidekc.org. Estab. 1984. Fine arts & crafts fair held annually in May. Outdoors. Accepts handmade crafts and other mediums. Juried. Awards/prizes: Best of Show, Best in Category. Exhibitors: 180. Number of attendees: 70,000. Free to public. Apply online.

ADDITIONAL INFORMATION Deadline for entry: see website. Application fee: see website. Space fee: see website. Exhibition space: see website. For more information, crafters should e-mail, visit website or call.

BRUCE MUSEUM OUTDOOR ARTS FESTIVAL

1 Museum Dr., Greenwich CT 06830-7157. (203) 869-6786, ext. 336. E-mail: sue@brucemuseum.org. Website: www.brucemuseum.org. Contact: Sue Brown Gordon, festival director. Estab. 1981. Fine arts & crafts fair held annually in October. Outdoors. Accepts handmade crafts, painting, sculpture, mixed media, graphics/drawing (including computer-generated works), photography. Juried. Exhibitors: see website. Number of attendees: varies. Free to public. Apply online.

ADDITIONAL INFORMATION Deadline for entry: June. Application fee: $20. Space fee: $350. Exhibition space: 10×12. For more information, crafters should e-mail, visit website or call.

BUCKHEAD SPRING ARTS & CRAFTS FESTIVAL

4469 Stella Dr., Atlanta GA 30327. (404)873-1222. E-mail: lisa@affps.com. Website: www.buckheadartsfestival.com. Contact: Lisa Windle, festival director. Estab. 2009. Annual arts & crafts show. Held mid May. Outdoors. Accepts handmade crafts, paintings, photography, sculpture, leather, metal, glass, jewelry. Juried. Awards/prizes: ribbons. Number of exhibitors: 185. Number of attendees: 40,000. Free to public. Apply at Zapplication.org.

ADDITIONAL INFORMATION Deadline for entry: March 14. Application fee: $25. Space fee: $200. Exhibition space: 10×10 ft. For more information, crafters should visit website.

BUCKTOWN ARTS FEST

Holstein Park, 2200 N. Oakley Ave., Chicago IL 60647. E-mail: inquiries@bucktownartsfest.com. Website: www.bucktownartsfest.com. Estab. 1984. Fine arts & crafts fair held annually in August. Outdoors. Accepts handmade crafts and other mediums. Juried. Exhibitors: 200. Number of attendees: 40,000. Free to public. Apply online.

ADDITIONAL INFORMATION Deadline for entry: March. Application fee: $45. Space fee: $300; $200 (seniors 60 and over). Exhibition space: 10×10. For more information, crafters should e-mail, visit website or call.

BUFFALO GROVE INVITATIONAL ART FESTIVAL

Amdur Productions, P.O. Box 550, Highland Park IL 60035. (847)926-4300. Fax: (847)926-4330. E-mail: info@amdurproductions.com. Website: www.amdurproductions.com. Estab. 2002. Fine arts & crafts fair held annually in July. Outdoors. Accepts handmade crafts, ceramic, digital art, fiber, drawing, furniture, glass, jewelry, metal, 2D/3D mixed media, painting, photography, printmaking, wood. Juried. Exhibitors: 120. Number of attendees: 20,000. Free to public. Apply online.

ADDITIONAL INFORMATION Deadline for entry: see website. Application fee: $25. Space fee: $450. Exhibition space: 10×10. For more information, crafters should e-mail, visit website or call.

BUST MAGAZINE'S HOLIDAY CRAFTACULAR

E-mail: craftacular@bust.com. Website: www.bust.com. Fine arts & crafts fair held annually in June. Indoors. Accepts handmade crafts and other mediums. Exhibitors: see website. Number of attendees: varies. Admission: $3 adults; children 12 & under free. Apply online.

ADDITIONAL INFORMATION Deadline for entry: May. Application fee: $20. Space fee: see website. Exhibition space: see website. For more information, crafters should e-mail, visit website or call.

CABIN FEVER CRAFT SHOW

(215)850-1888. E-mail: frommyhand@gmail.com. Website: www.craftsatmolandhouse.com. Contact: Gwyn Duffy. "Chase away the winter blahs! We have gathered over 50 talented local crafters to lift your spirits with their creativity. Find the perfect gift, tasty treat or decoration for your home and leave here knowing that Spring is just around the corner. Spend some time wandering around the beautiful historic setting that was once the headquarters for General George Washington. $1 admission benefits the Moland House Restoration Project."

CAPE CORAL FESTIVAL OF THE ARTS

Cape Coral Festival of the Arts Committee, P.O. Box 101346, Cape Coral FL 33910. (239)699-7942. E-mail: info@capecoralfestival.com. Website: www.capecoralfestival.com. Estab. 1985. Fine arts & crafts fair held annually in January. Outdoors. Accepts handmade crafts and other mediums. Juried. Exhibitors: see website. Number of attendees: see website. Free to public. Apply online.

ADDITIONAL INFORMATION Deadline for entry: October 1. Application fee: $20. Space fee: $306. Exhibition space: see website. For more information, crafters should e-mail, visit website or call.

CAROLINA ONE STOP SHOP HOP

Hubbard Dr., Lancaster SC 29720. (803)273-3834. E-mail: dusawyer@comporium.net. Website: www.onestopshophop.wordpress.com. Contact: Donna Sawyer, co-chair. Estab. 2006. Annual shop hop held 2nd Saturday in February. Indoors. Accepts handmade crafts, fabric, yarns, thread, patterns, quilting tools and gadgets, vintage linens, buttons, quilting supplies. Awards/prizes: door prizes. Exhibitors: 25. Number of attendees: 300. Admission: $3. See website for application.

ADDITIONAL INFORMATION Deadline for entry: November. Space fee: $60-$200. Exhibition space: classroom, 10×10. For more information, e-mail.

TIPS "Reasonably priced and quality work."

CASA GRANDE HOLIDAY ARTS & CRAFTS FESTIVAL

7225 N. Oracle Rd., Suite 112, Tucson AZ 85704. (520)797-3959 ext. 0. Fax: (520)531-9225. E-mail: lauren@saaca.org. Website: www.saaca.org. Fine arts & crafts fair held annually in December. Outdoors. Accepts handmade crafts and other mediums. Exhibitors: 60. Number of attendees: see website. Free to public. Apply online.

ADDITIONAL INFORMATION Deadline for entry: December. Application fee: see website. Space fee: $185 (single); $310 (double). Exhibition space: 12×12 (single); 12×24 (double). For more information, crafters should e-mail, visit website or call.

CASTLEBERRY FAIRE

38 Charles St., Rochester NY 03867. (603)332-2616. E-mail: info@castleberryfairs.com. Website: www.castleberryfairs.com. Contact: Terry & Chris Mullen. Estab. 1995. Fine arts & crafts fair held annually in November, Thanksgiving weekend. Indoors. Accepts handmade crafts and other mediums. Juried. Exhibitors: see website. Number of attendees: see website. Admission: $8 adults; children 12 & under free. Apply online.

ADDITIONAL INFORMATION Deadline for entry: see website. Application fee: see website. Space fee: $375 (10×6); $475 (10×10). Exhibition space: 10×6; 10×10. For more information, crafters should e-mail, visit website or call.

CENTERFEST: THE ART LOVERS FESTIVAL

Durham Arts Council, 120 Morris St., Durham NC 27701. (919)560-2787. E-mail: centerfest@durhamarts. org. Website: www.centerfest.durhamarts.org. Estab. 1974. Fine arts & crafts fair held annually in September. Outdoors. Accepts handmade crafts, clay, drawing, fibers, glass, painting, photography, printmaking, wood, jewelry, mixed media, sculpture. Juried. Awards/prizes: Best in Show, 1st place, 2nd place, 3rd place. Exhibitors: 140. Number of attendees: see website. Admission: $5 donation accepted at gate. Apply online.

ADDITIONAL INFORMATION Deadline for entry: May. Application fee: see website. Space fee: $195 (single); $390 (double). Exhibition space: 10×10 (single); 10×20 (double). For more information, crafters should e-mail, visit website or call.

CENTRAL PENNSYLVANIA FESTIVAL OF THE ARTS

403 S. Allen St., Suite 205A, P.O. Box 1023, State College PA 16804. (814)237-3682. Website: www. arts-festival.com. Estab. 1966. Fine arts & crafts fair held annually in July. Outdoors. Accepts handmade crafts and other mediums. Exhibitors: see website. Number of attendees: see website. Admission: Free to public. Apply online.

ADDITIONAL INFORMATION Deadline for entry: June. Application fee: see website. Space fee: see website. Exhibition space: see website. For more information, crafters should visit website or call.

CHANGING SEASONS ARTS & CRAFTS SHOW

Changing Seasons, 307 Silver Springs Pl., Norco CA 92860. (951)735-4751. E-mail: changingseasons artsandcrafts@yahoo.com. Website: www.changing seasonscraftshows.com. Fine arts & crafts fair held annually 5 times a year. Outdoors. Accepts handmade crafts and other mediums. Exhibitors: see website. Number of attendees: see website. Admission: Free to public. Apply online.

ADDITIONAL INFORMATION Deadline for entry: June. Application fee: see website. Space fee: see website. Exhibition space: see website. For more information, crafters should visit website or call.

CHARLEVOIX WATERFRONT ART FAIR

Charlevoix Waterfront Art Fair, PO Box 57, Charlevoix, MI 49720. (231)547-2675. E-mail: cwaf14@gmail. com. Website: www.charlevoixwaterfrontfair.org. Fine arts & crafts fair held annually. Outdoors. Accepts handmade crafts and other mediums. Limited number of spaces available. Exhibitors: see website. Number of attendees: see website. Admission: Free to public. Apply online.

ADDITIONAL INFORMATION Deadline for entry: see website. Application fee: see website. Space fee: see website. Exhibition space: see website. For more information, crafters should visit website or call.

CHASTAIN PARK FESTIVAL

4469 Stella Dr., Atlanta GA 30327. (404)873-1222. E-mail: lisa@affps.com. Website: www.chastain parkartsfestival.com. Contact: Lisa Windle, festival director. Estab. 2008. Arts & crafts show held annually early November. Outdoors. Accepts handmade crafts, painting, photography, sculpture, leather, metal, glass, jewelry. Juried by a panel. Awards/prizes: ribbons. Number of exhibitors: 175. Number of attendees: 45,000. Free to public. Apply online via Zapplication.org.

ADDITIONAL INFORMATION Deadline for entry: August 29. Application fee: $25. Space fee: $275. Exhibition space: 10×10. For more information, see website.

CHEROKEE TRIANGLE ART FAIR

Cherokee Triangle Association, PO Box 4306, Louisville, KY 40204. (502)459-0256. E-mail: cherokeetriangle@bellsouth.net. Website: www.cherokeetriangle.org/art-fair/. Juried fine arts & crafts fair held annually with over 200 vendors. Outdoors. Accepts handmade crafts and other mediums. Exhibitors: see website. Number of attendees: see website. Admission: Free to public. Apply online.

ADDITIONAL INFORMATION Deadline for entry: see website. Application fee: see website. Space fee: see website. Exhibition space: see website. For more information, crafters should visit website or call.

CHERRY CREEK ARTS FESTIVAL

Cherry Creek Arts, 2 Steele St, B100, Denver, CO 80206. (303)355-2787. E-mail: management@cherryarts.org. Website: www.cherryarts.org. Fine arts & crafts fair held annually. Outdoors. Award-winning three-day celebration of the visual, culinary and performing arts. Exhibitors: see website. Number of attendees: see website. Admission: Free to public. Apply online.

ADDITIONAL INFORMATION Deadline for entry: see website. Application fee: see website. Space fee: see website. Exhibition space: see website. For more information, crafters should visit website or call.

CHERRYWOOD ART FAIR

P.O. Box 4283, Austin TX 78765. E-mail: cherrywoodartfair@gmail.com. Website: www.cherrywoodartfair.org. Estab. 2001. "Cherrywood Art Fair is an art filled two-day event showcasing local artists, live music, kids activities and great food in a free, family-friendly environment. More than 8,000 visitors stroll through the fairgrounds looking at art, listening to beautiful music and sampling some of Austin's finest food trailer cuisine. Since its inception, the fair has served as a destination for discerning holiday shoppers seeking unique and artful items from Texas artists."

CHESTER CRAFT SHOW

Chester Craft Show, PO Box 613, Madison, NJ 07940. (973)377-6600. Website: www.chestercraftshow.com. Fine arts & crafts fair held twice annually. Outdoors. Accepts a wide variety of handmade items including traditional crafts, fine art and country crafts as well as antiques, home furnishings and specialty items. Exhibitors: see website. Number of attendees: see website. Admission: see website. Apply online.

ADDITIONAL INFORMATION Deadline for entry: see website. Application fee: see website. Space fee: see website. Exhibition space: see website. For more information, crafters should visit website or call.

CHESTERTON ART FAIR

Chesterton Art Center, 115 S. 4th St., Chesterton, IN 46304. (219)926-4711. Website: www.chestertonart.com/ChestertonArtFair.html. Fine arts & crafts fair held annually. Outdoors. Accepts painting, drawing, photography, jewelry, sculputre, glass, pottery and other mediums. Exhibitors: see website. Number of attendees: see website. Admission: $5 for both days. Apply online.

ADDITIONAL INFORMATION Deadline for entry: see website. Application fee: see website. Space fee: see website. Exhibition space: see website. For more information, crafters should visit website or call.

CHICAGO BOTANIC ART FESTIVAL

E-mail: info@amdurproductions.com. Website: www.amdurproductions.com. Fine arts & crafts fair held in July. Outdoors. Accepts handmade crafts and other mediums. Exhibitors: 95. Number of attendees: 30,000. Free to public. Apply online.

ADDITIONAL INFORMATION Deadline for entry: January. Application fee: $35. Space fee: $625. Exhibition space: see website. For more information, crafters should e-mail, visit website or call.

CHICAGO TRIBUNE MAGNIFICENT MILE ART FESTIVAL

270 Central Blvd. suite 107B, Jupiter, FL 33458. (561)746-6615. E-mail: info@artfestival.com. Website: www.artfestival.com. Fine arts & crafts fair held twice annually. Outdoors. Accepts handmade crafts and other mediums. Exhibitors: see website. Number of attendees: see website. Admission: see website. Apply online.

ADDITIONAL INFORMATION Deadline for entry: see website. Application fee: see website. Space fee: see website. Exhibition space: see website. For more information, crafters should visit website or call.

CHICAGO TRIBUNE NORTH MICHIGAN AVE. ART FESTIVAL

270 Central Blvd, Suite 107B, Jupiter FL 33458. (561)746-6615. Fax: (561)746-6528. E-mail: info@artfestival.com. Website: www.artfestival.com. "This venerable event continues to highlight the talents of hundreds of artists, while also providing Chicago with one of its more enjoyable summer traditions. Original artwork will be on display for the entirety of the weekend. Visitors will have the opportunity to meet the creators of the art on display; commission a

specific piece, ask questions about techniques, learn the sources of their inspirations, and purchase fine works of art." See website for more information.

CHRISTMAS IN SEATTLE GIFT & GOURMET FOOD SHOW

Washington State Convention Center, 800 Convention Place, Seattle WA 98101. (800)521-7469. Fax: (425)889-8165. E-mail: seattle@showcaseevents.org. Website: www.showcaseevents.org. Contact: Dena Sablan, show manager. Estab. 1992. Seasonal holiday show held annually in November. Indoors. Accepts handmade crafts, art, photography, pottery, glass, jewelry, clothing, fiber. Juried. Exhibitors: 300. Number of attendees: 15,000. Admission: $14.50 (for all 3 days); 12 & under free. Apply via website or call or e-mail for application.

ADDITIONAL INFORMATION Deadline for entry: October 31. Space fee: see website. Exhibition space: 10×10. For more information, e-mail, call, send SASE or visit website.

TIPS "Competitive pricing, attractive booth display, quality product, something unique for sale, friendly & outgoing personality."

CHRISTMAS IN THE COUNTRY CRAFT FAIR

(910)799-9424. E-mail: wnypremier@ec.rr.com. Website: www.wnypremierpromotions.com/christmas-in-the-country. "Christmas in the Country has been recognized as the #2 contemporary and classic artisan market in the nation by *Sunshine Artist*, the leading publication in the art and craft event industry. The event has been ranked either #1 or #2 in the nation for the past 10 years. Now, drawing almost 60,000 visitors over four days, the event is widely recognized as the preeminent holiday artisan market in the United States. Christmas in the Country is held in November at the Hamburg Fairgrounds. Christmas in the Country will welcome over 400 artisans spread out over five buildings. Attendees to Christmas in the Country will find unique and only handcrafted creations including home décor, gourmet foods and wine, original music, trendsetting jewelry, handpoured aromatic candles, children's toys and clothing, stylish pottery, original wall art, gifts for pets, and holiday gift items galore."

CHURCH ON THE HILL ANNUAL FINE ARTS AND HANDMADE CRAFTS FAIR

(413)637-1001. E-mail: ucclenox@verizon.net. Website: www.churchonthehilllenox.org/events/crafts-fair. "For more than a quarter of a century we've brought you this juried craft fair with the finest quality local handmade crafts from this region." See website for more information.

CITYPLACE ART FAIR

270 Central Blvd., Suite 107B, Jupiter FL 33458. (561)746-6615. Fax: (561)746-6528. E-mail: info@artfestival.com. Website: www.artfestival.com. "CityPlace, located in downtown West Palm Beach, is a beautiful downtown shopping district. This retail empire, rich in European architecture, includes ten fine restaurants, a 20 screen theater, a cultural city theatre, scores of high end shops, and private high end residences. Combine beautiful architecture, breathtaking fountains, and quaint sidewalk cafés and we have the next great venue in fine art festival." See website for more information.

CLEVELAND FINE ART EXPO

Sankofa Fine Art Plus, 540 E 105th St., Cleveland, OH 44108. (216)541-2787. E-mail: info@sankofafineartplus.org. Website: www.sankofafineartplus.org. Fine arts & crafts fair held annually. Accepts handmade crafts and other mediums. Exhibitors: see website. Number of attendees: see website. Admission: see website. Apply online.

ADDITIONAL INFORMATION Deadline for entry: see website. Application fee: see website. Space fee: see website. Exhibition space: see website. For more information, crafters should visit website or call.

CLEVELAND HANDMADE

Cleveland Handmade Markets. E-mail: info@clevelandhandmade.com. Website: www.clevelandhandmade.com/market/. Fine arts & crafts fairs held throughout the year. Accepts handmade crafts and other mediums. Exhibitors: see website. Number of attendees: see website. Admission: see website. Apply online.

ADDITIONAL INFORMATION Deadline for entry: see website. Application fee: see website. Space fee: see website. Exhibition space: see website. For more information, crafters should visit website or call.

COARSEGOLD CHRISTMAS FAIRE

Coarse Gold Historic Village, PO Box 1514, Coarsegold, CA 93614. Contact Diane Boland (559)683-3900. Website: coarsegoldca.com/CVGevents.html. "Christmas Spirit mountain style. Listen to carolers, visit with Father Christmas, and do some Christmas shopping at the craft booths in the park." Exhibitors: see website. Number of attendees: see website. Admission: see website. Apply online.
ADDITIONAL INFORMATION Deadline for entry: see website. Application fee: see website. Space fee: see website. Exhibition space: see website. For more information, crafters should visit website or call.

COCONUT GROVE ARTS FESTIVAL

Coconut Grove Arts Festival, 3390 Mary St., Miami, FL 33133. (305)447-0401. E-mail: monty@cgaf.com. Website: www.cgaf.com. Three day event celebrating visual, culinary and performing arts. Held annually. Outdoors. "More than 360 internationally recognized artists from across the globe flock to Coconut Grove each winter to showcase their latest pieces." Exhibitors: see website. Number of attendees: see website. Admission: $15 per day. Apply online.
ADDITIONAL INFORMATION Deadline for entry: see website. Application fee: see website. Space fee: see website. Exhibition space: see website. For more information, crafters should visit website or call.

COCONUT POINT ART FESTIVAL

270 Central Blvd., Suite 107B, Jupiter FL 33458. (561)746-6615. Fax: (561)746-6528. E-mail: info@artfestival.com. Website: www.artfestival.com. "Fine art, music and more will occupy the streets for two fun-filled days during this art fest that has earned the title of 'The Big One!' This art show features life-size sculptures, spectacular paintings, one-of-a-kind jewels, photography, ceramics, and much more. Visitors will have the opportunity to meet the creators of the art on display, commission a specific piece, ask questions about techniques, learn the sources of their in-spirations, and purchase fine works of art." See website for more information.

COLLEGE HILL ARTS FESTIVAL

College Hill Arts Festival, PO Box 544, Cedar Falls, IA 50613. Website: www.collegehillartsfestival.com. Fine arts & crafts fair held annually. Accepts handmade crafts and other mediums. Juried event featuring 75 artists from around the United States. Exhibitors: see website. Number of attendees: see website. Admission: see website. Apply online.
ADDITIONAL INFORMATION Deadline for entry: see website. Application fee: see website. Space fee: see website. Exhibition space: see website. For more information, crafters should visit website or call.

COLORADO COUNTRY CHRISTMAS GIFT SHOW

Denver Mart, 451 E. 58th Ave., Denver CO 80216. (800)521-7469. Fax: (425)889-8165. E-mail: denver@showcase.events.org. Website: www.showcaseevents.org. Contact: Kim Peck, show manager. Estab. 2003. Annual holiday show held early November. Indoors. Accepts handmade crafts, art, photography, pottery, glass, jewelry, fiber, clothing. Juried. Exhibitors: 400. Number of attendees: 25,000. Admission: see website. Apply by e-mail, call or website.
ADDITIONAL INFORMATION Deadline for entry: see website. Space fee: see website. Exhibition space: 10×10. For more information, e-mail, call, send SASE or see website.
TIPS "Competitive pricing, attractive booth display, quality product, something unique for sale, friendly & outgoing personality."

COLUMBIANA ARTIST MARKET

Shelby County Arts Council, PO Box 624, 104 Mildred St., Columbiana, AL 35051. (205)669-0044. E-mail: info@shelbycountyartscouncil.com. Website: www.shelbycountyartscouncil.org. Fine arts & crafts fair held annually. Accepts pottery, jewelry, watercolors, oil paintings, acrylic paintings, clothing accessories, culinary arts and other mediums. Exhibitors: see website. Number of attendees: see website. Admission: see website. Apply online.

ADDITIONAL INFORMATION Deadline for entry: see website. Application fee: see website. Space fee: see website. Exhibition space: see website. For more information, crafters should visit website or call.

THE COLUMBUS ARTS FESTIVAL

100 E. Broad St., Suite 2250, Columbus OH 43216. (614)221-8531. Fax: (614)224-7461. E-mail: shuntley @gcac.org. Website: www.columbusartsfestival.org. Contact: Scott Huntley, director. Estab. 1962. Fine art show held annually the first full weekend in June. Outdoors. Accepts fine art, 2D/3D mixed media, ceramics, digital art, drawing, fiber, glass, jewelry, leather, painting, metal, photography, printmaking, sculpture, wood. Juried. Awards/prizes: Best in show, Jurors' Choice, Merit Award, Best Presentation, Best Emerging Artist. Exhibitors: 220. Number of attendees: 450,000. Free to public. Apply via Zapplication. org.
ADDITIONAL INFORMATION Deadline for entry: mid-January. Application fee: $35. Space fee: 495. Exhibition Space: 10×10; double booths available by invitation. Average sales: $6,000. For more information, e-mail.

COMMONWHEEL ARTISTS ANNUAL LABOR DAY ARTS & CRAFTS FESTIVAL

(719)577-7700. E-mail: festival@commonwheel.com. Website: www.commonwheel.com/festival. Contact: festival committee (by e-mail). Estab. 1975. Arts & crafts show held annually in September. Outdoors. Accepts handmade crafts and all mediums. Juried. Awards/prizes: ribbons in all categories and free both for following year. Exhibitors: 110. Number of attendees: 15,000. Free to public. Artists should apply via website.
ADDITIONAL INFORMATION Deadline for entry: May 15. Application fee: $25. Space fee: $300 (artists); $400 (food). Exhibition space: 10×10. (artists); 12×14 ft. (food). For more information, crafters should e-mail or visit website.

CORAL SPRINGS FESTIVAL OF THE ARTS

270 Central Blvd., Suite 107B, Jupiter FL 33458. (561)746-6615. Fax: (561)746-6528. E-mail: info@ artfestival.com. Website: www.artfestival.com. "The Coral Springs Festival of the Arts has grown considerably over the years into a two-day celebration of arts and culture with a fine art show, contemporary craft festival, theatrical performances and full line-up of live music. Held in conjunction with the Coral Springs Art Festival Committee and the City, this event brings 250 of the nation's best artists and crafters to South Florida. Stroll amidst life-size sculptures, spectacular paintings, one-of-a-kind jewels, photography, ceramics, a separate craft festival, Green Market and much more. No matter what you're looking for, you'll be sure to find it among the various array of artists and crafters participating in this arts & crafts fair."

CORN HILL ARTS FESTIVAL

133 S. Fitzhugh St., Rochester NY 14608-9956. (585)262-3142. E-mail: chna@cornhill.org. Website: www.cornhillartsfestival.com. Fine arts & crafts fair held annually in July. Outdoors. Accepts handmade crafts and other mediums. Exhibitors: see website. Number of attendees: see website. Admission: Free to public. Apply online.
ADDITIONAL INFORMATION Deadline for entry: early July. Application fee: $35. Space fee: $265 (single); $530 (double). Exhibition space: 10×10 (single); 10×20 (double). For more information, crafters should visit website, send e-mail or call.

CORVALLIS FALL FESTIVAL

(541)752-9655. E-mail: director@corvallisfallfestival. com. Website: www.corvallisfallfestival.org. Corvallis Fall Festival is a not-for-profit event with the mission to help sustain local arts and crafts while serving, supporting and showcasing the Corvallis community.

COTTONWOOD ART FESTIVAL

Cottonwood Art Festival. Contact Serri Ayers (972)744-4582. E-mail: serri.ayers@cor.gov. Website: www.cottonwoodartfestival.com. Fine arts & crafts fair held semi annually. Jurors select over 240 artists to exhibit their museum-quality work. Exhibitors: see website. Number of attendees: see website. Admission: free. Apply online.
ADDITIONAL INFORMATION Deadline for entry: see website. Application fee: see website. Space fee: see

website. Exhibition space: see website. For more information, crafters should visit website or call.

COUNTRY FOLK ARTS AND CRAFTS SHOW

E-mail: shows@countryfolkart.com. Website: www.countryfolkart.com. "Country Folk Art Shows has grown to 17 shows in 5 states. Every participant is juried and hand selected for their outstanding workmanship and integrity of creative design. Some of the more popular decorating items found at our shows are handcrafted furniture, home and garden decor, jewelry, textiles, holiday decor, wearable art, handmade candles and soaps, quilts, paintings, framed art, florals, iron work, wood carvings, baskets, stained glass and much more."

COUNTRYSIDE VILLAGE ART FAIR

Countryside Village Art Fair. E-mail: artfair@countryside-village.com. Website: www.countryside-village.com. Fine arts & crafts fair held annually. "Omaha's oldest and most prestigious annaul fine and decorative art fair. Established in 1969." Exhibitors: see website. Number of attendees: see website. Admission: see website. Apply online.
ADDITIONAL INFORMATION Deadline for entry: see website. Application fee: see website. Space fee: see website. Exhibition space: see website. For more information, crafters should visit website or call.

COVINGTON ART FAIR

Website: www.facebook.com/CovingtonArtFair. Fine arts & crafts fair held annually. "Two-day juried event showcases watercolor, oils, photography, sculpture, pottery, jewelry, fiber art, wearable art and more. Over 75 local, regional and national artists." Exhibitors: see website. Number of attendees: see website. Admission: see website. Apply online. Artist applications are posted each January for that year's show.
ADDITIONAL INFORMATION Deadline for entry: see website. Application fee: see website. Space fee: see website. Exhibition space: see website. For more information, crafters should visit website or call.

CRAFT & FINE ART FESTIVAL AT THE NASSAU COUNTY MUSEUM OF ART

American Concern for Artistry and Craftsmanship, P.O. Box 650, Montclair NJ 07042. (973)746-0091. Fax: (973)509-7739. E-mail: acacinfo@gmail.com. Website: www.craftsatlincoln.org. Fine art & craft show held annually in September. Outdoors. Accepts handmade crafts. Juried. Number exhibitors: 90. Number attendees: varies. Free to public. Apply online or via Zapplication.org.
ADDITIONAL INFORMATION Deadline for entry: June. Application fee: none. Space fee: varies. Exhibition space: varies. For more information, crafters should call, e-mail or visit website.

CRAFT & SPECIALTY FOOD FAIR (NEW HAMPSHIRE)

38 Charles St., Rochester NH 03867. (603)332-2616. E-mail: info@castleberryfairs.com. Website: www.castleberryfairs.com. Art & craft show held annually in November. Indoors. Accepts handmade crafts and other mediums. Juried. Number exhibitors: see website. Number attendees: varies. Admission: $7 adults; children 12 & under free. Apply online.
ADDITIONAL INFORMATION Deadline for entry: see website. Application fee: see website. Space fee: $350 (10×6); $450 (10×10). Exhibition space: 10×6; 10×10. For more information, crafters should e-mail, call or visit website.

CRAFT ALASKA ARTS AND CRAFTS SHOW

Website: www.yelp.com/events/anchorage-craft-alaska-arts-and-crafts-show. Craft Alaska features live entertainment and dozens of Alaska-made arts and crafts vendors.

CRAFTAPALOOZA & FABULOUS VINTAGE MARKET—ABILENE

E-mail: montagefestivals@earthlink.net. Website: www.montagefestivals.com. Arts & crafts show held twice a year (see website for dates). Indoors. Accepts handmade crafts, artisan designs, antique & vintage, home décor & inspiration, and more. Exhibitors: varies. Number of attendees: varies. Admission: $3 adults; under 12 free. Apply via website.

ADDITIONAL INFORMATION Deadline for entry: see website. Application fee: see website. Space fee: $95 (10×10); $165 (10×20). Exhibition space: 10×10; 10×20. For more information send e-mail or visit website.

CRAFTAPALOOZA & FABULOUS VINTAGE MARKET—SALINA

E-mail: montagefestivals@earthlink.net. Website: www.montagefestivals.com. Arts & crafts show held in March. Indoors. Accepts handmade crafts, artisan designs, antique & vintage, home décor & inspiration, and more. Exhibitors: varies. Number of attendees: varies. Admission: $3 adults; under 12 free. Apply via website.

ADDITIONAL INFORMATION Deadline for entry: see website. Application fee: see website. Space fee: $70 (10×10); $105 (10×20). Exhibition space: 10×10; 10×20. For more information send e-mail or visit website.

CRAFTAPALOOZA & FABULOUS VINTAGE MARKET—WICHITA

E-mail: montagefestivals@earthlink.net. Website: www.montagefestivals.com. Arts & crafts show held twice a year (see website for dates). Indoors. Accepts handmade crafts, artisan designs, antique & vintage, home décor & inspiration, and more. Exhibitors: varies. Number of attendees: varies. Admission: $3 adults; under 12 free. Apply via website.

ADDITIONAL INFORMATION Deadline for entry: see website. Application fee: see website. Space fee: $95 (8×10); $165 (8×20). Exhibition space: 8×10; 8×20. For more information send e-mail or visit website.

CRAFTBOSTON

The Society of Arts & Crafts, 175 Newbury St., Boston MA 02116. (617)266-1810. Fax: (617)266-5654. E-mail: show@craftboston.org. Website: www.societyofcrafts. org. "Presented by The Society of Arts and Crafts, CraftBoston Spring and Holiday are New England's premiere juried exhibitions and sales of contemporary craft. This twice annual, well-established show features the most outstanding artists of our time, showcasing one-of-a-kind and limited edition pieces in baskets, ceramics, decorative fiber, wearables, furniture, glass, jewelry, leather, metal, mixed media, paper, and wood."

CRAFT FAIR OF THE SOUTHERN HIGH-LANDS

Southern Highland Craft Guild. Folk Art Center, PO Box 9545, Asheville, NC 22815. (828)298-7928. Website: www.craftguild.org. Fine arts & crafts fair held twice annually. "Fine traditional and contemporary crafts. Nearly 200 craftspeople fill the two levels of the center selling their works of clay, fiber, glass, leather, metal, mixed media, natural materials, paper, wood and jewelry." Exhibitors: must be guild member. Number of attendees: see website. Admission: $8. Apply online.

ADDITIONAL INFORMATION Deadline for entry: see website. Application fee: see website. Space fee: see website. Exhibition space: see website. For more information, crafters should visit website or call.

CRAFT LAKE CITY DIY FESTIVAL

351 Pierpont Ave., 4B, Salt Lake City UT 84101. (801)487-9221. Fax: (801)487-1359. Website: www. craftlakecity.com. Fine arts & crafts fair held annually in June. Outdoors. Accepts handmade crafts and other mediums. Exhibitors: 200. Number of attendees: see website. Admission: Free to public. Apply online.

ADDITIONAL INFORMATION Deadline for entry: early May. Application fee: $15. Space fee: varies. Exhibition space: varies. For more information, crafters should visit website or call.

CRAFTLAND

235 Westminster St., Providence RI 02903. (401)272-4285. E-mail: info@craftlandshop.com. Website: www.craftlandshop.com/pages/show. Craftland Show is an annual holiday craft show featuring the work of 170 artists from Rhode Island and nationwide. It celebrates all kinds of handmade objects and the people who make them.

◎ CRAFTOBERFEST

E-mail: chelsiehellige@gmail.com. Website: www. craftoberfest.com. "Craftoberfest is St. Louis' first lantern-lit outdoor night market featuring local beer, live music, and some of the best handmade & vintage finds our fair city has to offer."

CRAFTS AT MOLAND HOUSE

1641 Old York Rd., Warminser/Hartsville PA 18974. (215)850-1888. E-mail: frommyhand@gmail.com. Website: www.craftsatmolandhouse.com. Contact: Gwyn Duffy, event coordinator. Estab. 2010. Arts & crafts show held annually in March & November. Indoors. Accepts handmade crafts. Juried. Exhibitors: 55. Number of attendees: 5,000. Admission: $1. E-mail for application.

ADDITIONAL INFORMATION Deadline for entry: rolling. Application fee: $50. Space fee: 25% of sales. Exhibition Space: varies. For more information, e-mail or visit website.

CRAFTS IN THE BARN

4130 Thistlwood Rd., Hatboro PA 19040. (215)850-1888. E-mail: frommyhand@gmail.com. Website: www.craftsinthebarn.com. Contact: Gwyn Duffy, show coordinator. Estab. 1985. Arts & crafts show held annually in May & October. Indoors. Accepts handmade crafts. Exhibitors: 75. Number of attendees: 6,000. Free to the public. E-mail for application.

ADDITIONAL INFORMATION Deadline for entry: rolling. Application fee: $50. Space fee: 25% of sales. Exhibition Space: varies. For more information, e-mail or visit website.

CRAFTY BASTARDS ARTS & CRAFTS FAIR

Washington City Paper, 1400 Eye St., NW, Suite 99, Washington, DC 20005. (202)332-8500. Website: www.washingtoncitypaper.com/craftybastards. Fine arts & crafts fair held annually. Accepts handmade crafts and other mediums. "An exhibition and sale of handmade alternative arts and crafts from independent artists "Exhibitors: see website. Number of attendees: see website. Admission: $5. Apply online.

ADDITIONAL INFORMATION Deadline for entry: see website. Application fee: see website. Space fee: see website. Exhibition space: see website. For more information, crafters should visit website or call.

CRAFTY SUPERMARKET

Cincinnati OH. E-mail: craftysupermarket@gmail.com. Website: www.craftysupermarket.com. Contact: Chris Salley Davis & Grace Dobush, co-organizers. Estab. 2009. Semi-annual indie arts & crafts show held late April & late November. Indoors. Accepts handmade crafts, art & design, ocassionally accepts edible gifts. Juried. Exhibitors: Spring show 50; holiday show 90. Number of attendees: Spring show, 2,000; holiday show 4,000. Free to public. Apply online.

ADDITIONAL INFORMATION Deadline for entry: check website. Application fee: $10. Space fee: see website. Exhibition space: varies. For more information, see website.

TIPS "Our shows are very competitive (usually less than a quarter of applications are accepted), but we aim to make sure at least a third of the vendors at each show are new to us. We draw modern artists, crafters and designers from all over the eastern U.S. and bring in shoppers from Ohio, Indiana, Kentucky and beyond. Attend one of our shows or check out the lists of past vendors on our website to get an understanding of our style. We're a modern indie craft show with a serious eye for design."

CRAFTY WONDERLAND

E-mail: craftywonderland@yahoo.com. Website: www.craftywonderland.com. "Crafty Wonderland is the place to go to find the best handmade goods in the NW, as well as affordable work from talented visual artists. It's an event meant to bring together crafty people with those who appreciate cool handmade items, to support artists, and to spread the joy of craft throughout our community. The show even offers a kids' area where budding young artists can set up and sell their work! Each Crafty Wonderland features a free DIY area where local artists share their talent and teach visitors how to make a craft of their own to take home."

CREATIVE HAND

E-mail: info@creativehandkc.org. Website: www.creativehandkc.org. "Handcrafted fiber show sponsored by the Kansas City Fiber Guild and the Kansas City Weaver's Guild. Artists from both groups come together for the Creative Hand Show and Sale. The show is both exhibition and sale of art-to-wear that members of both groups have created by hand."

CRESTED BUTTE ARTS FESTIVAL

P.O. Box 324, Crested Butte CO 81224. (970)349-1184. E-mail: juliette@crestedbutteartsfestival.com. Website: www.crestedbutteartsfestival.com. "The Crested Butte Arts Festival, Crested Butte's signature cultural event and one of Colorado's top 5 fine art and fine craft shows, features 175 well-known, established artists from around the world and is recognized as a top-quality, juried show."

CROCKER PARK FINE ART FAIR

270 Central Blvd., Suite 107B, Jupiter FL 33458. (561)746-6615. Fax: (561)746-6528. E-mail: info@artfestival.com. Website: www.artfestival.com. "Over 100 fine artists and crafters will be on hand to display at this first-class affair. With mediums such as paintings, sculpture, jewelry, photography, pottery and much, much more there, is something for everyone at this top notch event. Crocker Park creates the perfect setting for this event featuring a sophisticated mix of retail stores, great restaurants, cafés, a multi-screen movie theater, luxury apartments—all together in a congenial neighborhood of parks and tree-lined streets."

CROSBY FESTIVAL OF THE ARTS

Toledo Botanical Garden, 5403 Elmer Drive, Toledo, OH 43615. (419)536-5566. E-mail: info@toledogarden.org. Website: www.toledogarden.org. Fine arts & crafts fair held annually. Accepts handmade crafts and other mediums. Exhibitors: see website. Number of attendees: see website. Admission: see website. Apply online.

ADDITIONAL INFORMATION Deadline for entry: see website. Application fee: see website. Space fee: see website. Exhibition space: see website. For more information, crafters should visit website or call.

CUSTER'S LAST STAND FESTIVAL OF THE ARTS

Custer Fair, PO Box 6013, Evanston, IL 60204. (847)328-2204. E-mail: office@custerfair.com. Website: www.custerfair.com. Fine arts & crafts fair held annually. Accepts handmade crafts and other mediums. "Artists, craftspeople, antique dealers, restauranteurs, entertainers and the business community

get together with 70,000 attendees for this award-winning Northshore tradition. "Exhibitors: see website. Number of attendees: see website. Admission: see website. Apply online.

ADDITIONAL INFORMATION Deadline for entry: see website. Application fee: see website. Space fee: see website. Exhibition space: see website. For more information, crafters should visit website or call.

DELAND OUTDOOR ART FESTIVAL

(386)717-1888. E-mail: delandoutdoorartfestival@cfl.rr.com. Website: www.delandoutdoorartfest.com. Annual festival held in March. Admission is free. Fine artists from throughout the Southeast will be competing for thousands of dollars in cash prizes and awards. The festival offers a craft section with items for sale ranging from handmade jewelry, carved wooden toys to Adirondack lawn furniture. More than 4,000 spectators visit the festival.

DES MOINES ARTS FESTIVAL

Des Moines Arts Festival, 601 Locust St. Suite 700, Des Moines, IA 50309. (515)286-4950. E-mail: info@desmoinesartsfestival.org. Website: desmoinesartsfestival.org. Fine arts & crafts fair held annually. Accepts handmade crafts and other mediums. Exhibitors: see website. Number of attendees: see website. Admission: see website. Apply online.

ADDITIONAL INFORMATION Deadline for entry: see website. Application fee: see website. Space fee: see website. Exhibition space: see website. For more information, crafters should visit website or call.

DETROIT URBAN CRAFT FAIR

E-mail: vendors@detroiturbancraftfair.com. Website: www.detroiturbancraftfair.com. "The Detroit Urban Craft Fair (DUCF) is a two-day alternative craft fair held annually in the city of Detroit. The fair features 100 handmade crafters and indie artists. DUCF is a community market that encourages the interaction of maker and buyer. It is unique opportunity for shoppers to find one-of-a-kind items and meet the people who made them. Participating crafters have the chance to connect with a large, supportive audience. The Detroit Urban Craft Fair's mission is to elevate handmade goods as an alternative to mass-produced items, support and elevate small craft business by providing a place for them to sell during the busy holiday shopping season, and raise awareness of handmade craft." See website for more information.

DICKENS HOLIDAY CRAFTS FAIR

Finley Community Center, Attn: Crafts Fair, 2060 W. College Avenue, Santa Rosa CA 95401. (707)543-3755. E-mail: craftsfair@srcity.org. Website: www.http://ci.santa-rosa.ca.us/departments/recreationandparks/programs/specialevents/craftfair/Pages/default.aspx. Craft fair held annually in December. Indoors. Accepts handmade crafts. Exhibitors: 70. Number of attendees: see website. Admission: $2; children 12 & under free. Apply online.

ADDITIONAL INFORMATION Deadline for entry: July. Application fee: $25. Space fee: varies. Exhibition space: varies. For more information, crafters should visit website or call.

DILLON ART FESTIVAL

Lake Dillon Arts Festival, 4214 E Colfax Ave., Denver, CO 80220. (720)941-6088. Website: www.summitcountyartfestival.com. Fine arts & crafts fair held annually. Accepts handmade crafts and other mediums. Exhibitors: see website. Number of attendees: see website. Admission: see website. Apply online.

ADDITIONAL INFORMATION Deadline for entry: see website. Application fee: see website. Space fee: see website. Exhibition space: see website. For more information, crafters should visit website or call.

DIYPSI—AN INDIE ART FAIR

Website: www.diypsi.com. Indie art fair occuring in late summer and early December. "Our intent is to be one component of a thriving community of entrepreneurs, artists, organizations and events that serve to build it up. Our contribution to this endeavor is DIYpsi (dip-see)– a handmade art fair that takes place in Ypsilanti's Depot Town District biannually. For two weekends each year, we host the best indie artists our city and region have to offer for a one of a kind holiday shopping experience that will take care of everyone on your list." See website for more information and to apply.

DIY STREET FAIR

E-mail: info@diystreetfair.com. Website: www.diystreetfair.com. "The DIY Street Fair is a free 2-day, 3-night event in Ferndale, MI where local artists, crafters, businesses, groups and organizations, musicians, restaurants, food trucks, brewers and others whose lives and work adhere to do-it-yourself ethic converge for one big celebration. The event, which launched its first weekend fair in 2008, showcases the immense creative energy, independent spirit and innovative talent that can be found throughout the area. Open to the public, free to attend and all are welcome." See website for more information and to apply.

DOWNTOWN ASPEN ART FESTIVAL

270 Central Blvd, Suite 107B, Jupiter FL 33458. (561)746-6615. Fax: (561)746-6528. E-mail: info@artfestival.com. Website: www.artfestival.com. "Downtown Aspen Art Festival will provide you an exclusive opportunity to experience a broad range of phenomenal creations ranging from life-size sculptures, photography, glass, paintings, ceramics, one-of-a-kind jewelry, and mixed media. Take in fabulous views of Downtown Aspen, grab a delicious bite at a local eatery, and purchase original artwork from the artists themselves, as you enjoy this weekend of visual inspiration." See website for more information.

DOWNTOWN DELRAY BEACH FESTIVAL OF THE ARTS

207 Central Blvd., Suite 107B, Jupiter FL 33458. (561)746-6615. Fax: (561)746-6528. E-mail: info@artfestival.com. Website: www.artfestival.com. "This annual juried art festival of hand-crafted artwork including glass, photography, painting, mixed media, fiber, jewelry and much more. This much anticipated, premiere Delray Beach art festival hosts hundreds of artists exhibiting and selling their work in an outdoor gallery that spans one mile of Atlantic Avenue from US1 all the way to A1A." See website for more information.

DOWNTOWN DOWNERS GROVE FESTIVAL

Changing Seasons, 307 Silver Springs Pl., Norco CA 92860. (951)735-4751. E-mail: changingseasons artsandcrafts@yahoo.com. Website: www.changing

seasonscraftshows.com. Fine arts & crafts fair held annually 5 times a year. Outdoors. Accepts handmade crafts and other mediums. Exhibitors: see website. Number of attendees: see website. Admission: Free to public. Apply online.

ADDITIONAL INFORMATION Deadline for entry: June. Application fee: see website. Space fee: see website. Exhibition space: see website. For more information, crafters should visit website or call.

DOWNTOWN DOWNERS GROVE FESTIVAL (ILLINOIS)

Amdur Productions, P.O. Box 550, Highland Park IL 60035. (847)926-4300. Fax: (847)926-4330. E-mail: info@amdurproductions.com. Website: www.amdurproductions.com. Art & craft show held annually in September. Outdoors. Accepts handmade crafts and other mediums. Juried. Awards/prizes: given at festival. Number exhibitors: 100. Number attendees: 30,000. Free to public. Apply online.

ADDITIONAL INFORMATION Deadline for entry: early January. Application fee: $20. Space fee: $335. Exhibition space: 10×10. For more information, crafters should e-mail, call or visit website.

DOWNTOWN DUNEDIN ART FESTIVAL

270 Central Blvd., Suite 107B, Jupiter FL 33458. (561)746-6615. Fax: (561)746-6528. E-mail: info@artfestival.com. Website: www.artfestival.com. "Meet 150 of the nation's most talented artists showcasing a broad spectrum of mediums including sculpture, photography, glass, paintings, ceramics, jewelry, mixed media and more! Howard Alan Events offer patrons the opportunity to personally meet with the artists, commission a work of art, and learn what inspires the artists' work."

DOWNTOWN DUNEDIN CRAFT FESTIVAL

270 Central Blvd., Suite 107B, Jupiter FL 33458. (561)746-6615. Fax: (561)746-6528. E-mail: info@ArtFestival.com. Website: www.artfestival.com. "If Tampa is on your travel agenda this June, you can't miss out on this terrific craft event in the city's most desirable suburb of Dunedin. It is here, a short drive from Tampa, along Dunedin's Main Street, you will meet some of the country's finest crafters with products all handmade in the U.S.A. Botanical hotplates, ceramic planters, functional pottery, hair accessories, handmade one-of-a-kind jewelry pieces and an expansive Green Market offers something for every taste & budget."

DOWNTOWN FESTIVAL AND ART SHOW

302 NE 6th Ave., Gainesville FL 32601. (352)393-8536. Fax: (352)334-2249. E-mail: piperlr@cityofgainesville.org. Website: www.gvlculturalaffairs.org. Contact: Linda Piper, events coordinator. Estab. 1981. Fine art show held annually in November. Outdoors. Accepts handmade crafts and fine art. Juried. Awards/prizes: $16,700 in cash awards. Exhibitors: 240. Number of attendees: 100,000. Free to public. Apply online .

ADDITIONAL INFORMATION Deadline for entry: May 4. Application fee: $23.50. Space fee: $272. Exhibition space: 12×12. Average sales: $5,000. For more information, send e-mail.

DOWNTOWN SARASOTA ART & CRAFT FESTIVAL

270 Central Blvd., Suite 107B, Jupiter FL 33458. (561)746-6615. Fax: (561)746-6528. E-mail: info@ArtFestival.com. Website: www.artfestival.com. "Behold contemporary crafts from more than 100 of the nation's most talented artisans. A variety of jewelry, pottery, ceramics, photography, painting, clothing and much more—all handmade in America—will be on display, ranging from $15 to $3,000. An expansive Green Market with plants, orchids, exotic flora, handmade soaps, gourmet spices and freshly popped kettle corn further compliments the weekend, blending nature with nurture."

DOWNTOWN STUART ART FESTIVAL

270 Central Blvd., Suite 107B, Jupiter FL 34458. (561)746-6615. Fax: (561)746-6528. E-mail: info@artfestival.com. Website: www.artfestival.com. "The Stuart Festival of the Arts is set up along Osceola Street in Stuart's historic downtown area. This event brings together some of the best artists in the nation,

displaying life-size sculptures, spectacular paintings, one-of-a-kind jewels, photography and more. Howard Alan Events offer patrons the opportunity to personally meet with the artists, commission a work of art, and learn what inspires the artists' work."

DOWNTOWN VENICE ART CLASSIC

270 Central Blvd., Suite 107B, Jupiter FL 33458. (561)746-6615. Fax: (561)746-6528. E-mail: info@artfestival.com. Website: www.artfestival.com. "The annual Venice Art Classic is becoming as popular as its counter-part Venice show in the fall. Set up along West Venice Avenue in the heart of Downtown Venice, you will meet 150 of the nation's most talented artists showcasing a broad spectrum of mediums including sculpture, photography, glass, paintings, ceramics, jewelry, mixed media and more! Howard Alan Events offer patrons the opportunity to personally meet with the artists, commission a work of art, and learn what inspires the artists' work." See website for more information.

DOYLESTOWN ARTS FESTIVAL

E-mail: info@doylestownalliance.org. Website: www.doylestownartsfestival.com. "This two-day festival is the largest event of the year in the heart of beautiful Doylestown Borough in Bucks County PA. This annual festival has grown to include more than 160 exhibitors and a food court. Diverse activities are available at numerous locations throughout the downtown area. Live music features solo acts as well as rock, pop, folk, big band and music for kids. The festival is a free event for the community."

DRIFTLESS AREA ART FESTIVAL

E-mail: info@driftlessareaartfestival.com. Website: www.driftlessareaartfestival.com. The Driftless Area Art Festival celebrates the visual, performing, and culinary arts of the Driftless Area.

DUBUQUEFEST FINE ARTS FESTIVAL

8 Lindberg Terrace, Dubuque IA 52001. (563)564-5290. E-mail: paula@dubuquefest.org. Website: www.dubuquefest.org. Contact: Paula Neuhaus, art fair director. Estab. 1977. Fine arts & crafts fair held annually in May. Outdoors. Accepts handmade crafts and other mediums. Juried. Awards/prizes: 1st place, 2nd place, 3rd place. Exhibitors: 70. Number of attendees: varies. Admission: Free to public. Apply online.
ADDITIONAL INFORMATION Deadline for entry: see website. Application fee: $15. Space fee: $110. Exhibition space: 12×12. For more information, crafters should e-mail, visit website or call.

EAGLE RIVER WATERMELON DAYS CRAFT & GIFT FESTIVAL

705 Bugbee Ave., Wausau WI 54401. (715)675-6201. Fax: (715)675-7649. E-mail: mmccallin@charter.net. Website: www.macproductionllc.com. Contact: Mac & Bonnie McCallin. Fine arts & crafts fair held annually in July. Outdoors. Accepts handmade crafts and other mediums. Juried. Exhibitors: see website. Number of attendees: varies. Admission: Free to public. Apply online.
ADDITIONAL INFORMATION Deadline for entry: see website. Application fee: see website. Space fee: varies. Exhibition space: 12×10. For more information, crafters should e-mail, visit website or call.

EAST LANSING ART FESTIVAL

410 Abbot Rd., East Lansing MI 48823. (517)319-6804. E-mail: info@elartfest.com. Website: www.elartfest.com. Contact: Michelle Carlson, festival director. Estab. 1963. Fine arts & crafts fair held annually in May. Outdoors. Accepts handmade crafts and other mediums. Juried. Awards/prizes: over $5,500 in cash awards. Exhibitors: see website. Number of attendees: varies. Admission: Free to public. Apply online.
ADDITIONAL INFORMATION Deadline for entry: November. Application fee: $25. Space fee: $300 (single); $600 (double). Exhibition space: 10×10 (single); 10×10 (double). For more information, crafters should e-mail, visit website or call.

EASTON ART AFFAIR

(330)284-1082. E-mail: bhuff@eastonartaffair.com. Website: www.eastonartaffair.com. Contact: Barb Huff. Estab. 1999. Fine arts & crafts fair held annually in June. Outdoors. Accepts handmade crafts, ceramics, digital art, drawing, glass, jewelry, metal work, mixed media, painting, photography, printmaking & graphics, sculpture, wearable art, wood. Juried. Awards/prizes: Best of Show, Honorable Mention. Exhibitors: 105. Number of attendees: varies. Admission: Free to public. Apply online.

ADDITIONAL INFORMATION Deadline for entry: March 1. Application fee: $25. Space fee: $300 (single); $600 (double). Exhibition space: 10×10 (single); 10×20 (double). For more information, crafters should e-mail, visit website or call.

ECHO PARK CRAFT FAIR

Website: www.echoparkcraftfair.com. "The EPCF is a bi-annual design event in Silverlake featuring over 70 artists and designers. Beatrice Valenzuela and Rachel Craven founded the Echo Park Craft Fair (EPCF) in 2009. The pair visualized a space that would showcase and nurture the many talented artisans, designers and craftspeople living in their inspired community on the eastside of Los Angeles. Originally held in Valenzuela's backyard featuring just a handful of friends, The Echo Park Craft Fair has grown into a highly anticipated bi-annual arts event, attracting thousands of visitors from around Los Angeles...and beyond."

EDINA ART FAIR

(952)922-1524. Fax: (952)922-4413. Website: www.edinaartfair.com. Fine arts & crafts fair held annually in June. Outdoors. Accepts handmade crafts, ceramics, enamel, fiber, glass, jewelry, mixed media, photography, sculpture, wearable art, wood. Juried. Awards/prizes: Best of Show, Best Display, Awards of Excellence, Merit Awards. Number exhibitors: 300. Number attendees: 165,000. Free to public. Apply online

ADDITIONAL INFORMATION Deadline for entry: February. Application fee: $35. Space fee: $425 (single); $850 (double). Exhibition space: 10×10 (single); 10×20 (double). For more information, crafters should visit website or call.

EDMOND QUILT FESTIVAL

(405)348-2233. E-mail: wonderland48@cox.net. Website: www.edmondquiltguild.us. Contact: Alice Kellog. Quilt show held annually in July. Indoors. Accepts handmade quilts. Entry only open to Edmond Quilt Guild members. Juried. Awards/prizes: Founder's Award, Best Hand Quilting, Best of Show, Judges' Choice, Viewers' Choice. Number exhibitors: see website. Number attendees: see website. Free to public. Apply online.

ADDITIONAL INFORMATION Deadline for entry: mid-July. Application fee: see website. Space fee: see website. Exhibition space: see website. For more information, crafters should e-mail, visit website or call.

ELK RIVER ARENA'S FALL CRAFT SHOW

1000 School St., Elk River MN 55330. (763)635-1145. Fax: (763)635-1144. E-mail: lestby@elkrivermn.gov. Website: www.elkriverarena.com. Contact: Laura Estby, office assistant. Estab. 1997. Annual fine arts & crafts show held mid-September. Indoors & outdoors. Accepts handmade crafts, paintings, ceramics, photography, woodwork. Juried. Exhibitors: 85+. Number of attendees: 1,500. Free to public. Apply online at elkriverarena.com.

ADDITIONAL INFORMATION Deadline for entry: until filled. Space fee: $50-$75. Exhibition space: 90-126 sq. ft. For more information e-mail or see website.

TIPS "Bring good quality items, typically $25 and under. Be pleasant!"

ELK RIVER ARENA'S SPRING CRAFT SHOW

1000 School St., Elk River MN 55330. (763)635-1145. Fax: (763)635-1144. E-mail: lestby@elkrivermn.gov. Website: www.elkriverarena.com. Contact: Laura Estby, office assistant. Estab. 1990. Annual fine arts & crafts show held early May. Indoors. Accepts handmade crafts, paintings, ceramics, photography, upcycled items. Juried. Exhibitors: 85+. Number of attendees: 1,200. Free to public. Apply online at elkriverarena.com.

ADDITIONAL INFORMATION Deadline for entry: until filled. Space fee: $50-$75. Exhibition space: 90-126 sq. ft. For more information, e-mail or see website.

TIPS "Be pleasant to customers; have unique items that are well crafted!"

EVANSTON ART & BIG FORK FESTIVAL

Amdur Productions, P.O. Box 550, Highland Park IL 60035. (847)926-4300. Fax: (847)926-4330. E-mail: info@amdurproductions.com. Website: www.amdurproductions.com. Art & craft show held annually in September. Outdoors. Accepts handmade crafts and other mediums. Juried. Awards/prizes: given at artist breakfast. Number exhibitors: 30. Number attendees: varies. Free to public. Apply online.

ADDITIONAL INFORMATION Deadline for entry: early May. Application fee: $25. Space fee: $430. Exhibition space: 10×10. For more information, crafters should e-mail, call or visit website.

EVANSTON ETHNIC ARTS FAIR

Evanston Cultural Arts Programs, Morton Civic Center, Parks, Recreation & Community Services, 2100 Ridge Ave., Room 1116, Evanston IL 60201. (847)448-8260. Fax: (847)448-8051. E-mail: pbattaglia@cityofevanston.org. Website: www.cityofevanston.org/festivals-concerts/ethnic-arts-festival. Contact: Patricia Battaglia. Estab. 1984. Fine arts & crafts fair held annually in July. Outdoors. Accepts handmade crafts and other media. Juried. Awards/prizes: see website. Number exhibitors: see website. Number attendees: varies. Free to public. Apply online.

ADDITIONAL INFORMATION Deadline for entry: see website. Application fee: see website. Space fee: see website. Exhibition space: see website. For more information, crafters should e-mail, visit website or call.

FALL CRAFT FEST

Ozark Regional Promotions, 5557 Walden St., Lowell AR 72745. (479)756-6954. E-mail: karenlloyd@juno.com. Website: www.ozarkregionalartsandcrafts.com. Art & craft show held annually in October. Indoors. Accepts handmade crafts and other mediums. Juried. Number exhibitors: see website. Number attendees: varies. Free to public. Apply online.

ADDITIONAL INFORMATION Deadline for entry: mid August. Application fee: none. Space fee: varies. Exhibition space: varies. For more information, crafters should e-mail, call or visit website.

FALL FESTIVAL OF THE ARTS OAKBROOK CENTER

Amdur Productions, P.O. Box 550, Highland Park IL 60035. (847)926-4300. Fax: (847)926-4330. E-mail: info@amdurproductions.com. Website: www.amdurproductions.com. Estab. 1962. Fine arts & crafts fair held annually in September. Outdoors. Accepts handmade crafts, jewelry, ceramics, painting, photography, digital, printmaking and more. Juried. Number exhibitors: see website. Number attendees: varies. Admission: Free to public. Apply online.

ADDITIONAL INFORMATION Deadline for entry: see website. Application fee: $25. Space fee: $460. Exhibition space: 10×10. For more information, crafters should e-mail, call or visit website.

FALL FESTIVAL ON PONCE

Olmstead Park, North Druid Hills, 1451 Ponce de Leon, Atlanta GA 30307. (404)873-1222. E-mail: Lisa@affps.com. Website: festivalonponce.com. Contact: Lisa Windle, festival director. Estab. 2011. Arts & crafts show held annually mid-October. Outdoors. Accepts handmade crafts, painting, photography, sculpture, leather, metal, glass, jewelry. Juried by a panel. Awards/prizes: ribbons. Number of exhibitors: 125. Number of attendees: 45,000. Free to public. Apply online at Zapplication.org.

ADDITIONAL INFORMATION Deadline for entry: August 22. Application fee: $25. Space fee: $250. Exhibition space: 10×10. For more information, see website.

FAUST HERITAGE FESTIVAL

15185 Olive Blvd., Chesterfield MO 63017. (314)615-8328. Fax: (314)615-8325. E-mail: jfoley@stlouisco.com. Website: www.stlouisco.com/parksandrecreation/parkpages/faust. Contact: Jim Foley, site coordinator. Historic craft fair held annually the end of September. Indoor & outdoor. Accepts handmade crafts. Exhibitors: 15+. Number of attendees: 2,000-4,000. Admission: $5 adults; $2 children 4-12; 3 & under free. Apply by contacting festival coordinator.

ADDITIONAL INFORMATION Deadline for entry: Septermber 15. Space fee: 15% of profit. For more information, crafters should e-mail or call.

FESTIVAL FETE

P.O. Box 2552, Newport RI 02840. (401)207-8115. E-mail: pilar@festivalfete.com. Website: www.festival-fete.com. Fine arts & crafts fair held annually in July. Outdoors. Accepts handmade crafts, painting, sculpture, photography, drawing, fabric, crafts, ceramics, glass and jewelry. Juried. Awards/prizes: see website. Number exhibitors: 150. Number attendees: varies. Free to public. Apply online.

ADDITIONAL INFORMATION Deadline for entry: see website. Application fee: see website. Space fee: $175. Exhibition space: 10×10. For more information, crafters should e-mail, visit website or call.

⊙ FESTIVAL FOR THE ENO

(919)620-9099 ext. 203. E-mail: crafts@enoriver.org. Website: www.enoriver.org/festival. "The Festival for the Eno is presented by the Eno River Association to celebrate and preserve the natural, cultural and historic resources of the Eno River Valley. All participants must recognize that the festival is a combined effort toward this specific goal. As one of its chief attractions, the festival features the excellence and diversity of the region's arts and crafts. The festival is held at West Point on the Eno, a Durham City Park on Roxboro Road, open to residents of the Carolinas, Virginia, Georgia and Tennessee only, and all items must be the handiwork of the participant, who must be present." See website for more information.

FESTIVAL OF THE VINE

8 S. Third St., Geneva IL 60134. (630)232-6060. Fax: (630)232-6083. E-mail: chamberinfo@genevachamber.com. Website: www.genevachamber.com. Contact: Ellen Townsley, volunteer coordinator. Estab. 1981. Arts & crafts show held annually in mid September. Outdoors. Accepts handmade crafts. Juried. Exhibitors: 100. Number of attendees: 200,000. Free to public. Apply online.

ADDITIONAL INFORMATION Deadline for entry: June 1. Application fee: none. Space fee: $175. Exhibition space: 10×10. For more information, crafters should e-mail, visit website or call.

FESTIVAL OF TREES CRAFT & GIFT SHOW

The Family Tree Center, 2520 5th Ave., S, Billings MT 59101-4342. (406)252-9799. Fax: (406)256-3014. Website: www.familytreecenterbillings.org. Estab. 1985. "Begun in 1985, the Festival of Trees has become synonymous with the holiday season in Billings. For many residents and visitors, the holidays would not be complete without at least one visit to view the trees or participate in the weekend activities. Each year, the Festival of Trees provides an opportunity for community members to help prevent child abuse and neglect in Yellowstone County and the surrounding area. Donating or buying a tree, sponsoring the event, or participating in one of the many weekend activities during the festival helps raise money and awareness; both help the Family Tree Center. Over the course of this 4-day event, over 10,000 people pass through the doors to view the unique holiday trees and participate in the assortment of activities. All dollars raised at the Festival go where they are needed most—toward the many child abuse prevention programs in place at The Family Tree Center. Referrals are increasing, and the number of families that we serve continues to grow. Now more than ever, the Family Tree Center needs your support." See Website for more details.

FIESTA ARTS FAIR

Southwest School of Art, 300 Augusta St., San Antonio TX 78205. (210)224-1848. Fax: (210)224-9337. Website: www.swschool.org/fiestaartsfair. Art & craft market/show held annually in April. Outdoors. Accepts handmade crafts, Ceramics, paintings, jewelry, glass, photography, wearable art and other mediums. Juried. Number exhibitors: 125. Number attendees: 12,000. Admission: $16 weekend pass; $10 daily adult pass; $5 daily children pass; children 5 & under free. Apply via Zapplication.org.

ADDITIONAL INFORMATION Deadline for entry: November. Application fee: none. Space fee: varies. Exhibition space: varies. For more information, crafters should call or visit website.

FINE ART FAIR

Foster Arts Center Building, 203 Harrison St., Peoria IL 61602. (309)637-2787. E-mail: events@peoriaartguild.org. Website: www.peoriaartguild.org. Contact: special events coordinator. Estab. 1962. Fine arts

& crafts fair held annually in September. Outdoors. Accepts handmade crafts, painting, sculpture, photography, drawing, fabric, crafts, ceramics, glass and jewelry. Juried. Number exhibitors: 150. Number attendees: varies. Admission: $7 adults; children 12 & under free; Peoria Art Guild members free. Apply online.

ADDITIONAL INFORMATION Deadline for entry: see website. Application fee: see website. Space fee: see website. Exhibition space: see website. For more information, crafters should e-mail, visit website or call.

FINE CRAFT SHOW

Memorial Art Gallery of the University of Rochester, 500 University Ave., Rochester NY 14607. (585)276-8900. Fax: (585)473-6266. E-mail: maginfo@mag.rochester.edu. Website: www.mag.rochester.edu/events/fine-craft-show/. Estab. 2000. Fine arts & crafts fair held annually in October. Indoors. Accepts handmade crafts, ceramics, glass, jewelry, metal, leather, wood, wearable art and more. Juried. Number exhibitors: 40. Number attendees: varies. Admission: $12; $5 college students w/ ID. Apply online.

ADDITIONAL INFORMATION Deadline for entry: see website. Application fee: see website. Space fee: see website. Exhibition space: see website. For more information, crafters should e-mail, visit website or call.

FINE CRAFT SHOW AND SALE—MEMORIAL ART GALLERY

500 University Ave., Rochester NY 14607. (585)276-8910. E-mail: smcnamee@mag.rochester.edu. Website: www.magrochester.edu. Contact: Sharon McNamee, gallery council assistant. Estab. 2000. Fine craft show held annually late October/early November. Indoors. Accepts handmade crafts, glass, ceramics, leather, wearables, jewelry, wood, furniture, metal. Juried. Awards/prizes: Best in Show; Award of Excellence (2). Exhibitors: 40. Number of attendees: 2,000. Admission: $10-12. Apply online.

ADDITIONAL INFORMATION Deadline for entry: March 31. Application fee: $35. Space fee: $475. Exhibition space: 10×10. Average sales: $1,500-6,000. For more information, crafters should e-mail or visit website.

TIPS "One of a kind or limited edition."

FIREFLY ART FAIR

Wauwatosa Historical Society, 7406 Hillcrest Drive, Wauwatosa WI 53213. (414)774-8672. E-mail: staff@wauwatosahistoricalsociety.org. Website: www.wauwatosahistoricalsociety.org. Estab. 1985. Fine arts & crafts fair held annually in August. Outdoors. Accepts handmade crafts, painting, sculpture, photography, ceramics, jewelry, fiber, printmaking, glass, paper, leather, wood. Juried. Number exhibitors: 150. Number attendees: varies. Free to public. Apply online.

ADDITIONAL INFORMATION Deadline for entry: March. Application fee: $15. Space fee: $140. Exhibition space: 10×10. For more information, crafters should e-mail, visit website or call.

FIREFLY HANDMADE MARKET

P.O. Box 3195, Boulder CO 80307. E-mail: fireflyhandmade@gmail.com. Website: www.fireflyhandmade.com. Estab. 2010. Fine crafts fair held annually 3 times a year. Outdoors. Accepts handmade crafts. Juried. Number exhibitors: 100. Number attendees: 6,000. Free to public. Apply online.

ADDITIONAL INFORMATION Deadline for entry: May. Application fee: $25. Space fee: varies. Exhibition space: varies. For more information, crafters should e-mail or visit website.

FIRST FRIDAY & SATURDAY ON THE RIVER

404 E. Bay St., Savannah GA 31401. (912)234-0295. Fax: (912)234-4904. E-mail: info@riverstreetsavannah.com. Website: www.riverstreetsavannah.com. Contact: Scott Harris, artist relations manager. Arts & crafts show held annually first Friday & Saturday of each month March-December. Outdoors. Accepts handmade crafts. Juried. Exhibitors: 30-50. Number of attendees: 10,000. Free to public.

ADDITIONAL INFORMATION Deadline for entry: early January. Application fee: $15. Space fee: $150-$300. Exhibition space: 10×10 ft. (double booth space also available). For more information, crafters should e-mail or visit website.

FLINT ART FAIR

(810)695-0604. E-mail: committee@flintartfair.org. Website: www.flintartfair.org. Fine arts & crafts fair held annually in June. Outdoors. Accepts handmade crafts and other mediums. Juried. Number exhibitors: see website. Number attendees: varies. Admission: $5 adults; $3 children 12 & under, seniors and FOMA members. Apply online.

ADDITIONAL INFORMATION Deadline for entry: see website. Application fee: see website. Space fee: see website. Exhibition space: see website. For more information, crafters should e-mail, visit website or call.

FOUNTAIN HILLS GREAT FAIR

P.O. Box 17598, Fountain Hills AZ 85269. E-mail: sharon@fountainhillschamber.com. Website: www. fountainhillschamber.com/the-great-fair.asp. Contact: Sharon Morgan. "This three day juried art fair features nearly 500 artists and artisans from across the United States and around the globe, and attracts 200,000+ visitors. Food booths, beer garden and seating areas abound throughout the venue, with great breakfast, lunch and rest stops situated at locations in the middle and at both ends of the festival area. Live musical entertainment." See website for more information.

FREDERICK FESTIVAL OF THE ARTS

11 West Patrick St., Suite 201, Frederick MD 21701. (301)662-4190. E-mail: kris.fair.ffota@gmail.com. Website: www.frederickartscouncil.org. Estab. 1993. Fine arts & crafts fair held annually in June. Outdoors. Accepts handmade crafts, jewelry, photography, painting, glass, wood, metal, drawing, digital, sculpture, fiber, and other forms of mixed media. Juried. Number exhibitors: 110. Number attendees: varies. Free to public. Apply online.

ADDITIONAL INFORMATION Deadline for entry: see website. Application fee: see website. Space fee: see website. Exhibition space: see website. For more information, crafters should e-mail, visit website or call.

FREDERICKSBURG FALL HOME & CRAFTS FESTIVAL

Ballantine Management Group of Virginia, 2371 Carl D. Silver Parkway, Fredericksburg VA 22401. (540)548-5555 ext.108. Fax: (540)548-5577 . E-mail: csilversmith@bmg1.com. Website: www. fredericksburgartsandcraftsfaire.com. Contact: Casey

Silversmith. Estab. 2009. Fine arts & crafts fair held annually in October. Indoors. Accepts handmade arts & crafts only. Juried. Number exhibitors: see website. Number attendees: varies. Admission: $8 at door; $7 online & seniors 60+; children 12 & under free. Apply online.

ADDITIONAL INFORMATION Deadline for entry: see website. Application fee: see website. Space fee: varies. Exhibition space: varies. For more information, crafters should e-mail, visit website or call.

FREDERICKSBURG JEWELRY & ACCESSORY SHOWCASE

Ballentine Management Group of Virginia, 2371 Carl D. Silver Parkway, Fredericksburg VA 22401. (540)5478-5555 ext.108 . Fax: (540)548-5577. E-mail: csilversmith@bmg1.com. Website: www. fredericksburgartsandcraftsfaire.com. Contact: Casey Silversmith. Fine jewelry & accesories fair held annually in April. Indoors. Accepts handmade jewelry & accessories. Juried. Number exhibitors: see website. Number attendees: varies. Admission: $8 at door; $7 online & seniors 60+; children 12 & under free. Apply online.

ADDITIONAL INFORMATION Deadline for entry: see website. Application fee: see website. Space fee: varies. Exhibition space: varies. For more information, crafters should e-mail, visit website or call.

FREDERICKSBURG SPRING ARTS & CRAFTS FAIRE

Ballantine Management Group of Virginia, 2371 Carl D. Silver Parkway, Fredericksburg VA 22401. (540)548-5555 ext. 108. Fax: (540)548-5577. E-mail: csilversmith@bmg1.com. Website: www.fredericks burgartsandcraftsfaire.com. Contact: Casey Silversmith. Estab. 2009. Fine arts & crafts fair held annually in March. Indoors. Accepts handmade crafts and other mediums. Juried. Number exhibitors: see website. Number attendees: varies.Admission: $8 at door; $7 online & seniors 60+; children 12 & under free. Apply online.

ADDITIONAL INFORMATION Deadline for entry: see website. Application fee: see website. Space fee: varies. Exhibition space: varies. For more information, crafters should e-mail, visit website or call.

FRIENDS OF THE KENOSHA PUBLIC MUSE-UMS ART FAIR

5500 First Ave., Kenosha WI 53140. (262)653-4140. Fax: (262)653-4437. E-mail: pgregorski@kenosha.org. Website: www.kenoshapublicmuseum.org. Contact: Peggy Gregorski, deputy director. Estab. 1964. Fine arts & crafts show held annually 3rd Sunday of July. Indoors & outdoors. Accepts handmade crafts. Juried. Awards/prizes: 5 awards totaling $2,000. Exhibitors: 125. Number of attendees: 7,000. Free to public. Apply online.

ADDITIONAL INFORMATION Deadline for entry: May 1. Application fee: none. Space fee: $125-200. Exhibition space: 10×10 (indoors); 15×15 (outdoors). For more information, crafters should e-mail or visit website.

FUNKY JUNK ROUNDUP

E-mail: montagefestivals@earthlink.net. Website: www.montagefestivals.com. One-day shopping extravaganza held in May. Indoors. Accepts handmade crafts, junktiques, artisan designs, antique & vintage, home décor & inspiration, and more. Exhibitors: varies. Number of attendees: varies. Admission: $3 adults; under 12 free. Apply via website.

ADDITIONAL INFORMATION Deadline for entry: see website. Application fee: see website. Space fee: $95 (10×10); $165 (10×20). Exhibition space: 10×10; 10×20. For more information, e-mail or visit website.

GARAGE SALE ART FAIR

E-mail: bonnie@garagesaleartfair.com. Website: www.garagesaleartfair.com. Fine arts & crafts fair held annually in February. Indoors. Accepts handmade crafts and other mediums. Juried. Number exhibitors: 125. Number attendees: 3,500. Free to public. Apply online.

ADDITIONAL INFORMATION Deadline for entry: see website. Application fee: see website. Space fee: varies. Exhibition space: varies. For more information, crafters should e-mail, visit website.

GASLIGHT CRAFT FAIR

7010 E. Broadway Blvd., Tucson AZ 85710. (520)886-4116. Fax: (520)722-6232. E-mail: glt@qwestoffice.net. Contact: Teresa, bookkeeper. Estab. 2012. Art & craft show/seasonal/holiday show held every Saturday (weather permitting); Friday-Sunday in November & December. Outdoors. Accepts handmade crafts. Exhibitors: 30. Number of attendees: 300. Free to public. Apply online.

ADDITIONAL INFORMATION Deadline for entry: 1 week before event. Application fee: none. Space fee: $10/space per day; $30 in November & December. Exhibition space: 8×10 (under tent); 12×12 (in parking lot). For more information, crafters should e-mail, call or visit Facebook page.

GASPARILLA FESTIVAL OF THE ARTS

P.O. Box 10591, Tampa FL 33679. (813)876-1747. E-mail: info@gasparillaarts.com. Website: www.gasparilla-arts.com. Estab. 1970. Fine arts & crafts fair held annually in March. Outdoors. Accepts handmade crafts, a ceramic, digital, drawing, fiber, glass, jewelry, mixed media, painting, photography, printmaking, sculpture, watercolor and wood. Juried. Awards/prizes: $74,500 in cash awards. Number exhibitors: 300. Number attendees: 250,000. Free to public. Apply online.

ADDITIONAL INFORMATION Deadline for entry: September. Application fee: $40. Space fee: $375. Exhibition space: 10×10. For more information, crafters should e-mail, visit website or call.

GATHERING AT THE GREAT DIVIDE

Mountain Art Festivals, P.O. Box 3578, Breckenridge CO 80424. (970)547-9326. E-mail: info@mountainartfestivals.com. Website: www.mountainartfestivals.com. Estab. 1975. Fine arts & crafts fair held annually in August. Outdoors. Accepts handmade crafts, painting, sculpture, photography, drawing, fabric, crafts, ceramics, glass and jewelry. Juried. Number exhibitors: see website. Number attendees: varies. Free to public. Apply online.

ADDITIONAL INFORMATION Deadline for entry: April. Application fee: $35. Space fee: $500. Exhibition space: 10×10. For more information, crafters should e-mail, visit website or call.

GERMANTOWN FRIENDS SCHOOL JURIED CRAFT SHOW

31 W. Coulter St., Philadelphia PA 19144. (215)900-7734. E-mail: craftshow@gfsnet.org. Website: www.germantownfriends.org/parents/parents-association/craft-show/index.aspx. "This jewel of a show, located on the GFS campus, has been ranked among the top 10 percent of the nation's craft shows by the authoritative *ArtFair SourceBook*." See website for more information.

GLAM INDIE CRAFT SHOW

E-mail: glamcraftshow@gmail.com. Website: www.glamcraftshow.com. Fine arts & crafts fair held annually in December. Outdoors. Accepts handmade crafts, painting, sculpture, photography, drawing, fabric, crafts, ceramics, glass and jewelry. Juried. Number exhibitors: varies. Number attendees: varies. Admission: $3 adults; children 10 & under free. Apply online.

ADDITIONAL INFORMATION Deadline for entry: September. Application fee: see website. Space fee: varies. Exhibition space: varies. For more information, crafters should e-mail or visit website.

GLENCOE FESTIVAL OF ART

Amdur Productions, P.O. Box 550, Highland Park IL 60035. (847)926-4300. E-mail: info@amdurproductions.com. Website: www.amdurproductions.com. Fine arts & crafts fair held annually in August. Outdoors. Accepts handmade crafts, painting, sculpture, photography, drawing, fabric, crafts, ceramics, glass and jewelry. Juried. Number exhibitors: 120. Number attendees: 35,000. Free to public. Apply online.

ADDITIONAL INFORMATION Deadline for entry: see website. Application fee: $25. Space fee: varies. Exhibition space: varies. For more information, crafters should e-mail or visit website.

GLENVIEW OUTDOOR ART FAIR

Glenview Art League, P.O. Box 463, Glenview IL 60025-0463. (847)724-4007. E-mail: glenviewartleague@att.net. Website: www.glenviewartleague.org. Fine arts & crafts fair held annually in July. Outdoors. Accepts handmade crafts, Paintings, sculpture, hand-pulled artist's prints (e.g., etchings), drawings,

mixed media, ceramics, photography and jewelry. Juried. Awards/prizes: Best of Show, Awards of Excellence, Merit Awards. Number exhibitors: see website. Number attendees: varies. Free to public. Apply online.

ADDITIONAL INFORMATION Deadline for entry: May. Application fee: $10. Space fee: varies. Exhibition space: 12×12. For more information, crafters should e-mail, call or visit website.

GLENWOOD AVENUE ARTS FEST

E-mail: info@glenwoodave.org. Website: www.glenwoodave.org. "The Glenwood Avenue Arts Fest (GAAF) is a free, weekend-long event that features artists, open studios and live entertainment on three outdoor stages. Experience art, theater, music, as well as food and drink, on the brick-laid streets of the Glenwood Avenue Arts District in Chicago's historic Rogers Park neighborhood." See website for more details.

GOLD CANYON ARTS FESTIVAL

5301 S. Superstition Mountain Dr., Suite 104, #183, Gold Canyon AZ 85118. E-mail: info.gcartsfest@gmail.com. Website: www.gcartsfest.com. Fine arts & crafts fair held annually the 4th Saturday in January. Outdoors. Accepts handmade crafts and other mediums. Juried. Number exhibitors: 85. Number attendees: 6,000. Free to public. Apply online.

ADDITIONAL INFORMATION Deadline for entry: November. Application fee: none. Space fee: $60. Exhibition space: 10×10. For more information, crafters should e-mail, call or visit website.

GOLD COAST ART FAIR

Amdur Productions, P.O. Box 550, Highland Park IL 60035. (847)926-4300. E-mail: info@amdurproductions.com. Website: www.amdurproductions.com. Fine arts & crafts fair held annually in June. Outdoors. Accepts handmade crafts and other mediums. Juried. Awards: announced at festival. Number exhibitors: 300. Number attendees: 100,000. Free to public. Apply online.

ADDITIONAL INFORMATION Deadline for entry: see website. Application fee: $35. Space fee: $595. Exhibition space: see website. For more information, crafters should e-mail, call or visit website.

GOLDEN FINE ARTS FESTIVAL

Golden Fine Arts Festival, 1010 Washington Ave., Golden CO 80401. (303)279-3113. E-mail: info@ goldencochamber.org. Website: www.goldenfinearts festival.org. Fine arts & crafts fair held annually in August. Outdoors. Accepts handmade crafts, ceramics, fiber, glass, jewelry, mixed media, 2D, painting, photography, and sculpture. Juried. Number exhibitors: see website. Number attendees: 40,000. Free to public. Apply online.

ADDITIONAL INFORMATION Deadline for entry: April. Application fee: $25. Space fee: $350. Exhibition space: 10×10. For more information, crafters should e-mail, call or visit website.

GOT CRAFT?

E-mail: info@gotcraft.com. Website: www.gotcraft. com. "Founded in 2007, Got Craft? is held twice a year in May and December featuring 75+ handmade designers, craft workshops, tasty treats, music, FREE swag bags, and an average attendance of 6,000 a year." See website for more information.

GRAND LAKE STREAM FOLK ART FESTIVAL

P.O. Box 465, Princeton ME 04668-0465. (207)796-8199. E-mail: grandlakestreamfolkartfestival@gmail. com. Contact: Cathy or Bill Shamel. Estab. 1994. Arts & crafts show held annually last full weekend in July. Outdoors. Accepts handmade crafts, canoe building. Juried. Exhibitors: 60. Number of attendees: 3,000. Admission: $8. Apply via e-mail or call.

ADDITIONAL INFORMATION Deadline for entry: none. Application fee: none. Space fee: $300 (10×10); $450 (10×15); $600 (10×20). Exhibition space: 10×10; 10×15; 10×20. For more information, crafters should e-mail or call.

TIPS "Upscale display and good lighting."

GREAT GULFCOAST ARTS FESTIVAL

Website: www.ggaf.org. "The Great Gulfcoast Arts Festival is a juried art show. Each year, we receive more than 600 applications for the festival. Each applicant is required to submit three images of their work and one image of their display area along with their application. Qualified jurors are shown each art-

ist's images simultaneously and anonymously, and collectively choose more than 200 artists who will be invited to exhibit their work. Best of Show, Awards of Distinction, Awards of Excellence, Awards of Honor, and Awards of Merit winners from the previous year's festival are exempt from the jurying process." See website for more information.

GREAT LAKES ART FAIR

46100 Grand River Rd., Novi MI 48374. (248)348-5600 ext. 208. Fax: (248)347-7720. E-mail: jmc mahon@suburbanshowplace.com. Website: www. greatlakesartfair.com. Contact: Jackie McMahon, event manager. Estab. 2009. Fine art show held annually in April. Indoors. Accepts handmade crafts, wood, ceramics, painting, 3D mixed media, photography. Juried. Awards/prizes: $900 in cash & prizes; free booth next show. Exhibitors: 200. Number of attendees: 10,000. Admission: $7. Apply online.

ADDITIONAL INFORMATION Deadline for entry: early February. Application fee: $30. Space fee: $400. Exhibition space: 10×12. For more information, crafters should e-mail, call or visit website.

GREAT MIDWEST ART FEST

Amdur Productions, P.O. Box 550, Highland Park IL 60035. (847)926-4300. Fax: (847)926-4330. E-mail: info@amdurproductions.com. Website: www. amdurproductions.com. Art & craft show held annually in July. Outdoors. Accepts handmade crafts and other mediums. Juried. Number exhibitors: see website. Number attendees: varies. Free to public. Apply online.

ADDITIONAL INFORMATION Deadline for entry: early May. Application fee: $15. Space fee: $185. Exhibition space: 10×10. For more information, crafters should e-mail, call or visit website.

GREEN VALLEY ART FESTIVAL

2050 W. State Route 89A Lot 237, Cottonwood AZ 86326. (928)300-4711. E-mail: alan@runningbear-productions.net. Website: www.runningbearpro-ductions.net. Contact: Alan Smith. Fine art and craft show held three times a year. See website or e-mail for more information.

GREEN WITH INDIE

E-mail: stlouiscraftmafia@gmail.com. Website: www.greenwithindiecraftshow.com. Fine arts & crafts fair held annually in March. Indoors. Accepts handmade crafts and vintage items. Juried. Number exhibitors: 65. Number attendees: varies. Free to public. Apply online.

ADDITIONAL INFORMATION Deadline for entry: January. Application fee: none. Space fee: varies. Exhibition space: varies. For more information, crafters should e-mail or visit website.

GUMTREE FESTIVAL

P.O. Box 786, Tupelo MS 38802. (662)844-2787. Website: www.gumtreefestival.com. "The festival is highly respected, and brings an influx of 30,000 people to downtown Tupelo the actual weekend of the Festival. GumTree festival showcases the artwork of around 100 artists from all over the south and beyond. GumTree Festival is an iconic institution for the fine arts." See website for more details.

HALIFAX ART FESTIVAL

P.O. Box 2038, Ormond Beach FL 32175-2038. (386)304-7247; (407)701-1184. E-mail: halifaxartfest@aol.com. Website: www.halifaxartfestival.com. Estab. 1962. Fine arts & crafts fair held annually in November. Outdoors. Accepts handmade crafts, ceramics, fiber, glass, jewelry, mixed media, 2D, painting, photography, and sculpture. Juried. Awards/prizes: Best of Show, Judges Choice, Awards of Excellence, Awards of Distinction, Awards of Honor, Awards of Merit, Student Art Awards, Purchase Award, Patron Purchase Award. Number exhibitors: 200. Number attendees: 45,000. Free to public. Apply online.

ADDITIONAL INFORMATION Deadline for entry: August. Application fee: $30. Space fee: $225 (competitive); $125 (non competitive). Exhibition space: see website. For more information, crafters should e-mail, call or visit website.

HAMPTON FALLS CRAFT FESTIVAL

Castleberry Fairs & Festivals, 38 Charles St., Rochester NH 03867. (603)332-2616. E-mail: info@castleberryfairs.com. Website: www.castleberryfairs.com. Estab. 2008. Fine arts & crafts fair held annually in September. Outdoors. Accepts handmade crafts and other mediums. Juried. Number exhibitors: see website. Number attendees: varies. Free to public. Apply online.

ADDITIONAL INFORMATION Deadline for entry: see website. Application fee: see website. Space fee: $225. Exhibition space: 10×10. For more information, crafters should e-mail, call or visit website.

HANDMADE ARCADE

E-mail: info@handmadearcade.com. Website: www.handmadearcade.com. "Handmade Arcade (HA), founded in 2004, is Pittsburgh's first and largest independent craft fair. HA brings young, innovative crafters and progressive do-it-yourself designers to the David L. Lawrence Convention Center to sell their handmade, locally produced, and offbeat wares at a bustling marketplace. A highly anticipated annual event, HA attracts more than 8,000 attendees in one day. HA provides craft artists working outside mainstream and fine arts sectors with a grassroots, high-visibility venue to sell wares, build community, network, and share their artistic practice." See website for more information.

◎ HANDMADE BABY FAIR

Om Baby, 2201 Rear Market St., Camp Hill PA 17011. (717)761-4975. E-mail: holly@ombabycenter.com. Website: www.ombabycenter.com/Handmade_Baby.html. Fine craft fair featuring local, handmade, natural and sustainable baby products. "If you are seeking unique, handmade, local baby and children's items, then this is the event to attend! You'll find everything from bibs to diapers, clothing and nursery decor for your special little one!" See website for more details.

HANDMADE CITY SPRING FAIR

E-mail: handmadecityinfo@gmail.com. Website: www.handmade-city.com. Fine arts & crafts fair held annually in December. Indoors. Accepts handmade crafts and other mediums. Juried. Number exhibitors: see website. Number attendees: varies. Free to public. Apply online.

ADDITIONAL INFORMATION Deadline for entry: October. Application fee: none. Space fee: $40. Exhibition space: 6×10. For more information, crafters should e-mail or visit website.

HANDMADE HARVEST

(613)461-2211. E-mail: hello@handmadeharvest. com. Website: www.handmadeharvest.com. "The Handmade Harvest Craft Show takes place in Almonte, Ontario, a quaint little tourist town about 30 minutes west of Ottawa. Founded in 2010, the show is the brainchild of former co-workers-cum-friends Emily Arbour and Colleen Hewitt. Upon bonding over their love of all things handmade, Emily and Colleen embarked on a new adventure: crafting as a business. In no time at all, what started as a few after-hours workshops (an ingenious way to fund their nasty little craft supply habits) became a business unto itself." See website for details.

HANDMADE MADISON

E-mail: info@handmademadison.com. Website: www.handmademadison.com. "Handmade Madison pop-up markets are an opportunity for artists and craftspeople to showcase the things they love to make and for those who appreciate good craftsmanship to find something they will truly love, or love to give! We pride ourselves on our wonderful vendors—people who create with sincerity and passion. We provide a wide variety of handcrafted items. Customers can experience firsthand the gratitude of our makers and delight in supporting local and regional independent artists." See website for more details.

HANDMADE MARKET CHICAGO

Website: www.handmadechicago.com. "Handmade Market is a unique event to connect the makers of beautiful things to people who appreciate the unique and handmade." See website for details.

HANDMADE TOLEDO MAKER'S MART

Website: www.handmadetoledo.com. "45+ handmade vendors from all over the Midwest will showcase their wares for a one day pop up shop. Grab some grub from local food trucks and bakeries, sip on some locally roasted coffee, enjoy the sounds of some of Toledo's talented buskers, shop handmade and celebrate 419

Day with us! Handmade fun for the whole family! There will be kid friendly activities, crafty make and takes, and much more!" See website for details.

HANDWEAVERS GUILD OF BOULDER ANNUAL SALE

2111 Hermosa Dr., Boulder CO 80304. (303)444-1010. E-mail: frey.barb@gmail.com. Website: www.handweaversofboulder.org. Contact: Barbara Olson. Fine arts & crafts fair held annually in October. Outdoors. Accepts handmade crafts. Juried. Open to members only. Awards/prizes: Juror's Award, People's Choice Award. Number exhibitors: see website. Number attendees: varies. Free to public. Apply online.
ADDITIONAL INFORMATION Deadline for entry: October. Application fee: $15. Space fee: see website. Exhibition space: see website. For more information, crafters should e-mail, call or visit website.

HARVEST FESTIVAL ORIGINAL ART & CRAFT SHOW

2181 Greenwich St., San Francisco CA 94123. (415)447-3205. Fax: (415)346-4965. E-mail: harvest@weshows.com. Website: www.harvestfestival.com. Contact: Lori Walker. Estab. 1972. Arts & crafts show held annually September-December. Indoors. Accepts handmade crafts. Juried. Number of exhibitors: varies. Number of attendees: varies. Admission fee: $9 adults; $7 seniors; $4 youth; 12 & under free. Apply online.
ADDITIONAL INFORMATION Deadline for entry: until filled. Space fee: varies. Exhibition space: 10×10; 10×15; 10×20; 10×30. Exhibition space: varies by location and size; corners additional $125. For more information, e-mail or visit website.
TIPS "We look for quality and variety."

HEARTFEST

Stookey Companies, P.O. Box 31083, Des Moines IA 50310. (515)278-6200. Fax: (515)276-7513. E-mail: suestookey@att.net. Website: www.stookeyshows. com. Fine arts & crafts fair held annually in February. Indoors. Accepts handmade crafts and other mediums. Juried. Number exhibitors: see website. Number attendees: see website. Free to public. Apply online.

ADDITIONAL INFORMATION Deadline for entry: January. Application fee: $25. Space fee: varies. Exhibition space: varies. For more information, crafters should e-mail, call or visit website.

HIGHLAND PARK FESTIVAL OF FINE CRAFT

Amdur Productions, P.O. Box 550, Highland Park IL 60035. (847)926-4300. E-mail: info@amdur productions.com. Website: www.amdurproductions. com. Fine arts & crafts fair held annually in June. Outdoors. Accepts handmade crafts, ceramics, fiber, glass, jewelry, wood and more. Juried. Number exhibitors: 130. Number attendees: varies. Free to public. Apply online.

ADDITIONAL INFORMATION Deadline for entry: April. Application fee: $35. Space fee: $455. Exhibition space: 10×10. For more information, crafters should e-mail, call or visit website.

HIGHLAND LAST CALL ART FAIR

Amdur Productions, P.O. Box 550, Highland Park IL 60035. (847)926-4300. Fax: (847)926-4330. E-mail: info@amdurproductions.com. Website: www.amdur-productions.com. "The Highwood Last Call Art Fair features great art at great prices. The show gives the public the chance to buy end of the season original art, leftover inventory, slightly damaged, bruised and odd pieces at discounted prices. Artists decide how much to discount their work and can use festival stickers to mark work at 10% to 50% off." See website for more information.

HILTON HEAD ISLAND ART FESTIVAL

270 Central Blvd., Suite 107B, Jupiter FL 33458. (561)746-6615. Fax: (561)746-6528. E-mail: info@artfestival.com. Website: www.artfestival.com. "More than 150 of America's finest artists will descend on Hilton Head Island at Shelter Cove Harbour. This now annual event has become a favorites of both tourists and locals alike. Visit with artists displaying paintings, jewelry, sculpture, photography, pottery and much more. There is something from every budget. This show will contain a segregated craft market place. Also available at the venue is fine dining, exquisite retail, and live entertainment making this a fun, free family event. Take a break from the beaches and golf courses and come to this unique event. We look forward to seeing you on Memorial Day Weekend! Free parking; dune buggy transportation is available 10am-5pm from visitor parking located at the adjacent lot behind HS1 building; the chamber lot behind the arts center to the show site at Neptune Circle." See website for details.

HISTORIC SHAW ART FAIR

(314)773-3935. E-mail: greg@gobdesign.com. Website: www.shawartfair.org. Contact: Greg Gobberdiel, coordinator. Fine arts & crafts fair held annually in October. Outdoors. Accepts handmade crafts, ceramics, fiber, glass, jewelry, mixed media, painting, photography, and sculpture. Juried. Number exhibitors: see website. Number attendees: varies. Free to public. Apply online.

ADDITIONAL INFORMATION Deadline for entry: April. Application fee: $25. Space fee: $280. Exhibition space: 10×10. For more information, crafters should e-mail, call or visit website.

HOBE SOUND FESTIVAL OF THE ARTS

270 Central Blvd., Suite 107B, Jupiter FL 33458. (561)746-6615. Fax: (561)746-6528. E-mail: info@artfestival.com. Website: www.artfestival.com. "The Atlantic coast village of Hobe Sound, located in Martin County, lies just north of Palm Beach and south of Stuart—next to America's most affluent in Jupiter Island. Hobe Sound boasts magnificent surroundings including unspoiled national parks, beautiful beaches, premier golf courses, and world class restaurants and shops. Hobe Sound will transform four blocks of A1A/Dixie Highway into a living, breathing, art gallery for two days with the Hobe Sound Festival of the Arts. Life-size sculptures, spectacular paintings, one-of-a-kind jewels, photography, ceramics, and much more make for one fabulous weekend. No matter what you're looking for, you'll be sure to find it among the various array of artists participating in this juried art fair. As always, admission and parking are free." See website for details.

HOLIDAY HANDMADE CAVALCADE

Website: www.handmadecavalcade.com. "The Handmade Cavalcade is a biannual craft fair in NYC, put together by the dedication and DIY drive of Etsy New York—local New York metro area Etsy Sellers. Come out and shop the unique handmade gifts of your local Etsy shops while snacking on locally made sweets and connecting with other small crafty businesses." See website for details.

HOLIDAY SIZZLE—POTOMAC FIBER ARTS GALLERY

Website: www.potomacfiberartsgallery.com. "Potomac Fiber Arts Gallery (Studio 18) announces the opening of the juried show 'Holiday Sizzle.' In this show, our artists excel in holiday spirit and sparkle. Whether for self or gifts, jewelry, sculpture, clothing, and wall pieces are some of the items that will be exhibited." See website for details.

HOMEWOOD FINE ARTS & CRAFTS FESTIVAL

Pacific Fine Arts Festivals, P.O. Box 280, Pine Grove CA 95665. (209)267-4394. Fax: (209)267-4395. E-mail: pfa@pacificfinearts.com. Website: www.pacificfinearts.com. "This free event brings together an exciting group of more than 50 artists showcasing an assortment of collectable arts and crafts in a variety of media including paintings, ceramics, jewelry, woodwork, photography and much more." See website for more information.

HONOLULU GLASS ART & BEAD FESTIVAL

Soft Flex Company, P.O. Box 80, Sonoma CA 95476. (707)732-3513. Fax: (707)938-3097. E-mail: thomas@softflexcompany.com; sara@softflexcompany.com. Website: www.softflexcompany.com/WSWrapper.jsp?mypage=FestivalHI_Main.html. Contact: Sara Oehler or Scott Clark. Beading event held annually in March & September. Indoors. Accepts beads, gemstones, findings, collectible glass art & jewelry. Juried. Number exhibitors: see website. Number attendees: see website. Free to public. Apply online.
ADDITIONAL INFORMATION Deadline for entry: March. Application fee: see website. Space fee: varies.

Exhibition space: varies. For more information, crafters should e-mail, call or visit website.

HOPI FESTIVAL OF ARTS & CULTURE

(928)774-5213. Website: www.musnaz.org/hp/hopi_fest.shtml. "A Fourth of July tradition since the 1930s, the Hopi Festival of Arts & Culture is the oldest Hopi show in the world. Attendees will enjoy two days of authentic food, artist demonstrations, musical performances, dancing and a not-to-be missed children's area that will entertain the young at heart with take-home crafts related to Hopi culture." See website for more information.

HUDSON MOHAWK WEAVERS GUILD ANNUAL SHOW & SALE

Website: www.hmwg.org/showandsale.html. "For 4 days each November, the Guild takes over the historic Pruyn House and turns it into a showcase for the best of modern handweaving, from traditional to contemporary. Guild members work all year to produce a tremendous variety of handwoven items, from rugs and other homegoods to clothing pieces such as scarves, shawls and jackets. Holiday gifts such as cards and ornaments are also available. Each room in the Pruyn House is devoted to a particular class of items such as linens or scarves and staffed with an accomplished local weaver to assist and answer questions. Admission is free, and visitors can watch fashion shows featuring woven goods or take in demonstrations of handweaving and spinning." See website for more information.

HUNGRY MOTHER ARTS & CRAFTS FESTIVAL

Website: www.hungrymotherfestival.com. "Every summer the Hungry Mother State Park, in Marion, Virginia, opens its doors to visitors and artisans from all over the country. Â Three days of art, entertainment, food and fun are guaranteed." See website for more information and to apply.

HYDE PARK SQUARE ART SHOW

P.O. Box 8402, Cincinnati OH 45208. (513)353-2045. E-mail: hpartshowinfo@aol.com. Website: www.hydeparksquare.org/hydeparkartshow.html. Fine arts

& crafts fair held annually in August. Outdoors. Accepts handmade crafts, ceramics, fiber, glass, jewelry, mixed media, 2D, painting, photography, and sculpture. Juried. Awards/prizes: Best of Show, 1st Place, 2nd Place, 3rd Place, Honorable Mention. Number exhibitors: see website. Number attendees: see website. Free to public. Apply online.

ADDITIONAL INFORMATION Deadline for entry: March. Application fee: $35. Space fee: $125. Exhibition space: see website. For more information, crafters should e-mail, call or visit website.

HYDE PARK VILLAGE ART FAIR
270 Central Blvd., Suite 107B, Jupiter FL 33458. (561)746-6615. Fax: (561)746-6528. E-mail: info@artfestival.com. Website: www.artfestival.com. "Located just outside the city of Tampa, along several city and residential blocks, Hyde Park provides upscale shopping in high-end boutiques, as well as premier dining in various restaurants and cafés. Locals and tourists alike find Hyde Park Village to be a prime area for any and all ages. It's been just over 2 decades since it's inception, and this esteemed community art festival continues to highlight the talents of more than 150 exhibitors displaying a wide range of works from life-size sculptures to photography and jewelry. There are all sorts of opportunities to appreciate and purchase art, during this weekend of visual inspiration." See website for details.

IDAHO ARTISTRY IN WOOD SHOW
(208)466-4899. E-mail: marlies-schmitt@clearwire. net. Website: www.idahoartistryinwood.org. Contact: Marlies Schmitt, publicity chair. Estab. 2009. Fine arts & crafts show held annually last weekend of February. Indoors. Accepts handmade crafts, artwork made from wood or gourds. Awards/prizes: prize ribbons. Number exhibitors: 120 competitors; 7 vendors. Number of attendees: 1,000. Admission: $4; 12 & under free. Artists should apply online.

ADDITIONAL INFORMATION Deadline for entry: February 15 for advance registration; registration can be done at exhibit site on day before show opens. Application fee: $3 per piece in advacne; $5 at the door. Space fee: $75. Exhibition space: 100 sq. ft. For more information, crafters should e-mail or visit website.

TIPS "This show is primarily a competition and exhibition. Although opportunities for sales are given, the focus is not on sales, so there are no guarantees, especially for high price items."

IMAGES—A FESTIVAL OF THE ARTS
E-mail: images@imagesartfestival.org. Website: www. imagesartfestival.org. Fine arts & crafts fair held annually in January. Outdoors. Accepts handmade crafts, ceramics, fiber, glass, jewelry, mixed media, 2D, painting, photography, and sculpture. Juried. Awards/prizes: $100,000 in awards and prizes. Number exhibitors: 225. Number attendees: 45,000. Free to public. Apply online.

ADDITIONAL INFORMATION Deadline for entry: October. Application fee: $40. Space fee: $250. Exhibition space: 11×12. For more information, crafters should e-mail, call or visit website.

INDIE CRAFT BAZAAR
E-mail: indiecraftbazaar@gmail.com. Website: www. getupandcraft.com/Indie_Craft_Bazaar.html. "Indie Craft Bazaar is your local source for orginal art, handmade items, vintage, recycled and vegan goods! These 'ain't your grandma's crafts! ICB is a pop-up shop filled with all sorts of imaginative, impressive and, often-times quirky, handmade curiosities! Support our community, small business, and the arts by joining us at the next show! Admission is $5." See website for more information.

INDIE CRAFT EXPERIENCE
E-mail: craft@ice-atlanta.com. Website: www.ice-atlanta.com. "The Indie Craft Experience was founded in January 2005. With a vision to provide indie crafters an opportunity to sell and promote their creations in Atlanta, ICE quickly caught on as a favorite event for participants and attendees alike. ICE is a grass-roots effort, organized by two Atlanta crafters—Christy Petterson and Shannon Mulkey. Inspired by indie craft markets in Chicago and Austin, the Indie Craft Experience was founded in order to provide Atlanta with a major indie craft event. In addition to craft markets, ICE also organizes a vintage market called Salvage and an annual Pop-Up Shop during the holiday season." See website for more information and to apply.

INDIE CRAFT PARADE

E-mail: info@indiecraftparade.com. Website: www.indiecraftparade.com. Contact: Elizabeth Ramos, executive director. Estab. 2010. Annual arts & crafts show held annually in September 2 weekends after Labor Day. Indoors. Accepts handmade crafts, 2D/3D fine art, fiber art, paper goods, handmade wearables, and an etc. category (toys, home & garden, artisan food, supplies). Juried. Awards/prizes: small cash prize for best booth display. Exhibitors: 75. Number of attendees: 6,500. Admission: $2; children free. Apply via website.

ADDITIONAL INFORMATION Deadline for entry: June 25. Application fee: $20. Space fee: $65 & $95. Exhibition space: 32 sq. ft.; 16 sq. ft. Average sales: $2,500. For more information, e-mail or see website.

TIPS "To sell successfully, understand your market. Attendees at Indie Craft include a vast range from high school/college students to well-established families to retired adults. Have products that fit within a variety of price ranges; make a well-built display that prominently shows your products; be engaging with your potential customers."

INDIEMADE CRAFT MARKET

P.O. Box 3204, Allentown PA 18106. (610)703-8004. E-mail: ann@indiemadecraftmarket.com. Website: www.indiemadecraftmarket.com. Contact: Ann Biernat-Rucker, co-producer. Estab. 2007. Arts & craft show held annually the 1st Saturday in December. Indoors. Accepts handmade crafts. Juried. Exhibitors: see website. Number of attendees: see website. Admission: $3. Apply online.

ADDITIONAL INFORMATION Deadline for entry: April 1. Application fee: none. Space fee: $50. Exhibition space: 8 ft. table. For more information, crafters should visit website.

INDIE SOUTH FAIR

660 N. Chase St., Athens GA 30601. E-mail: indiesouthfair@gmail.com. Website: www.indiesouthfair.com. Contact: Serra Ferguson, organizer. Estab. 2007. Arts & Crafts show held annually the 1st weekends of May & December. Outdoors. Accepts handmade crafts and all other mediums. Exhibitors: 100. Number of attendees: 3,000. Free to public. Apply via website.

ADDITIONAL INFORMATION Deadline for entry: March 2nd for Spring show; September 28 for holiday market. Application fee: $15. Space fee: $175 (10×10); $90 (6×4). Exhibition space: 10×10; 6×4. Average sales: $800-1,200. For more information send e-mail.

TIPS "Create beautiful and functional Art, present it well, and have a friendly, outgoing demeanor."

ITASCA ART & WINE FESTIVAL

Village of Itasca, 550 W. Irving Park Rd., Itasca IL 60143-1795. (630)773-0835. Fax: (630)773-2505. Website: www.itasca.com. "Annual juried fine arts and wine festival, Benches on Parade, takes place in historic downtown Itasca, located in scenic Usher Park near the gateway to the newly created River Walk. There will be live music in the gazebo, a backdrop for meandering through the winding walkways of the park with wine tasting and painted iron benches (up for silent auction) on display throughout." See website or call for details.

JACKSON HOLE FALL ARTS FESTIVAL

Website: www.jacksonholechamber.com/fall_arts_festival. "The Jackson Hole Fall Arts Festival is widely recognized as one of the premier cultural events in the Rocky Mountain West. Thousands of art enthusiasts are drawn each year to experience the diverse artwork and breathtaking natural surroundings that make Jackson Hole a leading cultural center. Experience the world-class installments of contemporary, culinary, landscape, Native American, wildlife, and Western, arts. Visitors will appreciate the works of nationally and internationally acclaimed artists along with an exceptional array of art, music, cuisine, and wine. More than fifty events round out our eleven-day festival." See website for more information.

JAMAICA PLAIN OPEN STUDIOS

JPAC, P.O. Box 300222, Jamaica Plain MA 02130. (617)855-5767. E-mail: coordinator@jpopenstudios.com. Website: www.jpopenstudios.com/juried-show. "The Jamaica Plain Arts Council Juried Exhibition is an annual event designed to provide artists from around New England with a chance to show in a high traffic public space in Boston's most creative neighborhood." See website for more information.

JEFFERSON QUILT SHOW "QUILTS ON THE BAYOU"

(903)276-4639. Website: www.miller-bowiequilt-show.info. Contact: Gwen Scrivner. "Annual quilt show. Quilts, vendors, door prizes, special drawing, raffle quilt, community appreciation awards (Red Hearts, given by members of the business community) and excellence in quilting awards (a special ribbon and $25)." See website for more information and to apply.

JINGLE FEST HANDMADE CRAFT FAIR

Website: www.eventcalifornia.com. "One of the largest handmade table top craft fairs events in San Jose and in the San Francisco Bay Area. Jingle Fest Craft Fair is a curated handmade craft marketplace showcasing the best Bay Area talents in contemporary craft and artwork. Our show brings the best local artists and designers out of their studios and workshops and into the spotlight for a festive one-day celebration of everything handmade." See website for more information.

JUNO BEACH CRAFT FESTIVAL ON THE OCEAN

270 Central Blvd., Suite 107B, Jupiter FL 33458. (561)746-6615. Fax: (561)746-6528. E-mail: info@art-festival.com. Website: www.artfestival.com. "Join us in Jupiter for another fantastic weekend craft festival. Shop handcrafted leather goods, paintings, photography, personalized products, glassworks, and much more—all made in The USA! A Palm Beach favorite, this craft festival is not to be missed! Stroll along the scenic A1A and shop handmade fine crafts that suit every budget, while visiting with some of the nation's best crafters. Get a jump start on holiday gifts at this fabulous free craft event." See website for more information.

KEEPSAKE COLLECTION ART & CRAFT SHOWS

(989)681-4023; (989)781-9165. E-mail: craftpeddler@nethawk.com; bonnmur9@aol.com. Website: www.keepsakecollectionshows.com. Contact: Leslie Needham or Bonnie Murin. "The Keepsake Collection endeavors to connect quality artists and craftspeople with interested buyers of unique and desirable workmanship. To ensure this goal categories are limited both in scope and number. You'll always find professional quality exhibitors and merchandise at our shows as all are juried. Advertising is extensive; including direct mail, postcards, flyers, radio advertising, newspaper ads, in-ground signs, billboards, etc." See website for more information.

KENTUCKY CRAFTED

21st Floor, Capital Plaza Tower, 500 Mero St., Frankfort KY 40601-1987. (502)564-3757; (888)833-2787. Fax: (502)564-2839. E-mail: Ed.Lawrence@ky.gov. Website: www.artscouncil.ky.gov/KentuckyArt/Event_Market.htm. Art & craft market/show held annually in March. Indoors. Accepts handmade crafts, ceramics, fiber, metal and other mediums. Juried. Number exhibitors: 200. Number attendees: varies. Admission: $10, 1-day ticket; $15, 2-day ticket; children 15 & under free. Apply online.

ADDITIONAL INFORMATION Deadline for entry: see website. Application fee: see website. Space fee: varies. Exhibition space: varies. For more information, crafters should e-mail, call or visit website.

KEY WEST CRAFT SHOW

301 Front St., Key West FL 33040. (305)294-1243. E-mail: kwcraftshow@earthlink.net. Website: www.keywestartcenter.com/craft.html. Fine arts & crafts fair held annually in January. Outdoors. Accepts handmade crafts and other mediums. Juried. Number exhibitors: 100. Number attendees: 25,000. Free to public. Apply online.

ADDITIONAL INFORMATION Deadline for entry: September. Application fee: $25. Space fee: $225; $340. Exhibition space: 10×10; 10×15. For more information, crafters should e-mail, call or visit website.

KINGS BEACH FINE ARTS & CRAFTS ON THE SHORE

Pacific Fine Arts Festivals, P.O. Box 280, Pine Grove CA 95665. (209)267-4394. Fax: (209)267-4395. E-mail: pfa@pacificfinearts.com. Website: www.pacificfinearts.com. The annual Fine Arts and Crafts on the Shore at Kings Beach is one of Lake Tahoe's must-attend events, showcasing an outstanding array of creations that capture the imagination and inspire the heart. Set among the towering pine trees along the shores of Lake Tahoe at Kings Beach State Park, this free outdoor festival is sponsored by the North Tahoe Business Association and features original collectables including watercolor and oil paintings, glasswork, sculptures, photography, fine crafts, jewelry and much more." See website for more information.

KIRK SCHOOL SPRING SHOWCASE OF ARTS & CRAFTS

NSSEO, 799 W. Kensington Rd., Mount Prospect IL 60056. (847)463-8105. E-mail: showcase@nsseo.org. Website: www.nsseo.org. Fine arts & crafts fair held annually in March. Indoors. Accepts handmade crafts and other items. Juried. Number exhibitors: 90. Number attendees: 1,600. Free to public. Apply online.

ADDITIONAL INFORMATION Deadline for entry: March. Application fee: none. Space fee: $75. Exhibition space: 10×5. For more information, crafters should e-mail, call or visit website.

KPFA CRAFT FAIR

1929 MLK Jr. Way, Berkeley CA 94704. (510)848-6767 ext. 243. E-mail: events@kpfa.org. Website: www. kpfa.org/craftsfair/. Contact: Jan Etre, coordinator. Fine arts & crafts fair held annually in December. Outdoors. Accepts handmade crafts, ceramics, fiber, glass, jewelry, mixed media, 2D, painting, photography, and sculpture. Juried. Number exhibitors: 200. Number attendees: see website. Admission: $10; disabled, 65+ and children under 17 free. Apply online.

ADDITIONAL INFORMATION Deadline for entry: see website. Application fee: $20. Space fee: varies. Exhibition space: 10×10. For more information, crafters should e-mail, call or visit website.

KRIS KRINGLE HOLIDAY CRAFT SHOW

14735 National Pike, Clear Springs MD 21722. (301)582-1233. Website: www.kriskringlecraftshow. com. Contact: Linda Williams. Fine arts & crafts fair held annually in November. Indoors. Accepts handmade crafts and other mediums. Juried. Number exhibitors: see website. Number attendees: see website. Free to public. Apply online.

ADDITIONAL INFORMATION Deadline for entry: see website. Application fee: see website. Space fee: varies. Exhibition space: varies. For more information, crafters should call or visit website.

LABOR DAY WEEKEND CRAFT FAIR AT THE BAY

38 Charles St., Rochester NH 03867. (603)332-2616. E-mail: info@castleberryfairs.com. Website: www. castleberryfairs.com. Fine arts & crafts fair held annually in August. Indoors & outdoors. Accepts handmade crafts and other items. Juried. Number exhibitors: see website. Number attendees: see website. Free to public. Apply online.

ADDITIONAL INFORMATION Deadline for entry: see website. Application fee: see website. Space fee: $350. Exhibition space: varies. For more information, crafters should e-mail, call or visit website.

LA JOLLA FESTIVAL OF THE ARTS

(760)753-1670. E-mail: admin@ljfa.org. Website: www.ljfa.org. Contact: Ted Pena, executive director. Estab. 1987. Annual fine art show held the 3rd weekend in June. Outdoors. Accepts handmade crafts, sculpture, glass, ceramics, paper, wood, paint, mix, fiber/textile, photography, jewelry. Juried. Awards/prizes: Best of Show in each category. Exhibitors: 195. Number of attendees: 7,000. Admission: $9-$16. Apply via Zapplication.org.

ADDITIONAL INFORMATION Deadline for entry: March 1. Application fee: $25 Space fee: $500-$800. Exhibition space: 10×10, 10×20. For more information see website.

TIPS "Apply on Zaaplication as soon as registration opens in December of the previous year. Take full advantage of social networking and marketing tools to inform customers about the LJFA and how to obtain discount tickets to attend."

LAKE CABLE WOMAN'S CLUB CRAFT SHOW

5725 Fulton Dr., NW, Canton OH 44718. (330)323-3202. E-mail: lcwccraftshow@gmail.com. Contact: Connie Little, chairman. Estab. 1982. Craft show held semi-annually the first Sunday in March & November. Indoors. Accepts handmade crafts. Juried. Number of exhibitors: 60. Number of attendees: 500-800. Free to public. Call or e-mail for application.

ADDITIONAL INFORMATION Deadline for entry: varies. Space fee: Starting at $30. Exhibition space: 8×5. For more information, call or e-mail.

TIPS "We look for quality and variety."

LAKEFRONT FESTIVAL OF ART

700 N. Art Museum Dr., Milwaukee WI 53202. (414)224-3853. E-mail: lfoa@mam.org. Website: www.mam.org/lfoa. Contact: Krista Renfrew, festival director. Estab. 1963. Fine art show held annually the 3rd week in June. Indoors & outdoors. Accepts printmaking, sculpture, wood, painting, jewelry, ceramics, digital, drawing/pastel, MM2, fiber-non, wearable fiber, glass, photography, metal, NM. Juried. Awards/prizes: Artist Awards (10), Honorable Mention (10), Sculpture Garden. Exhibitors: 176. Number of attendees: 25,000. Admission: $17 general; $10 members & advance; 12 & under free. Apply via Zapplication.org.

ADDITIONAL INFORMATION Deadline for entry: November 25. Application fee: $35. Space fee: $500; $600 corner. Exhibition Space: 10×10. For more information send e-mail or visit website.

LAKE NORMAN FOLK ART FESTIVAL

Hickory Museum of Art, 243 Third Ave., N.E., Hickory NC 28601. (828)327-8576. E-mail: blohr@hickorymuseumofart.org. Website: www.lakenormanfolkartfestival.com. Fine arts & crafts fair held annually in October. Outdoors. Accepts handmade crafts and other mediums. Juried. Number exhibitors: see website. Number attendees: see website. Free to public. Apply online.

ADDITIONAL INFORMATION Deadline for entry: July. Application fee: none. Space fee: $75. Exhibition space: see website. For more information, crafters should e-mail, call or visit website.

LAKESHORE ART FESTIVAL

380 W. Western, Suite 202, Muskegon MI 49440. (231)724-3176. Fax: (231)728-7281. E-mail: artfest@muskegon.org. Website: www.lakeshoreartfestival.org. Contact: Carla Flanders, director. Estab. 2013. Fine arts & crafts show held annually the July 4 & 5.

Outdoors. Accepts handmade crafts. Juried. Awards/prizes: First place/Best in Show, $1,000; 2nd place, $800; 3rd place, $600; Honorable Mention, $400; Committee's Choice, $200. Exhibitors: 300. Number of attendees: 50,000. Free to public. Apply via website or Zapplication.org.

ADDITIONAL INFORMATION Deadline for entry: March. Application fee: $30. Space fee: $250 fine art/craft; $180 craft, Children's Lane, Artisan Food Market. Exhibition space: 12×12. Average sales: $800-1,200. For more information, e-mail, call or visit website.

TIPS "The Lakeshore Art Festival is seeking unique, quality, handcrafted products so be sure your items fall within these areas. Also, we strongly recommend that all images submitted are not only good quality images but also of your best pieces so that we can accurately access your work."

LAKE ST. LOUIS FARMERS AND ARTISTS MARKET

Lake St Louis Farmers and Artists Market, P.O. Box 91, Warrenton MO 63383-0091. (314)495-2531. E-mail: lakestlouisfarmersmarket@gmail.com. Website: www.themeadowsatlsl.com. Farmer & craft market held annually every Saturday, April-October. Outoors. Accepts handmade crafts, jewelry, art, pottery, soap, candles, clothing, wood crafts and other crafts. Exhibitors: varies. Number of attendees: varies. Free to public. Apply online.

ADDITIONAL INFORMATION Deadline for entry: see website. Application fee: none. Space fee: $325 (full season); $25 (daily vendor). Exhibition space: 10×10. For more information, crafters should e-mail, visit website or call.

LAKEVIEW EAST FESTIVAL OF THE ARTS

(773)348-8608. Website: www.lakevieweastfestivalofthearts.com. "The Lakeview East Festival of the Arts showcases more than 150 juried artists featuring paintings, sculpture, photography, furniture, jewelry and more. These original pieces are for sale in a wide range of price ranges. In addition to the art, the Festival has become a center of activity for the weekend with live demonstrations, entertainment stages, family activities and a garden oasis. Lakeview East is a dynamic and diversified neighborhood community rich in culture, history and the arts. The Lakeview East Chamber of Commerce works hand in hand with their local residents and business owners and is pleased to offer its neighbors and the Chicagoland area with one of the premier fine art outdoor festivals." For more information, sponsorship and volunteer opportunities, please call (773) 348-8608.

LAKEWOOD ARTS FESTIVAL

The Lakewood Arts Festival, P.O. Box 771288, Lakewood OH 44107. (216)529-6651. Website: www.lakewoodartsfest.org. Fine arts & crafts fair held annually in August. Outdoors. Accepts handmade crafts and other mediums. Juried. Number exhibitors: 164. Number attendees: 10,000. Free to public. Apply online.

ADDITIONAL INFORMATION Deadline for entry: March. Application fee: $10. Space fee: $100. Exhibition space: 10×10. For more information, crafters should call or visit website.

LAKE WORTH BEACH ART FEST

270 Central Blvd., Suite 107B, Jupiter FL 33458. (561)746-6615. Fax: (561)746-6528. E-mail: info@artfestival.com. Website: www.artfestival.com. "This oceanfront show will take place directly on the A1A (South Ocean Blvd) at Lake Avenue. This area is home to a beautiful beach, upscale restaurants and popular retail shops. Venue: A1A (South Ocean Blvd) & Lake Ave in Lake Worth Beach Public Admission: Free, no gate. Parking: Daytime Available for RVs and standard size vehicles. Spaces: 10×10, 10×15 and 10×20 booth spaces. Show hours: Saturday & Sunday 10am-5pm. Set-up: Saturday Morning at 5 a.m. Security: Overnight Security will be onsite." See website for more information.

LANDSDOWNE ARTS FESTIVAL

E-mail: jennifer@hoffcomm.com. Website: www.lansdowneartsfestival.com. "The Lansdowne Arts Festival is a weekend-long event featuring an array of creative and performing arts, including painting, crafts, sculpture, jewelry, live music, demonstrations, and children's events. Set in the historic suburb of Lansdowne, Pennsylvania, the festival has grown to include dozens of exhibiting artists and musical acts. All festival events will be held at the historic Twentieth Century Club at 84 S. Lansdowne Avenue." See website for more information.

LAS OLAS ART FAIR

270 Central Blvd., Suite 107B, Jupiter FL 33458. (561)746-6615. Fax: (561)746-6528. E-mail: info@ArtFestival.com. Website: www.artfestival.com. "The Las Olas Art Fair is ranked as one of the top 100 art festivals in the nation and continues to be one of the most anticipated art events in the area. People come out yearly to see more than 150 artists display their work in what looks like a mini art gallery lined along the street. Meet the creators of the art on display; commission a specific piece; ask questions about techniques; learn the sources of their inspirations; and purchase fine works of art at affordable prices. No matter what you're looking for, you'll be sure to find it on Las Olas at this always anticipated, juried art fair."

LATIMER HALL ARTS & CRAFT SHOW

103 Towne Lake Parkway, Woodstock GA 30188. (347)216-4691. E-mail: mainstreetcraftshow@yahoo.com. Website: www.mainstreetcraftshow.com. Contact: Deb Skroce, director. Estab. 2013. Monthly arts & crafts. Indoors & outdoors. Accepts handmade crafts, repurposed items. Exhibitors: 50. Number of attendees: 1,000. Free to public. Apply via e-mail or website.

ADDITIONAL INFORMATION Deadline for entry: see website or contact by e-mail. Space fee: $50 & $30. Exhibition space: 10×10, 10×9, 9×6. For more information, e-mail or see website.

TIPS "Share the event page on Facebook."

LAUDERDALE BY THE SEA CRAFT FESTIVAL

270 Central Blvd., Suite 107B, Jupiter FL 33458. (561)746-6615. Fax: (561)746-6528. E-mail: info@artfestival.com. Website: www.artfestival.com. "Come visit with more than 100 crafters exhibiting and selling their work in an outdoor gallery. From photog-

raphy, paintings, sculpture, jewelry and more showcased from local and traveling crafters, your visit to Lauderdale By the Sea is promised to be a feast for the senses. This spectacular weekend festival is not to be missed. Spanning along A1A and Commercial Blvd., the venue is right off the beach and is set up amongst the restaurants and retailers."

LEAGUE OF NH CRAFTSMEN ANNUAL FAIR

League of NH Craftsmen, 49 S. Main St., Suite 100, Concord NH 03301-5080. (603)224-3375. Fax: (603)225-8452. E-mail: twiltse@nhcrafts.org. Website: www.nhcrafts.org/craftsmens-fair-overview.php. Contact: Susie Lowe-Stockwell, executive director. See website for more information.

LEESBURG FINE ART FESTIVAL

Paragon Fine Art Festivals, 8258 Midnight Pass Rd., Sarasota FL 34242. (941)487-8061. Fax: (941)346-0302. E-mail: admin@paragonartfest.com. Website: www.paragonartevents.com/lee. Contact: Bill Kinney. Fine arts & crafts fair held annually in September. Outdoors. Accepts handmade crafts, ceramics, fiber, glass, jewelry, mixed media, painting, photography, and sculpture. Juried. Number exhibitors: 115. Number attendees: varies. Free to public. Apply online.

ADDITIONAL INFORMATION Deadline for entry: July. Application fee: $30. Space fee: $395. Exhibition space: see website. For more information, crafters should e-mail, call or visit website.

LEVIS COMMONS FINE ART FAIR

The Guild of Artists & Artisans, 118 N. Fourth Ave., Ann Arbor MI 48104. (734)662-3382 ext. 101. E-mail: info@theguild.org; nicole@theguild.org. Website: www.theguild.org. Contact: Nicole McKay, artist relations director. Fine arts & crafts fair held annually in September. Outdoors. Accepts handmade crafts, jewelry, ceramics, painting, glass, photography, fiber and more. Juried. Number exhibitors: 130. Number attendees: 35,000. Free to public. Apply online.

ADDITIONAL INFORMATION Deadline for entry: April. Application fee: $25 members; $30 nonmembers. Space fee: varies. Exhibition space: varies.

For more information, crafters should e-mail, call or visit website.

LEWISTON ART FESTIVAL

P.O. Box 1, Lewiston NY 14092. (716)754-0166. Fax: (716)754-9166. E-mail: director@artcouncil.org. Website: www.artcouncil.org. Estab. 1966. Arts & crafts show held annually in August. Outdoors. Accepts handmade crafts, drawing, printmaking, computer generated art, 2D/3D mixed media, photography, ceramics, fiber, glass, jewelry, sculpture, wood. Juried. Exhibitors: 175. Number of attendees: 35,000. Free to public. Apply online.

ADDITIONAL INFORMATION Deadline for entry: early May. Application fee: $15. Space fee: $175. Exhibition space: 10×10. For more information, crafters should e-mail, visit website.

LINCOLN ARTS FESTIVAL

E-mail: melissa@artscene.org. Website: www.artscene.org/lincoln-arts-festival. Fine arts & crafts fair held annually in September. Outdoors. Accepts handmade crafts, jewelry, ceramics, painting, glass, photography, fiber and more. Juried. Awards/prizes: $6,000 in awards & prizes. Number exhibitors: see website. Number attendees: varies. Free to public. Apply online.

ADDITIONAL INFORMATION Deadline for entry: May. Application fee: $25. Space fee: $190 (10×10); $310 (10×20). Exhibition space: 10×10; 10×20. For more information, crafters should e-mail or visit website.

LINCOLNSHIRE ART FESTIVAL

E-mail: info@amdurproductions.com. Website: www.amdurproductions.com. Fine arts & crafts fair held annually in August. Outdoors. Accepts handmade crafts, jewelry, ceramics, painting, glass, photography, fiber and more. Juried. Awards/prizes: given at festival. Number exhibitors: 130. Number attendees: 30,000. Free to public. Apply online.

ADDITIONAL INFORMATION Deadline for entry: January. Application fee: $25. Space fee: $430. Exhibition space: 10×10. For more information, crafters should e-mail or visit website.

LITTLE FALLS ARTS & CRAFTS FAIR

200 1st St. NW, Little Falls MN 56345-1365. (320)632-5155. Fax: (320)632-2122. E-mail: artsandcrafts@littlefallsmnchamber.com. Website: www.littlefalls mnchamber.com. Contact: Stacey, registrar. Estab. 1972. Arts & crafts show held annually in September. Outdoors. Accepts handmade crafts. Juried. Exhibitors: 600. Number of attendees: 125,000. Free to public. Apply online .

ADDITIONAL INFORMATION Deadline for entry: March 20. Application fee: $10. Space fee: $195. Exhibition space: 10×10. Average sales: $5,000. For more information send e-mail, call or visit website.

TIPS "Have quality product that is reasonably priced!"

LONG GROVE ART FEST

Star Events, 1609 W. Belmont Ave., 2nd Floor, Chicago IL 60657. E-mail: info@starevents.com. Website: www.starevents.com/festivals/long-grove-art-fest. "More than 100 local artists will captivate festival goers with their inspirations talents in various art forms including oil, acrylic, watercolor, jewelry, sculpture, photography, wood, fiber, glass, paper, metal, and mixed media, all in the relaxed setting of the streets of Long Grove. Artists will also be able to submit their 2D and 3D creations in to the festival's annual art competition." See website for more information.

LONG ISLAND STREET FAIRS

(516)442-6000. Fax: (516)543-5170. E-mail: alan@nassaucountycraftshows.com. Website: www.long islandstreetfairs.com. Contact: Alan Finchley, owner. Estab. 2008. Art & craft shows, seasonal/holiday and street fairs held year round on Long Island. Indoors & outdoors. Accepts handmade crafts and other mediums. Juried. Exhibitors: 100. Number of attendees: varies by event. Most events free to public. Apply online.

ADDITIONAL INFORMATION Deadline for entry: when events are sold out. Application fee: none. Space fee: $175. Exhibition space: 10×10. Average sales: $1,000. For more information, crafters should e-mail, call, send SASE or visit website.

LONG'S PARK ART & CRAFT FESTIVAL

Long's Park Amphitheater Foundation, 630 Janet Ave., Suite A-111, Lancaster PA 17601-4541. (717)735-8883. Website: www.longspark.org/art-craft-festival. Fine arts & crafts fair held annually Labor Day Weekend. Outdoors. Accepts handmade crafts, jewelry, ceramics, painting, glass, photography, fiber and more. Juried. Number exhibitors: 200. Number attendees: varies. Admission: see website. Apply online.

ADDITIONAL INFORMATION Deadline for entry: February. Application fee: see website. Space fee: $510 (single); $645 (double). Exhibition space: 10×10 (single); 10×20 (double) . For more information, crafters should call or visit website.

LORING PARK ART FESTIVAL

E-mail: info@loringparkartfestival.com. Website: www.loringparkartfestival.com. "The Loring Park Art Festival is produced by Artists for Artists LLP, an organization of experienced artists. The juried festival is a two day event in Loring Park near downtown Minneapolis. The hours are Saturday, 10-6 and Sunday 10-5. The festival consists of 140 visual artists displaying their orginal work in 12×12 booths, strolling musicians, scheduled stage performances, children's activities and food booths. The artwork presented will be from a variety of media including painting, photography, printmaking, handmade paper, wood, jewelry, clay, sculpture, fiber, mixed media and glass. Within these categories will be a variety of styles from traditional to abstract in a variety of price ranges with the goal being 'something for everyone.'" See website for more information.

LOS ALTOS ROTARY FINE ART SHOW

Website: www.rotaryartshow.com. "Each year, the Los Altos Rotary Club presents Fine Art in the Park—one of the Bay Area's premier open-air art shows, featuring original, juried works by some 170 artists. Fine art pieces range from paintings and sculpture to ceramics, jewelry and unique gifts. Entertainment, food and beverages make this an ideal occasion for shopping and family fun. As you stroll through the lovely park, viewing first-rate art, you'll take comfort knowing that your purchase goes to support a great cause. All proceeds of the Rotary Fine Art in the Park show go to support a wide range of community service agencies in the Bay Area, and support international development projects in places like Nepal, Mexico, Malaysia and Afghanistan. Come for a day of fun and great art. There is free parking at Los Altos High School, with shuttles to the park." See website for more information.

LOS OLAS ART FAIR

270 Central Blvd., Suite 107B, Jupiter FL 33458. (561)746-6615. Fax: (561)746-6528. E-mail: info@ artfestival.com. Website: www.artfestival.com. "The Las Olas Art Fair is ranked as one of the top 100 art festivals in the nation and continues to be one of the most anticipated art events in the area. People come out yearly to see more than 150 artists display their work in what looks like a mini art gallery lined along the street. Meet the creators of the art on display; commission a specific piece; ask questions about techniques; learn the sources of their inspirations; and purchase fine works of art at affordable prices. No matter what you're looking for, you'll be sure to find it on Las Olas at this always anticipated, juried art fair." See website for more information.

LOUISVILLE FESTIVAL OF THE ARTS

270 Central Blvd., Suite 107B, Jupiter FL 33458. (561)746-6615. Fax: (561)746-6528. E-mail: info@ artfestival.com. Website: www.artfestival.com. "Paddock Shops (formerly the Summit), located just East of downtown Louisville, brings culture and fine art to the art lovers of its community. Join us for a weekend of art in the city that defines southern hospitality. You'll have the opportunity to meet America's finest artisans and crafters and peruse their work. Purchase their handcrafted jewelry, pottery, sculptures, photography, and much more. Bring the family down to view the great artwork, dine at one of the many restaurants, and peruse the many shops and boutiques! This show will contain a segregated craft market place." See website for more information.

MADEIRA BEACH CRAFT FESTIVAL

270 Central Blvd., Suite 107B, Jupiter FL 33458. (561)746-6615. Fax: (561)746-6528. E-mail: info@art festival.com. Website: www.artfestival.com. "Join us in Madeira Beach to browse and purchase a wide va-

riety of ceramics, jewelry, stained glass, metal works and much more. Our Green Market offers live flora, freshly popped kettle corn, gourmet spices, and sauces. Come meet and visit with some of the nation's best crafters at this free, weekend event, where you're sure to find something for everyone on your gift list."

MAGNOLIA BLOSSOM FESTIVAL

Magnolia/Columbia County Chamber of Commerce, P.O. Box 866, Magnolia AR 71754. (870)901-2216; (870)693-5265. E-mail: jpate006@centurytel.net; jpate002@centurytel.net. Website: www.blossom festival.org. Craft show held annually in May. Outdoors. Accepts handmade crafts, ceramics, paintings, jewelry, glass, photography, wearable art and other mediums. Juried. Number exhibitors: see website. Number attendees: varies. Free to public. Apply online.

ADDITIONAL INFORMATION Deadline for entry: late March. Application fee: none. Space fee: varies. Exhibition space: varies. For more information, crafters should call, e-mail or visit website.

MAINE CRAFT GUILD'S MOUNT DESERT IS-LAND ANNUAL DIRECTIONS SHOW

The Maine Crafts Guild, 369 Old Union Rd., Washington ME 04574. (207)557-3276. E-mail: mdi. show@mainecraftsguild.com. Website: www.maine craftsguild.com/shows. "The Maine Craft Guild's Mount Desert Island Directions Show is often referred to as the most outstanding, most successful, and longest running craft show in Maine. At the annual show, 80 of Maine's finest craftspeople will fill the newly renovated gymnasium and cafeteria at the Mount Desert Island High School with their work, transforming the space into a gallery-like setting of carefully designed individual displays. Come and meet extraordinary artisans and purchase work of heirloom quality handmade here in Maine. Admission: $6 adults; children under 18 free."

MAINSAIL ARTS FESTIVAL

E-mail: artist@mainsailart.org. Website: www.main sailart.org. Fine arts & crafts fair held annually in April. Outdoors. Accepts handmade crafts, ceramics, digital art, fibers, glass, graphics, jewelry, metal, mixed media, oil/acrylic, photography, sculpture, watercolor and wood . Juried. Awards/prizes: $60,000 in cash awards. Number exhibitors: 270. Number attendees: 100,000. Free to public. Apply online.

ADDITIONAL INFORMATION Deadline for entry: December. Application fee: $35. Space fee: $275. Exhibition space: 10×10. For more information, crafters should e-mail or visit website.

MAIN STREET FORT WORTH ARTS FESTIVAL

777 Taylor St., Suite 100, Fort Worth TX 76102. (817)336-2787. Fax: (817)335-3113. E-mail: festival info@dfwi.org. Website: www.mainstreetartsfest.org. "Presented by Downtown Fort Worth Initiatives, Inc. MAIN ST. has a history of attracting tens of thousands of people annually during the four-day visual arts, entertainment and cultural event. MAIN ST. showcases a nationally recognized fine art and fine craft juried art fair, live concerts, performance artists and street performers on the streets of downtown Fort Worth. We invite a total of 223 artists to the show (including 12 Emerging Artists), which includes approximately 26 award artists from the previous years' event. We project our images at our jury using state-of-the-art projectors direct from the exact electronic files submitted by the artists." See website for more information.

MAIN STREET TO THE ROCKIES ART FESTIVAL

270 Central Blvd., Suite 107B, Jupiter FL 33458. (561)746-6615. Fax: (561)746-6528. E-mail: info@art festival.com. Website: www.artfestival.com. "Nestled in the magnificent area near the Rocky Mountains, Frisco offers visitors the authentic Colorado experience. Playing host to many signature events, and community gatherings, Frisco truly is the Main Street of the Rockies. The town of Frisco offers great dining, vacation rentals, hotels, restaurants, attractions and scenic places to visit in the mountains. Please join us for the Annual Main Street to the Rockies Art Festival. Browse and purchase art from the finest artists in the country. The original artists will be on-hand showcasing glass, sculpture, mixed media, paintings, photography, jewelry, ceramics, and more. No matter what you're looking for, you'll be sure to find it among the various array of artists participating in this juried art fair. As always, admission and parking are free." See website for more information.

MAKER FAIRE—BAY AREA

E-mail: makers@makerfaire.com. Website: www.makerfaire.com. "Part science fair, part county fair, and part something entirely new, Maker Faire is an all-ages gathering of tech enthusiasts, crafters, educators, tinkerers, hobbyists, engineers, science clubs, authors, artists, students, and commercial exhibitors. All of these makers come to Maker Faire to show what they have made and to share what they have learned. The launch of Maker Faire in the Bay Area in 2006 demonstrated the popularity of making and interest among legions of aspiring makers to participate in hands-on activities and learn new skills at the event. A record 195,000 people attended the two flagship Maker Faires in the Bay Area and New York in 2013, with 44% of attendees first timers at the Bay Area event, and 61% in New York. It's a family event, 50% attend the event with children. Maker Faire is primarily designed to be forward-looking, showcasing makers who are exploring new forms and new technologies. But it's not just for the novel in technical fields; Maker Faire features innovation and experimentation across the spectrum of science, engineering, art, performance and craft." See website for more information.

MAKER FAIRE—NEW YORK

E-mail: makers@makerfaire.com. Website: www.makerfaire.com. "Part science fair, part county fair, and part something entirely new, Maker Faire is an all-ages gathering of tech enthusiasts, crafters, educators, tinkerers, hobbyists, engineers, science clubs, authors, artists, students, and commercial exhibitors. All of these 'makers' come to Maker Faire to show what they have made and to share what they have learned. The launch of Maker Faire in the Bay Area in 2006 demonstrated the popularity of making and interest among legions of aspiring makers to participate in hands-on activities and learn new skills at the event. A record 195,000 people attended the two flagship Maker Faires in the Bay Area and New York in 2013, with 44% of attendees first timers at the Bay Area event, and 61% in New York. It's a family event, 50% attend the event with children. Maker Faire is primarily designed to be forward-looking, showcasing makers who are exploring new forms and new technologies. But it's not just for the novel in technical fields; Maker Faire features innovation and experimentation across the spectrum of science, engineering, art, performance and craft." See website for more information.

MAMMOTH LAKES FINE ARTS & CRAFTS FESTIVAL

Pacific Fine Arts Festivals, P.O. Box 280, Pine Grove CA 95665. (209)267-4394. Fax: (209)267-4395. E-mail: pfa@pacificfinearts.com. Website: www.pacificfinearts.com. "This free event, which runs from 10 a.m. to 5 p.m. each day, will give attendees the opportunity to meet with talented artists and artisans from throughout the western U.S. as they present their original works against the majestic background of the Sierra Nevada mountains. On display will be a wide variety of arts and crafts including photography, watercolor and oil paintings, ceramics, jewelry, woodwork and much more." See website for more information.

MANAYUNK ARTS FESTIVAL

4312 Main St., Philadelphia PA 19127. (215)482-9565. E-mail: info@manayunk.org. Website: www.manayunk.com. Contact: Caitlin Maloney, director of marketing & events. Estab. 1990. Arts & craft show held annually late June. Outdoors. Accepts handmade crafts, fiber, glass, ceramics, jewelry, mixed media, painting, photography, wood, sculpture. Juried. Awards/prizes: Best in each category; Best in Show. Exhibitors: 300. Number of attendees: 200,000. Free to public. Apply via Zapplication.org.

ADDITIONAL INFORMATION Deadline for entry: March 1. Application fee: $30. Space fee: $450. Exhibition Space: 10×10. Average sales: $2,000-7,000. For more information, e-mail or call.

TIPS "Displaying your work in a professional manner and offering items at a variety of price points always benefits the artist."

MANDEVILLE CRAFT SHOW

812 Park Ave., Mandeville LA 70448. (985)373-2307. E-mail: dasistas@outlook.com. Website: www.

mandevillecraftshow.com. Contact: Joy Frosch, manager. Estab. 2013. Bi-annual arts & crafts show held in early April & late September. Indoors & outdoors. Accepts handmade crafts. Juried. Exhibitors: 70. Number of attendees: 1,200. Admission: $2 adults; children 12 & under free. See website for application.

ADDITIONAL INFORMATION Deadline for entry: February 7. Space fee: varies. Exhibition space: 8×8, 8×16, 10×10, 10×20. Average sales: $3,700. For more information, e-mail, call or see website.

TIPS "Presentation is everything—look online for suggestions on set-up and presentation."

MARCO ISLAND FESTIVAL OF THE ARTS

270 Central Blvd., Suite 107B, Jupiter FL 33458. (561)746-6615. Fax: (561)746-6528. E-mail: info@artfestival.com. Website: www.artfestival.com. Fine arts & crafts show held on Marco Island. See website for more information and to apply.

MARION ARTS FESTIVAL

1225 6th Ave., Ste. 100, Marion IA 52302. Website: www.marionartsfestival.com. Fine arts & crafts fair held annually in May. Outdoors. Accepts handmade crafts, jewelry, ceramics, painting, photography, digital, printmaking and more. Juried. Awards/prizes: Best of Show, IDEA Award. Number exhibitors: 50. Number attendees: 14,000. Free to public. Apply via Zapplication.org.

ADDITIONAL INFORMATION Deadline for entry: January. Application fee: $25. Space fee: $225. Exhibition space: 10×10. For more information, crafters should visit website.

MARKET ON THE GREEN ARTS & CRAFTS FAIR

(203)333-0506. E-mail: crdraw9@aol.com. Outdoor show featuring 70 quality artisans, food vendors, bake booth, flowers and raffle booth. Held annually in May. Call or e-mail for more information.

MARSHFIELD ART FAIR

New Visions Gallery, 1000 N. Oak Ave., Marshfield WI 54449. (715)387-5562. E-mail: newvisions.gallery@frontier.com. Website: www.marshfieldartfair.

weebly.com. "Share a Marshfield tradition with family and friends at this FREE community celebration of the arts, held each year on Mother's Day. Marshfield Art Fair offers a wide variety of fine art and craft by more than 100 Midwestern artists. Musicians and performers entertain throughout the day. Hands-On-Art activities are available for kids." See website for more information.

MCGREGOR SPRING ARTS & CRAFTS FESTIVAL

McGregor-Marquette Chamber of Commerce, P.O. Box 105, McGregor IA 52157. (800)896-0910; (563)873-2186. E-mail: mcgregormarquettechamber@gmail.com. Website: www.mcgreg-marq.org. Fine arts & crafts fair held annually in May & October. Indoors & outdoors. Accepts handmade crafts, jewelry, ceramics, painting, photography, digital, printmaking and more. Number exhibitors: see website. Number attendees: varies. Free to public. Apply via online.

ADDITIONAL INFORMATION Deadline for entry: see website. Application fee: none. Space fee: $75 outdoor; $100 indoor. Exhibition space: 10×10. For more information, crafters should e-mail, call or visit website.

MESA ARTS FESTIVAL

Mesa Arts Center, One E. Main St., Mesa AZ 85201. (480)644-6627. Fax: (480)644-6503. E-mail: shawn.lawson@mesaartscenter.com. Website: www.mesaartscenter.com. Fine arts & crafts fair held annually in December. Outdoors. Accepts handmade crafts, jewelry, ceramics, painting, photography, digital, printmaking and more. Number exhibitors: see website. Number attendees: varies. Free to public. Apply online.

ADDITIONAL INFORMATION Deadline for entry: see website. Application fee: $25. Space fee: $250. Exhibition space: 10×10. For more information, crafters should e-mail, call or visit website.

MESA MACFEST

E-mail: info@macfestmesa.com. Website: www.macfestmesa.com. "The Mission of Mesa Arts and Crafts Festival (MACfest) is to provide an environment that encourages the economic and artistic growth of emerging and established artists and crafters while revitalizing downtown Mesa and building a sense of community. MACFest is a free event featuring unique artist creations, music and fun for the whole family." See website for more information.

MESQUITE QUILT SHOW

Rutherford Recreation Center, 900 Rutherford Dr., P.O. Box 850137, Mesquite TX 75185-0137. (972)523-7672. Website: www.mesquitequiltguildinc.com. Juried quilt show. See website for more information.

THE MIAMI PROJECT

Art Market Productions, 109 S. 5th St., Suite 407, Brooklyn NY 11249. (212)518-6912. Fax: (212)518-7142. E-mail: info@art-mrkt.com. Website: www.miami-project.com. "Miami Project is a contemporary and modern art fair that takes place during Miami's art fair week. Working with a focused selection of galleries from around the globe, Miami Project presents a diverse selection of work by today's leading artists. What sets Miami Project apart is its unique venue which is constructed for the optimal viewing experience for both dealers and collectors alike." See website for more information.

MICHIGAN FIRST SUMMER IN THE VILLAGE

City of Lathrup Village, 27400 Southfield Road, Lathrup Village MI 48076. (248)557-2600 ext. 224. E-mail: recreation@lathrupvillage.org. Website: www.summerinthevillage.com. Estab. 2003. Arts & crafts show held annually in June. Outdoors. Accepts handmade crafts, ceramics, fiber, glass, jewelry, metal, mixed media, painting, photography, printmaking, sculpture, wood. Juried. Exhibitors: varies. Number of attendees: varies. Free to public. Apply online.

ADDITIONAL INFORMATION Deadline for entry: see website. Application fee: $20. Space fee: $95. Exhibition space: 10×10. For more information, crafters should e-mail, visit website or call.

MIDSUMMER ARTS FAIRE

P.O. Box 24, Quincy IL 62306. (217)779-2285. Fax: (217)222-8698. E-mail: info@artsfaire.org. Website:

www.artsfaire.org. Contact: Kris Eyler, coordinator. Fine art show held annually in June. Outdoors. Accepts photography, paintings, pottery, jewelry. Juried. Awards/prizes: various totaling $5,000. Exhibitors: 60. Number of attendees: 7,000. Free to public. Apply via Zapplication.org.

ADDITIONAL INFORMATION Deadline for entry: February 28. Application fee: $20. Space fee: $100. Exhibition space: 10×10. Average sales: $2,500. For more information, crafters should e-mail, call, see Facebook page or visit website.

TIPS "Variety of price points with several options at a lower price point as well."

MIDWEST FIBER & FOLK ART FAIR

P.O. Box 754, Crystal Lake IL 60039-0754. (815)276-2537. E-mail: carol@artaffairs.org. Website: www.fiberandfolk.com. "The Midwest Fiber & Folk Art Fair annually on the 1st weekend of August. Come on out for shopping in the Marketplace, featuring both supplies and finished goods (wearable art), take a workshop, watch the demonstrations, listen to the music, pet an alpaca, or enjoy the food." See website for more information.

MILLENIUM ART FESTIVAL

Amdur Productions, P.O. Box 550, Highland Park IL, 60035. (847)926-4300. E-mail: info@amdurproductions.com. Website: www.amdurproductions.com. Fine arts & crafts fair held annually in May. Outdoors. Accepts handmade crafts and other mediums. Juried. Exhibitors: 110. Number of attendees: varies. Admission: Free to public. Apply online.

ADDITIONAL INFORMATION Deadline for entry: see website. Application fee: see website. Space fee: $495. Exhibition space: see website. For more information, crafters should e-mail, visit website or call.

MILL VALLEY FALL ARTS FESTIVAL

P.O. Box 300, Mill Valley CA 94942. (415)381-8090. E-mail: mvfafartists@gmail.com. Website: www.mvfaf.org. "The Mill Valley Fall Arts Festival has been recognized as a fine art and craft show of high-quality original artwork. The festival draws well-educated buyers from nearby affluent neighborhoods of Marin County and the greater San Francisco Bay Area. The

event provides an exceptional opportunity for the sale of unique, creative and high-end work." See website for more information.

MILWAUKEE AVENUE ARTS FESTIVAL

E-mail: info@iamlogansquare.com. Website: www.milwaukeeavenueartsfestival.org. A celebration of the art, music and culture of Logan Square. See website for more information.

MILWAUKEE DOMES ART FESTIVAL

Website: www.milwaukeedomesartfestival.com. Fine arts & crafts fair held annually in August. Indoors & outdoors. Accepts handmade crafts, jewelry, ceramics, painting, photography, digital, printmaking and more. Juried. Awards/prizes: $10,500 in awards and prizes. Number exhibitors: see website. Number attendees: varies. Free to public. Apply online.

ADDITIONAL INFORMATION Deadline for entry: see website. Application fee: $35. Space fee: $250 outdoor; $450 indoor. Exhibition space: 10×10. For more information, visit website.

MINNE-FAIRE: A MAKER AND DIY EXPOSITION

E-mail: fair@tcmaker.org. Website: www.tcmaker.org. "This two day event will be returning to its roots. Admission will be free, though we'll happily accept donations to keep it running. We'll be showing off our expanded space and capabilities and celebrating all things Maker—that is after all what this is all about. If you're interested in participating, feel free to e-mail us at fair@tcmaker.org." See website for more information.

☺ MINNESOTA WOMEN'S ART FESTIVAL

E-mail: naomiotr@aol.com. Website: www.womensartfestival.com. "The mission of the Women's Art Festival is to provide a welcoming place for women artists to show and sell their creations and to provide a fun and festive atmosphere for guest to shop, gather and enjoy community. Supporting local women artists of all experience levels, from first time exhibitors to experienced professionals. We are a non-juried show with the expectation that all goods are of excellent quality, made and sold by local women. We do not accept dealers or importers and define local as any woman who wants to travel to Minneapolis for a day of fun, camaraderie, community and creativity. Now held at the Midtown YWCA in Minneapolis, the event has grown to include over 100 women artists working in a large variety of media. There is live music by women performers throughout the day and a women-owned coffee shop providing food, beverages and treats. Artists and guests alike comment on the quality of the artistic work, the fun and comfortable atmosphere, the caliber of the music and the wonderful addition of good food, good coffee and the chance to see good friends." See website for more information.

MISSION FEDERAL ARTWALK

210 Columbia St., San Diego CA 92101. (619)615-1090. Fax: (619)615-1099. E-mail: info@artwalksandiego.org. Website: www.artwalksandiego.org. Fine arts & crafts fair held annually in April. Outdoors. Accepts handmade crafts, jewelry, ceramics, painting, photography, digital, printmaking and more. Juried. Number exhibitors: 350. Number attendees: 90,000. Free to public. Apply online.

ADDITIONAL INFORMATION Deadline for entry: January. Application fee: none. Space fee: varies. Exhibition space: varies. For more information, crafters should e-mail, call or visit website.

MOLLIE MCGEE'S HOLIDAY MARKET

Mollie McGee's Market, P.O. BOX 6324, Longmont CO 80501. (303)772-0649. E-mail: mollie@molliemcgee.com. Website: www.molliemcgee.com. Fine arts & crafts fair held annually in October & November. Outdoors. Accepts handmade crafts and other mediums. Juried. Number exhibitors: see website. Number attendees: varies. Free to public. Apply online.

ADDITIONAL INFORMATION Deadline for entry: see website. Application fee: none. Space fee: varies. Exhibition space: varies. For more information, crafters should e-mail, call or visit website.

MONTE SANO ART FESTIVAL

706 Randolph Ave., Huntsville AL 35801. (256)653-3654. E-mail: curtisbenzle@gmail.com. Website: www.montesanoartfestival.com. Contact: Curtis Benzle, director. Estab. 1998. Annual arts & crafts show held in September. Outdoors. Accepts handmade crafts, painting, sculpture, photography, prints. Juried. Exhibitors: 130. Number of attendees: 4,000. Admission: $7. Apply via website.

ADDITIONAL INFORMATION Deadline for entry: May 1. Application fee: $15. Space fee: $125. Exhibition space: 100 sq. ft. Average sales: $2,000. For more information see website.

TIPS "Apply with a quality booth slide."

MONUMENT SQUARE ART FESTIVAL

The Racine Arts Council, 316 Sixth St., Racine WI 53403. E-mail: jeff@theelementsgallery.com. Website: www.monumentsquareartfest.com. Fine arts & crafts fair held annually in May. Outdoors. Accepts handmade crafts and other mediums. Juried. Number exhibitors: see website. Number attendees: varies. Free to public. Apply online.

ADDITIONAL INFORMATION Deadline for entry: April. Application fee: none. Space fee: varies. Exhibition space: varies. For more information, crafters should e-mail or visit website.

MORNING GLORY FINE CRAFT FAIR

(262)894-0038. E-mail: bethhoffman@wi.rr.com. Website: www.wdcc.org. Contact: Beth Hoffman. Fine craft fair held annually in August. Outdoors. Accepts handmade crafts and other mediums. Juried. Awards/prizes: $3,000 in cash and prizes. Number exhibitors: see website. Number attendees: varies. Free to public. Apply via Zapplication.org.

ADDITIONAL INFORMATION Deadline for entry: March. Application fee: $35. Space fee: varies. Exhibition space: varies. For more information, crafters should e-mail, call or visit website.

MOUNT DORA ARTS FESTIVAL

Mount Dora Center for the Arts, 138 East Fifth Ave., Mount Dora FL 32757. (352)383-0880. Fax: (352)383-7753. Website: www.mountdoracenterforthearts.org/arts-festival. "A juried fine arts festival, for art lovers, casual festival-goers and families, nothing compares to the Mount Dora Arts Festival. In addition to the endless rows of fine art, including oil paintings, watercolors, acrylics, clay, sculpture and photography, the festival features local and regional musical entertainment at a main stage in Donnelly Park." See website for more information.

MOUNT MARY STARVING ARTIST SHOW
Website: www.mtmary.edu/alumnae/events/ starving-artists-show.html. Contact: Alumnae & Parent Engagement Office. "Always the Sunday after Labor Day! This annual outdoor art show features local and national artists that work in all mediums and sell original artwork for $100 or less." See website for more information.

MYSTIC OUTDOOR ARTS FESTIVAL
E-mail: Cherielin@MysticChamber.org. Website: www.mysticchamber.org/?sec=sec&s=44. "The annual Mystic Outdoor Art Festival has evolved in many ways from its humble beginnings. In 1957, Milton Baline and several other local business owners and art lovers proposed that Mystic pattern a festival after the famous Washington Square Festival in New York. That first show featured 105 artists and 500 paintings. Between 4,000 and 6,000 visitors came to admire and purchase art. Today the Mystic Outdoor Art Festival stretches over two miles and is the oldest of its kind in the Northeast. The Mystic Outdoor Art Festival has grown to over 250 artists who come from all corners of the U.S. and bring more than 100,000 works of art." See website for more information.

NAMPA FESTIVAL OF ARTS
131 Constitution Way, Nampa ID 83686. (208)468-5858. Fax: (208)465-2282. E-mail: rec@cityofnampa.us. Website: www.nampaparksandrecreation.org. Contact: Wendy Davis, program director. Estab. 1986. Fine art & craft show held annually mid-August. Outdoors. Accepts handmade crafts, fine art, photography, metal, anything handmade. Juried. Awards/prizes: cash. Exhibitors: 180. Number of attendees: 15,000. Free to public. See website for application.
ADDITIONAL INFORMATION Deadline for entry: July 10. Space fee: $40-90. Exhibition Space: 10×10, 15×15, 20×20. For more information, e-mail, call or visit website.
TIPS "Price things reasonably and have products displayed attractively."

NAPERVILLE WOMAN'S CLUB ART FAIR
(630)209-1246. E-mail: naperartfair@comcast.net. Website: www.napervillewomansclub.org. Contact: Roxanne Lang. "Over 100 local and national artists will be displaying original artwork in clay, fiber, glass, jewelry, mixed media, metal, painting, photography, sculpture and wood. Ribbons and cash prizes are awarded to winning artists by local judges and NWC. The Naperville Woman's Club Art Fair is the longest continuously running art fair in Illinois. Activities at this event include entertainment, a silent auction, artist demonstrations, the Empty Bowl Fundraiser to benefit local food pantries, and the Petite Picassos children's activities tent. This is the largest fundraiser of the year for the Naperville Woman's Club. Proceeds from the event help fund a local art scholarship and local charities. Admission and parking are free. For more information please e-mail us at: naperartfair@comcast.net."

NAPLES NATIONAL ART FESTIVAL
Website: www.naplesart.org. "The annual Naples National Art Festival is consistently voted among the top 10 art festivals in the country by Sunshine Artist Magazine, and the local community continues to count the Naples National Art Festival among its premiere, must-see events. This festival features the talents of more than 260 artists from around the country and awards $5,000 in cash to top artists. The festival draws crowds in excess of 22,000. Don't miss it!" See website for more information.

NATIVE AMERICAN FINE ART FESTIVAL
E-mail: tkramer@litchfield-park.org. Website: www.litchfield-park.org. Contact: Tricia Kramer. "The Native American Arts Festival highlights the finest southwest Native American artists including tradiional and contemporary Native American jewelry, pottery, basketry, weaving, katsinas, painting, and beadwork. The event includes a variety of Native American art, entertainment and learning opportunities. Admission fee is $5.00 per person, $3.00 students with I.D., children 12 and under admitted free. For more information call (623) 935-9040."

NEACA'S FALL CRAFT SHOW

NEACA Fall Show, 2100 Mythewood Dr., Huntsville AL 35803. (256)859-0511; (256)883-4028. Website: www.neaca.org. Contact: Annie Hannah. Craft show held annually in September. Indoors. Accepts handmade crafts, ceramics, paintings, jewelry, glass, photography, wearable art and other mediums. Juried. Number exhibitors: 150. Number attendees: 25,000. Free to public. Apply online.

ADDITIONAL INFORMATION Deadline for entry: August. Application fee: none. Space fee: $225. Exhibition space: 10×12. For more information, crafters should call, e-mail or visit website.

NEPTUNE ART AND CRAFT SHOW

E-mail: christie@virginiamoca.org. Website: www.virginiamoca.org/outdoor-art-shows/neptune-arts-craft-show. "The Neptune Festival Art & Craft Show is part of a citywide festival at the Virginia Beach oceanfront. The Art & Craft Show portion is produced by the Virginia Museum of Contemporary Art and showcases 250 artists and crafters." See website for more information.

NEW ENGLAND HOLIDAY CRAFT SPECTACULAR

38 Charles St., Rochester NH 03867. (603)332-2616. E-mail: info@castleberryfairs.com. Website: www.castleberryfairs.com. Fine arts & crafts fair held annually in December. Indoors. Accepts handmade crafts, jewelry, ceramics, painting, photography, digital, printmaking and more. Juried. Number exhibitors: see website. Number attendees: varies. Admission: $7 adults; children 12 & under free. Apply online.

ADDITIONAL INFORMATION Deadline for entry: see website. Application fee: see website. Space fee: varies. Exhibition space: varies. For more information, crafters should e-mail or visit website.

NEWTON ARTS FESTIVAL

Piper Promotions, 4 Old Green Rd., Sandy Hook CT 06482. (203)512-9100. E-mail: staceyolszewski@yahoo.com. Website: www.newtownartsfestival.com. Contact: Stacey Olszewski. Fine arts & crafts fair held annually in September. Outdoors. Accepts handmade crafts, jewelry, ceramics, painting, photography, digital, printmaking and more. Juried. Number exhibitors: see website. Number attendees: varies. Admission: $5; children 12 & under free. Apply online.

ADDITIONAL INFORMATION Deadline for entry: August. Application fee: none. Space fee: $105 (booth); $225 (festival tent). Exhibition space: 10×10. For more information, crafters should e-mail, call or visit website.

NIANTIC OUTDOOR ART & CRAFT SHOW

P.O. Box 227, Niantic CT 06357. (860)739-9128. E-mail: hapark@juno.com. Website: www.nianticartsandcraftshow.com. Contact: Howard Parkhurst. Fine art & craft show held annually in July. Outdoors. Accepts handmade crafts, ceramics, fiber, glass, graphics, jewelry, leather, metal, mixed media, painting, photography, printmaking, sculpture, woodworking. Juried. Number exhibitors: 142. Number attendees: varies. Free to public. Apply online.

ADDITIONAL INFORMATION Deadline for entry: March. Application fee: $20. Space fee: varies. Exhibition space: varies. For more information, crafters should e-mail, call or visit website.

NORTH CHARLESTON ARTS FESTIVAL

P.O. Box 190016, North Charleston SC 29419-9016. (843)740-5854. E-mail: culturalarts@northcharleston.org. Website: www.northcharlestonartsfest.com. Fine arts & crafts fair held annually in May. Outdoors. Accepts handmade crafts, jewelry, ceramics, painting, photography, digital, printmaking and more. Juried. Number exhibitors: see website. Number attendees: 30,000. Admission: see website. Apply online.

ADDITIONAL INFORMATION Deadline for entry: January. Application fee: see website. Space fee: see website. Exhibition space: see website. For more information, crafters should e-mail, call or visit website.

NORTHERN VIRGINIA FINE ARTS FESTIVAL

(703)471-9242. E-mail: info@restonarts.org. Website: www.northernvirginiafineartsfestival.org. Fine arts & crafts fair held annually in May. Outdoors. Accepts handmade crafts, jewelry, ceramics, painting, photography, digital, printmaking and more. Juried. Number exhibitors: 200. Number attendees: varies. Admission: $5; children 18 & under free. Apply online.

ADDITIONAL INFORMATION Deadline for entry: see website. Application fee: see website. Space fee: see website. Exhibition space: see website. For more information, crafters should e-mail, call or visit website.

NORTH IOWA EVENT CENTER'S SPRING EXTRAVAGANZA

(641)529-3003. E-mail: craftsunited@gmail.com. Contact: Jennifer Martin. Annual indoor craft show at the North Iowa Events Center in Mason City, Iowa. Hourly door prizes given away. Admission is free with donation to the North Iowa Humane Society. Hand crafted items, hand baked goods, and home based businesses allowed. E-mail or call for more information.

NORTH SHORE FESTIVAL OF ART

Amdur Productions, P.O. Box 550, Highland Park IL 60035. (847)926-4300. E-mail: info@amdurproductions.com. Website: www.amdurproductions.com. Fine arts & crafts fair held annually in July. Outdoors. Accepts handmade crafts, jewelry, ceramics, painting, photography, digital, printmaking and more. Juried. Number exhibitors: 100. Number attendees: 84,000. Free to public. Apply online.

ADDITIONAL INFORMATION Deadline for entry: see website. Application fee: $25. Space fee: $445. Exhibition space: 10×10. For more information, crafters should e-mail, call or visit website.

NORWAY ARTS FESTIVAL

Western Maine Art Group, P.O. Box 122, Norway ME 04268. (207)890-3649. E-mail: kahnig@yahoo.com. Website: www.norwayartsfestival.org. Contact: Irina Kahn. "Norway Arts Festival is a four day event held in Norway, Maine. The Festival starts on Thursday evening with a focus feature and continues Friday evening with music. Saturday is the art show and myriad events and performances that are held along Norway's historic Main Street. All events are free and open to all ages." See website for more information.

NOT YO MAMA'S CRAFT FAIR

E-mail: notyomamajc@gmail.com. Website: www.notyomamasaffairs.com. "Not Yo Mama's Craft Fair is an exclusive and unique event where the best and brightest creatives from the Jersey City metro area can hock their DIY wares to the coolest cats in Chill Town." See website for more information.

NOT YOUR GRANDMA'S CRAFT FAIR

E-mail: dizzycupcake@gmail.com. Website: www.nygcf.org. Contact: Jessie or Heather. "Not Your Grandma's Craft Fair spawned from the need to fill a gap in the local artsy craft market. After attending many local craft fairs, Dizzy Cupcakes realized they just didn't quite fit in. They wanted somewhere to not only sell their wares but also a place to see artists like them, a little estranged from the potholder/doily crowd. The Dizzy Cupcakes created Not Your Grandma's Craft Fair to be a showcase of the area's best artists and crafters, attracting crowds who might not make it to the average church basement bazaar." See website or e-mail for more information.

NUTS ABOUT ART

E-mail: nps@grics.net. Website: www.thenextpictureshow.com/pdf/NAA2014.pdf. Fine art show sponsored by The Next Picture Show at John Dixon Park. Free admission. See website for more information.

OCONOMOWOC FESTIVAL OF THE ARTS

P.O. Box 651, Oconomowoc WI 53066. Website: www.oconomowocarts.org. Estab. 1970. Fine arts & crafts fair held annually in August. Outdoors. Accepts handmade crafts, jewelry, ceramics, painting, photography, digital, printmaking and more. Juried. Awards/prizes: $3,500 in awards & prizes. Number exhibitors: 140. Number attendees: varies. Admission: Free to public. Apply online.

ADDITIONAL INFORMATION Deadline for entry: March. Application fee: $40. Space fee: $250. Exhibition space: 10×10. For more information, crafters should visit website.

ODD DUCK BAZAAR

2030 Polk St., Hollywood FL 33020. (954)243-9856. E-mail: info@oddduckbazaar.com. Website: www. oddduckbazaar.com. Contact: Shelley Mitchell, co-producer. Estab. 2010. Arts & crafts show (specializes in "odd" or unusual) held annually in late March or early April. Indoors. Accepts handmade crafts, vintage, antique. Juried. Exhibitors: 65. Number of attendees: 3,000. Admission: $5. Apply online.

ADDITIONAL INFORMATION Deadline for entry: see website. Application fee: $2. Space fee: $85-100. Exhibition space: 36-72 sq. ft. For more information, crafters should e-mail, visit website or see social media.

TIPS "We are looking for outside of the norm, so feel free to experiment."

OHIO MART

Stan Hywet Hall and Gardens, 714 N. Portage Path, Akron OH 44303. (330)836-5533; (888)836-5533. E-mail: info@stanhywet.org. Website: www.stanhywet. org. Estab. 1966. Fine arts & crafts fair held annually in October. Outdoors. Accepts handmade crafts, jewelry, ceramics, painting, photography, digital, printmaking and more. Juried. Number exhibitors: see website. Number attendees: varies. Admission: $9 adults; $2 youth. Apply online.

ADDITIONAL INFORMATION Deadline for entry: see website. Application fee: see website. Space fee: see website. Exhibition space: see website. For more information, crafters should call, e-mail or visit website.

OKLAHOMA CITY FESTIVAL OF THE ARTS

Arts Council of Oklahoma City, 400 W. California, Oklahoma City OK 73102. (405)270-4848. Fax: (405)270-4888. E-mail: info@artscouncilokc.com. Website: www.artscouncilokc.com. Estab. 1967. Fine arts & crafts fair held annually in April. Outdoors. Accepts handmade crafts, jewelry, ceramics, painting, photography, digital, printmaking and more. Juried. Number exhibitors: 144. Number attendees: varies. Free to public. Apply online.

ADDITIONAL INFORMATION Deadline for entry: see website. Application fee: see website. Space fee: see website. Exhibition space: see website. For more information, crafters should call, e-mail or visit website.

OLD CAPITOL ART FAIR

P.O. Box 5701, Springfield IL 62705. (405)270-4848. Fax: (405)270-4888. E-mail: artistinfo@yahoo.com. Website: www.socaf.org. Contact: Kate Baima. Estab. 1961. Fine arts & crafts fair held annually in May. Outdoors. Accepts handmade crafts, jewelry, ceramics, painting, photography, digital, printmaking and more. Juried. Awards/prizes: 1st Place, 2nd Place, 3rd Place, Awards of Merit. Number exhibitors: see website. Number attendees: varies. Free to public. Apply online.

ADDITIONAL INFORMATION Deadline for entry: November. Application fee: $35. Space fee: $300 (single); $550 (double). Exhibition space: 10×10 (single); 10×10 (double). For more information, crafters should call, e-mail or visit website.

OLD FOURTH WARD PARK ARTS FESTIVAL

592 N. Angier Ave., NE, Atlanta GA 30308. (404)873-1222. E-mail: Lisa@affps.com. Website: oldfourth wardparkartsfestival.com. Contact: Lisa Windle, festival director. Estab. 2013. Arts & crafts show held annually late June. Outdoors. Accepts handmade crafts, painting, photography, sculpture, leather, metal, glass, jewelry. Juried by a panel. Awards/prizes: ribbons. Number of exhibitors: 150. Number of attendees: 25,000. Free to public. Apply online at Zapplication.org.

ADDITIONAL INFORMATION Deadline for entry: April 25. Application fee: $25. Space fee: $200. Exhibition space: 10×10. For more information, see website.

OLD SAYBROOK ARTS & CRAFTS SHOW

Website: www.oldsaybrookchamber.com/pages/ ArtsCraftsFestival/. "From acrylics to photography, jewelry and oil painting, wood sculptures and glass creations, the 51st annual juried show will feature fine art and hand-made crafts sure to please a wide array of tastes and interests. Admission and ample parking are free." See website for more information and to apply.

OLD TOWN ART FESTIVAL

Old Town San Diego Chamber of Commerce, P.O. 82686, San Diego CA 92138. (619)233-5008. Fax: (619)233-0898. E-mail: rob-vslmedia@cox.net; otsd@ aol.com. Website: www.oldtownartfestival.com. Fine

arts & crafts fair held annually in September. Outdoors. Accepts handmade crafts, jewelry, ceramics, painting, photography, digital, printmaking and more. Juried. Number exhibitors: see website. Number attendees: 15,000. Free to public. Apply online.
ADDITIONAL INFORMATION Deadline for entry: September 1. Application fee: $25. Space fee: varies. Exhibition space: varies. For more information, crafters should call, e-mail or visit website.

OMAHA SUMMER ARTS FESTIVAL

Vic Gutman & Associates, P.O. Box 31036, Omaha NE 68131. (402)345-5401. Fax: (402)342-4114. E-mail: ebalazs@vgagroup.com. Website: www.summerarts. org. Estab. 1975. Fine arts & crafts fair held annually in June. Outdoors. Accepts handmade crafts, jewelry, ceramics, painting, photography, digital, printmaking and more. Juried. Number exhibitors: 135. Number attendees: varies. Free to public. Apply online.
ADDITIONAL INFORMATION Deadline for entry: see website. Application fee: see website. Space fee: varies. Exhibition space: varies. For more information, crafters should call, e-mail or visit website.

☉ ONE OF A KIND CRAFT SHOW

One of a Kind Show & Sale, 10 Alcorn Ave., Suite 100, Toronto ON M4V 3A9 Canada. (416)960-5399. Fax: (416)923-5624. E-mail: jill@oneofakindshow.com. Website: www.oneofakindshow.com. Contact: Jill Benson. Estab. 1975. Fine arts & crafts fair held annually 3 times a year. Outdoors. Accepts handmade crafts, jewelry, ceramics, painting, photography, digital, printmaking and more. Juried. Number exhibitors: varies per show. Number attendees: varies per show. Free to public. Apply online.
ADDITIONAL INFORMATION Deadline for entry: see website. Application fee: see website. Space fee: varies. Exhibition space: varies. For more information, crafters should call, e-mail or visit website.

ORANGE BEACH ARTS FESTIVAL

26389 Canal Road, Orange Beach AL 36561. (251)981-2787. Fax: (251)981-6981. E-mail: helpdesk@orangebeachartcenter.com. Website: www.orangebeachartsfestival.com. Fine art & craft show held annually in March. Outdoors. Accepts handmade crafts, ceram-

ics, paintings, jewelry, glass, photography, wearable art and other mediums. Juried. Number exhibitors: 90. Number attendees: varies. Free to public. Apply online.
ADDITIONAL INFORMATION Deadline for entry: See website. Application fee: see website. Space fee: varies. Exhibition space: varies. For more information, crafters should call, e-mail or visit website.

◑ THE ORIGINAL VINTAGE & HANDMADE FAIR

E-mail: info@cowboysandcustard.com. Website: www.vintageandhandmade.co.uk. "This popular event is always a joy to attend with 40 stalls brimming with scrumptious vintage goodies & divine handmade lovelies. Showcasing some of the best vintage dealers, artists & creative designer-makers from the South-West & beyond, it is a day not to be missed. With everything from vintage china & glass, toys & games, books & ephemera, fabrics & haberdashery, homewares, handmade hats, quilts, notebooks, cards, purses, bags & so much more, you will find much to inspire & delight you!" See website for more information.

PACIFIC INTERNATIONAL QUILT FESTIVAL

Mancuso Show Management, P.O. Box 667, New Hope PA 18938. (215)862-5828. Fax: (215)862-9753. E-mail: mancuso@quiltfest.com. Website: www.quiltfest. com. "This well-recognized and largest quilt show on the west coast, known to quilters as P.I.Q.F., is held at the Santa Clara Convention Center in the greater San Francisco Bay Area. Not only does this incredible event feature astounding works of quilt art, it also offers a wide array of workshops and lectures presented by world-renowned instructors. A 300 booth Merchants Mall can be found with the best in fabrics, notions, machines, wearable art and everything for the quilter, artist and home sewer." See website for more information.

PA GUILD OF CRAFTSMEN FINE CRAFT FAIRS

Center of American Craft, 335 N. Queen St., Lancaster PA 17603. (717)431-8706. E-mail: nick@pacrafts.org.

Website: www.pacrafts.org/fine-craft-fairs. Contact: Nick Mohler. Fine arts & crafts fair held annually 5 times a year. Outdoors. Accepts handmade crafts, jewelry, ceramics, painting, photography, digital, printmaking and more. Juried. Number exhibitors: varies per show. Number attendees: varies per show. Free to public. Apply online.

ADDITIONAL INFORMATION Deadline for entry: January. Application fee: $25. Space fee: varies. Exhibition space: 10×10. For more information, crafters should call, e-mail or visit website.

PALM BEACH FINE CRAFT SHOW

Crafts America, LLC, P.O. Box 603, Green Farms CT 06838. (203)254-0486. Fax: (203)254-9672. E-mail: info@craftsamericashows.com. Website: www.crafts americashows.com. Fine crafts fair held annually in February. Indoors. Accepts handmade crafts, basketry, ceramics, fiber, furniture, glass, jewelry, leather, metal, mixed media, paper, wood. Juried. Number exhibitors: 125. Number attendees: varies. Admission: $15 general; $14 senior citizens; children 12 & under free. Apply online.

ADDITIONAL INFORMATION Deadline for entry: October. Application fee: $45. Space fee: varies. Exhibition space: varies. For more information, crafters should e-mail, call or visit website.

PALM SPRINGS ARTS FESTIVAL

78206 Varner Rd., Ste D-114, Palm Desert CA 92211-4136. Website: www.palmspringsartsfestival. "In the birthplace of Western Chic, Palm Springs Arts Festival is pleased to present 175 of the finest traditional and contemporary artists from throughout the West, Southwest and the world to dazzle your eyes." See website for more information.

PALM SPRINGS DESERT ART FESTIVAL

West Coast Artists, P.O. Box 750, Acton CA 93510. (818)813-4478. E-mail: info@westcoastartists.com. Website: www.westcoastartists.com. Fine arts & crafts fair held annually several times a year. Outdoors. Accepts handmade crafts and other mediums. Juried. Number exhibitors: varies. Number attendees: varies. Free to public. Apply online.

ADDITIONAL INFORMATION Deadline for entry: varies. Application fee: see website. Space fee: varies. Exhibition space: varies. For more information, crafters should e-mail, call or visit website.

PALM SPRINGS FINE ART FAIR

HEG—Hamptons Expo Group, 223 Hampton Rd., Southampton NY 11968. (631)283-5505. Fax: (631)702-2141. E-mail: info@hegshows.com. Website: www.palmspringsfineartfair.com. Fine art fair held annually in February. Indoors. Accepts fine art from galleries. Juried. Number exhibitors: 60. Number attendees: 12,000. Admission: see website. Apply online.

ADDITIONAL INFORMATION Deadline for entry: see website. Application fee: none. Space fee: varies. Exhibition space: varies. For more information, crafters should e-mail, call or visit website.

PALO ALTO FESTIVAL OF THE ARTS

MLA Productions, 1384 Weston Rd., Scotts Valley CA 95066. (831)438-4751. E-mail: marylou@mla-productions.com. Website: www.mlaproductions.com/PaloAlto/index.html. "This high-quality, community-friendly event is sponsored by the Palo Alto Chamber of Commerce and the City of Palo Alto. In the past it has attracted over 150,000 people every year from throughout California and the West Coast. The festival takes place on tree-lined University Avenue in beautiful downtown Palo Alto, a vital economic area 35 miles south of San Francisco." See website for more details.

PARK CITY KIMBALL ARTS FESTIVAL

638 Park Ave., P.O. Box 1478, Park City UT 84060. (435)649-8882. Fax: (435)649-8889. E-mail: artsfest@kimballartcenter.org. Website: www.kimballart center.org. Estab. 1970. Fine art show held annually 1st weekend in August. Outdoors. Accepts ceramics, drawing, fiber, glass, jewelry, matalwork, mixed media, painting, photography, printmaking, sculpture, wood. Juried. Awards/prizes: Best in Show. Exhibitors: 220. Number of attendees: 55,000. Admission: see website. Apply online.

ADDITIONAL INFORMATION Deadline for entry: March 1. Application fee: $50. Space fee: $550-1,500.

Exhibition space: 100 sq.ft-200 sq. ft. For more information, crafters should visit website.

PARK POINT ART FAIR

(218)428-1916. E-mail: coordinator@parkpointart-fair.org. Website: www.parkpointartfair.org. Contact: Carla Tamburro, art fair coordinator. Estab. 1970. Fine arts & crafts fair held annually in June. Outdoors. Accepts handmade crafts, jewelry, ceramics, painting, photography, digital, printmaking and more. Juried. Awards/prizes: $1,300 in awards. Number exhibitors: 120. Number attendees: 10,000. Free to public. Apply online.

ADDITIONAL INFORMATION Deadline for entry: April. Application fee: $15. Space fee: $185. Exhibition space: 10×10. For more information, crafters should e-mail, call or visit website.

PATCHWORK SHOW

E-mail: hello@patchworkshow.com. Website: www.patchworkshow.com. Fine handmade fair held bi-annually in Spring & Fall in 4 locations. Outdoors. Accepts handmade crafts and other mediums. Juried. Number exhibitors: see website. Number attendees: varies. Free to public. Apply online.

ADDITIONAL INFORMATION Deadline for entry: see website. Application fee: $10. Space fee: varies. Exhibition space: varies. For more information, crafters should e-mail or visit website.

PEACHTREE HILLS FESTIVAL OF THE ARTS

285 Peachtree Hills Rd., NE, Atlanta GA 30305. (404)873-1222. E-mail: lisa@affps.com. Website: www.peachtreehillsfestival.com. Contact: Lisa Windle, festival director. Estab. 2011. Arts & crafts show held annually late May/early June. Outdoors. Accepts handmade crafts, painting, photography, sculpture, leather, metal, glass, jewelry. Juried by a panel. Awards/prizes: ribbons. Number of exhibitors: 125. Number of attendees: 25,000. Free to public. Apply online at Zapplication.org.

ADDITIONAL INFORMATION Deadline for entry: April 11. Application fee: $25. Space fee: $225. Exhibition space: 10×10. For more information, see website.

PEMBROKE ARTS FESTIVAL

Website: www.pembrokeartsfestival.org. Fine arts & crafts fair held annually in August. See website for more information.

PENROD ARTS FAIR

The Penrod Society, P.O. Box 40817, Indianapolis IN 46240. E-mail: artists@penrod.org. Website: www.penrod.org. Fine handmade fair held annually in September. Outdoors. Accepts handmade crafts and other mediums. Juried. Awards/prizes: Best in Show. Number exhibitors: 350. Number attendees: varies. Admission: see website. Apply via Zapplication.org.

ADDITIONAL INFORMATION Deadline for entry: April. Application fee: see website. Space fee: varies. Exhibition space: varies. For more information, crafters should e-mail or visit website.

PENTWATER FINE ARTS & CRAFT FAIR

Pentwater Jr. Women's Club, P.O. Box 357, Pentwater MI 49449. E-mail: pentwaterjuniorwomensclub@yahoo.com. Website: www.pentwaterjuniorwomensclub.com. "Always the 2nd Saturday in July, the fair is held on the beautiful Village Green located in downtown Pentwater, Michigan, during the height of the summer resort season. The fair is held regardless of the weather, and space is limited for this juried show." See website for more information and to apply.

PETERS VALLEY FINE CRAFT FAIR

Sussex County Fair Grounds, 37 Plains Rd., Augusta NJ 07822. (973)948-5200. Fax: (973)948-0011. E-mail: craftfair@petersvalley.org. Website: www.petersvalley.org. Contact: craft fair director. Estab. 1970. Fine craft show held annually the last full weekend in September that doesn't conflict with a holiday. Indoors. Accepts handmade crafts. Juried. Awards/prizes: free booth space next year. Exhibitors: 150. Number of attendees: 7,000. Admission: $9/day; $12/2-day; group rates also available. Apply via Zapplication.org.

ADDITIONAL INFORMATION Deadline for entry: see website. Application fee: $35. Space fee: $415+. Exhibition space: 10×10. For more information, crafters should e-mail, call or visit website.

PHILADELPHIA MUSEUM OF ART CONTEMPORARY CRAFT SHOW

P.O. Box 7646, Philadelphia PA 19101-7646. (215)684-7930. E-mail: twcpma@philamuseum.org. Website: www.pmacraftshow.org. Estab. 1977. Fine craft show (specializes in "odd" or unusual) held annually 2nd weekend in November. Indoors. Accepts handmade crafts, clay, glass, wood, fiber, metal. Juried. Exhibitors: 195. Number of attendees: 18,000. Admission: $15. Apply online.

ADDITIONAL INFORMATION Deadline for entry: April 1. Application fee: $50. Space fee: $1,200+. Exhibition space: see website. For more information, crafters should send visit website.

PICCOLO SPOLETO FINE CRAFTS SHOW

Fine Craft Shows Charleston, P.O. Box 22152, Charleston SC 29413-2152. (843)364-0421. E-mail: piccolo@finecraftshowscharleston.com. Website: www.finecraftshowscharleston.com. Fine handmade fair held annually in May. Outdoors. Accepts handmade crafts and other mediums. Juried. Awards/prizes: $5-6,000 in cash awards. Number exhibitors: 95. Number attendees: 9,000. Admission: $3 adults; children 18 & under free. Apply via Zapplication.org.

ADDITIONAL INFORMATION Deadline for entry: February. Application fee: $30. Space fee: $250. Exhibition space: 10×10. For more information, crafters should e-mail, call or visit website.

PICNIC MUSIC & ARTS FESTIVAL

E-mail: picnicportland@gmail.com. Website: www.picnicportland.com. Estab. 2008. Indie craft fair & music festival held annually in August. Outdoors. Accepts handmade crafts and other mediums. Juried. Number exhibitors: 100. Number attendees: varies. Free to public. Apply online.

ADDITIONAL INFORMATION Deadline for entry: mid May. Application fee: $10. Space fee: $175. Exhibition space: 10×10. For more information, crafters should e-mail or visit website.

PIEDMONT PARK ARTS FESTIVAL

1701 Piedmont Ave., Atlanta GA 30306. (404)873-1222. E-mail: lisa@affps.com. Website: www.piedmontparkartsfestival.com. Contact: Lisa Windle, festival director. Estab. 2011. Arts & crafts show held annually in mid August. Outdoors. Accepts handmade crafts, painting, photography, sculpture, leather, metal, glass, jewelry. Juried by a panel. Awards/prizes: ribbons. Number of exhibitors: 250. Number of attendees: 60,000. Free to public. Apply online at Zapplication.org.

ADDITIONAL INFORMATION Deadline for entry: June 6. Application fee: $25. Space fee: $275. Exhibition space: 10×10. For more information artists should visit website.

PITTSBURGH ART, CRAFT & LIFESTYLE SHOW

Huff's Promotions, Inc., 4275 Fulton Rd., N.W., Akron OH 44718. (330)493-4130. Fax: (330)493-7607. E-mail: shows@huffspromo.com. Website: www.huffspromo.com. Art & Craft show held annually several times a year. Indoors. Accepts handmade crafts and other mediums. Juried. Number exhibitors: see website. Number attendees: varies. Free to public. Apply online.

ADDITIONAL INFORMATION Deadline for entry: varies. Application fee: see website. Space fee: varies. Exhibition space: see website. For more information, crafters should e-mail, call or visit website.

PLAZA ART FAIR

Highwoods Properties, 4706 Broadway, Suite 260, Kansas City MS 64112. (816)753-0100. Fax: (816)753-4625. E-mail: countryclubplaza@highwoods.com. Website: www.countryclubplaza.com. Contact: Melissa Anderson. Estab. 1931. Art & craft show held annually in September. Outdoors. Accepts handmade crafts and other mediums. Juried. Awards/prizes: $10,000 in cash awards. Number exhibitors: 240. Number attendees: 300,000. Free to public. Apply via Zapplication.org.

ADDITIONAL INFORMATION Deadline for entry: May. Application fee: $35. Space fee: $425. Exhibition space: 12×12. For more information, crafters should e-mail, call or visit website.

PORT CLINTON ART FESTIVAL

Amdur Productions, P.O. Box 550, Highland Park IL 60035. (847)926-4300. Fax: (847)926-4330. E-mail: info@amdurproductions.com. Website: www.

amdurproductions.com. Art & craft show held annually in August. Outdoors. Accepts handmade crafts and other mediums. Juried. Awards/prizes: bestowed at artist breakfast. Number exhibitors: 260. Number attendees: 250,000. Free to public. Apply online.

ADDITIONAL INFORMATION Deadline for entry: early January. Application fee: $50. Space fee: $765. Exhibition space: 10×10. For more information, crafters should e-mail, call or visit website.

POWDERHORN ART FAIR

PPNA, 821 E. 35th St., Minneapolis MN 55407. (612)767-3515. E-mail: dixie@powderhornartfair.org. Website: www.powderhornartfair.com. Estab. 1991. Art & craft show held annually in August. Outdoors. Accepts handmade crafts and other mediums. Juried. Awards/prizes: Best in Show, 2nd Place, 3rd Place, Merit Award, Spirit of Powderhorn. Number exhibitors: 184. Number attendees: varies. Free to public. Apply via Zapplication.org.

ADDITIONAL INFORMATION Deadline for entry: early March. Application fee: $35. Space fee: $240. Exhibition space: 11×11. For more information, crafters should e-mail, call or visit website.

PRAIRIE VILLAGE ART FAIR

Website: www.prairievillageshops.com. Annual art fair held in May. See website for more information.

PROMENADE OF ART

Amdur Productions, P.O. Box 550, Highland Park IL 60035. (847)926-4300. Fax: (847)926-4330. E-mail: info@amdurproductions.com. Website: www.amdurproductions.com. Art & craft show held annually in June. Outdoors. Accepts handmade crafts and other mediums. Juried. Awards/prizes: given at festival. Number exhibitors: 125. Number attendees: 35,000. Free to public. Apply online.

ADDITIONAL INFORMATION Deadline for entry: early January. Application fee: $25. Space fee: $460. Exhibition space: 10×10. For more information, crafters should e-mail, call or visit website.

PUNTA GORDA SULLIVAN STREET CRAFT FESTIVAL

270 Central Blvd., Suite 107B, Jupiter FL 33458. (561)746-6615. Fax: (561)746-6528. E-mail: info@ArtFestival.com. Website: www.artfestival.com. "Since it's inception, the Punta Gorda craft fair continues to grow and highlight the talents of many unique crafters, providing the area with one of its most enjoyable summer traditions. Come meet and visit with some of the nation's best crafters while enjoying the charming streets of Punta Gorda."

QUILT & FIBER ARTS SHOW

P.O. Box 3481, Pahrump NV 89041. (775)751-6776. E-mail: pahrumppacinfo@gmail.com. Website: www.pvpac.org. "This three day event offers a chance to see gorgeous quilts of all sizes, as well as needlework, wearable art and other fiber arts. The show also offers demonstrations, a bed turning, door prizes, vendors, a silent auction, quilt appraiser, theme challenge, featured quilter, food counter and a pick-a-prize raffle. And each year an Opportunity Quilt with a custom quilt display rack is raffled off to one lucky winner on the last day." See website for more information.

QUILT, CRAFT & SEWING FESTIVAL

Website: www.quiltcraftsew.com/phoenix.html. "At the Quilt, Craft & Sewing Festival in Phoenix, Arizona, you will find a wide variety of sewing, quilting, needle-art and craft supply exhibits from many quality companies." See website for more information.

RED RIVER QUILTER'S ANNUAL QUILT SHOW

Website: www.redriverquilters.com. Judged quilt show held annually in October. See website for more information.

THE RENEGADE CRAFT FAIR—AUSTIN

1910 S. Halsted St., Suite #2, Chicago IL 60608. E-mail: rachel@renegadecraft.com. Website: www.renegadecraft.com. "Renegade Craft Fair is the world's premier network of events serving the DIY craft community. RCF was the first event of its kind when it was founded in 2003, and we are still the largest and most far-reaching with 14 annual events in Chicago, IL; New York, NY; San Francisco, CA; Los Angeles, CA; Austin, TX; Portland, OR; London, UK. On average, our events are attended by over 250,000 people annually, and hundreds of craft-based businesses have been launched successfully out of the fairs." See website for more information and specific details about each city and how to apply.

THE RENEGADE CRAFT FAIR—BROOKLYN

Renegade Craft Fair, 1910 S. Halsted St., Suite #2, Chicago IL 60608. E-mail: rachel@renegadecraft.com. Website: www.renegadecraft.com. "Renegade Craft Fair is the world's premier network of events serving the DIY craft community. RCF was the first event of its kind when it was founded in 2003, and we are still the largest and most far-reaching with 14 annual events in Chicago, IL; New York, NY; San Francisco, CA; Los Angeles, CA; Austin, TX; Portland, OR; London, UK. On average, our events are attended by over 250,000 people annually, and hundreds of craft-based businesses have been launched successfully out of the fairs." See website for more information and specific details about each city and how to apply.

THE RENEGADE CRAFT FAIR—CHICAGO

Renegade Craft Fair, 1910 S. Halsted St., Suite #2, Chicago IL 60608. E-mail: rachel@renegadecraft.com. Website: www.renegadecraft.com. "Renegade Craft Fair is the world's premier network of events serving the DIY craft community. RCF was the first event of its kind when it was founded in 2003, and we are still the largest and most far-reaching with 14 annual events in Chicago, IL; New York, NY; San Francisco, CA; Los Angeles, CA; Austin, TX; Portland, OR; London, UK. On average, our events are attended by over 250,000 people annually, and hundreds of craft-based businesses have been launched successfully out of the fairs." See website for more information and specific details about each city and how to apply.

THE RENEGADE CRAFT FAIR—LONDON

Renegade Craft Fair, 1910 S. Halsted St., Suite #2, Chicago IL 60608. E-mail: rachel@renegadecraft.com. Website: www.renegadecraft.com. "Renegade Craft Fair is the world's premier network of events serv-

ing the DIY craft community. RCF was the first event of its kind when it was founded in 2003, and we are still the largest and most far-reaching with 14 annual events in Chicago, IL; New York, NY; San Francisco, CA; Los Angeles, CA; Austin, TX; Portland, OR; London, UK. On average, our events are attended by over 250,000 people annually, and hundreds of craft-based businesses have been launched successfully out of the fairs." See website for more information and specific details about each city and how to apply.

THE RENEGADE CRAFT FAIR—LOS ANGELES

Renegade Craft Fair, 1910 S. Halsted St., Suite #2, Chicago IL 60608. E-mail: rachel@renegadecraft.com. Website: www.renegadecraft.com. "Renegade Craft Fair is the world's premier network of events serving the DIY craft community. RCF was the first event of its kind when it was founded in 2003, and we are still the largest and most far-reaching with 14 annual events in Chicago, IL; New York, NY; San Francisco, CA; Los Angeles, CA; Austin, TX; Portland, OR; London, UK. On average, our events are attended by over 250,000 people annually, and hundreds of craft-based businesses have been launched successfully out of the fairs." See website for more information and specific details about each city and how to apply.

THE RENEGADE CRAFT FAIR—PORTLAND

Renegade Craft Fair, 1910 S. Halsted St., Suite #2, Chicago IL 60608. E-mail: rachel@renegadecraft.com. Website: www.renegadecraft.com. "Renegade Craft Fair is the world's premier network of events serving the DIY craft community. RCF was the first event of its kind when it was founded in 2003, and we are still the largest and most far-reaching with 14 annual events in Chicago, IL; New York, NY; San Francisco, CA; Los Angeles, CA; Austin, TX; Portland, OR; London, UK. On average, our events are attended by over 250,000 people annually, and hundreds of craft-based businesses have been launched successfully out of the fairs." See website for more information and specific details about each city and how to apply.

THE RENEGADE CRAFT FAIR—SAN FRAN-CISCO

Renegade Craft Fair, 1910 S. Halsted St., Suite #2, Chicago IL 60608. E-mail: rachel@renegadecraft.com. Website: www.renegadecraft.com. "Renegade Craft Fair is the world's premier network of events serving the DIY craft community. RCF was the first event of its kind when it was founded in 2003, and we are still the largest and most far-reaching with 14 annual events in Chicago, IL; New York, NY; San Francisco, CA; Los Angeles, CA; Austin, TX; Portland, OR; London, UK. On average, our events are attended by over 250,000 people annually, and hundreds of craft-based businesses have been launched successfully out of the fairs." See website for more information and specific details about each city and how to apply.

RIDGELAND FINE ARTS FESTIVAL

(253)344-1058. E-mail: bobmcfarland2@hotmail.com. Website: www.ridgelandartsfest.com. Fine art & craft show held annually in April. Outdoors. Accepts handmade crafts and other mediums. Juried. Awards/prizes: $7,500 in awards. Number exhibitors: 80. Number attendees: varies. Free to public. Apply via Zapplication.org.

ADDITIONAL INFORMATION Deadline for entry: November. Application fee: see website. Space fee: varies. Exhibition space: varies. For more information, crafters should e-mail, call or visit website.

RISING SUN FESTIVAL OF FINE ARTS & CRAFTS

E-mail: andrea@enjoyrisingsun.com. Website: www.enjoyrisingsun.com. Fine arts & craft show held annually in September. Outdoors. Accepts handmade crafts and other mediums. Juried. Awards/prizes: $8,000 in awards. Number exhibitors: see website. Number attendees: varies. Free to public. Apply via Zapplication.org.

ADDITIONAL INFORMATION Deadline for entry: July. Application fee: $15. Space fee: $100 (single); $200 (double). Exhibition space: 10×10 (single); 10×10 (double). For more information, crafters should e-mail or visit website.

RIVERWALK FINE ART FAIR

Naperville Art League, 508 N. Center St., Naperville IL 60563. (630)355-2530. Fax: (630)355-3071. E-mail: naperartleague@aol.com. Website: www.napervilleartleague.com. Estab. 1984. Art & craft show held annually in September. Outdoors. Accepts handmade crafts and other mediums. Juried. Awards/prizes: Best of Show, 1st Place, Honorable Mentions, Purchase Awards. Number exhibitors: see website. Number attendees: varies. Free to public. Apply via Zapplication.org.

ADDITIONAL INFORMATION Deadline for entry: early April. Application fee: $35. Space fee: $400. Exhibition space: 10×12. For more information, crafters should e-mail, call or visit website.

ROCK 'N ROLL CRAFT SHOW

(314)649-7727. E-mail: info@rocknrollcraftshow.com. Website: www.rocknrollcraftshow.com. "Rock 'n Roll Craft Show is St. Louis' original alternative art, craft, and music event! RRCS showcases unique items handcrafted from new and recycled materials by talented artisans, as well as locally and nationally acclaimed bands!" See website for more information.

ROCKPORT ART FESTIVAL

Rockport Center for the Arts, 902 Navigation Circle, Rockport TX 78382. (361)729-5519. E-mail: info@rockportartcenter.com. Website: www.rockportartcenter.com. "Over 120 artists, live music & food, and A/C party tent, kids' activities, and more just steps away from Aransas Bay and Rockport Beach Park!" See website for more information.

ROTARY KEY BISCAYNE ART FESTIVAL

270 Central Blvd, Suite 107B, Jupiter FL 33458. (561)746-6615. Fax: (561)746-6528. E-mail: info@artfestival.com. Website: www.artfestival.com. Estab. 1963. "The annual Key Biscayne Art Festival benefits our partner and co producer, The Rotary Club of Key Biscayne. Held in Key Biscayne, an affluent island community in Miami-Dade County, just south of downtown Miami, the Annual Key Biscayne Art Festival is one not to be missed! In fact, visitors plan their springtime vacations to South Florida around this terrific outdoor festival that brings together long-

time favorites and the newest names in the contemporary art scene. Life-size sculptures, spectacular paintings, one-of-a-kind jewels, photography, ceramics, and much more make for one fabulous weekend." See website for more information.

ROUND THE FOUNTAIN ART FAIR
Round the Fountain Art, P.O. Box 1134, Lafayette IN 47902. (765)491-6298. Website: www.roundthefountain.org. Estab. 1973. Art & craft show held annually in May. Outdoors. Accepts handmade crafts and other mediums. Juried. Awards/prizes: Best of Show, 2nd Place, 3rd Place, Merit Awards, Aldo Award. Number exhibitors: 100. Number attendees: varies. Free to public. Apply via Zapplication.org.
ADDITIONAL INFORMATION Deadline for entry: early April. Application fee: $35. Space fee: $150 (single); $300 (double). Exhibition space: 10×10 (single); 10×20 (double). For more information, crafters should call or visit website.

RUBBER STAMP & PAPER ARTS FESTIVALS
(541)574-8000. E-mail: info@heirloompro.com. Website: www.heirloompro.com. Estab. 1993. "Retail consumer events featuring art stamps, cardmaking, scrapbooking and paper arts. You will find art stamps, paper, cardstock and envelopes, inks and pads, diecuts, brass stencils, glitter, embossing powder, tools, pencils, pens and markers, embellishments, and more. Classes, workshops, Design & Treasure, make 'n takes, demonstrations. Learn, become inspired, and shop." See website for more information.

SACRAMENTO ARTS FESTIVAL
American Art Festivals Inc., P.O. Box 3037, Atascadero CA 93423. (805)461-6700. E-mail: americanartfestivals@yahoo.com. Website: www.sacartsfest.com. Art & craft show held annually in November. Outdoors. Accepts handmade crafts and other mediums. Juried. Number exhibitors: see website. Number attendees: 10,000. Free to public. Apply via Zapplication.org.
ADDITIONAL INFORMATION Deadline for entry: April. Application fee: $10. Space fee: varies. Exhibition space: varies. For more information, crafters should e-mail, call or visit website.

SALEM ART FAIR & FESTIVAL
Salem Art Association, 600 Mission St., SE, Salem OR 97302. (503)581-2228. Fax: (503)371-3342. Website: www.salemart.org. "SAA is the proud organization behind the nationally ranked Salem Art Fair & Festival which is both our largest annual fundraiser and the largest festival of its kind in Oregon. Each year, the SAF&F attracts approximately 35,000 visitors from all over the nation and is committed to upholding the importance of fine arts and crafts by providing access to a range of artistic mediums appealing to both art appreciators and art collectors alike. With a variety of different activities and offerings, the art fair is an experience the whole family can enjoy." See website for more information.

SALEM ARTS FESTIVAL
(978)744-0004 ext.15. E-mail: kylie@salemmainstreets.org. Website: www.salemartsfestival.com. Contact: Kylie Sullivan. "The Salem Arts Festival promotes the arts in downtown Salem through a collaborative festival for residents and visitors providing opportunities to highlight the existing artist community and encourage general community participation in the arts. The festival regularly draws over 4,000 visitors. The festival is looking for art and performance for the sophisticated art patron as well as for the art novice including interactive events for children. It will engage participants of diverse backgrounds and ages by reaching out to current art patrons, local students, and the community at large." See website for more information.

SALT FORK ARTS & CRAFTS FESTIVAL
P.O. Box 250, Cambridge OH 43725. (740)439-9379. E-mail: director@saltforkfestival.org. Website: www.saltforkfestival.org. "The Salt Fork Arts & Crafts Festival (SFACF) is a juried festival that showcases high quality art in a variety of mediums, painting, pottery, ceramics, fiber art, metal work, jewelry, acrylics, mixed media, photography, and more. Between 90 and 100 artists come from all over the U.S., for this 3-day event. In addition, the festival heralds Heritage of the Arts. This program offers a look at Early American and Appalachian arts and crafts. Many of which are demonstrated by craftsmen practicing arts such as basket weaving, flint knapping, spindling, flute mak-

ing, quilting, blacksmithing, and more. Area students are given the opportunity to display their work , visitors are entertained throughout the weekend by a variety of talented performing artists, concessionaires offer satisfying foods and there are crafts for kids and adults." See website for more information.

SALT LAKE'S FAMILY CHRISTMAS GIFT SHOW

South Towne Exposition Center, 9575 S. State St., Sandy UT 84070. (800)521-7469. Fax: (425)889-8165. E-mail: saltlake@showcaseevents.org. Website: www.showcaseevents.org. Contact: Kristine Vannoy, show manager. Estab. 1999. Seasonal holiday show held annually in November. Indoors. Accepts handmade crafts, art, photography, pottery, glass, jewelry, clothing, fiber. Juried. Exhibitors: 400. Number of attendees: 25,000. Admission: $11.50 (for all 3 days); 13 & under free. Apply via website or call or e-mail for application.

ADDITIONAL INFORMATION Deadline for entry: October 31. Space fee: see website. Exhibition space: 10×10. For more information send e-mail, call, send SASE or visit website.

TIPS "Competitive pricing, attractive booth display, quality product, something unique for sale, friendly & outgoing personality."

SANDY SPRINGS ARTSAPALOOZA

6100 Lake Forrest Dr., N.E., Sandy Springs GA 30328. (404)873-1222. E-mail: lisa@affps.com. Website: www.sandyspringsartsapalooza.com. Contact: Lisa Windle, festival director. Estab. 2011. Arts & crafts show held annually mid April. Outdoors. Accepts handmade crafts, painting, photography, sculpture, leather, metal, glass, jewelry. Juried by a panel. Awards/prizes: ribbons. Number of exhibitors: 150. Number of attendees: 25,000. Free to public. Apply online at Zapplication.org.

ADDITIONAL INFORMATION Deadline for entry: February 14. Application fee: $25. Space fee: $200. Exhibition space: 10×10. For more information, see website.

SANDY SPRINGS FESTIVAL & ARTISTS MARKET

6075 Sandy Springs Circle, Sandy Springs GA 30328. (404)873-1222. E-mail: lisa@affps.com. Website: www.sandyspringsfestival.com. Contact: Lisa Windle, festival director. Estab. 1986. Arts & crafts show held annually late June. Outdoors. Accepts handmade crafts, painting, photography, sculpture, leather, metal, glass, jewelry. Juried by a panel. Awards/prizes: ribbons. Number of exhibitors: 120. Number of attendees: 40,000. Free to public. Apply online at Zapplication.org. For more information, see website.

ADDITIONAL INFORMATION Deadline for entry: July 25. Application fee: $25. Space fee: $250. Exhibition space: 10×10. For more information, see website.

SAN FRANCISCO BAZAAR

1559B Sloat Blvd. #198, San Francisco CA 94132. (415)684-8447. E-mail: sf_info@sanfranciscobazaar. org. Website: www.sanfranciscobazaar.org. Contact: Jamie Chan, director. Estab. 2007. Handmade, independent DIY art & design festival held annually 5 times a year (see website for dates). Indoors & outdoors. Accepts handmade crafts, locally and domestically designed goods. Juried. Exhibitors: 150. Number of attendees: 10,000. Free to public. Apply online at www.sanfranciscobazaar.org/apply.

ADDITIONAL INFORMATION Deadline for entry: varies (see website). Application fee: $0-$20 per show. Space fee: $90-$400. Exhibition space: 10×10 ft. For more information, crafters should see website.

TIPS "Each year San Francisco Bazaar curates hundreds of carefully juried artists and designers. Shoppers can expect to find the crème de la crème of indie goods: handbags, pottery, letterpress stationary, silk-screened T-shirts, baby clothes, zines, posters, body products and more! Please make sure you have a comprehensive website, e-commerce shop or photo album at the time of application so that we may best understand your products offered and your artistic mission."

SAN FRANCISCO FINE CRAFT SHOW

American Craft Council Shows, 155 Water St., 4th Floor, Unit 5, Brooklyn NY 11201. (800)836-3470. Fax: (612)355-2330. E-mail: shows@craftcouncil.org. Website: www.craftcouncil.org. Art & craft show held annually in August. Indoors. Accepts handmade crafts, ceramics, fiber, metal and other mediums. Juried. Awards/prizes: Awards of Excellence. Number exhibitors: 225. Number attendees: varies. Free to public. Apply online.

ADDITIONAL INFORMATION Deadline for entry: August. Application fee: $30 + $10 handling/processing fee for each set of images. Space fee: varies. Exhibition space: varies. For more information, crafters should e-mail, call or visit website.

SAN MARCO ART FESTIVAL

270 Central Blvd., Suite 107B, Jupiter FL 33458. (561)746-6615. Fax: (561)746-6528. E-mail: info@artfestival.com. Website: www.artfestival.com. "Browse and purchase original handmade works including: glass, photography, painting, mixed media, fiber, jewelry and much more. Artists will be on-hand all weekend to share their inspirations for each uniquely-crafted piece. No matter what you're looking for, you'll be sure to find it among the numerous artisans participating in this greatly anticipated, juried, community art fair."

SANTA CRUZ HERITAGE HOLIDAY CRAFT & GIFT FAIR

Freedom Post Office, P.O. Box 1806, Freedom CA 95019. (831)612-9118. E-mail: heritageholidayfair@gmail.com. Website: www.sccfheritage.org/heritage-holiday-craft-fair. "This festive event full of holiday cheer includes crafts, folk art, antiques, collectibles, gift foods, delicious refreshments at the food courts, and free parking. The 25-foot Christmas tree will light up your child's eyes! The Agricultural History Project will host a County Christmas. General admission is $3.00, children under 5 are free." See website for more information.

SANTA FE COLLEGE SPRING ARTS FESTIVAL

3000 NW 83rd St., Gainesville FL 32606. (352)395-5355. Fax: (352)336-2715. E-mail: kathryn.lehman@sfcollege.edu. Website: www.springartsfestival.com. Contact: Kathryn Lehman, cultural program coordinator. Estab. 1969. Fine art show held annually in March or April. Outdoors. Accepts painting, photography, fabrics, glass, watercolor, wood, 2D/3D mixed media, grapics, sculpture. Juried. Awards/prizes: $20,000 cash awards; ribbons. Exhibitors: 190. Number of attendees: 110,000. Free to public. Apply via Zapplication.org.

ADDITIONAL INFORMATION Deadline for entry: December. Application fee: see website. Space fee: see website. Exhibition space: 12×12. For more information, crafters should e-mail, call or visit website.

TIPS "Original, medium prices."

SARASOTA CRAFT FAIR

270 Central Blvd., Suite 107B, Jupiter FL 33458. (561)746-6615. Fax: (561)746-6528. E-mail: info@artfestival.com. Website: www.artfestival.com. "Behold contemporary crafts from more than 100 of the nation's most talented artisans. A variety of jewelry, pottery, ceramics, photography, painting, clothing and much more—all handmade in America—will be on display, ranging from $15 to $3,000. An expansive Green Market with plants, orchids, exotic flora, handmade soaps, gourmet spices and freshly popped kettle corn further compliments the weekend, blending nature with nurture." See website for more information.

SAULT SAINTE MARIE ARTS, CRAFTS & FAMILY FUN FAIR

EUP Community Dispute Resolution Center, P.O. Box 550, Sault Sainte Marie MI 49783. (906)253-9840. Fax: (888)664-6402. E-mail: coordinator@saultcraftfair.org. Website: www.saultcraftfair.org. "This event is held annually on the last Friday of June. Please join us on the lawn of Historic City Hall, overlooking the east end of the Sault Locks and the St. Mary's River." See website for more information.

SAWDUST ART FESTIVAL

935 Laguna Canyon Rd., Laguna Beach CA 92651. (949)494-3030. Fax: (949)494-7390. Website: www. sawdustartfestival.org. Contact: Tom Klingenmeier, general manager. Estab. 1966. Arts & crafts show held annually June-August (see website for dates; also has winter shows). Outdoors. Accepts handmade crafts, all art mediums. Awards/prizes: peer awards. Exhibitors: 200 (summer); 175 (winter). Number of attendees: 200,000 (summer); 20,000 (winter). Admission: $8.50 adults. Application release date varies (see website). **ADDITIONAL INFORMATION** Deadline for entry: varies (see website). Application fee: $30 per show. Space fee: $1,250+ (summer). Exhibition space: 10×8. For more information, call, e-mail or see website. **TIPS** "Be here on the grounds exhibiting your artwork."

SCOTTSDALE CELEBRATION OF FINE ARTS

7900 E. Greenway Rd., Suite 101, Scottsdale AZ 85260-1714. (480)443-7695. Fax: (480)596-8179. E-mail: info@celebrateart.com. Website: www.celebrateart. com. "The Celebration of Fine Art™ is a juried show. We jury not only for quality but variety. This helps insure that direct competition is minimized and that you will have the best opportunity for success. All styles of art in all mediums are welcome. In addition to painting and sculpture, we also have fine crafts such as furniture, jewelry, ceramics basketry and weaving. Only work created by the artist and handmade work is accepted. We do not allow manufactured goods of any kind. Artists who have previously been selected for the show will be juried in the two months following the current exhibit. Additional details, prices and other information are contained in the artist application packet." See website for more information.

SCRAPBOOK EXPO

1353 Walker Ln., Corona CA 92879. (951)734-4307. Fax: (951)848-0711. E-mail: exhibitors@scrapbook-expo.com. Website: www.scrapbookexpo.com. "Scrapbook Expo combines scrapbooking, paper crafting and stamping and offers YOU the crafter the most amazing crafting experience you'll ever find." See website for dates and more information.

SEASONS OF THE HEART CRAFT, DECOR & GIFT FAIRE

P.O. Box 191, Ramona CA 92064. (760)445-1330. E-mail: seasonsoftheheart@cox.net. Website: seasons oftheheartcraftfaire.com. Contact: Linda or Ron Mulick, owners/promoters. Estab. 1988. Arts & crafts show, seasonal/holiday show held annually in November. Indoors. Accepts handmade crafts, collectibles, gourmet foods. Exhibitors: 100. Number of attendees: 6,000. Free to public. Apply online. **ADDITIONAL INFORMATION** Deadline for entry: October 1. Application fee: none. Space fee: $225 + 15% of sales. Exhibition space: 10×10. Average sales: $2,000. For more information, crafters should e-mail, visit website or call. **TIPS** "Do quality work and price your items reasonably."

SEATTLE HANDMADE HOLIDAY SHOW

Website: www.seattlehandmade.com. "Enjoy the official beginning of the Holiday gift shopping season and find the perfect gifts for the loved ones on your list at the Seattle Handmade Holiday Show (formerly etsyRAIN Handmade Holiday Show). Celebrating many fabulous years of supporting the handmade community of Seattle and the greater Pacific NW." See website for more details.

SEATTLE'S HOLIDAY DIY FAIR

The Vera Project, 305 Harrison St., Seattle WA 98109. E-mail: fundraising@theveraproject.org. Website: www.theveraproject.org. "This extravaganza features several independent NW record and cassette labels, musicians, silk-screened show posters, vintage record dealers, local artists, craft-makers, and designers selling their wares throughout Vera's venue. This is the perfect opportunity to find a one-of-a-kind gift just in time for the holidays. Interactive entertainments will take place throughout the day, including the Surrealist Songwriting Project and live silkscreening lessons, and the event will also include Hollow Earth DJs spinning on site, a bake sale, and a raffle for rare posters, records and more!" See website for more information.

SEATTLE WEAVERS GUILD ANNUAL SHOW & SALE

Seattle Weavers' Guild, 1245 10th Ave., E, Seattle WA 98102. E-mail: sale@seattleweaversguild.com. Website: www.seattleweaversguild.com. "The annual sale showcases one-of-a-kind handcrafted items, including towels, rugs, blankets, tapestries, exquisite jewelry, accessories for pets, children's items, handmade cards, household goods, hats, bags, wall art, jackets, scarves, wraps, sculptural basketry, liturgical weaving, handspun and/or hand-dyed yarns along with weaving and spinning tools. There will also be demonstrations of spinning, weaving and other fiber crafts during the sale. Proceeds from the sale are used to fund the guild's volunteer outreach program and to bring talented practicing artists to Seattle Weavers' Guild to educate both its members and the public. Parking and entrance to the sale are free." See website for more information.

SELDAN HANDMADE FAIR

(757)664-6880. "Selden HandMade Fair showcases the work of contemporary indie-craft artists. Crafters and do-it-yourselfers will offer original handmade goods in a wide variety of media. Enjoy live artist demonstrations and a variety of musical performances. FREE and open to the public!" See website for more information.

SELL-A-RAMA

Tyson Wells Sell-A-Rama, P.O. Box 60, Quartzsite AZ 85346. (928)927-6364. E-mail: tysonwells@tds.net. Website: www.tysonwells.com. Arts & craft show held annually in January. Outdoors & indoors. Accepts handmade crafts, ceramics, paintings, jewelry, glass, photography, wearable art and other mediums. Juried. Number exhibitors: see website. Number attendees: varies. Free to public. Apply online. **ADDITIONAL INFORMATION** Deadline for entry: see website for dates. Application fee: none. Space fee: varies. Exhibition space: varies. For more information, crafters should call, e-mail or visit website.

SFUSD ARTS FESTIVAL

(415)695-2441. Fax: (415)695-2496. E-mail: sfusdaf2014@gmail.com. Website: sfusdartsfestival.org. "The San Francisco Unified School District proudly presents the SFUSD Arts Festival, a celebration of student creativity in visual, literary, media and performing arts. This unique San Francisco event (formerly Young at Art) has been a point of destination for families, teachers, artists and community members from San Francisco and beyond. The promise of equity and access in arts education for all students K-12 during the curricular day, made real by the SFUSD's groundbreaking Arts Education Master Plan, finds its point of destination in this festival, where all who attend may see for themselves the inspiration and creativity inherent in all of our youngest San Franciscans!" See website for more information.

SHIPSHEWANA QUILT FESTIVAL

P.O. Box 245, Shipshewana IN 46565. (260)768-4887. E-mail: info@shipshewanaquiltfest.com. Website: www.shipshewanaquiltfest.com. Contact: Nancy Troyer, show organizer. Estab. 2009. Quilt & vendor show held annually late June. Indoors. Accepts handmade crafts and other mediums. Juried. Awards/prizes: cash. Exhibitors: 20. Number of attendees: 4,000. Admission: $8/day; $12/week. Apply online.
ADDITIONAL INFORMATION Deadline for entry: see website. Application fee: none. Space fee: varies. Exhibition space: varies. Average sales: $5,000-10,000. For more information, crafters should e-mail, call or visit website.
TIPS "Booth presentation and uniqueness of product a must."

SIESTA KEY CRAFT FESTIVAL

270 Central Blvd., Suite 107B, Jupiter FL 33458. (561)746-6615. Fax: (561)746-6528. E-mail: info@artfestival.com. Website: www.artfestival.com. "Join us at the annual Siesta Key Craft Festival and take in the sand and the sea along Ocean Boulevard and Beach Road as you discover wonderful creations from more than 100 crafters exhibiting and selling their work in an outdoor gallery. From photography, paintings, sculpture, jewelry and more showcased from local and traveling crafters, your visit to Siesta Key is promised to be a feast for the senses. This spectacular weekend festival is not to be missed." See website for more information.

SLIDELL NEWCOMERS SELL-A-BRATION ARTS & CRAFTS SHOW

P.O. Box 2681, Slidell LA 70459. (985)641-2021. E-mail: ncsellabration@aol.com. Website: www.sell-a-brationcraftshow.webs.com. Contact: Linda Tate, show chair. Estab. 1982. Arts & crafts show held annually in October. Indoors. Accepts handmade crafts, origianl artwork, original photography. Number of exhibitors: 70-80. Number of attendees: 2,200-2,300. Free to public. Apply online.

ADDITIONAL INFORMATION Deadline for entry: October 5. Space fee: Starting at $100. Exhibition space: 10×10. For more information, see website.

SMITHSONIAN CRAFT SHOW

MRC 037 P.O. Box 37012, SIB Room T472, Washington, D.C. 20013-7012. E-mail: austrpr@si.edu. Website: www.smithsoniancraftshow.org. Art & craft show held annually in April. Indoors. Accepts handmade crafts basketry, ceramics, decorative fiber, furniture, glass, jewelry, leather, metal, mixed media, paper, wearable art, and wood. Juried. Awards/prizes: Gold Award, Silver Award, Bronze Award, Excellence Awards, Exhibitor's Choice Awards. Number exhibitors: 121. Number attendees: varies. Admission: see website for rates. Apply online.

ADDITIONAL INFORMATION Deadline for entry: September. Application fee: $50. Space fee: varies. Exhibition space: varies. For more information, crafters should e-mail or visit website.

SMOKY HILL RIVER FESTIVAL FINE ART SHOW

(785)309-5770. E-mail: sahc@salina.org. Website: www.riverfestival.com. Fine art & craft show held annually in June. Outdoors. Accepts handmade crafts ceramics, jewelry, fiber, mixed media, painting, drawing/pastels, glass, metal, wood, graphics/printmaking, digital, paper, sculpture, and photography. Juried. Awards/prizes: Jurors' Merit Awards, Purchase Awards. Number exhibitors: 90. Number attendees: 60,000. Admission: $10 in advance; $15 at gate; children 11 & under free. Apply via Zapplication.org.

ADDITIONAL INFORMATION Deadline for entry: February. Application fee: $30. Space fee: $275. Exhibition space: 10×10. For more information, crafters should e-mail or visit website.

SMOKY HILL RIVER FESTIVAL FOUR RIVERS CRAFT SHOW

(785)309-5770. E-mail: sahc@salina.org. Website: www.riverfestival.com. Fine art & craft show held annually in June. Outdoors. Accepts handmade crafts ceramics, folk art, leather, paper, clothing, glass, metal, herbal/soaps, basketry, wood, mixed media, jewelry, fiber and more. Juried. Awards/prizes: Jurors' Merit Awards. Number exhibitors: 50. Number attendees: 60,000. Admission: $10 in advance; $15 at gate; children 11 & under free. Apply via Zapplication.org.

ADDITIONAL INFORMATION Deadline for entry: February. Application fee: $30. Space fee: $325. Exhibition space: 10×10. For more information, crafters should e-mail or visit website.

SNAKE ALLEY ART FAIR

Website: www.snakealley.com/artfair.html. Art fair held annually on Father's Day. Features 104 selected artists from throughout the Midwest. See website for more information.

SOFA

(800)563-7632. Fax: (773)326-0660. Website: www.sofaexpo.com. The annual Exposition of Sculpture Objects & Functional Art + Design Fair (SOFA) is a gallery-presented, international art exposition dedicated to bridging the worlds of design, decorative and fine art. Works by emerging and established artists and designers are available for sale by premier galleries and dealers. See website for more information.

SONORAN FESTIVAL OF FINE ART

(623)734-6526; (623)386-2269. E-mail: cvermillion12@cox.net; info@vermillionpromotions.com. Website: www.vermillionpromotions.com. Contact: Candy Vermillion. "The prestigious Sonoron Festival of Fine Art is one of the largest open air fine art venues in the Southwest featuring more than 125 local and nationally-acclaimed artists. Sponsored each year by the Sonoran Arts League, the festival is a juried show open to artists from around the country. With more than 400 members, the Arts League is a vital contributor to the cultural life in the foothills, and a focal point for artists and art patrons." See website for more information.

SOUTHWEST ARTS FESTIVAL

81800 Avenue 51, Indio CA 92201. (760)347-0676. Fax: (760)347-6069. E-mail: swaf@indiochamber.org. Website: www.indiochamber.org. Contact: Joshua R. Bonner, president/CEO. Estab. 1986. Fine art show held annually in January. Outdoors. Accepts handmade crafts, clay, drawing, glass, jewelry, metalworks and some art that does not fit into listed categories. Juried. Awards/prizes: Best of Show. Exhibitors: 250. Number of attendees: 10,000-15,000. Admission: $8; $12 2 day pass; 16 & under free. Apply online .

ADDITIONAL INFORMATION Deadline for entry: see website. Application fee: earlybird, $45; regular, $55 (fee is non-refundable). Space fee: $250 + 15% of all sales. Exhibition space: 12×12. For more information, visit website.

SPACE COAST ART FESTIVAL

P.O.Box 320135, Cocoa Beach FL 32932. (321)784-3322. Fax: (866)815-3322. E-mail: info@spacecoastartfestival.com. Website: www.spacecoastartfestival.com. Art & craft show held annually in November. Outdoors. Accepts handmade crafts and other mediums. Juried. Awards/prizes: up to $50,000 in awards. Number exhibitors: 250. Number attendees: varies. Admission: see website. Apply online.

ADDITIONAL INFORMATION Deadline for entry: early July. Application fee: $40. Space fee: $300. Exhibition space: 12×12. For more information, crafters should e-mail, call or visit website.

SPANKER CREEK FARM ARTS & CRAFTS FAIR

P.O. Box 5644, Bella Vista AR 72714. (479)685-5655. E-mail: info@spankercreekfarm.com. Website: www.spankercreekfarm.com. Arts & craft show held annually in the spring & fall. Outdoors & indoors. Accepts handmade crafts, ceramics, paintings, jewelry, glass, photography, wearable art and other mediums. Juried. Number exhibitors: see website. Number attendees: varies. Free to public. Apply online.

ADDITIONAL INFORMATION Deadline for entry: see website for dates. Application fee: none. Space fee: varies. Exhibition space: varies. For more information, crafters should call, e-mail or visit website.

SPRING CRAFT FEST

Ozark Regional Promotions, 5557 Walden St., Lowell AR 72745. (479)756-6954. E-mail: karenlloyd@juno.com. Website: www.ozarkregionalartsandcrafts.com. Art & craft show held annually in May. Indoors. Accepts handmade crafts and other mediums. Juried. Number exhibitors: see website. Number attendees: varies. Free to public. Apply online.

ADDITIONAL INFORMATION Deadline for entry: March. Application fee: none. Space fee: varies. Exhibition space: varies. For more information, crafters should e-mail, call or visit website.

SPRING FESTIVAL: AN ARTS & CRAFTS AFFAIR

Huffman Productions, Inc., P.O. Box 655, Antioch IL 60002. (402)331-2889. E-mail: hpifestivals@cox.net. Website: www.hpifestivals.com. Fine arts & crafts fair held annually 3 times a year in the Spring. Indoors. Accepts handmade crafts and other mediums. Juried. Number exhibitors: see website. Number of attendees: varies per show. Admission: varies per show. Apply online.

ADDITIONAL INFORMATION Deadline for entry: see website. Application fee: none. Space fee: see website. Exhibition space: 10×10. For more information, crafters should e-mail, visit website or call.

SPRING FESTIVAL OF THE ARTS OAKBROOK CENTER

Amdur Productions, P.O. Box 550, Highland Park IL 60035. (847)926-4300. Fax: (847)926-4330. E-mail: info@amdurproductions.com. Website: www.amdurproductions.com. Art & craft show held annually in May. Outdoors. Accepts handmade crafts and other mediums. Juried. Number exhibitors: see website. Number attendees: varies. Free to public. Apply online.

ADDITIONAL INFORMATION Deadline for entry: early April. Application fee: $25. Space fee: $460. Exhibition space: 10×10. For more information, crafters should e-mail, call or visit website.

SPRING FESTIVAL ON PONCE

Olmstead Park, North Druid Hills, 1451 Ponce de Leon, Atlanta GA 30307. (404)873-1222. E-mail:

Lisa@affps.com. Website: festivalonponce.com. Contact: Lisa Windle, festival director. Estab. 2011. Arts & crafts show held annually early April. Outdoors. Accepts handmade crafts, painting, photography, sculpture, leather, metal, glass, jewelry. Juried by a panel. Awards/prizes: ribbons. Number of exhibitors: 125. Number of attendees: 40,000. Free to public. Apply online at Zapplication.org.

ADDITIONAL INFORMATION Deadline for entry: February 7. Application fee: $25. Space fee: $250. Exhibition space: 10×10. For more information, see website.

SPRING GREEN ARTS & CRAFTS FAIR

Spring Green Arts & Crafts Fair Committee, P.O. Box 96, Spring Green WI 53588. E-mail: springgreenartfair@gmail.com. Website: www.springgreenartfair.com. Fine arts & crafts fair held annually June. Indoors. Accepts handmade crafts, glass, wood, painting, fiber, graphics, pottery, sculpture, jewelry, photography. Juried. Awards/prizes: Best of Show, Award of Excellence. Number exhibitors: see website. Number of attendees: varies per show. Admission: varies per show. Apply online.

ADDITIONAL INFORMATION Deadline for entry: mid February. Application fee: $10-$20. Space fee: $150. Exhibition space: 10×10. For more information, crafters should e-mail or visit website.

SPRINGTIME IN OHIO

P.O. Box 586, Findlay OH 45839-0586. (419)436-1457. Fax: (419)435-5035. E-mail: hello@cloudshows.biz. Website: www.cloudshows.biz. Estab. 1988. Arts & crafts show held annually in May. Indoors & outdoors. Accepts handmade crafts and other items. Exhibitors: 280. Admission: $5; children 12 & under free. Apply online.

ADDITIONAL INFORMATION Deadline for entry: see website. Application fee: see website. Space fee: see website. Exhibition space: see website. For more information, crafters should e-mail, visit website.

SQUARE TOMATOES CRAFT FAIR

P.O. Box 4471, Davis CA 95617. (530)758-4903. E-mail: squaretcrafts@gmail.com. Website: www.squaretomatoescrafts.com. Contact: Sally Parker. Fine arts

& crafts fair held annually July. Outdoors. Accepts handmade crafts and other mediums. Juried. Number exhibitors: see website. Number of attendees: varies. Free to public. Apply online.

ADDITIONAL INFORMATION Deadline for entry: see website. Application fee: none. Space fee: $25. Exhibition space: 10×10. For more information, crafters should e-mail, call or visit website.

ST. ARMANDS CIRCLE CRAFT FESTIVAL

270 Central Blvd., Suite 107B, Jupiter FL 33458. (561)746-6615. Fax: (561)746-6528. E-mail: info@artfestival.com. Website: www.artfestival.com. "For two days, festival-goers will enjoy works from the state's best talent of crafters and long-time festival favorites along with the newest names on the contemporary craft scene. Come see some of America's best crafters displaying one of a kind jewelry, pottery, plant holders, soaps, and much much more. Also included will be an expansive green market with unique orchids and delicious dips and sauces!"

ST. CLAIR ART FAIR

Alice W. Moore Center for the Arts, 201 N. Riverside Ave. (in Riverview Plaza), Saint Clair MI 48079. (810)329-9576. Fax: (810)329-9464. Website: www.stclairart.org. The annual St. Clair Art Fair is one of the oldest art fairs in eastern Michigan. This juried Art Fair is traditionally the last full weekend in June, Saturday and Sunday. See website for more information.

ST. JOHN MEDICAL CENTER FESTIVAL OF THE ARTS

(440)808-9201. E-mail: ardis.radak@csauh.com. Website: www.www.sjws.net/festival_of_arts.aspx. Contact: Ardis Radak. Art & craft show held annually in July. Outdoors. Cleveland OH. Accepts handmade crafts, ceramics, glass, fiber, glass, graphics, jewelry, leather, metal, mixed media, painting, photography, printmaking, sculpture, woodworking. Juried. Awards/prizes: Best of Show, 1st Place, 2nd Place, Honorable Mention. Number exhibitors: 200. Number attendees: 15,000. Free to public. Apply via Zapplication.org.

ADDITIONAL INFORMATION Deadline for entry: May. Application fee: $15. Space fee: $300 (single); $600 (double). Exhibition space: 10×10 (single); 10×20 (double). For more information, crafters should e-mail, call or visit website.

ST. MARY'S SAUER KRAUT FESTIVAL CRAFT FAIR

301 W. Tielky St., Bear Creek WI 54929. (715)460-5202. Fax: (715)823-6010. E-mail: songofbernadette@gmail.com. Website: www.ssrmparishes.org. Contact: Jennifer Wood, chair. Estab. 2010. Arts & crafts show held annually the 1st week of August. Outdoors. Accepts handmade crafts, party plans, unique gifts, antiques. Exhibitors: 30. Number of attendees: 200. Free to public. Apply via website.

ADDITIONAL INFORMATION Deadline for entry: see website. Space fee: $25. Exhibition space: 10×10. For more information, e-mail.

TIPS "The festival is a family event with carnival games, car show, parade, and dinner. It is located in a high traffic area. Keep displays simple and bright to attract attention."

ST. PAUL FINE CRAFT SHOW

American Craft Council Shows, 155 Water St., 4th Floor, Unit 5, Brooklyn NY 11201. (800)836-3470. Fax: (612)355-2330. E-mail: shows@craftcouncil.org. Website: www.craftcouncil.org. Art & craft show held annually in April. Indoors. Accepts handmade crafts, ceramics, fiber, metal and other mediums. Juried. Awards/prizes: Awards of Excellence. Number exhibitors: 240. Number attendees: varies. Free to public. Apply online.

ADDITIONAL INFORMATION Deadline for entry: August. Application fee: $30 + $10 handling/processing fee for each set of images. Space fee: varies. Exhibition space: varies. For more information, crafters should e-mail, call or visit website.

ST. PETE BEACH COREY AREA CRAFT FESTIVAL

270 Central Blvd., Suite 107B, Jupiter FL 33458. (561)746-6615. Fax: (561)746-6528. E-mail: info@artfestival.com. Website: www.artfestival.com. "Corey Avenue in St. Pete Beach comes alive with the nation's best crafters displaying their handmade pottery, jewelry, paintings, and so much more! This open-air craft

festival also includes a Green Market featuring exotic live plants, handmade soaps, savory dips, and gourmet sauces. Join us for a fun, free event in the heart of St. Pete Beach."

STITCHES IN BLOOM QUILT SHOW AT THE OREGON GARDEN

879 W. Main St., Silverton OR 97381. (503)874-8100. E-mail: info@oregongarden.org. Website: www.oregongarden.org. Contact: Mary Ridderbusch, events coordinator. Estab. 2005. Arts & crafts/quilt show held annually in late January. Indoors. Accepts handmade crafts and quilts. Awards/prizes: Peoples' Choice; Challenge Quilt. Exhibitors: 20. Number of attendees: 2,300. Admission: $11. Apply online at www.oregongarden.org/events/quiltshow.

ADDITIONAL INFORMATION Deadline for entry: January 9. Application fee: $10. Space fee: $150-260, Exhibition space: 9,000 sq. ft. For more information e-mail or see website.

STITCH ROCK

E-mail: info@rockthestitch.com. Website: www.rockthestitch.com. "Stitch Rock is South Florida's largest annual indie craft fair & bazaar bringing back old school crafting techniques with new school flare! Wth over 80 vendors the show is full of uncommon handmade goods like D.I.Y fashion, funky home deco items, adorable plushies, natural bath & body goodies, vintage finds, hot rod paintings, pin up photography, & much more!" See website for more information.

STONE MOUNTAIN OKTOBERFEST & ARTIST MARKET

6655 James B. Rivers Dr., Stone Mountain GA 30083. (404)873-1222. E-mail: lisa@affps.com. Website: www.stonemountainvillage.com/oktoberfest0809.html. Contact: Lisa Windle, festival director. Estab. 2011. Arts & crafts show held annually mid October. Outdoors. Accepts handmade crafts, painting, photography, sculpture, leather, metal, glass, jewelry. Juried by a panel. Awards/prizes: ribbons. Number of exhibitors: 150. Number of attendees: 7,500. Free to public. Apply online at Zapplication.org.

ADDITIONAL INFORMATION Deadline for entry: August 22. Application fee: $25. Space fee: $150.

Exhibition space: 10×10. For more information, see website.

SUGARLOAF CRAFT FESTIVALS

Sugarloaf Mountain Works, Inc., 19807 Executive Park Circle, Germantown MD 20874. (301)990-1400; (800)210-9900. Fax: (301)253-9620. E-mail: sugarloafinfo@sugarloaffest.com. Website: www. sugarloafcrafts.com. "For over 30 years, the nation's most talented artisans have personally sold their contemporary crafts and fine art at Sugarloaf Craft Festivals. You will find Sugarloaf Craft Festivals in five great locations in the Mid-Atlantic area. Sugarloaf art fairs and craft festivals are among the nation's best and largest shows of their kind. Each show features a variety of work by the most talented craft designers and fine artists. From blown glass and sculpture to fine art and designer clothing, you'll find the handcrafted creations you're looking for at Sugarloaf!" See website for more information.

SUGAR PLUM BAZAAR

E-mail: sugarplumbazaar@yahoo.com. Website: www.sugarplumbazaar.com. Handmade and vintage event. Juried. Apply online. See website for more details.

SUGARPLUM MARKETPLACE

E-mail: sugarplum1market@yahoo.com. Website: www.jltheshoals.org/sugarplummarketplace.htm. "This three-day marketplace includes an array of children's events, and shopping opportunities. Shoppers from across the Southeast will enjoy more than 90 merchants from throughout the U.S. offering unique gifts and holiday trends in a festive, family-friendly atmosphere. The Sugarplum Marketplace serves as a major fundraiser for the Junior League of the Shoals. Funds raised support the league's ongoing efforts to improve the Shoals community through the effective action and leadership of trained volunteers." See website for more information.

SUMMER ON SOUTHPORT

Amdur Productions, P.O. Box 550, Highland Park IL 60035. (847)926-4300. Fax: (847)926-4330. E-mail: info@amdurproductions.com. Website: www.am durproductions.com. Art & craft show held annually in July. Outdoors. Accepts handmade crafts and other mediums. Juried. Number exhibitors: 100. Number attendees: varies. Admission: $5 donation to Southport Neighbors Association. Apply online.
ADDITIONAL INFORMATION Deadline for entry: early January. Application fee: $25. Space fee: $335. Exhibition space: 10×10. For more information, crafters should e-mail, call or visit website.

SUMMIT ART FESTIVAL

Website: www.summitartfest.org. Fine arts & crafts fair held annually October. Outdoors. Accepts handmade crafts, jewelry, ceramics, painting, glass, photography, fiber and more. Juried. Awards/prizes: Best of Show, 2nd place, 3rd place, Mayor's Award, Juror's Merit Award. Number exhibitors: see website. Number attendees: varies. Free to public. Apply online.
ADDITIONAL INFORMATION Deadline for entry: July. Application fee: $25. Space fee: $255. Exhibition space: 10×10. For more information, crafters should visit website.

SUNCOAST ARTS FESTIVAL

E-mail: info@suncoastartsfest.com. Website: www. suncoastartsfest.com. "The Suncoast Arts Fest (SAF) has brought together quality fine artists and craftspeople with area art lovers who are motivated to buy. The event takes place in the heart of the Tampa Bay area, convenient to major interstates. SAF is a family-oriented cultural event. Artwork exhibited must be appropriate for viewers of all ages. The SAF committee has the sole exclusive and final authority to determine if any work is not acceptable for display." See website for more information.

SUN VALLEY CENTER ARTS & CRAFTS FESTIVAL

P.O. Box 656, Sun Valley ID 83353. (208)726-9491. Fax: (208)726-2344. E-mail: festival@sunvalleycenter. org. Website: www.sunvalleycenter.org. Contact: Sarah Kolash, festival director. Estab. 1968. Annual fine art & craft show held 2nd weekend in August. Outdoors. Accepts handmade crafts, ceramics, drawing, fiber, glass, jewelry, metalwork, mixed media, painting, photography, printmaking, sculpture, woodwork. Juried. Exhibitors: 130. Number of attendees: 12,000. Free to public. Apply via Zapplication.org.

ADDITIONAL INFORMATION Deadline for entry: February 28. Application fee: $30 before February 1; $35 on/after February 1. Space fee: $450 & $900. Exhibition space: 10×10 & 10×20. Average sales: $3,700. For more information, e-mail or see website.

TACOMA HOLIDAY FOOD & GIFT FESTIVAL

Tacoma Dome, 2727 E. D St., Tacoma WA 98421. (800)521-7469. Fax: (425)889-8165. E-mail: tacoma@showcaseevents.org. Website: www.showcaseevents.org. Contact: Susie O'Brien Borer, show manager. Estab. 1982. Seasonal holiday show held annually in October. Indoors. Accepts handmade crafts, art, photography, pottery, glass, jewelry, clothing, fiber. Juried. Exhibitors: 500. Number of attendees: 40,000. Admission: $13.50 (for all 5 days); 12 & under free. Apply via website or call or e-mail for application.

ADDITIONAL INFORMATION Deadline for entry: October 7. Space fee: see website. Exhibition space: 6×10, 7×10, 10×10. For more information, e-mail, call, send SASE or visit website.

TIPS "Competitive pricing, attractive booth display, quality product, something unique for sale, friendly & outgoing personality."

TAHOE ARTS PROJECT ART FESTIVAL

(530)542-3632. E-mail: tahoearts@aol.com. Website: www.tahoeartsproject.org. "Tahoe Arts Project Art Festival is an art show nestled in a pine forest in the heart of South Lake Tahoe. Festival admission and parking will be free for artists." See website for more information.

TAHOE CITY FINE ARTS & CRAFTS FESTIVAL

Pacific Fine Arts Festivals, P.O. Box 280, Pine Grove CA 95665. (209)267-4394. Fax: (209)267-4395. E-mail: pfa@pacificfinearts.com. Website: www.pacificfinearts.com. The annual Tahoe City Fine Arts & Crafts Festival will give visitors a special opportunity to meet with more than 45 artisans and craftspeople showcasing a wide variety of arts and crafts including photography, oil paintings, ceramic vessels, jewelry and much more." See website for more information.

TALBOT STREET ART FAIR

Talbot Street Art Fair, P.O. Box 489, Danville IN 46122. (317)745-6479. E-mail: talbotstreetartfair@hotmail.com. Website: www.talbotstreet.org. "With over 270 artists from across the nation, this juried art fair continues to be ranked as one of the finest fairs in the country. Talbot Street Art Fair is located between 16th & 20th / Delaware & Pennsylvania—Indianapolis in the historic Herron-Morton neighborhood.This is a family-friendly event with plenty to see and do for everyone." See website for more information.

⊚ TAOS FALL ARTS FESTIVAL

P.O. Box 675, Taos NM 87571. (575)758-4648. E-mail: tfafvolunteer@gmail.com. Website: www.taosfallarts.com. Contact: Patsy S. Wright. Estab. 1974. "This festival is the oldest art festival in Taos, premiering in 1974 and only showcasing artist that reside in Taos County. It includes three major art shows: the curated exhibit titled 'Distinguished Achievement Award Series,' a juried exhibit titled 'Taos Select,' and the 'Taos Open,' as its name implies, an exhibit open to all artists working in Taos County. The festival represents over 250 Taos County artists working in a variety of mediums. Each year a limited edition poster is printed to commemorate the arts festival. The proceeds from the shows will benefit art programs for Taos County children." See website for more information.

THIRD WARD ART FESTIVAL

Amdur Productions, P.O. Box 550, Highland Park IL 60035. (847)926-4300. Fax: (847)926-4330. E-mail: info@amdurproductions.com. Website: www.amdurproductions.com. Art & craft show held annually in August. Outdoors. Accepts handmade crafts and other mediums. Juried. Awards/prizes: given at festival. Number exhibitors: 135. Number attendees: 30,000. Free to public. Apply online.

ADDITIONAL INFORMATION Deadline for entry: early January. Application fee: $25. Space fee: $450. Exhibition space: 10×10. For more information, crafters should e-mail, call or visit website.

THOUSAND OAKS ART FESTIVAL

City of Thousand Oaks, Cultural Affairs Department, 2100 E. Thousand Oaks Blvd., Thousand Oaks CA 91362. (805)498-6591. E-mail: richardswilliams@roadrunner.com. Website: www.toartsfestival.com. "2-day festival with more than 60 visual art exhibitors. Continuous live performances, children's hands-on artistic and interactive art exhibits, and over 12,000 visitors. Free admission and parking. Smoke free premises. Wine Tasting at the lakes." See website for more information.

THREE RIVERS ART FESTIVAL

P.O. Box 633, Covington LA 70434. (985)327-9797. E-mail: info@threeriversartfestival.com. Website: www.threeriversartfestival.com. "With 200 artists from more than 20 states. A juried show of original works. Tent after colorful tent ranged along the streets of historic downtown Covington, Louisiana. Arts and fine crafts demonstrations. Music. Food. Three Rivers Run. And lots of activities just for kids. It's the Covington Three Rivers Art Festival. Where the fun starts with art and goes on for two wonderful days." See website for more information.

TALUCA LAKE FINE ARTS FESTIVAL

West Coast Artists, P.O. Box 750, Acton CA 93510. (818)813-4478. Fax: (661)526-4575. E-mail: info@westcoastartists.com. Website: www.westcoastartists.com. "Open to all media of original fine art and fine crafts. All work will be juried. Categories will be limited. No commercial, manufactured, imported, mass produced or purchased for resale items will be accepted. No clothing. No representatives." See website for more information.

◗ TORRIANO CRAFT & HANDMADE FAIR

E-mail: torrianoparents@gmail.com. Website: www.facebook.com/TorrianoCraftMarket/info. "Bi-annual pop-up market selling affordable and original creations. Have-a-go craft demos, portraits and facepainting for children." See website for more information.

○ TRENTON AVENUE ARTS FESTIVAL

E-mail: info@trentonaveartsfest.org. Website: www.trentonaveartsfest.org. "Free and open to the public, the Trenton Avenue Arts Festival celebrates East Kensington's incredible mix of local artists, musicians and eateries. Organized by the dedicated volunteers of the East Kensington Neighbors Association and featuring over 200 local arts and food vendors, TAAF attracts 10k+ attendees to raise funds for neighborhood projects and revitalization. The festival is held on Trenton Avenue, a wide cobblestone street that has been part of Kensington's rich creative history for over a hundred years. By hosting the Trenton Avenue Arts Festival, EKNA continues that tradition." See website for more information.

○ UNIQUE LA

Website: www.stateofunique.com. "Unique LA was created by community leader and designer Sonja Rasula as a way to bring local-made design and art to the masses while helping to grow and support the U.S. economy and small businesses. Currently 20,000+ attendees come to discover independent designers/artists and buy local (an estimated $1.5 million is spent at each two-day show). At the largest independent design show in the country, attendees get the rare chance to meet and shop directly from hundreds of hand-selected designers and artists in one space. All of the products at the show are made right here in the USA. Unique LA makes it easy for shoppers to support the local economy, discover great design and deals, join in community, and have a blast with DJs/free drinks/free craft projects and workshops and more." See website for more information.

○ UNPLAZA ART FAIR

E-mail: PeaceWorksKC@gmail.com. Website: www.peaceworkskc.org/unplaza.html. Art fair. Annual fundraiser for Peace Works Kansas City. See website for more information and to apply.

UPPER ARLINGTON LABOR DAY ARTS FESTIVAL

(614)583-5000. Website: www.uaoh.net/egov/docs/1389217117601.htm. Fine art & craft show held annually in September. Outdoors. Accepts handmade crafts, ceramics, fiber, glass, graphics, jewelry, leather, metal, mixed media, painting, photography, printmaking, sculpture, woodworking. Juried. Awards/prizes: $1,350 in award. Number exhibitors: 200. Number attendees: 25,000. Free to public. Apply via Zapplication.org.

ADDITIONAL INFORMATION Deadline for entry: February. Application fee: see website. Space fee: varies. Exhibition space: varies. For more information, crafters should call or visit website.

URBAN CRAFT UPRISING

E-mail: kristen@urbancraftuprising.com. Website: www.urbancraftuprising.com. "Urban Craft Uprising is Seattle's largest indie craft show! At UCU, now in its eighth year, fans can choose from a wide variety of hand-crafted goods, including clothing of all types, jewelry, gifts, bags, wallets, buttons, accessories, aprons, children's goods, toys, housewares, paper goods, candles, kits, art, food, and much, much more. Each show is carefully curated and juried to ensure the best mix of crafts and arts, along with quality and originality. This bi-annual show showcases over 100 vendors excelling in the world of craft, art and design." See website for more information.

UTAH ARTS FESTIVAL

230 S. 500 W. #120, Salt Lake City UT 84101. (801)322-2428. E-mail: lisa@uaf.org. Website: www.uaf.org. "The annual festival takes place the 4th weekend of June each summer and is held downtown in Salt Lake City at Library and Washington Squares. A full time staff of four and one part-time person work year-round to produce the Festival. In addition, we engage seasonal coordinators to help plan and implement artistic programs each year. A technical staff, stage and production crews, along with more than 1,000 volunteers rounds out the personnel needed to produce the annual event. The Utah Arts Festival is the largest outdoor multi-disciplinary arts event in Utah with attendance hovering over 80,000 each summer. Having garnered numerous awards internationally, nation-ally and locally, the event remains one of the premiere events that kicks off the summer in Utah each June." See website for more information.

VAGABOND INDIE CRAFT FAIR

E-mail: urbanbazaarsf@gmail.com. Website: www.vagabondsf.wordpress.com. "This event, which includes more than 20 talented local artists and craftspeople selling their work over 2 days (different vendors each day!), takes place in the back garden of Urban Bazaar. The merchandise offered at Vagabond will include all manner of gifts, with a focus on jewelry, accessories, and affordable artwork." See website for more information.

VERMONT MAPLE FESTIVAL

E-mail: info@vtmaplefestival.org. Website: www.vtmaplefestival.org. "Glittery jewelry, taste-tempting specialty foods, classy clothing, assorted artwork, wooden things, fine photographs, and so much more! Now enlarged to more than 60 vendors, the show offers both traditional and the latest in craft innovations, as well as the fine specialty foods for which Vermont is famous! It's one of the first large craft shows of the year, and it's admission free—a show that folks who delight in creativity have on their 'don't miss' list." See website for more information.

VICTORIAN CHRISTMAS IN LANDMARK PARK

Arts and Crafts Landmark Park, P.O/ Box 6362, Dothan AL 36302. (334)794-3452. Website: www.landmarkpark.com/events.html#current. "Warm up to some holiday hospitality during an afternoon centered on the pleasures of Christmas' past. Visitors are invited to sample turn-of-the-century desserts and sip hot chocolate or mulled cider while children try their hand at making traditional Christmas decorations. A circuit-riding preacher will arrive on horseback to deliver a Christmas message at the church. Arts and crafts, holiday music, wagon rides and more. Free admission; visitors are encouraged to bring a nonperishable food item for donation to the Wiregrass Area United Way Food Bank." See website for more information.

VILLAGES CRAFT FESTIVAL AT COLONY PLAZA

270 Central Blvd., Suite 107B, Jupiter FL 33458. (561)746-6615. Fax: (561)746-6528. E-mail: info@art festival.com. Website: www.artfestival.com. "There's something for everyone at this craft festival, featuring arts and crafts all created in the USA. Handmade one-of-a-kind jewelry pieces you will not find anywhere else, personalized wall hangings, art for your pets, ceramics—functional and decorative, and much, much more. An expansive green market lends plants, exotic flora and homemade soaps. Come find that unique gift and we will see you there!"

THE VILLAGES CRAFT FESTIVAL AT LA PLAZA GRANDE

270 Central Blvd., Suite 107B, Jupiter FL 33458. (561)746-6615. Fax: (561)746-6528. E-mail: info@art festival.com. Website: www.artfestival.com. Arts & crafts show held annually in January. Outdoors. Accepts handmade crafts and other items. Juried. Exhibitors: see website. Number of attendees: varies. Admission: see website. Apply online.
ADDITIONAL INFORMATION Deadline for entry: see website. Application fee: see website. Space fee: see website. Exhibition space: see website. For more information, crafters should e-mail, visit website or call.

VINTAGE DAYS CRAFTS FAIRE

(559)278-2741. E-mail: vintagecraftsfaire@gmail. com. Website: www.fresnostate.edu/studentaffairs/ studentinvolvement/traditions/vintagedays/crafts. html. "The Vintage Days Crafts Faire is a marketplace for over 100 exhibitors specializing in handmade items including jewelry, children's toys, home decor, and more. To ensure high quality and innovative items, all applications are juried." See website for more information.

WALK IN THE WOODS ART FAIR

Hawthorn Hollow, 880 Green Bay Rd., Kenosha WI 53144. (334)794-3452.. E-mail: hawthornhollow@ wi.rr.com. Website: www.hawthornhollow.org/ events/art-fair. "The Walk in the Woods Art Fair has grown to be one of the more popular and well respected in southeastern Wisconsin, where over 60 artists display their creations along the wooded trails and gardens of Hawthorn Hollow. Fine art ranging from jewelry to acrylic and watercolor paintings, from photography to wood sculpting, glass and garden art will all be available for purchase. We also feature live entertainment throughout the day, face painting, food/ beverages for sale, and a silent auction. A $5.00 donation per vehicle is requested. Come and enjoy a beautiful day combining fine art with music and nature." See website for more information.

WALNUT CREEK SIDEWALK FINE ARTS & CRAFTS FESTIVAL

Pacific Fine Arts Festivals, P.O. Box 280, Pine Grove CA 95665. (209)267-4394. Fax: (209)267-4395. E-mail: pfa@pacificfinearts.com. Website: www.pacificfinearts.com. "The annual fine arts and crafts festival is free to the public and will feature more than 150 professional artists traveling from throughout California and the Western United States to showcase original paintings, sculpture, photography, jewelry, clothing and other fine works." See website for more information.

WASHINGTON CRAFT SHOW

Crafts America, LLC, P.O. Box 603, Green Farms CT 06838. (203)254-0486. Fax: (203)254-9672. E-mail: info@craftsamericashows.com. Website: www.crafts americashows.com/WASH_main.htm. Fine crafts fair held annually in October. Indoors. Accepts handmade crafts, basketry, ceramics, fiber, furniture, glass, jewelry, leather, metal, mixed media, paper, wood. Juried. Awards/prizes: cash awards. Number exhibitors: see website. Number attendees: varies. Admission: $15 general; $14 seniors; children 12 & under free. Apply online.
ADDITIONAL INFORMATION Application deadline: mid October. Application fee: $45. Space fee: varies. Exhibition space: varies. For more information, crafters should e-mail, call or visit website.

WATERFRONT INVITATIONAL ART FAIR

Saugatuck Douglas Art Club, Box 176, Saugatuck MI 49453-0176. (334)794-3452. E-mail: artclub@ saugatuckdouglasartclub.org. Website: www.

saugatuckdouglasartclub.org. Juried art & craft fair. See website for more information.

WASAU FESTIVAL OF ARTS

P.O. Box 1763, Wausau WI 54402. (715)842-1676. E-mail: artclub@saugatuckdouglasartclub.org. Website: www.wausaufoa.org. "Since its inception in 1965, this outdoor celebration of the arts has become an annual event in the heart of Wausau's historic downtown and an integral part of Wausau's Artrageous weekend. Patrons can enjoy and purchase artwork in a variety of styles and price ranges from over 120 juried, professional artists from all over the United States." See website for more information.

⊙ WEDGWOOD ART FESTIVAL

P.O. Box 15246, Seattle WA 98115. E-mail: wafestival@gmail.com. Website: www.wedgwoodfestival.com. "The Wedgwood Art Festival is a 2-day event supporting and celebrating arts for the community of Wedgwood, Seattle. Most participating artists reside in Seattle and the Puget Sound area. A few guest Northwest artists who live outside the Puget Sound area are also included to add variety to the show." See website for more information.

WELLS STREET ART FESTIVAL

E-mail: rrobinson@chicagoevents.com. Website: www.chicagoevents.com. "One of the city's largest and most acclaimed fine arts happenings, it's held in the heart of Chicago's historic Old Town neighborhood. The annual art extravaganza features the works of more than 250 juried artists with the eclectic mix running the gamut from paintings, sculptures and glasswork to photography, ceramics, woodwork and much more. It also features the tasty cuisine of Old Town restaurants, the always-hoppin' music stage, and a silent auction." See website for more information.

WILLOUGHBY ARTSFEST

28 Public Square, Willoughby OH 44094. (440)942-1632. E-mail: info@wwlcchamber.com. Website: www.wwlcchamber.com. "Historical Downtown Willoughby, in the hub of Lake County, is located 20 miles east of Cleveland and easily accessible from both Interstate 2 and 90. Featuring over 125 artists, entertainment & food, this show welcomes over 10,000 people. Willoughby ArtsFest—you won't want to miss it!" See website for more information.

⟳ WINNIPEG FOLK FESTIVAL HANDMADE VILLAGE

203-211 Bannatyne Avenue, Winnipeg MB R3B 3P2, Canada. (204)231-0096; (866)301-3823. Fax: (204)231-0076. E-mail: info@winnipegfolkfestival.ca. Website: www.winnipegfolkfestival.ca. "The Hand-Made Village celebrates the long-standing history that folk art shares with folk music festivals. Our village features the handmade work of up to 50 artisans from across Canada." See website for more information.

WINTER PARK SIDEWALK ART FESTIVAL

Winter Park Sidewalk Art Festival, P.O. Box 597, Winter Park FL 32790-0597. (407)644-7207. E-mail: wpsaf@yahoo.com. Website: www.wpsaf.org. "The Winter Park Sidewalk Art Festival is one of the nation's oldest, largest and most prestigious juried outdoor art festivals, consistently rated among the top shows by *Sunshine Artist* and *American Style* magazines. Each year more than 350,000 visitors enjoy the show." See website for more information.

WOODLANDS WATERWAY ARTS FESTIVAL

P.O. Box 8184, The Woodlands TX 77387. E-mail: info@woodlandsartsfestival.com. Website: www.woodlandsartsfestival.com. "The Woodlands Waterway Arts Festival (WWAF) weekend event is a celebration of visual, culinary and performing arts. The festival gives patrons the rare and special opportunity to meet and talk with artists from around the country, sample great food, watch the Art of Food demos, enjoy live music and entertain their families at our interactive 'ARTOPOLY' area. Adult tickets are $12.00, a weekend pass is $15.00, and children 12 and under are admitted free. Cash ONLY at all gates and food vendors." See website for more information.

WOODSSTOCK MUSIC & ARTS FESTIVAL

(419)862-3182. Website: www.woodsstock.org. Fine art & craft show held annually in August. Outdoors. Accepts handmade crafts, ceramics, drawing, fiber, glass, jewelry, leather, metal, mixed media, painting, photography, sculpture, wood. Juried. Awards/prizes: Best of Show, Honorable Mention. Number exhibitors: see website. Number attendees: varies. Admission: $25 general; $45 VIP. Apply via Zapplication.org.

ADDITIONAL INFORMATION Deadline for entry: June. Application fee: $20. Space fee: $100 (single); $150 (double). Exhibition space: 10×10 (single); 10×20 (double). For more information, crafters should visit website.

YELLOW DAISY FESTIVAL

E-mail: ydf@stonemountainpark.com. Website: www.stonemountainpark.com/events/Yellow-Daisy-Festival.aspx. "More than 400 artists and crafters from 38 States and two countries display their works for your appreciation and purchase. Daily live entertainment, Children's Corner activities, and crafter demonstrations throughout the event as well as fabulous festival foods. Yellow Daisy Festival is free with paid parking admission. Vehicle entry to the park is $10 for a one day permit or $35 for an annual permit." See website for more information.

ONLINE MARKET-PLACES

Most crafters are aware of Etsy, but there are other on-line marketplaces that provide support for craft artisans. Whether you choose to diversify your on-line presence by selling across multiple platforms, or choose to focus on one or two sites, you need to be aware of the ever-changing landscape of online sales. Visit their website and take a look around. Do they offer a functionality that would be helpful to your online sales? Do you recognize anyone who is selling on that site? What is the competition? How do images appear? What is the site's financial take of your sales, or do they charge a flat fee per listing? Consider all of your options and do your research to make sure you are maximizing your online opportunities. Also, be sure to read Kristen Robinson's article, "Finding Success on Etsy" for insight into starting and maintaining a successful Etsy shop. Kristen's article provides information specific to Etsy as well as across-the-board insight into online selling.

The listings here are only the tip of the iceberg. More an more online venues sprout up everyday. As a crafter and business person, get to know the venues before. If you can, order from a vendor to gain a first-hand understanding of the user's experience. Try to talk with someone who has a shop on the site—or sites—you're interested in.

KEY TO SYMBOLS & ABBREVIATIONS

Symbol	Meaning
☢	Canadian market
🌐	market located outside of the U.S. and Canada
⌂	market prefers to work with local artists/designers
b&w	black & white (photo or illustration)
SASE	self-addressed, stamped envelope
SAE	self-addressed envelope
IRC	International Reply Coupon, for use when mailing to countries other than your own

COMPLAINT PROCEDURE

If you feel you have not been treated fairly by a company listed in *Crafter's Market*, we advise you to take the following steps:

- First, try to contact the company. Sometimes one e-mail or letter can quickly clear up the matter.
- Document all your correspondence with the company. If you write to us with a complaint, provide the details of your submission, the date of your first contact with the company, and the nature of your subsequent correspondence.
- We will enter your complaint into our files.
- The number and severity of complaints will be considered in our decision whether to delete the listing from the next edition.
- We reserve the right to not list any company for any reason.

ARTFIRE

E-mail: service@artfire.com. Website: www.artfire.com. Geared towards handmade items. Provides shopping cart feature. Products sold: handmade items, vintage, supplies, PDF downloads, patterns/books. Setup costs: $12.95/month. Accepted payment methods: Visa, Mastercard, American Express, PayPal, Bill Me Later, ProPay, Amazon Payments. Sales disputes: dedicated customer service team to resolve disputes and answer queries. Provided to sellers: community forums/chats, additional free marketing opportunities, groups.

ARTFUL HOME

E-mail: help@artulis.com. Website: www.artulis.com. Geared towards handmade items & other merchandise. Provides shopping cart feature. Products sold: handmade, craft, art, vintage. Provided to sellers: community forums/chats, additional free marketing opportunities, groups.

BONANZA

109 W. Denny Way, #312, Seattle WA, 98119. E-mail: support@bonanza.com. Website: www.bonanza.com. Products sold: handmade items, vintage, supplies, art, crafts, accessories, apparel. Setup costs: free. Accepted payment methods: see website. Sales disputes: dedicated customer service team to resolve disputes and answer queries. Provided to sellers: community forums/chats.

CAFEPRESS

Website: www.cafepress.com. "CafePress is where the world's creative minds join forces to provide an unparalleled marketplace. We give you the power to create custom products and personalized gifts on a variety of high-quality items such as T-shirts, hoodies, posters, bumper stickers and mugs. CafePress also allows you to set up online shops where you can design and sell your own unique merchandise. Our design tools make it easy to add photos, text, images, and even create cool designs or logos from scratch. As if it couldn't get any better, you can even find content from major entertainment partners such as *The Hunger Games*, *Big Bang Theory* and *Star Trek* as well as products dedicated to hobbies, birthdays, the mili-tary and more. At CafePress we print each item as it's ordered and many products ship within 24 hours."

☻ CORIANDR

Mookle Studios Limited, 12 Parklands Close, Chandlers Ford, Eastleigh Hants SO53 2EQ, United Kingdom. E-mail: support@coriandr.com. Website: www.coriandr.com. Geared towards handmade items. Setup costs: see website. Accepted payment methods: credit card, PayPal. Provided to sellers: community forums/chats, groups.

CRAFT IS ART

Las Vegas NV. Website: www.craftisart.com. Estab. 2009. Geared towards handmade items. Provides shopping cart feature. Setup costs: free option; premium option $79.99/yr. Accepted payment methods: Visa, Mastercard, American Express, PayPal, Amazon Payments, Google Checkout. Provided to sellers: community forums/chats, Facebook integration, customizable store, coupons, business cards, postcards.

CRAFTSY

999 18th St., Suite 240, Denver CO 80202. Website: www.craftsy.com. Estab. 2010. "Craftsy provides education and tools to help you bring your creativity to life. Our hundreds of classes in quilting, sewing, knitting, cake decorating, art, photography, cooking and many more categories, bring the world's best instructors to you. Learn at your pace with easy-to-follow HD video lessons you can access on your computer and mobile device anytime, anytime, anywhere, forever. Craftsy's Supplies Shop is carefully curated to bring you the best brands at incredible values, ensuring you always have exactly what you need for your next project. Find your new favorite fabric collections, designer yarns, art supplies, books, class materials and more. Find your next project in Craftsy's Pattern Marketplace, featuring thousands of beautiful patterns from the world's best independent designers. All proceeds go directly to supporting passionate designers, and you can instantly download high-quality patterns for chic shawls, adorable baby booties, couture dresses, scalloped lace hats and so much more!"

DAWANDA

Windscheidstr 18, Berlin 10627, Germany. (44)20 3608 1414. E-mail: english@dawanda.com. Website: en.dawanda.com. Estab. 2006. Geared towards handmade items. Provides shopping cart feature. Products sold: handmade items, vintage, supplies, PDF downloads, patterns/books. Setup costs: free; 5% commission on successful sales. Handling and tax should be included by seller in item price; shipping is added automatically at checkout. Accepted payment methods: Visa, Mastercard, American Express, PayPal, checking account, Wirecard, voucher, cash on collection. Sales disputes: dedicated customer service team to resolve disputes and answer queries within 24 hours. Standard listings: 4 photos & 5,000 characters. Other listing features: detailed product description, size/dimensions/weight, materials utilized, production method, customization options, keywords. Site statistics: 250,000 designers, 4 million products, 3.8 million members, over 200 million page impressions a month, 18 million page visits per month, strong social media presence. Provided to sellers: community forums/chats, additional free marketing opportunities, groups.

TIPS "As an international community, we would recommend sellers translate their listings into a selection of our 7 languages available. In addition, we would recommend uploading high-quality photos with your product on a light, neutral background—Dawanda is a very visual community. Don't forget to tell the story behind your products, too! Dawanda is the online marketplace for unique and handmade products and gives creatives and designers the opportunity to offer their one-of-a-kind and limited edition products for sale. Dawanda centers around the idea of 'social commerce,' allowing customers to interact with designers, comment on favorite products and pass on recommendations. Our lively and passionate community allows buyers and sellers to interact and personalise the shopping experience—going against the grain of mass produced products. Dawanda is an international community available in 7 languages and offers a space for designers and creatives to develop their business, talents and success in turn allowing them to make a living from doing what they love."

ELECTRONIC COTTAGE

Website: www.electroniccottage.com. Estab. 2010. "This arts portal is first and foremost a direct connection between those individuals who enjoy purchasing originally created handmade art & craft work, and those professionals who enjoy creating that work. The extent of this connection is only made possible through the use of computers and the internet, exactly as Joseph Deken predicted decades ago. At EC Gallery, there is no need to join a club, become a member, make up a username, remember a password, leave us your e-mail, or jump through any other hoops. All we ask is that you sit back and enjoy your visits to the studio websites of the immensely talented people from around the world who exhibit via this online gallery. At EC Gallery you can connect directly to make purchases from the distinct websites of over 2,000 contemporary and traditional artists & craftspeople. Each cyberstudio is a truly unique experience, so explore and have fun … you will find much amazing work throughout our community of talented professionals."

ETSY

Website: www.etsy.com. Geared towards handmade items. Shopping cart checkout feature. Products sold: handmade items, vintage, craft supplies. Setup costs: $0.20 to list an item; 3.5% fee on sale price. Listing features: user profiles, photos, shop banner.

FARMMADE

3300 NW 185th #129, Portland OR 97229. Contact: Rex Long, CEO. Estab. 2010. Geared towards handmade items and other merchandise. Provides shopping cart feature. Products sold: handmade items, vintage, supplies, patterns/books. Setup costs: none; also has free trial period. Ongoing fees: after trial period, monthly subscription fee of $5. Per listing fee: none; allow unlimited listings per seller. Transaction fee: 5% per sale. Shipping/handling & tax: added automatically. Accepted payment methods: Visa, Mastercard, American Express, PayPal. Sales disputes: sellers are required to set up their own shop policies for returns, etc. In the event there is a dispute, the seller is responsible for resolving it with the understanding that all transactions are subject to be reviewed by their customers. Standard listings: photos & words. Other listing features: each seller has the ability to tell their personal farm story and to connect their shop to supported social media platforms including personal blogs. Site statistics: startup company with a newsletter, blog and social media presence with followers reaching into the thousands. Provided to sellers: additional free marketing opportunities.

TIPS "A sellers farm story is essential to selling their product. A buyer will connect with a farmer if they can visualize who that farmer is, where they live and how they created their product. This connection is the key to creating a customer for life. A farmer's reputation for being hardworking, fair and honest are well known traits. We qualify our sellers to be involved in agriculture and/or livestock on some scale, whether that is in their backyard or 100 acres of rural farmland, our handmade artists strongly identify with a farmer's way of life. Being self-sufficient and using sustainable practices creates this web of interconnectedness that you can't replicate anywhere else. This is reflected in the quality of their products."

☻ FOLKSY

Harland Works, 72 John Street, Sheffield S2 4QU, United Kingdom. Website: www.folksy.com. Geared towards handmade items. Setup costs: see website. Folksy currently only supports sellers who are living and working in the UK.

GLC CRAFT MALL

(604)946-8041. E-mail: info@glcmall.com. Website: www.glccraftmall.com. Geared towards handmade items. Setup costs: see website. Provides shopping cart checkout feature. Shipping & handling handled by individual shops. Payments accepted: Credit cards, PayPal.

GOODSMITHS

218½ 5th St., West Des Moines IA 50265. Website: www.goodsmiths.com. Geared towards handmade items. Setup costs: see website. Provides shopping cart checkout feature. Payments accepted: MasterCard, Visa, PayPal.

HANDMADE ARTISTS' SHOP

Website: www.handmadeartists.com. Geared towards handmade items. Setup costs: must have a subscription to the Handmade Artists' Shop ($5/month; $50/year). Provides shopping cart checkout feature. Payments accepted: MasterCard, Visa, Discover, American Express, PayPal. Provided to sellers: items added to Google Product Search and The Find, search engine optimization (SEO), internal PM system, coupons, forums, community.

HANDMADE CATALOG

(800)851-0183. E-mail: pam@handmadecatalog.com. Website: www.handmadecatalog.com. Estab. 2002. Geared towards handmade items. Setup costs: see website. Provides shopping cart checkout feature. Provided to sellers: website maintenance, marketing, feature in weekly e-mail newsletter, no contracts & cancel anytime.

ICRAFT

Website: www.icraftgifts.com. Geared towards handmade items. Setup costs: $25 + monthly subscription fee. Provides shopping cart checkout feature. Provided to sellers: search engine optimization (SEO), Facebook & Twitter integration, free Seller's Bootcamp, free blogging software, iCraft community.

I MADE IT! MARKETPLACE

P.O. Box 9613, Pittsburgh PA 15226. (412)254-4464. Website: www.imadeitmarket.com. Contact: Carrie Nardini, director. Estab. 2007. Geared towards handmade items. Products sold: handmade items. Setup costs: currently no online for sales. Ongoing fees: see website. Provided to sellers: community forums/chats, additional paid marketing opportunities, additional free marketing opportunities, seminars, social events, workshops.

TIPS "We have built a reputation for fun, unique, high quality handmade wares including a wide variety of work that is ideal for anyone on a shopper's list."

MADE IT MYSELF

P.O. Box 888, Fresno CA 93714. E-mail: support@madeitmyself.com. Website: www.madeitmyself.com.

Geared towards handmade items. Setup costs: none; 3% fee for every item sold.

MAIN STREET REVOLUTION

Website: www.overstock.com/Main-Street-Revolution/39/store.html. "Main Street Revolution is Overstock.com showing its commitment to small businesses across the United States. By giving local shopkeepers a broader audience, we're supporting the American Dream."

MELA ARTISANS

Website: www.melaartisans.com. "Mela Artisans is a luxury lifestyle brand that combines traditional handcrafting techniques with the freshness and functionality of contemporary design. Our distinctive and original collections fuse modern designs with enduring techniques passed down through generations in artisan communities."

● MISI

27 Old Gloucester Street, London WC1N 3AX, United Kingdom. E-mail: admin@misi.co.uk. Website: www.misi.co.uk. Estab. 2008. Geared towards handmade items. Setup costs: none; 3% fee for every item sold. Provided to sellers: crafters blog, free domain, 12 month listing, forum.

● NOT MASS PRODUCED

Orchard Cottage, Station Road, Longstanton, Cambridge, Cambridgeshire CB24 3DS, United Kingdomm. 01954 261066. E-mail: enquiries@notmassproduced.com. Website: www.notmassproduced.com. Estab. 2008. Geared towards handmade items. All artisans are vetted. "Designers are from the UK and no further than Europe."

REDBUBBLE

650 Castro St., Suite 120-275, Mountain View CA, 94041. Website: www.redbubble.com. "Redbubble is a free marketplace that helps thousands of artists reach new audiences and sell their work more easily. RB gives you access to a wide range of high-quality products, just waiting for your designs to make them more amazing. We coordinate everything from printing and shipping through to ongoing customer service, giving you more time to focus on creating great art and design (and occasionally watching cat videos on the internet)."

SHOP HANDMADE

11901 137th Ave., Ct. KPN, Gig Harbor WA, 98329-6617. E-mail: Service@ShopHandmade.com. Website: www.shophandmade.com. Geared towards handmade items. Setup fee: none. Payments accepted: PayPal.

SILK FAIR

Website: www.silkfair.com. Geared towards handmade items and other merchandise. Setup fee: see website.

SPOONFLOWER

2810 Meridian Parkway, Suite 176, Durham NC 27713. (919)886-7885. Website: www.spoonflower.com. Geared towards handmade items. Products sold: fabric, wallpaper, decals and gift wrap. Setup fee: see website. "At Spoonflower we make it possible for individuals to design, print and sell their own fabric, wallpaper, decals and gift wrap. It was founded in May 2008 by two Internet geeks who had crafty wives but who knew nothing about textiles. The company came about because Stephen's wife, Kim, persuaded him that being able to print her own fabric for curtains was a really cool idea. She wasn't alone. The Spoonflower community now numbers over a million individuals who use their own fabric to make curtains, quilts, clothes, bags, furniture, dolls, pillows, framed artwork, costumes, banners and much, much more. The Spoonflower marketplace offers the largest collection of independent fabric designers in the world."

STORENVY

Website: www.storenvy.com. Geared towards handmade items. Setup costs: none. Payments accepted: all major credit cards, PayPal. Provided to sellers: customizable options, Facebook integration, visitor stats, mobile & tablet friendly sites, custom domain option, inventory & order tracking.

SUPERMARKET

E-mail: thisisawesome@supermarkethq.com. Website: www.supermarkethq.com. Geared towards hand-made items. "Supermarket is a curated collection of awesome design products."

ZIBBET

Website: www.zibbet.com. Geared towards handmade items. Products sold: handmade goods, fine art, vintage, craft supplies. Setup costs: see website. Provided

BOOK PUBLISHERS

//

Seeing your name on the cover of a book is both a dream and a goal for many professional crafters. This section of listings is dedicated to book publishers that publish craft books of some kind. Keep in mind that a large publisher may have many different imprints, or trade names, under which books for a more specific demographic are published. For example, F+W Media, Inc., publishes mixed-media craft books under the North Light imprint and quilting books under the Fons & Porter imprint. Where appropriate, we have included different imprints in order to specify the type of craft that imprint publishes.

Before sending off queries to book publishers, make sure you have a strong idea with industry research to back it up. Just like you, publishers are trying to generate a profit, so make sure your idea is well thought out and is unique but relevant. Most successful book proposals will be accompanied by photos of potential projects. However, until they are specifically requested by an editor, never send physical materials to a publisher; it is possible you will never see those samples again. Instead, take some simple but beautiful photos of your samples for inclusion in your proposal.

Each publisher is different in the way they accept submissions and draft proposals, so read the instructions for each publisher's information to understand their process. Also, do further research on any company in which you are interested in submitting a proposal. Visit the company's website, look at books they have published and where those books are sold. Do you respect the authors they have worked with previously? Do you like the content they produce? What is the reputation of the company or of their books? Do you like the photography and design? Although each book is different, keep in mind that similarities amongst an entire publisher's line of books will likely impact yours as well.

- Mass market paperbacks are sold at supermarkets, newsstands, drugstores, etc. They include romance novels, diet books, mysteries, and novels by popular authors such as Stephen King.
- Trade books are the hardcovers and paperbacks found only in bookstores and libraries. The paperbacks are larger than those on the mass market racks, and are printed on higher-quality paper and often feature matte-paper jackets.
- Textbooks contain plenty of illustrations, photographs, and charts to explain their subjects.
- Small press books are produced by small, independent publishers. Many are literary or scholarly in theme and often feature fine art on their covers.
- Backlist titles or reprints refer to publishers' titles from past seasons that continue to sell year after year. These books are often updated and republished with freshly designed covers to keep them up to date and attractive to readers.

Tonia Jenny, the acquisitions editor for North Light Books, has written an excellent article about the book proposal process. Be sure to read "Crafting a Book Proposal" for more insight into this process, and to find tips and tricks to submitting a successful book proposal. Then read Margot Potter's article, "Write and Publish a Craft Book," about the overall process for some real-life insight into what writing a book might mean for you.

Before signing a contract, identify your goals for writing a book and make sure that your contract is meeting those expectations. Where will your book be sold? What kind of marketing and promotional assistance will the publisher give you? Will you receive an advance and royalty on book sales, or will you receive one flat fee for the book, regardless of sales? Is it important for you to have a say in the photography or not? Don't sign a contract before making sure that your goals are in line with your publisher and specified in the contract.

Writing a book is a lot of hard work, but sharing your craft with the world through a published book will provide you with a strong foothold in the professional craft world. Good luck with your book proposal!

ALL AMERICAN CRAFTS

7 Waterloo Rd., Stanhope NJ 07874. (973)347-6900. Fax: (973)347-6909. E-mail: sales@allamericancrafts. com. Website: www.allamericancrafts.com. Estab. 1981. Types of books published: knitting, quilting, general craft, decorative painting, and more.

⊛ ANNESS PUBLISHING LTD./ SOUTHWATER

Blaby Road, Wigston Leicester LE18 4SE, United Kingdom. 0116 275 9060. Fax: 0116 275 9090. E-mail: info@anness.com. Website: www.annesspublishing. com. Estab. 1999.

ANNIE'S PUBLISHING

Website: www.annies-publishing.com. Estab. 1985. "Annie's is the media division of DRG. Its products—including magazines, books, kits and supplies, online classes and TV programming—are targeted to home and family interests, including crafts, nostalgia and home décor."

AXIS PUBLISHING

Huntsville AL. Website: www.axis-publishing.webs. com. Estab. 2008. "Our mission is to empower authors across the globe, through cutting edge and innovative writings, recordings, techniques and technologies."

BRYNMORGEN PRESS

318 Bath Rd., Brunswick ME 04011. (207)761-8217. E-mail: tim@brynmorgen.com. Website: www. brynmorgen.com. Contact: Tim McCreight. Estab. 1981.

C&T PUBLISHING

1651 Challenge Dr., Concord CA 94520. (925)677-0377. Fax: (925)677-0377. E-mail: ctinfo@ctpub.com. Website: www.ctpub.com. Contact: Roxane Cerda, acquisitions manager. Estab. 1983. Types of books published: sewing, quilting, mixed media art. Publishes trade paperback originals, CD ROMs, DVDs, art materials, totes, journals, umbrellas, notecards. Specialty: quilting books. Titles can be found at JoAnn's Fabric, Michael's and Hobby Lobby. Publishes 50+ titles/year.

HOW TO CONTACT Accepts unsolicited proposals and manuscripts; guidelines available on website at www.ctpub.com/client_pages/submissions.cfm. Keeps information on file. Samples not filed are returned. Considers simultaneous submissions.

NEEDS Buys all rights. Finds authors through submissions. Works with never-before-published authors frequently. Look for original concept, popluar concept, on-trend concept, large following on social media, existing fan base. Average book has 60-144 pages. Average craft/DIY book contains 6-20+ projects/patterns. Provides print-ready illustrations in-house. Provides photography.

TERMS Books undergo technical edit prior to publication. Payment based on royalty/advance and royalty only.

RECENT TITLE(S) *Me and My Sewing Adventure*; *All-in-One Quilter's Reference Tool, 2nd Ed.*; *The Modern Appliqué Workbook*; *Foolproof Crazy Quilting*

TIPS "Provide a lot of visuals with your proposal. Try to really show me what you envision for your book and what makes your work special. Sell your author bio and your audience. I want to know how you reach your audience and how strong the number of followers you enjoy. Tell me what makes you the right person to write the book you are proposing. The biggest gimmie an author can offer is to be able to summarize in one sentence what makes their book stand out from the crowd. If a book's topic and uniqueness cannot be explained in a sentence (long sentences are okay), the resulting book will be hard to sell."

CHRONICLE BOOKS

680 Second St., San Francisco CA 94107. E-mail: submissions@chroniclebooks.com. Website: www. chroniclebooks.com. "We publish an exciting range of books, stationery, kits, calendars, and novelty formats. Our list includes children's books and interactive formats; young adult books; cookbooks; fine art, design, and photography; pop culture; craft, fashion, beauty, and home décor; relationships, mind-body-spirit; innovative formats such as interactive journals, kits, decks, and stationery; and much, much more." Publishes 90 titles/year. Book catalog for 9×12 SAE and 8 first-class stamps.

HOW TO CONTACT Submit via mail or e-mail (prefers e-mail for adult submissions; only by mail for children's submissions). Submit proposal (guidelines online) and allow 3 months for editors to review. If submitting by mail, do not include SASE since our staff will not return materials.

TERMS Generally pays authors in royalties based on retail price, "though we do occasionally work on a flat fee basis." Advance varies. Illustrators paid royalty based on retail price or flat fee.

DK PUBLISHING

Penguin Random House, 375 Hudson St., New York NY 10014. Website: www.dk.com. Contact: John Searcy; Nancy Ellwood, editorial director. "DK publishes photographically illustrated nonfiction for children of all ages."

DOVER PUBLICATIONS, INC.

31 E. Second St., Mineola NY 11501. (516)294-7000. Fax: (516)873-1401. E-mail: hr@doverpublications. com. Website: www.doverpublications.com. Contact: John Grafton (math/science reprints). Estab. 1941. Publishes trade paperback originals and reprints. Publishes 660 titles/year. Book catalog available online.

HOW TO CONTACT Query with SASE.

TERMS Makes outright purchase.

RECENT TITLE(S) *The Waning of the Middle Ages*, by John Huizenga.

ELLA PUBLISHING CO.

E-mail: submissions@ellapublishing.com. Website: www.ellapublishing.com. Estab. 1983. Types of books published: scrapbooking. Publishes ebooks. Specialty: scrapbooking. Publishes 12 titles/year.

HOW TO CONTACT See website for guidelines and proposal questionnaire. "Complete questions in a word-processing document and e-mail it as an attachment to submissions@ellapublishing.com. Please include 'eBook Idea' as your subject line. You may also include up to three visuals that demonstrate your scrapbooking style. Include 'Book Proposal' as your subject line."

NEEDS "To evaluate your proposal, we DON'T need (or want!) a finished document with all your images and photographs completed. What we DO need is a carefully thought-out topic, some background information, and a good sense of your familiarity with and enthusiasm for the project. Remember, you're selling us on YOU as much as you are selling us on your topic. Even if we can't use your proposal right now, we'll remember excited, talented people and keep you in mind for the future."

TERMS "When you e-mail us your proposal, you'll receive an automated confirmation e-mail letting you know it was received. Each proposal is then reviewed by our editorial board. If we believe your proposal will fit in our catalog, we will contact you with assignment details." Pays based on professional qualifications, the length of the book, and several other factors.

☉ FIREFLY BOOKS

50 Staples Ave., Unit 1, Richmond Hill ON L4B 0A7, Canada. (416)499-8412. E-mail: service@fireflybooks. com. E-mail: valerie@fireflybooks.com. Website: www.fireflybooks.com. Estab. 1974. Publishes high-quality nonfiction.

HOW TO CONTACT Prefers images in digital format, but will accept 35mm transparencies.

NEEDS "We're looking for book-length ideas, not stock. We pay a royalty on books sold, plus advance."

TERMS Send query letter with résumé of credits. Does not keep samples on file; include SAE/IRC for return of material. Simultaneous submissions OK. Payment negotiated with contract. Credit line given.

FONS & PORTER BOOKS

F+W Media, Inc., 10151 Carver Rd., Suite 200, Blue Ash OH 45242. E-mail: vanessa.lyman@fwmedia. com. Contact: Vanessa Lyman, content director. Publishes hardcover and trade paperback how-to books. "Fons & Porter Books, formerly KP Craft Books, publishes books on quilting, sewing, knitting and crochet, polymer clay, beading, jewelry-making, and general craft." Publishes 25-30 titles/year.

HOW TO CONTACT Send query letter with photographs, digital images. Accepts e-mail submissions. Samples are not filed and are returned.

NEEDS Buys all rights.

WALTER FOSTER PUBLISHING, INC.

3 Wrigley, Suite A, Irvine CA 92618. (800)426-0099. Fax: (949)380-7575. E-mail: info@walterfoster.com. Website: www.walterfoster.com. Estab. 1922. Pub-

lishes trade paperback originals. "Walter Foster publishes instructional how-to/craft instruction as well as licensed products."

FOX CHAPEL PUBLISHING

1970 Broad St., East Petersburg PA 17520. (800)457-9112. Fax: (717)560-4702. E-mail: acquisitions@fox chapelpublishing.com. Website: www.foxchapelpub lishing.com. Contact: Peg Couch, acquisitions editor. Publishes hardcover and trade paperback originals and trade paperback reprints. Fox Chapel publishes woodworking, woodcarving, and design titles for professionals and hobbyists. Publishes 25-40 titles/year.

HOW TO CONTACT Reviews artwork/photos. Send photocopies.

TERMS Pays royalty or makes outright purchase. Pays variable advance.

RECENT TITLE(S) *Celebrating Birch*; *Pinewood Derby Design Secrets*; *Woodworker's Guide to Veneering and Inlay*.

TIPS "We're looking for knowledgeable artists, craftspeople and woodworkers, all experts in their fields, to write books of lasting value."

⊜ GUILD OF MASTER CRAFTSMAN PUBLICATIONS

166 High Street, Lewes East Sussex BN7 1XU, United Kingdom. 44 01273 477374. E-mail: helen.chrystie@ thegmcgroup.com. Website: www.thegmcgroup.com. Types of books published: photography, woodworking, DIY, gardening, cookery, art, puzzles, all manner of craft subjects—from knitting and sewing to jewelery-making, dolls' house, upholstery, paper crafts and more. "Publishes and distributes over 3,000 books and magazines which are both valued by professional craftsmen/women and enjoyed by keen amateurs."

INTERWEAVE PRESS

201 E. Fourth St., Loveland CO 80537. (970)669-7672. Fax: (970)667-8317. Website: www.interweave.com. Estab. 1975. Publishes hardcover and trade paperback originals. Interweave Press publishes instructive titles relating to the fiber arts and beadwork topics. Publishes 40-45 titles/year. Book catalog available online.

HOW TO CONTACT Submit outline, sample chapters. Accepts simultaneous submissions if informed of non-exclusivity.

NEEDS Subjects limited to fiber arts (spinning, knitting, dyeing, weaving, sewing/stiching, art quilting, mixed media/collage) and jewelrymaking (beadwork, stringing, wireworking, metalsmithing).

RECENT TITLE(S) *Mark Making* by Helen Parrott, *Fair Isle Style* by Mary Jane Mucklestone, *Explorations in Beadweaving* by Kelly Angeley.

TIPS "We are looking for very clear, informally written, technically correct manuscripts, generally of a how-to nature, in our specific fiber and beadwork fields only. Our audience includes a variety of creative self-starters who appreciate inspiration and clear instruction. They are often well educated and skillful in many areas."

KALMBACH PUBLISHING CO.

21027 Crossroads Circle, P.O. Box 1612, Waukesha WI 53187. (262)796-8776. Fax: (262)798-6468. E-mail: books@kalmbach.com. Website: www.kalm bach.com. Contact: Ronald Kovach, senior editor. Estab. 1934. Publishes paperback originals and reprints. Publishes 40-50 titles/year.

NEEDS 10-20% require freelance illustration; 10-20% require freelance design. Book catalog free upon request. Approached by 25 freelancers/year. Prefers freelancers with experience in the hobby field. Uses freelance artists mainly for book layout/design and line art illustrations. Freelancers should have the most recent versions of Adobe InDesign, Photoshop and Illustrator. Projects by assignment only.

TERMS Send query letter with résumé, tearsheets and photocopies. No phone calls please. Samples are filed and will not be returned. Art director will contact artist for portfolio review. Finds artists through word of mouth, submissions. Assigns 10-12 freelance design jobs/year. Pays by the project. Assigns 3-5 freelance illustration jobs/year. Pays by the project.

RECENT TITLE(S) *The Model Railroader's Guide to Coal Railroading*, by Tony Koester; *Polymer Pizzazz: 27 Great Polymer Clay Jewelry Projects*.

TIPS "Our how-to books are highly visual in their presentation. Any author who wants to publish with us must be able to furnish good photographs and rough drawings before we'll consider his or her book."

KANSAS CITY STAR QUILTS

The Kansas City Star, 1729 Grand Blvd, Kansas City MO 64108. E-mail: dweaver@kcstar.com. Website: www.pickledish.com. Types of books published: quilt books.

KRAUSE PUBLICATIONS

A Division of F+W Media, Inc., 700 E. State St., Iola WI 54990. (715)445-2214. Fax: (715)445-4087. Website: www.krausebooks.com. Contact: Paul Kennedy (antiques and collectibles, music, sports, militaria, humor, numismatics); Corrina Peterson (firearms); Brian Lovett (outdoors); Brian Earnest (automotive). Publishes hardcover and trade paperback originals. "We are the world's largest hobby and collectibles publisher." Publishes 80 titles/year. Book catalog for free or on website.

HOW TO CONTACT Submit proposal package, including outline, table of contents, a sample chapter, and letter explaining your project's unique contributions. Reviews artwork/photos. Accepts only digital photography. Send sample photos.

RECENT TITLE(S) *Antique Trader Antiques & Collectibles 2014*; *The Geek Handbook*, by Alex Langley; *Standard Catalog of Firearms*, by Jerry Lee; Collecting *Rocks, Gems & Minerals*, by Patti Polk.

TIPS Audience consists of serious hobbyists. "Your work should provide a unique contribution to the special interest."

LANDAUER PUBLISHING

3100 101st St., Suite A, Urbandale IA 50322. (800)557-2144; (515)287-2144. Fax: 515-276-5102. E-mail: info@landauercorp.com. E-mail: jeramy@landauercorp.com; books@landauercorp.com. Website: www.landauerpub.com. Contact: Jeramy Landauer. Estab. 1991.

HOW TO CONTACT In preparing a book proposal for review/discussion, please include the following: 1. Author profile and the book concept: a brief paragraph about the author followed by the concept, namely, the vision for the book, the intended audience and why the book is needed/different from what is currently available. Please include tentative specs for the book: projects (how many/range), special features (e. g., an essay promoting/romancing the history/concept/author, unique teaching section, video,

location photography, special needs such as full-size patterns). Also, please include author website. 2. Table of contents: the TOC gives the preliminary project list and shows project variety/balance. 3. Sample projects showing the quality of your work (at least one or two completed projects must accompany the proposal along with photo samples or print-outs of your work). 4. A sample of how-to instructions, diagrams and illustrations (can be rough or finished). 5. Author expectations from the publisher re: guarantees, royalty rates, etc. 6. Timing.

NEEDS "Landauer strives to publish books that are more than project books. We require quality. We look for clear concepts. Books often include a technique section or other features enabling us to enhance the book and expand the audience. Most importantly, we prefer to publish works that will sell for many seasons and lend themselves to add-on product and new editions."

TERMS Authors are expected to take an active role in promoting their books such as attending and introducing their book at Quilt Market, engaging in teaching, maintaining a website/blog, creating a promotional project pattern for social media and/or magazines.

LARK CRAFTS

67 Broadway, Asheville NC 28801. (828)253-0467. E-mail: info@larkbooks.com. Website: www.larkcrafts.com. Estab. 1979.

HOW TO CONTACT Send query letter via e-mail or mail (with information your skills and qualifications in the subject area of your submission), résumé and images of your work or a link to your website. Include SASE if you would like materials returned to you. Submissions should be sent to the attention of the category editor, e.g., the material on a ceramics book should be addressed to the Ceramics Editor; a craft book proposal should be addressed to the Craft Acquisitions Editor; and so on.

TERMS "Please note that, due to the volume of mail received, we cannot guarantee the return of unsolicited material. Please do not send original art or irreplaceable work of any kind; while we will make every effort to return your submissions, we are not responsible for any loss or damage."

⦿ LAURENCE KING PUBLISHING LTD.

361–373 City Rd., London EC1V 1LR, United Kingdom. 44 (0)20 7841 6900. Fax: 44 (0)20 7841 6910. E-mail: commissioning@laurenceking.com. Website: www.laurenceking.com.

HOW TO CONTACT See website for details.

LEISURE ARTS

104 Champs Blvd., Suite 100, Maumelle AR 72113. E-mail: submissions@leisurearts.com. Website: www.leisurearts.com. Estab. 1971. Leisure Arts is a leading publisher of lifestyle and instructional craft publications. In addition to printed publications, the Leisure Arts product line also includes ebooks, digital downloads, and DVDs.

HOW TO CONTACT Submit an email letter with a PDF file or JPEG attachments to: submissions@leisurearts.com. Please do not send the actual designs or instructions unless asked to do so.

MACMILLAN

175 Fifth Ave., New York NY 10010. (646)307-5151. Website: www.us.macmillan.com. Publishes hardcover, trade paperback and paperback books.

MARTINGALE PUBLISHING

19021 120th Ave., N.E., Suite 102, Bothell WA 98011. (800)426-3126; (425)483-3313. Fax: (425)486-7596. E-mail: creitan@martingale-pub.com. Website: www.shopmartingale.com. Contact: Cathy Reitan, editorial author liaison. Estab. 1976. Types of books published: quilting, sewing, knitting, and crochet. Publishes books and ebooks.

HOW TO CONTACT Please email your submission to Cathy Reitan, editorial author liaison, at creitan@martingale-pub.com.

TERMS "Manuscript proposals are reviewed on a monthly basis. Editorial, marketing, and production personnel are involved in the review. The final decision will be based on your proposal, your work sample, your completed author questionnaire, and our feasibility analysis. The feasibility analysis investigates such basics as our cost of producing the book and our ability to market your work successfully and competitively. Part of this process may also include a customer survey to test the concept. If your pro-posal is approved for publication, you will receive a call from one of the editors regarding a publishing contract. We pay quarterly royalty based on net sales of your book, as spelled out in the publishing contract that you will be asked to sign. As a service to you, Martingale applies for the copyright on your book in your name. After you have signed your contract, you will receive detailed guidelines for preparing your manuscript. You are responsible for sending the completed manuscript and projects for photography to us at your own expense by the due date specified in the contract. From then on, Martingale pays all expenses for book production, shipping and handling. These expenses include editing, design, layout, illustration and photography."

MEREDITH BOOKS

1716 Locust St., Des Moines IA 50309-3023. (515)284-3000. Website: www.meredith.com. Types of books published: food, home, family. "Meredith Books feature more than 300 titles focusing on food, home and family."

⦿ NEW HOLLAND PUBLISHERS

The Chandlery, Unit 114, 50 Westminster Bridge Rd., London SE1 7QY, Uniedt Kingdom. 44(0) 207 953 75 65. Fax: 44(0) 207 953 76 05. E-mail: enquiries@nhpub.co.uk. Website: www.newhollandpublishers.com. "New Holland is a publishing house dedicated to the highest editorial and design standards."

NORTH LIGHT BOOKS

F+W Media, Inc., 10151 Carver Rd., Suite 200, Blue Ash OH 45242. Fax: (513)891-7153. E-mail: mona.clough@fwmedia.com. Website: www.artistsnetwork.com. Contact: Mona Clough, content director art and mixed media. Publishes hardcover and trade paperback how-to books. "North Light Books publishes art books, including watercolor, drawing, mixed media, acrylic that emphasize illustrated how-to art instruction. Currently emphasizing drawing including traditional as well as creativity and inspiration." Publishes 70-75 titles/year. Visit www.northlightshop.com .

HOW TO CONTACT Send query letter with photographs, digital images. Accepts e-mail submissions. Samples are not filed and are returned. Responds only if interested. Company will contact artist for portfolio review if interested.

NEEDS Buys all rights. Finds freelancers through art competitions, art exhibits, submissions, internet and word of mouth.

NORTHRIDGE PUBLISHING

Website: www.northridgepublishing.com. "At Northridge Publishing we share the passion of creating with our readers as we provide inspiration, support, and resources to crafters everywhere. Reader layouts, cards, and projects are featured throughout our publications as we provide a forum for readers to share the latest and best ideas."

PAGE STREET PUBLISHING

27 Congress St., Suite 103, Salem MA 01970. (978)594-8295. E-mail: info@pagestreetpublishing.com. Website: www.pagestreetpublishing.com. Publishes paperback originals. Publishes 20+ titles/year.

PENGUIN/PERIGEE TRADE

Website: www.penguin.com/meet/publishers/perigee. **HOW TO CONTACT** "Due to the high volume of manuscripts received, most Penguin Group (USA) imprints do not normally accept unsolicited manuscripts. Neither the corporation nor its imprints assume responsibility for any unsolicited manuscripts which we may receive. As such, it is recommended that sole original copies of any manuscript not be submitted, as the corporation is not responsible for the return of any manuscript (whether sent electronically or by mail), nor do we guarantee a response. Further, in receiving a submission, we do not assume any duty not to publish a book based on a similar idea, concept or story."

POTTER CRAFT/RANDOM HOUSE

1745 Broadway, New York NY 10019. Website: www.crownpublishing.com/imprint/potter-craft. Estab. 2006. Types of books published: knitting, crochet, sewing, papercrafts, jewelry making.
HOW TO CONTACT Random House LLC does not accept unsolicited submissions, proposals, manuscripts, or submission queries via e-mail at this time.

QUAYSIDE PUBLISHING GROUP

400 First Ave., N., Suite 400, Minneapolis MN 55401. E-mail: editor@quaysidepub.com. Website: www.qbookshop.com. Types of books published: general craft, sewing, crochet, knitting, quilting, papercraft, scrapbooking, mixed media art. Publishes hardcover originals, trade paperback originals, trade paperback reprints. Titles can be found at Barnes & Noble, Amazon, craft chains, independents and internationally. Publishes 100 titles/year. Catalog available online or free on request.
HOW TO CONTACT Accepts unsolicited proposals and manuscripts; guidelines available on website. Does not keep information on file. If not filed, returned by SASE. Responds only if interested. Considers simultaneous submissions and previously published work.
NEEDS Rights purchased vary according to project. Will negotiate with those unwilling to sell rights. Finds authors through agents/reps, submissions, word-of-mouth, magazines, internet. Works with never-before-published authors frequently. Looks for original concept, popular concept, on-trend concept, large following on social media, existing fan base. Average book has 128-160 pages. Average craft/DIY book contains 20-52 projects/patterns. Author provides print-ready illustrations when possible.
TERMS Some books undergo technical edits. Typical timeframe from contract to manuscript due date is 4-6 months. Payment based on project. First time authors typically paid $5,000-6,000.
RECENT TITLE(S) *One Zentangle a Day* by Beckah Krahula; *3D Art Lab for Kids* by Susan Schwake; *20 Ways to Draw a Cat*.
TIPS "Do your research. Be familiar with the other competitive books on your topic. Think about how your book is better and different."

QUIRK BOOKS

215 Church Street, Philadelphia PA 19106. (215)627-3581. Fax: (215)627-5220. E-mail: tiffany@quirkbooks.com. Website: www.quirkbooks.com. Contact: Tiffany Hill. Estab. 2002. Types of books published: unconventional, cookbooks, craft books, children's books and nonfiction. Publishes books and ebooks. Publishes 25 titles/year. Catalog available online.
HOW TO CONTACT "E-mail a query letter to one of our editors. The query letter should be a short de-

scription of your project. Try to limit your letter to a single page. If you have sample chapters, go ahead and include them. You can also mail materials directly to our office. If you would like a reply, please include a self-addressed stamped envelope. If you want your materials returned, please include adequate postage."

RODALE BOOKS

(610)967-5171. Fax: (610)967-8961. Website: www. rodaleinc.com. Estab. 1932. "Rodale Books publishes adult trade titles in categories such health & fitness, cooking, spirituality and pet care."

RYLAND PETERS & SMALL

519 Broadway, 5th Floor, New York NY 10012. (646)613-8682; (646)613-8684; (646)613-8685. Fax: (646)613-8683. E-mail: enquiries@rps.co.uk. Website: www.rylandpeters.com.

HOW TO CONTACT See website for details.

SEARCH PRESS USA

1338 Ross Street, Petaluma CA 94954-1117. (800)289-9276; (707)762-3362. Fax: (707)762-0335. E-mail: info@searchpressusa.com. Website: www.search pressusa.com. Types of books published: art, craft. "We have 30+ years experience in publishing art and craft instruction books exclusively."

SIMON & SCHUSTER

1230 Avenue of the Americas, New York NY 10020. (212)698-7000. Website: www.simonandschuster. com.

HOW TO CONTACT Send query letter with tearsheets. Accepts disk submissions. Samples are filed and are not returned. Responds only if interested. Portfolios may be dropped off every Monday and Wednesday and should include tearsheets.

NEEDS Works with 50 freelance illustrators and 5 designers/year. Prefers freelancers with experience working with models and taking direction well. Uses freelancers for hand lettering, jacket/cover illustration and design and book design. 100% of design and 75% of illustration demand knowledge of Illustrator and Photoshop. Works on assignment only.

TERMS Buys all rights. Originals are returned at job's completion.

SKYHORSE PUBLISHING

307 W. 36th St., 11th Floor, New York NY 10018. (212)643-6816. Fax: (212)643-6819. E-mail: crenfrow@skyhorsepublishing.com. Website: www. skyhorsepublishing.com. Contact: Constance Renfrow, assistant editor. Estab. 2006. Types of books published: general craft, sewing, crochet, knitting, papercraft, woodworking, interior decorating, household crafts, holiday crafts. Publishes hardcover originals, trade paperback originals, trade paperback reprints. Specialty: nonfiction. Titles can be found at Barnes & Noble, Amazon, Michael's. Publishes 10+ titles/year. Catalog available online.

HOW TO CONTACT Accepts unsolicited proposals and manuscripts; guidelines available on website. Does not keep information on file. If not filed, returned by SASE when specifically requested. Responds only if interested. Considers simultaneous submissions and previously published work.

NEEDS Negotiates rights. Finds authors through submissions, word-of-mouth, internet. Works with never-before-published authors frequently. Looks for original concept, popular concept, on-trend concept, large following on social media, existing fan base. Average book has 96-200 pages. Average craft/DIY book contains 45-100 projects/patterns. Author provides print-ready illustrations if book will be illustrated. Author provides photography.

TERMS Typical timeframe from contract to manuscript due date is 6 months, but can vary. Payment based on royalty/advance. First time authors typically paid $1,000-10,000.

RECENT TITLE(S) *Loom Magic, Souped Up* (and other Instructables.com titles); *Vintage Crafts*; *Warm Mittens and Socks*; *Fun with Yarn and Fabric*; *Swedish Christmas Crafts.*

TIPS "Please be sure to read submission guidelines and be courteous. Should you not receive a response from us, we often appreciate receiving one follow up e-mail. We wish every craft author will submit full proposal: a summary, author bio, projected TOC, comp titles, sample projects and sample photography."

STC CRAFT/MELANIE FALICK BOOKS

115 W. 18th St., New York NY 10011. (212)206-7715. Fax: (212)519-1210. E-mail: stccraft@abramsbooks.com. Website: www.abramsbooks.com. Estab. 1949. Types of books published: art, photography, cooking, interior design, craft, fashion, sports, pop culture, as well as children's books and general interest. Publishes high quality art and illustrated books. Titles can be found at Amazon.com, Barnes & Noble, Books-A-Million, Indie Bound, !ndigo.

HOW TO CONTACT Accepts unsolicited proposals and manuscripts for STC Craft. No submission will be returned without a SASE. Please submit via email to stccraft@abramsbooks.com or mail your submission along with a SASE.

STOREY PUBLISHING

210 MASS MoCA Way, North Adams MA 01247. (800)793-9396. Fax: (413)346-2196. E-mail: webmaster@storey.com. Website: www.storey.com. Contact: Deborah Balmuth, editorial director (building, sewing, gift). Estab. 1983. Publishes hardcover and trade paperback originals and reprints. "The mission of Storey Publishing is to serve our customers by publishing practical information that encourages personal independence in harmony with the environment. We seek to do this in a positive atmosphere that promotes editorial quality, team spirit, and profitability. The books we select to carry out this mission include titles on gardening, small-scale farming, building, cooking, homebrewing, crafts, part-time business, home improvement, woodworking, animals, nature, natural living, personal care, and country living. We are always pleased to review new proposals, which we try to process expeditiously. We offer both work-for-hire and standard royalty contracts." Publishes 40 titles/year. Book catalog available free.

HOW TO CONTACT Reviews artwork/photos.

RECENT TITLE(S) *The Veggie Gardener's Answer Book*, by Barbara W. Ellis; *The Home Creamery*, by Kathy Farrell-Kingsley; *Happy Dog, Happy You*, by Arden Moore.

TATE PUBLISHING

127 East Trade Center Terrace, Mustang OK 73064. (888)361-9473; (405)376-4900. Fax: (405)376-4401. Website: www.tatepublishing.com. "Tate Publishing & Enterprises, LLC, is a Christian-based, family-owned, mainline publishing organization with a mission to discover unknown authors. We combine unknown authors' undiscovered potential with Tate Publishing's unique approach to publishing and provide them with the highest quality books and the most inclusive benefits package available."

HOW TO CONTACT "If you have a manuscript you would like us to consider for publication and marketed on nationwide television, please fill out the form on our website. If you choose to submit by postal mail or electronically, those manuscripts will not be returned and will be deleted or destroyed if not accepted for publication. Please retain at least one copy of your manuscript when submitting a hard copy or electronic version for our consideration and review."

THAMES & HUDSON

500 Fifth Ave., New York NY 10110. (212)354-3763. Fax: (212)398-1252. E-mail: bookinfo@thames.wwnorton.com. Website: www.thamesandhudsonusa.com. Estab. 1949.

HOW TO CONTACT "To submit a proposal by e-mail, please paste the text of your query letter and/or proposal into the body of the e-mail message. Please keep your proposal under six pages, and do not send attachments. Please note that we cannot accept complete manuscripts via e-mail. We cannot open packages that are unsolicited or do not have a return address."

TUTTLE PUBLISHING

364 Innovation Dr., North Clarendon VT 05759. (802)773-8930. Fax: (802)773-6993. E-mail: submissions@tuttlepublishing.com. Website: www.tuttlepublishing.com. Estab. 1832. Publishes hardcover and trade paperback originals and reprints. Tuttle is America's leading publisher of books on Japan and Asia. Publishes 125 titles/year.

HOW TO CONTACT Query with SASE.

NEEDS "Familiarize yourself with our catalog and/or similar books we publish. Send complete book proposal with cover letter, table of contents, 1-2 sample chapters, target audience description, SASE. No e-mail submissions."

TERMS Pays 5-10% royalty on net or retail price, depending on format and kind of book.
RECENT TITLE(S) *The Complete Book of Sushi*, by Hideo Dekura, Brigid Treloar, and Ryuichi Yoshii; *Aikido Basics*, by Phong Thong Dany and Lynn Seiser; *Contemporary Asian Kitchens and Dining Rooms*, by Chami Jotisalikorn and Karina Zabihi.

ULYSSESS PRESS

Ulysses Press Main Office, P.O. Box 3440, Berkeley CA 94703. (510)601-8301. Fax: (510)601-8307. E-mail: ulysses@ulyssespress.com. Website: www.ulysses press.com. Catalog available online.
HOW TO CONTACT "We review unsolicited manuscripts on an ongoing basis." See website for submission guidelines. Please do not send e-mail submissions, attachments or disks. Do not send original artwork, photographs or manuscripts of which you do not retain a copy.
NEEDS "When it comes to finding new books, we are especially interested in titles that fill demonstrated niches in the trade book market. We seek books that take a specific and unique focus, a focus that can differentiate a book and make it stand out in a crowd."

● USBORNE PUBLISHING

83-85 Saffron Hill, London En EC1N 8RT, United Kingdom. (44)207430-2800. Fax: (44)207430-1562. E-mail: mail@usborne.co.uk. Website: www.usborne. com. "Usborne Publishing is a multiple-award winning, world-wide children's publishing company publishing almost every type of children's book for every age from baby to young adult."
HOW TO CONTACT Works with 100 illustrators per year. Illustrations only: Query with samples. Samples not returned; samples filed.
TERMS Pays authors royalty.
TIPS "Do not send any original work and, sorry, but we cannot guarantee a reply."

WILEY PUBLISHING (WILEY CRAFT)

John Wiley & Sons, Inc., Global Education, 111 River St., Hoboken NJ 07030-5774. Website: www.wiley. com.

WORKMAN PUBLISHING CO.

Website: www.workman.com. Contact: Suzanne Rafer, executive editor (cookbook, child care, parenting, teen interest); Ruth Sullivan, Margot Herrera, Kylie Foxx-McDonald, Jay Schaefer, senior editors. Raquel Jaramillo, senior editor (juvenile); Megan Nicolay, Savannah Ashour (associate editors).. Estab. 1967. Publishes hardcover and trade paperback originals, as well as calendars "We are a trade paperback house specializing in a wide range of popular nonfiction. We publish no adult fiction and very little children's fiction. We also publish a full range of full-color wall and Page-A-Day calendars." Publishes 40 titles/ year.
HOW TO CONTACT Query with SASE first for guidelines.
RECENT TITLE(S) *Gallop!*, by Rufus Butler Seder; *1,000 Recordings to Hear Before You Die*, by Tom Moon; *I Will Teach You To Be Rich*, by Ramit Sethi.
TIPS "No phone calls, please. We do not accept submissions via fax."

MAGAZINES

//

A big part of building your craft business and boosting sales is name recognition. In an ever-growing sea of crafty celebrities, getting your name out there is critical to establishing yourself in the market as a resource, an expert and a professional. Building name recognition requires constant work, especially in the beginning. Consistent social media, blogging and representation at popular shows are important to making sure you are recognized in the industry, and magazines are a great way to reach your target demographic all at once. The listings in this section are geared toward craft magazines across the sub-genres.

Start by reading Shannon Miller's article, "Publishing a DIY Magazine Article," about submitting projects to magazines. Her insight as a magazine editor and art director will be invaluable to you as you consider submitting projects, patterns and content to various magazines. Then, do your research. Peruse the listings in this book, visit your local bookstore and search online to find the magazines that will be the best fit for your work, and that reach your target demographic. For example, all quilt magazines are not geared toward the same audience; some are specifically targeting art quilters, while others cater to traditional or modern quilters. Be sure that you spend your precious time only submitting to those magazines that are a likely fit for your work and that will help grow your audience.

As Shannon mentions in her article, be sure to follow directions when submitting content to magazines. Editors are busy people with tight deadlines and failure to follow submission instructions might immediately disqualify your awesome project. Also, be patient after submitting. While it may feel like a lifetime to you, there are a million reasons why you may not hear back immediately from the editor. Don't get disheartened and don't give up!

Also, think creatively when it comes to magazine submissions. Is there a certain magazine that serves a demographic you'd like to reach but currently don't? Is there a way to tailor a project for them that still represents you while meeting the needs of their audience? Or maybe you are an expert at crochet joining techniques; instead of submitting a project idea, pitch an idea for an article—or, better yet, a series of articles—on different crochet joining methods.

As with book publishing, make sure that your goals and needs are in line with those of the magazine. If your primary goal is to build your audience, driving more people to your website or blog, or increasing your social media following, make sure that the magazine is willing to include your name, website and social media information before signing an agreement.

Remember that magazines need a lot of quality content to fill the pages. If you have great ideas to share with the craft world, persistence pays off. Stick with it, keep generating quality content, and you're certain to find success in magazine publishing.

KEY TO SYMBOLS & ABBREVIATIONS

Symbol	Meaning
✪	Canadian market
●	market located outside of the U.S. and Canada
⌂	market prefers to work with local artists/designers
b&w	black & white (photo or illustration)
SASE	self-addressed, stamped envelope
SAE	self-addressed envelope
IRC	International Reply Coupon, for use when mailing to countries other than your own

- A great source for new magazine leads is in the business section of your local library. Ask the librarian to point out the business and consumer editions of the *Standard Rate and Data Service* (*SRDS*) and *Bacon's Media Directory*. These huge directories list thousands of magazines and will give you an idea of the magnitude of magazines published today. Another good source is a yearly directory called *Samir Husni's Guide to New Magazines*, also available in the business section of the public library and online at www.mrmagazine.com. *Folio* magazine provides information about new magazine launches and redesigns.

- Each year the Society of Publication Designers sponsors a juried competition, the winners of which are featured in a prestigious exhibition. For information about the annual competition, contact the Society of Publication Designers at (212)223-3332 or visit their website at www.spd.org.

- Networking with fellow artists and art directors will help you find additional success strategies. The Graphic Artists Guild (www.gag.org), The American Institute of Graphic Artists (www.aiga.org), your city's Art Directors Club (www.adcglobal.org) or branch of the Society of Illustrators (www.societyillustrators.org) hold lectures and networking functions. Attend one event sponsored by each organization in your city to find a group you are comfortable with, then join and become an active member.

MAGAZINES

ALTERED COUTURE

22992 Mill Creek Dr., Laguna Hills CA 92653. E-mail: alteredcouture@stampington.com. Website: www. stampington.com/altered-couture. *Altered Couture* is a 160-page publication dedicated to altered and embellished clothing and accessories. It is filled with gorgeous photographs of altered jackets, T-shirts, sweaters, jeans, skirts, and more, accompanied by easy-to-understand techniques and endless inspiration.

HOW TO CONTACT "We prefer submissions of original art. If original art is not available, our next preference is high resolution digital images (300 dpi at 8½ × 10). If hi-res digital images are not available, we will very rarely consider professional-quality transparencies or color slides. Color-copy submissions are not accepted. All artwork must be identified with the artist's name, address, e-mail and phone number clearly printed on a label attached to each sample. Inscribe your name and address somewhere on each piece of art. If you desire acknowledgment of artwork receipt, please include a self-addressed stamped postcard. If the artwork is three-dimensional, please attach your identification with a removable string, or pack the sample in a plastic bag with your identification. If you have a unique artistic technique you'd like to share with others, please send samples of your artwork accompanied by a query letter outlining your article idea to the respective Managing Editor at *Altered Couture*. Managing editors also welcome brief e-mail inquiries."

NEEDS "Managing editors seek first-rate projects and encourage artists who have not published articles before to submit ideas, as editorial assistance will be provided."

TERMS Competitive editorial compensation is provided for all published articles. "We may hold your sample for an extended period of tim—9 to 12 months is common. Due to the large volume of artwork we receive, Somerset Studio will return only those submissions accompanied by sufficient postage in the form of cash, check or money order made out to Stampington & Company. We can not offer delivery confirmation; however, we are happy to put insurance on the submission. If you wish to have your artwork insured for the return journey, please include sufficient funds and indicate your preference in a postcard or letter enclosed with your submission. Please do not attach postage to packaging, and do not send loose postage stamps. Contributors from outside the US, please send cash, check, or money order in US funds to Stampington & Company. For questions regarding your artwork, please send inquiries to artmanagement@ stampington.com."

AMERICAN PATCHWORK & QUILTING

E-mail: apq@meredith.com. Website: www.allpeoplequilt.com/magazines-more/american-patchwork-and-quilting. "*American Patchwork & Quilting* magazine, part of the Better Homes and Gardens family, is the leading quilting magazine in the country."

AMERICAN QUILTER

American Quilter's Society, 5801 Kentucky Dam Rd., Paducah KY 42003. E-mail: micheleduffy@aqsquilt. com; ginnyharris@aqsquilt.com. Website: www. americanquilter.com.

CONTACT: Michele Duffy, editor-in-chief; Ginny Harris, editorial assistant. *American Quilter* is published six times per year and is the official publication of the American Quilter's Society.

HOW TO CONTACT Article ideas or queries may be submitted via e-mail to Editor-in-Chief Michele Duffy at micheleduffy@aqsquilt.com. Manuscripts may be submitted on a CD in .doc or .docx format with a hardcopy printout accompanying the disk or via e-mail with "submission" in the subject field to Editorial Assistant Ginny Harris at ginnyharris@aqsquilt.com. Articles may range from 500 to 1,500 words and have accompanying images. "Furthermore, the inclusion of high-quality photos increases the chance of article acceptance; several images of each quilt or project allow the committee to see your submission at its best."

APRONOLOGY

22992 Mill Creek Dr., Laguna Hills CA 92653. E-mail: apronology@stampington.com. Website: www. stampington.com/apronology. This new publication flirts with the many uses and looks of the apron.

HOW TO CONTACT "We prefer submissions of original art. If original art is not available, our next preference is high resolution digital images (300 dpi at 8½ × 10). If hi-res digital images are not available, we will very rarely consider professional-quality transparencies or color slides. Color-copy submissions are not accepted. All artwork must be identified with the artist's name, address, e-mail and phone number clearly printed on a label attached to each sample. Inscribe your name and address somewhere on each piece of art. If you desire acknowledgment of artwork receipt, please include a self-addressed stamped postcard. If the artwork is three-dimensional, please attach your identification with a removable string, or pack the sample in a plastic bag with your identification. If you have a unique artistic technique you'd like to share with others, please send samples of your artwork accompanied by a query letter outlining your article idea to the respective Managing Editor at: *Apronology*, 22992 Mill Creek Drive, Laguna Hills, CA 92653. Managing editors also welcome brief e-mail inquiries."

NEEDS "Managing editors seek first-rate projects and encourage artists who have not published articles before to submit ideas, as editorial assistance will be provided."

TERMS Competitive editorial compensation is provided for all published articles. "We may hold your sample for an extended period of time—9 to 12 months is common. Due to the large volume of artwork we receive, Somerset Studio will return only those submissions accompanied by sufficient postage in the form of cash, check or money order made out to Stampington & Company. We can not offer delivery confirmation; however, we are happy to put insurance on the submission. If you wish to have your artwork insured for the return journey, please include sufficient funds and indicate your preference in a postcard or letter enclosed with your submission. Please do not attach postage to packaging, and do not send loose postage stamps. Contributors from outside the US, please send cash, check, or money order in US funds to Stampington & Company. For questions regarding your artwork, please send inquiries to artmanagement@stampington.com."

ART DOLL QUARTERLY

Art Doll Quarterly, 22992 Mill Creek Dr., Laguna Hills CA 92653. E-mail: artdollquarterly@stampington.com. Website: www.stampington.com/art-doll-quarterly. "This full-color, 128-page publication is dedicated to art dolls and sculptural figures made from cloth, polymer clay, Creative Paperclay®, wire armatures, mixed-media, and much more. In each is-

sue, you will find original doll patterns, creative challenges, doll-artist profiles, convention listings and reviews, book & video reviews, and a 35-page gallery of art dolls made by our readers."

HOW TO CONTACT "We prefer submissions of original art. If original art is not available, our next preference is high resolution digital images (300 dpi at 8½ × 10). If hi-res digital images are not available, we will very rarely consider professional-quality transparencies or color slides. Color-copy submissions are not accepted. All artwork must be identified with the artist's name, address, e-mail and phone number clearly printed on a label attached to each sample. Inscribe your name and address somewhere on each piece of art. If you desire acknowledgment of artwork receipt, please include a self-addressed stamped postcard. If the artwork is three-dimensional, please attach your identification with a removable string, or pack the sample in a plastic bag with your identification. If you have a unique artistic technique you'd like to share with others, please send samples of your artwork accompanied by a query letter outlining your article idea to the respective Managing Editor at: *Art Doll Quarterly*, 22992 Mill Creek Drive, Laguna Hills, CA 92653. Managing editors also welcome brief e-mail inquiries."

NEEDS "Managing editors seek first-rate projects and encourage artists who have not published articles before to submit ideas, as editorial assistance will be provided."

TERMS Competitive editorial compensation is provided for all published articles. "We may hold your sample for an extended period of time—9 to 12 months is common. Due to the large volume of artwork we receive, Somerset Studio will return only those submissions accompanied by sufficient postage in the form of cash, check or money order made out to Stampington & Company. We can not offer delivery confirmation; however, we are happy to put insurance on the submission. If you wish to have your artwork insured for the return journey, please include sufficient funds and indicate your preference in a postcard or letter enclosed with your submission. Please do not attach postage to packaging, and do not send loose postage stamps. Contributors from outside the US, please send cash, check, or money order in US funds to Stampington & Company. For questions regarding your artwork, please send inquiries to artmanagement@stampington.com."

ARTFUL BLOGGING

22992 Mill Creek Dr., Laguna Hills CA 92653. E-mail: artfulblogging@stampington.com. Website: www. stampington.com/artful-blogging. "Allow yourself to be inspired as you flip through the pages of *Artful Blogging*. Join along with the growing community of artful bloggers as they continue to share their mesmerizing stories and captivating photographs."

HOW TO CONTACT "We prefer submissions of original art. If original art is not available, our next preference is high resolution digital images (300 dpi at 8½ × 10). If hi-res digital images are not available, we will very rarely consider professional-quality transparencies or color slides. Color-copy submissions are not accepted. All artwork must be identified with the artist's name, address, e-mail and phone number clearly printed on a label attached to each sample. Inscribe your name and address somewhere on each piece of art. If you desire acknowledgment of artwork receipt, please include a self-addressed stamped postcard. If the artwork is three-dimensional, please attach your identification with a removable string, or pack the sample in a plastic bag with your identification. If you have a unique artistic technique you'd like to share with others, please send samples of your artwork accompanied by a query letter outlining your article idea to the respective Managing Editor at: *Artful Blogging*, 22992 Mill Creek Drive, Laguna Hills, CA 92653. Managing editors also welcome brief e-mail inquiries."

NEEDS "Managing editors seek first-rate projects and encourage artists who have not published articles before to submit ideas, as editorial assistance will be provided."

TERMS Competitive editorial compensation is provided for all published articles. "We may hold your sample for an extended period of time—9 to 12 months is common. Due to the large volume of artwork we receive, Somerset Studio will return only those submissions accompanied by sufficient postage in the form of cash, check or money order made out to Stampington & Company. We can not offer delivery confirmation; however, we are happy to put insurance on the submission. If you wish to have your artwork insured for the return journey, please include sufficient funds and indicate your preference in a postcard or letter enclosed with your submission. Please do not attach postage to packaging, and do not send loose postage stamps. Contributors from outside the US, please send cash, check, or money order in US funds to Stampington & Company. For questions regarding your artwork, please send inquiries to artmanagement@stampington.com."

ART JEWELRY MAGAZINE

E-mail: editor@artjewelrymag.com. Website: www. art.jewelrymakingmagazines.com. *Art Jewelry*'s mission is to teach the beginning jewelry maker, broaden the skills of those at the intermediate level, challenge the advanced artisan—and inspire them all.

ART JOURNALING

22992 Mill Creek Dr., Laguna Hills CA 92653. E-mail: artjournaling@stampington.com. Website: www. stampington.com/art-journaling. "In every quarterly issue of *Art Journaling*, artists open their journals and share creative techniques for capturing their emotions. From stamping and collage art to painting and sketching, each journal is filled with innovative techniques that you'll want to try in your own art journal. Detailed photos and commentary will help you discover your journaling style, with hints and tricks for creating a stand-out page."

HOW TO CONTACT "We prefer submissions of original art. If original art is not available, our next preference is high resolution digital images (300 dpi at 8½ × 10). If hi-res digital images are not available, we will very rarely consider professional-quality transparencies or color slides. Color-copy submissions are not accepted. All artwork must be identified with the artist's name, address, e-mail and phone number clearly printed on a label attached to each sample. Inscribe your name and address somewhere on each piece of art. If you desire acknowledgment of artwork receipt, please include a self-addressed stamped postcard. If the artwork is three-dimensional, please attach your identification with a removable string, or pack the sample in a plastic bag with your identification. If you have a unique artistic technique you'd like to share with others, please send samples of your artwork accompanied by a query letter outlining your article idea to the respective Managing Editor at: *Art Journaling*, 22992 Mill Creek Drive, Laguna Hills, CA 92653. Managing editors also welcome brief e-mail inquiries."

NEEDS "Managing editors seek first-rate projects and encourage artists who have not published articles before to submit ideas, as editorial assistance will be provided."

TERMS Competitive editorial compensation is provided for all published articles. "We may hold your sample for an extended period of time—9 to 12 months is common. Due to the large volume of artwork we receive, Somerset Studio will return only those submissions accompanied by sufficient postage in the form of cash, check or money order made out to Stampington & Company. We can not offer delivery confirmation; however, we are happy to put insurance on the submission. If you wish to have your artwork insured for the return journey, please include sufficient funds and indicate your preference in a postcard or letter enclosed with your submission. Please do not attach postage to packaging, and do not send loose postage stamps. Contributors from outside the US, please send cash, check, or money order in US funds to Stampington & Company. For questions regarding your artwork, please send inquiries to artmanagement@stampington.com."

ART QUILTING STUDIO

22992 Mill Creek Dr., Laguna Hills CA 92653. E-mail: artquiltingstudio@stampington.com. Website: www.stampington.com/art-quilting-studio. "*Art Quilting Studio* magazine provides a playful and informative forum where quilt enthusiasts from all walks of life can cross-pollinate to share techniques, ideas, and inspiration."

HOW TO CONTACT "We prefer submissions of original art. If original art is not available, our next preference is high resolution digital images (300 dpi at 8½ × 10). If hi-res digital images are not available, we will very rarely consider professional-quality transparencies or color slides. Color-copy submissions are not accepted. All artwork must be identified with the artist's name, address, e-mail and phone number clearly printed on a label attached to each sample. Inscribe your name and address somewhere on each piece of art. If you desire acknowledgment of artwork receipt, please include a self-addressed stamped postcard. If the artwork is three-dimensional, please attach your identification with a removable string, or pack the sample in a plastic bag with your identification. If you have a unique artistic technique you'd like to share with others, please send samples of your artwork accompanied by a query letter outlining your article idea to the respective Managing Editor at: *Art Quilting Studio*, 22992 Mill Creek Drive, Laguna Hills, CA 92653. Managing editors also welcome brief e-mail inquiries."

NEEDS "Managing editors seek first-rate projects and encourage artists who have not published articles before to submit ideas, as editorial assistance will be provided."

TERMS Competitive editorial compensation is provided for all published articles. "We may hold your sample for an extended period of time—9 to 12 months is common. Due to the large volume of artwork we receive, Somerset Studio will return only those submissions accompanied by sufficient postage in the form of cash, check or money order made out to Stampington & Company. We can not offer delivery confirmation; however, we are happy to put insurance on the submission. If you wish to have your artwork insured for the return journey, please include sufficient funds and indicate your preference in a postcard or letter enclosed with your submission. Please do not attach postage to packaging, and do not send loose postage stamps. Contributors from outside the US, please send cash, check, or money order in US funds to Stampington & Company. For questions regarding your artwork, please send inquiries to artmanagement@stampington.com."

● BEAD

E-mail: usoffice@ashdown.co.uk. Website: www.beadmagazine.co.uk. "Created by bead lovers, for bead lovers, each issue of *Bead* is packed full of beautiful beadwork, wirework and stringing projects. Plus stylish and quality lampwork, metal clay, and polymer clay designs, and much more!"

BEAD & BUTTON

E-mail: editor@beadandbutton.com. Website: www.bnb.jewelrymakingmagazines.com. *Bead&Button* is a bimonthly magazine devoted to techniques, projects, and designs of beaded jewelry and accessories.

❾ BEADS & BEYOND

Traplet Publications Ltd., Traplet House, Pendragon Close Malvern WR14 1GA, United Kingdom. Website: www.beadsandbeyondmagazine.com. A "monthly, design-led craft magazine featuring jewellery making projects, new techniques, stunning photography and inspiration, interviews, reviews, best buys, competitions and prizes."

BEAD DESIGN STUDIO

7 Waterloo Rd., Stanhope NJ 07874. (973)347-6900. Fax: (973)347-6909. E-mail: editors@beaddesignstudiomag.com. Website: www.beaddesignstudiomag.com. Contact: Pamela Hawkins. *Bead Design Studio* is a perfect-bound bimonthly publication that showcases how beads can accent every aspect of readers' lives. *Bead Design Studio* is published six times a year, and is sold via subscription, on newsstands, and in craft and bead shops.

HOW TO CONTACT Submissions should include beginner to advanced skill levels, originality of design and use of materials, techniques used to complete the project, indicate if project would need photography to illustrate step-by-step instructions or pattern. *Bead Design Studio* prefers original designs, but will discuss alternative arrangements on a case-by-case basis. Submission format: send using FTP, CD-ROM or Zip disc. Include sketch, photo or other rendition with size info.

BEADIT... TODAY

E-mail: editor@bead-it-today.com. Website: www.bead-it-today.com. *Bead-It...Today* is a bimonthly how-to magazine that features trendy, budget-friendly jewelry and accessory designs that can be made, from start to finish, on the quick.

BEAD STYLE

21027 Crossroads Circle, P.O. Box 1612, Waukesha WI 53187-1612. Website: www.bds.jewelrymakingmagazines.com. *Bead Style*, the world's leading magazine for beaders. In every issue, *Bead Style* will deliver dozens of projects that show you how to make fast, fashionable, and fun jewelry that is uniquely you."

BEADWORK

Interweave Press, 201 E. Fourth St., Loveland CO 80537. E-mail: beadworksubmissions@interweave.com. Website: www.beadingdaily.com. "*Beadwork* is a bimonthly magazine devoted to everything about beads and beadwork. Our pages are filled with projects for all levels of beaders, with a focus on the learning needs of those who seek to master beadweaving stitches. We pride ourselves on our easy-to-follow instructions and technical illustrations as well as our informative and entertaining features."

HOW TO CONTACTGUIDELINES available on website. Query by e-mail or mail. If submitting a project idea, include high-resolution photo of project and contact info. If querying for a feature, submit proposal and contact info.

TERMS Acquires first rights and subsequent nonexclusive rights for use in print, electronic, or other Interweave publications and promotions.

BELLE ARMOIRE

Belle Armoire, 22992 Mill Creek Dr., Laguna Hills CA 92653. E-mail: bellearmoire@stampington.com. Website: www.stampington.com/belle-armoire. "*Belle Armoire* marries fabric arts with rubber stamping and embellishments – showcasing one-of-a-kind, handmade fashions and wearable-art projects. Whether you're an art stamper, embroidery artist, custom jewelry designer, fabric painter or knitting and crocheting enthusiast, *Belle Armoire* provides the opportunity and inspiration to create fashions that are uniquely you."

HOW TO CONTACT "We prefer submissions of original art. If original art is not available, our next preference is high resolution digital images (300 dpi at 8½ × 10). If hi-res digital images are not available, we will very rarely consider professional-quality transparencies or color slides. Color-copy submissions are not accepted. All artwork must be identified with the artist's name, address, e-mail and phone number clearly printed on a label attached to each sample. Inscribe your name and address somewhere on each piece of art. If you desire acknowledgment of artwork receipt, please include a self-addressed stamped postcard. If the artwork is three-dimensional, please attach your identification with a removable string, or pack the sample in a plastic bag with your identification. If you have a unique artistic technique you'd like to share with others, please send samples of your artwork accompanied by a query letter outlining your article idea to the respective Managing Editor at *Belle Armoire*."

NEEDS "Managing editors seek first-rate projects and encourage artists who have not published articles before to submit ideas, as editorial assistance will be provided."

TERMS Competitive editorial compensation is provided for all published articles. "We may hold your sample for an extended period of time—9 to 12 months is common. Due to the large volume of artwork we receive, Somerset Studio will return only those submissions accompanied by sufficient postage in the form of cash, check or money order made out to Stampington & Company. We can not offer delivery confirmation; however, we are happy to put insurance on the submission. If you wish to have your artwork insured for the return journey, please include sufficient funds and indicate your preference in a postcard or letter enclosed with your submission. Please do not attach postage to packaging, and do not send loose postage stamps. Contributors from outside the US, please send cash, check, or money order in US funds to Stampington & Company. For questions regarding your artwork, please send inquiries to artmanagement@stampington.com."

BELLE ARMOIRE JEWELRY

Belle Armoire Jewelry, 22992 Mill Creek Dr., Laguna Hills CA 92653. E-mail: bellearmoirejewelry@stampington.com. Website: www.stampington.com/belle-armoire-jewelry. "Belle Armoire Jewelry magazine is overflowing with exciting projects, such as necklaces, bracelets, earrings, and brooches. You'll be inspired by all of the projects, tips and techniques you will find. Whether your passion is stringing or making polymer clay beads, incorporating found or natural objects, you'll enjoy the artisan made creations inside *Belle Armoire Jewelry*."

HOW TO CONTACT "We prefer submissions of original art. If original art is not available, our next preference is high resolution digital images (300 dpi at 8½ × 10). If hi-res digital images are not available, we will very rarely consider professional-quality transparencies or color slides. Color-copy submissions are not accepted. All artwork must be identified with the artist's name, address, e-mail and phone number clearly printed on a label attached to each sample. Inscribe

your name and address somewhere on each piece of art. If you desire acknowledgment of artwork receipt, please include a self-addressed stamped postcard. If the artwork is three-dimensional, please attach your identification with a removable string, or pack the sample in a plastic bag with your identification. If you have a unique artistic technique you'd like to share with others, please send samples of your artwork accompanied by a query letter outlining your article idea to the respective Managing Editor at *Belle Armoire Jewelry*."

NEEDS "Managing editors seek first-rate projects and encourage artists who have not published articles before to submit ideas, as editorial assistance will be provided."

TERMS Competitive editorial compensation is provided for all published articles. "We may hold your sample for an extended period of time—9 to 12 months is common. Due to the large volume of artwork we receive, Somerset Studio will return only those submissions accompanied by sufficient postage in the form of cash, check or money order made out to Stampington & Company. We can not offer delivery confirmation; however, we are happy to put insurance on the submission. If you wish to have your artwork insured for the return journey, please include sufficient funds and indicate your preference in a postcard or letter enclosed with your submission. Please do not attach postage to packaging, and do not send loose postage stamps. Contributors from outside the US, please send cash, check, or money order in US funds to Stampington & Company. For questions regarding your artwork, please send inquiries to artmanagement@stampington.com."

BETTER HOMES & GARDENS

Website: www.bhg.com. *Better Homes & Gardens* is "the vibrant, down-to-earth guide for the woman who is passionate about her home and garden and the life she creates there."

● BRITISH PATCHWORK & QUILTING

Traplet Publications Ltd., Traplet House, Pendragon Close Malvern WR14 1GA, United Kingdom. E-mail: joanna.kent@traplet.com. Website: www.pandqmagazine.com.

CONTACT: Joanna Kent, editor. *British Patchwork and Quilting Magazine* is a monthly publication written by quilters, for quilters, with projects and features specifically to do with patchwork, quilting, appliqué and textiles.

CARDMAKER

E-mail: submissions@cardmakermagazine.com. Website: www.cardmakermagazine.com. *CardMaker* is the leading print-and-digital publication for card-making enthusiasts on the market. Published bi-monthly.

HOW TO CONTACT "We prefer to receive submissions via e-mail. Please send a completed submittal form, including an image of your project, along with your complete contact information, to Submissions@CardMakerMagazine.com. Your e-mail subject line should include the publication title and issue and project name—for example: CardMaker Winter 2014, Warm Holiday Wishes. Please keep the attached file size under 2MG. Please send one project submission per e-mail."

NEEDS Original, attractive designs and patterns for card projects that will appeal to readers of all skill levels. Technique-based projects and articles that include, but are not limited to: rubber stamping, paper folding, interactive card construction, quilling, die cutting, paper piecing, dry and heat embossing, paper cutting, handmade paper, etc. Your ideas for issue themes, new techniques and project types to feature

TERMS "When your project and instructions are approved, we will send an agreement with our payment offer and a business reply envelope. You should complete it with your signature and date, and return the original to us in the postage-paid envelope—the photocopy we send is for your records. If this is the first time we've worked with you or if it has been a while since we've accepted a project, you will also receive a W-9 (or a W-8 if you live outside the United States) which must be completed and returned before payments can be issued. You will be issued a check for payment within 45 days of the date we received your signed contract. We will keep your project until the magazine issue is published. Your project will be returned to you after publication. All manuscripts, diagrams, etc., remain our property. Since we purchase all rights to designs, you should not sell that design—or one very similar to it—to another publication. If you have questions as to what constitutes an original design, please contact us."

CARD MAKING & PAPERCRAFT

Website: www.cardmakingandpapercraft.com. *Cardmaking & Papercraft* is published 13 times a year by Immediate Media.

CARVING MAGAZINE

7 Waterloo Rd., Stanhope NJ 07874. (973)347-6900. Fax: (973)347-6909. E-mail: editors@carvingmagazine.com. Website: www.carvingmagazine.com. Contact: Chris Whillock, editor. "We feature carving projects that satisfy a wide range of experience levels and carving styles. Our beginning projects show detailed step-by-step instruction, with lots of photographs. The advanced projects show special tips and techniques from experienced woodcarvers. We also explore a wide range of carving styles, from relief to carving in-the-round, chip carving, wildlife, decorative, caricature, and much more. All of our projects feature high-quality, detailed photographs. Our project articles are written by actual woodcarvers—some beginners and some advanced. You'll learn their techniques, see what tools they use, and benefit from their carving experiences. They know what questions you might have because they've probably asked the same questions themselves."

HOW TO CONTACT Submissions should include introduction, complete list of materials, thorough step-by-step instructions, patterns, safety tips, teacher's tips, high-quality color photos.

TERMS "Please include a photograph of yourself and anything you'd like to promote for your sidebar. Please include as many photos, drawings and as much text as you think is necessary for the project. We will be editing the articles for grammar, spelling, length, and clarity. Any articles sent to us need to be your original design and not previously published anywhere else. Due to the number of articles we receive, we do not guarantee when and if we are able to publish it. If we are not able to publish your article it will be returned to you. If we do choose your article, we will contact you with the issue and date it will publish."

CLOTH PAPER SCISSORS

E-mail: submissions@clothpaperscissors.com. Website: www.clothpaperscissors.com. Published 6 times a year, *Cloth Paper Scissors* covers all types of fiber arts and collage work, including mixed media, assemblage, art dolls, visual art journals, rubber stamping, stamp carving, printmaking, creative embroidery, and book arts. Geared for the beginning artist/crafter as well as the advanced, *Cloth Paper Scissors* has a playful, positive tone, encouraging both the beginning and seasoned artist to try new techniques and share their work and expertise with a greater audience.

HOW TO CONTACT Please send the following to submissions@clothpaperscissors.com: 2-3 photos and/or sketches of the project(s) you'd like to write about; a short outline of the project, including a materials list; a 100-word bio; and your full address and contact information, including blog, website, and social-media information. Please put "I HEART PAPER" in the subject line.

NEEDS Beautiful, decorative, and/or practical projects that showcase paper.

COMPLETE CARDMAKING

Website: www.papercraftmagazines.com/the-magazines/complete-cardmaking. *Complete Cardmaking* is "the UK's first and only magazine dedicated to digital crafts, helping you make beautiful cards with your PC. This bi-monthly magazine is the ideal accompaniment for the avid digital crafter, providing a free CD-ROM with every issue."

COUNTRY SAMPLER

707 Kautz Rd., St. Charles IL 60174. (630)377-8000. Fax: (630)377-8194. E-mail: editors@countrysampler.com. Website: www.countrysampler.com. "*Country Sampler* is a must-have, all-in-one resource for any country decorator. Our unbeatable combination of country-lifestyle articles and a complete catalog of decorating products provide all the tips and tools you need to make your house a country home."

● CRAFTS

E-mail: crafts@craftscouncil.org.uk. Website: www.craftsmagazine.org.uk. Published 6 times a year and covering all disciplines, this is the perfect magazine for makers, collectors and lovers of craft.

● CRAFTS BEAUTIFUL

Aceville Publications. E-mail: sarah.crosland@aceville.co.uk. Website: www.crafts-beautiful.com. Contact: Sarah Crosland, editor. "Britain's best-selling craft magazine. Card making, papercraft, stitching, baking and knits—we love it all!"

CRAFTSELLER

E-mail: yourletters@craft-seller.com. Website: www.craft-seller.com. "An exciting magazine packed with projects, inspiration and advice for anyone who loves crafting and wants to make and sell their handmade crafts."

● CRAFT STAMPER

Traplet Publications Ltd., Traplet House, Pendragon Close Malvern WR14 1GA, United Kingdom. E-mail: alix.merriman@traplet.com. Website: www.crafts-tamper.com. Contact: Alix Merriman, editor. "The UK's best magazine for rubber stamping enthusiasts."

CREATE & DECORATE

7 Waterloo Rd., Stanhope NJ 07874. (973)347-6900. Fax: (973)347-6909. E-mail: editors@createanddecorate.com. Website: www.createanddecorate.com. Contact: Beverly Hotz, editor. "The very best magazine for primitive country and vintage-inspired crafts. *Create & Decorate* magazine guides your endeavors in punch needle, rug hooking, painting, stitching and mixed medium projects to decorate your home. Find inspiration in feature articles that offer a glimpse inside artists' work spaces, and read how creativity may start a successful business. Let us bring you on an antique junking journey, lead you in a fun new crafting technique, and introduce you to a different recipe every issue."

HOW TO CONTACT Submissions should include introduction, complete list of materials, thorough step-by-step instructions, patterns, source of products. Submission format: send as Microsoft Word document.

TERMS "We ask that you submit only original material that has not been published elsewhere, shared on the Internet, or is currently under consideration by another publisher. We request that you first submit several good quality photographs of the project for our consideration. Upon acceptance, we would require the finished item for our photography."

CREATE WITH ME

22992 Mill Creek Dr., Laguna Hills CA 92653. E-mail: createwithme@stampington.com. Website: www.stampington.com/create-with-me. "The articles cover a complete spectrum from fabric and wearable art to paint, papier mâché, card making, and bedroom décor—and there is something for every age group."
HOW TO CONTACT "We prefer submissions of original art. If original art is not available, our next preference is high resolution digital images (300 dpi at 8½ × 10). If hi-res digital images are not available, we will very rarely consider professional-quality transparencies or color slides. Color-copy submissions are not accepted. All artwork must be identified with the artist's name, address, e-mail and phone number clearly printed on a label attached to each sample. Inscribe your name and address somewhere on each piece of art. If you desire acknowledgment of artwork receipt, please include a self-addressed stamped postcard. If the artwork is three-dimensional, please attach your identification with a removable string, or pack the sample in a plastic bag with your identification. If you have a unique artistic technique you'd like to share with others, please send samples of your artwork accompanied by a query letter outlining your article idea to the respective Managing Editor at: *Create With Me*, 22992 Mill Creek Drive, Laguna Hills, CA 92653. Managing editors also welcome brief e-mail inquiries."
NEEDS "Managing editors seek first-rate projects and encourage artists who have not published articles before to submit ideas, as editorial assistance will be provided."
TERMS Competitive editorial compensation is provided for all published articles. "We may hold your sample for an extended period of time—9 to 12 months is common. Due to the large volume of artwork we receive, Somerset Studio will return only those submissions accompanied by sufficient postage in the form of cash, check or money order made out to Stampington & Company. We can not offer delivery confirmation; however, we are happy to put insurance on the submission. If you wish to have your artwork insured for the return journey, please include sufficient funds and indicate your preference in a postcard

or letter enclosed with your submission. Please do not attach postage to packaging, and do not send loose postage stamps. Contributors from outside the US, please send cash, check, or money order in US funds to Stampington & Company. For questions regarding your artwork, please send inquiries to artmanagement@stampington.com."

CREATING KEEPSAKES

E-mail: editorial@creatingkeepsakes.com. Website: www.creatingkeepsakes.com. Estab. 1996. "*Creating Keepsakes* magazine is the leading magazine for inspiration and techniques for scrapbookers."

● CREATIVE CARDMAKING

Website: www.creativemagazines.com. Each issue of *Creative Cardmaking* "includes a free cardmaking kit and is packed full of fantastic ideas for using your craft stash as well as all of the latest products from your favourite craft companies."

CREATIVE KNITTING

E-mail: editor@creativeknittingmagazine.com. Website: www.creativeknittingmagazine.com. "*Creative Knitting* features clear instructions for classic and current trends in knitting design."

CREATIVE MACHINE EMBROIDERY

E-mail: info@cmemag.com. Website: www.cmemag.com. *Creative Machine Embroidery* is a bi-monthly magazine devoted to all things embroidery.

CREATIVE STAMPING

Website: www.creativemagazines.com. "*Creative Stamping* is an amazing magazine devoted to the wonderful world of stamping."

CREATIVE WOODWORKS & CRAFTS

7 Waterloo Rd., Stanhope NJ 07874. (973)347-6900. Fax: (973)347-6909. E-mail: editors@woodworksandcrafts.com. Website: www.woodworksandcrafts.com. Contact: Debbie McGowan, editor. "*Creative Woodworks & Crafts* magazine is the best source available for original scroll saw, intarsia, and other small wood-

working project patterns. Every project and feature article is new and exclusive—'see it first in Creative Woodworks & Crafts!' Whether you are a professional woodcrafter or a hobbyist, you will find much in this publication to interest and inspire you to greater heights of woodworking achievement."

HOW TO CONTACT Submissions should include professional photographs, a complete and accurate supplies list formatted like those in the magazine.

TERMS "Please allow us at least eight weeks to review your project and get back to you. All designs must be completely original and we must have first exclusive publishing rights (your designs cannot be featured in any other publication until after the off-sale date)."

CROCHET!

E-mail: editor@crochetmagazine.com. Website: www.crochetmagazine.com. Contact: Ellen Gormley, editor. *Crochet!* is a full-color, 100-page full-size magazine published quarterly.

CROCHET 1-2-3

E-mail: editors@crochet1-2-3.com. Website: www.crochet1-2-3.com. *Crochet 1-2-3* is a bi-monthly magazine that features easy, creative, affordable crochet projects for you, your home and your family.

CROCHET TODAY!

E-mail: feedback@crochettoday.com. Website: www.crochettoday.com. "*Crochet Today* features fresh and modern crochet patterns, including gorgeous fashions, beautiful home decor, and sweet baby gifts. We focus on enriching the crocheter's skill set with step-by-step tutorials on the latest crochet stitch trends."

CROCHET WORLD

E-mail: editor@crochet-world.com. Website: www.crochet-world.com. Contact: Carol Alexander, editor. *Crochet World* magazine is published bimonthly. This 68-page magazine offers techniques and patterns with complete directions for all types of crochet.

HOW TO CONTACT Begin each submission with a sentence or two about why you designed it. Include all contact information with your query, including name, address, phone number, and e-mail address. If you want your projects returned, they must be accompanied by correct return postage, either check or money order ONLY. Project review: Reviews are held approximately every eight weeks. Check the Editorial Calendar for dates. Many of these projects are seasonal.

TERMS "If we accept your design(s), we will contact you within two weeks after the review date. We may choose to hold on to a project that might fit in another issue. All others will be returned as soon as possible."

CROSS-STITCH & NEEDLEWORK

E-mail: jfranchuk@c-sn.com. Website: www.c-sn.com. "From beginner to advanced, there's something for every stitcher in *Cross-Stitch & Needlework* magazine. Each issue is packed with captivating designs, engaging feature articles and designer profiles, large full-color charts, fantastic finishing ideas, and easy-to-follow instructions for cross-stitch, needlepoint, embroidery, Hardanger, and more." Published bimonthly.

HOW TO CONTACT "We are always open to design submissions. Please send photos of stitched models or copies of the charted designs via e-mail, or mail to Design Submissions, Bayview Publishing, P.O. Box 157, Plover WI 54467."

TERMS "All designs must be your original creations, and may not have been previously published or sold. Please, do not send actual stitched models before contacting us first."

CROSS STITCH CARD SHOP

Website: www.cross-stitching.com/magazines/cross-stitch-card-shop.

CROSS STITCH COLLECTION

E-mail: csc@futurenet.com. Website: www.crossstitchcollection.com. "*Cross Stitch Collection* offers the most beautiful cross stitch projects from the best designers, with high value, top quality charts."

CROSS STITCH CRAZY

Website: www.cross-stitching.com/magazines/cross-stitch-crazy.

❥ CROSS STITCH FAVOURITES

Website: www.cross-stitching.com/magazines/cross-stitch-favourites. Based in the United Kingdom.

❥ CROSS STITCH GOLD

Website: www.cross-stitching.com/magazines/cross-stitch-gold. Based in the United Kingdom.

❥ DESIGNER KNITTING

E-mail: helen.chrystie@thegmcgroup.com. Website: www.designerknittingmag.com. "*Designer Knitting* offers undeniable style. For fascinating features, seasonable fashion, yarn news and book reviews, this magazine is all you need and more." Based in the United Kingdom.

❥ EMBELLISH MAGAZINE

Website: www.artwearpublications.com.au/subscriptions/embellish-magazine.html. "*Embellish Magazine* aims to fuse fashion, fantasy and art into everyday items, gifts and homewares. You will find in each issue a mix of techniques and articles as well as ideas and inspirational stories. Expect to see a range of projects including dye processes; fabric manipulation; knit and/or crochet embellished finishes; couture techniques; hand embellishing; machine embellishing; prints; custom designs; repurposed textiles and projects related to textile applications that incorporate fabric, yarn, felt and/or fibre." Based in Australia.

❥ ENJOY CROSS STITCH

Website: www.cross-stitching.com/magazines/enjoy-cross-stitch. Based in the United Kingdom.

❥ FELT MAGAZINE

Website: www.artwearpublications.com.au/subscriptions/felt-magazine.html. "*Felt Magazine* aims to inspire a new generation of fibre enthusiasts with comprehensive projects, articles and an inspirational gallery. It includes a mix of easy, intermediate and technical projects to suit a wide range of skill levels." Based in Australia.

❥ FLAIR MAGAZINE

E-mail: liz@flairmagazine.co.uk. Website: www.flairmagazine.co.uk. "*Flair Magazine* for embroidery machine enthusiasts, full of projects, info, free embroidery designs and much more." Published quarterly in the United Kingdom.

GENERATION Q MAGAZINE

6102 Ash St., Simi Valley CA 93063. E-mail: melissa@generationqmagazine.com. Website: www.generationqmagazine.com. Contact: Melissa Thompson Maher. Estab. 2011. Bimonthly consumer magazine. *Generation Q Magazine* is a lifestyle publication reflecting the interests and obsessions of the modern and contemporary quilter and sewist. Circ. 10,000. Sample available for $5.

HOW TO CONTACT Submission guideleins available for SAE and on website. Accepts unsolicited submissions. Approached by 30 project/pattern designers/year. Works with almost all freelancers. Has featured projects/patters by Sara Lawson, Victoria Findlay Wolfe, Brigitte Heitland, Julie Herman, Heather Jones. Preferred subjects: sewing, quilting. Submission format: DOC files. Include sketch, photo or other rendition with size info. Submit print-ready step-by-step/assembly diagrams. Model and property release preferred. Once agree to publish project, submit via e-mail as JPEG at 300 dpi. Only accept DOC files for instructions and JPEGs or PDFs for illustrations.

TERMS Send e-mail with project concepts. Does not keep samples on file; samples are not returned. Responds in 2 months. Pays $200 minimum for project/pattern design and industry related articles. Credit line given. Pays on publication. Buys rights for 6 months. Finds freelancers by submissions, word-of-mouth, online. Undergoes technical edit before publication.

TIPS "Our audience is a niche within the quilting/sewing world. We want projects that reflect modern and contemporary styles. We don't like working with single fabric collection projects and we love new comers!"

❥ GET STAMPING

Website: www.papercraftmagazines.com/the-magazines/get-stamping. "*Get Stamping* is the number 1 magazine for stamping ideas and inspiration. Every issue comes with an A4 stamping kit, packed with a large collection of exclusively designed contemporary stamps."

GOOD OLD DAYS

E-mail: editor@goodolddaysmagazine.com. Website: www.goodolddaysmagazine.com. *Good Old Days* magazine tells the real stories of the people who lived and grew up in "the good old days" (about 1935–1960). available for $2

HOW TO CONTACT "Manuscripts should be typed (preferably double-spaced) with the author's name, address and phone number in the upper left-hand corner. Our preferred word length is 600–1,000 words. Please submit one manuscript at a time and enclose an SASE (self-addressed stamped envelope) if you want your material acknowledged and/or returned. If your story is not accepted and you have enclosed an SASE, you will receive it back after the review process has taken place—generally about 6 months. Send your submissions to: Good Old Days Submissions, 306 E. Parr Rd., Berne, IN 46711. If you do not enclose an SASE, you will hear from us only if we offer you a contract for your story. We do accept submissions via e-mail (Editor@GoodOldDaysMagazine.com) or fax [260] 589-8093), but treat them the same as mailed unsolicited manuscripts without an SASE."

GREEN CRAFT

22992 Mill Creek Dr., Laguna Hills CA 92653. E-mail: greencraft@stampington.com. Website: www.stampington.com/greencraft-magazine. "*Green Craft Magazine* provides ideas for upcycling trash to treasures by showcasing projects where waste is repurposed into ecologically-chic creations. To support sustainable production, the entire publication is printed on 100% recycled paper."

HOW TO CONTACT "We prefer submissions of original art. If original art is not available, our next preference is high resolution digital images (300 dpi at 8½ × 10). If hi-res digital images are not available, we will very rarely consider professional-quality transparencies or color slides. Color-copy submissions are not accepted. All artwork must be identified with the artist's name, address, e-mail and phone number clearly printed on a label attached to each sample. Inscribe your name and address somewhere on each piece of art. If you desire acknowledgment of artwork receipt, please include a self-addressed stamped postcard. If the artwork is three-dimensional, please attach your identification with a removable string, or pack the sample in a plastic bag with your identification. If you have a unique artistic technique you'd like to share with others, please send samples of your artwork accompanied by a query letter outlining your article idea to the respective Managing Editor at: *Green Craft Magazine*, 22992 Mill Creek Drive, Laguna Hills, CA 92653. Managing editors also welcome brief e-mail inquiries."

NEEDS "Managing editors seek first-rate projects and encourage artists who have not published articles before to submit ideas, as editorial assistance will be provided."

TERMS Competitive editorial compensation is provided for all published articles. "We may hold your sample for an extended period of time—9 to 12 months is common. Due to the large volume of artwork we receive, Somerset Studio will return only those submissions accompanied by sufficient postage in the form of cash, check or money order made out to Stampington & Company. We can not offer delivery confirmation; however, we are happy to put insurance on the submission. If you wish to have your artwork insured for the return journey, please include sufficient funds and indicate your preference in a postcard or letter enclosed with your submission. Please do not attach postage to packaging, and do not send loose postage stamps. Contributors from outside the US, please send cash, check, or money order in US funds to Stampington & Company. For questions regarding your artwork, please send inquiries to artmanagement@stampington.com."

HANDWOVEN

Interweave Press, 24520 Melott Rd., Hillsboro OR 97123. E-mail: aosterhaug@interweave.com. Website: www.weavingdaily.com. Contact: Anita Osterhaug. "The main goal of *Handwoven* articles is to inspire our readers to weave. Articles and projects should be accessible to weavers of all skill levels, even when the material is technical. The best way to prepare an article for *Handwoven* is to study the format and style of articles in recent issues."

HOW TO CONTACT Guidelines available on website.

HAUTE HANDBAGS

22992 Mill Creek Dr., Laguna Hills CA 92653. E-mail: hautehandbags@stampington.com. Website: www.stampington.com/haute-handbags. "How do you carry it? That's the question *Somerset Studio* & *Belle Armoire* would like to help answer through our exciting special publication titled *Haute Handbags*. Whether we use purses, clutches, totes, portfolios, sacks, bags, or attachés, there are many styles made with an astounding array of materials emerging from all corners of the creative world—all vying to be made and enjoyed!"

HOW TO CONTACT "We prefer submissions of original art. If original art is not available, our next preference is high resolution digital images (300 dpi at 8½ × 10). If hi-res digital images are not available, we will very rarely consider professional-quality transparencies or color slides. Color-copy submissions are not accepted. All artwork must be identified with the artist's name, address, e-mail and phone number clearly printed on a label attached to each sample. Inscribe your name and address somewhere on each piece of art. If you desire acknowledgment of artwork receipt, please include a self-addressed stamped postcard. If the artwork is three-dimensional, please attach your identification with a removable string, or pack the sample in a plastic bag with your identification. If you have a unique artistic technique you'd like to share with others, please send samples of your artwork accompanied by a query letter outlining your article idea to the respective Managing Editor at: *Haute Handbags*, 22992 Mill Creek Drive, Laguna Hills, CA 92653. Managing editors also welcome brief e-mail inquiries."

NEEDS "Managing editors seek first-rate projects and encourage artists who have not published articles before to submit ideas, as editorial assistance will be provided."

TERMS Competitive editorial compensation is provided for all published articles. "We may hold your sample for an extended period of time—9 to 12 months is common. Due to the large volume of artwork we receive, Somerset Studio will return only those submissions accompanied by sufficient postage in the form of cash, check or money order made out to Stampington & Company. We can not offer delivery confirmation; however, we are happy to put insurance on the submission. If you wish to have your artwork insured for the return journey, please include suffi-cient funds and indicate your preference in a postcard or letter enclosed with your submission. Please do not attach postage to packaging, and do not send loose postage stamps. Contributors from outside the US, please send cash, check, or money order in US funds to Stampington & Company. For questions regarding your artwork, please send inquiries to artmanagement@stampington.com."

HOLIDAYS & CELEBRATIONS

22992 Mill Creek Dr., Laguna Hills CA 92653. E-mail: holidaysandcelebrations@stampington.com. Website: www.stampington.com/somerset-holidays-and-celebrations. Learn how to create a lasting impression on special occasions like birthdays, Halloween, Christmas, Mother's Day, Valentine's Day, and more in each annual issue of *Somerset Holidays & Celebrations*—an endless source of handcrafted inspiration.

HOW TO CONTACT "We prefer submissions of original art. If original art is not available, our next preference is high resolution digital images (300 dpi at 8½ × 10). If hi-res digital images are not available, we will very rarely consider professional-quality transparencies or color slides. Color-copy submissions are not accepted. All artwork must be identified with the artist's name, address, e-mail and phone number clearly printed on a label attached to each sample. Inscribe your name and address somewhere on each piece of art. If you desire acknowledgment of artwork receipt, please include a self-addressed stamped postcard. If the artwork is three-dimensional, please attach your identification with a removable string, or pack the sample in a plastic bag with your identification. If you have a unique artistic technique you'd like to share with others, please send samples of your artwork accompanied by a query letter outlining your article idea to the respective Managing Editor at: *Holidays and Celebrations*, 22992 Mill Creek Drive, Laguna Hills, CA 92653. Managing editors also welcome brief e-mail inquiries."

NEEDS "Managing editors seek first-rate projects and encourage artists who have not published articles before to submit ideas, as editorial assistance will be provided."

TERMS Competitive editorial compensation is provided for all published articles. "We may hold your sample for an extended period of time—9 to 12 months is common. Due to the large volume of artwork we receive, Somerset Studio will return only those submissions accompanied by sufficient postage in the form of cash, check or money order made out to Stampington & Company. We can not offer delivery confirmation; however, we are happy to put insurance on the submission. If you wish to have your artwork insured for the return journey, please include sufficient funds and indicate your preference in a postcard or letter enclosed with your submission. Please do not attach postage to packaging, and do not send loose postage stamps. Contributors from outside the US, please send cash, check, or money order in US funds to Stampington & Company. For questions regarding your artwork, please send inquiries to artmanagement@stampington.com."

● HOMESTYLE SEWING

Website: www.cross-stitching.com/magazines/homestyle-sewing. Based in the United Kingdom.

INTERWEAVE CROCHET

Interweave Press, 201 E. 4th St., Loveland CO 80537. E-mail: lindsay.jarvis@fwmedia.com (queries only). Website: www.crochetme.com. "*Interweave Crochet* is a quarterly publication of Interweave for all those who love to crochet. In each issue we present beautifully finished projects, accompanied by clear step-by-step instructions, as well as stories and articles of interest to crocheters. The projects range from quick but intriguing projects that can be accomplished in a weekend to complex patterns that may take months to complete. Engaging and informative feature articles come from around the country and around the world. Fashion sensibility and striking examples of craft technique are important to us."
HOW TO CONTACT Guidelines available on website.

INTERWEAVE KNITS

Interweave Press, 201 E. 4th St., Loveland CO 80537. Website: www.knittingdaily.com. "*Interweave Knits* is a quarterly publication of Interweave Press for all those who love to knit. In each issue we present beautifully finished projects, accompanied by clear step-by-step instruction, and stories and articles of interest to knitters. The projects range from quick but intriguing items that can be accomplished in a weekend, to complex patterns that may take months to complete. Feature articles (personally arresting but information-rich) come from around the country and around the world. Fashion sensibility and striking examples of craft technique are important to us." Interweave Knits is published quarterly.
HOW TO CONTACT Guidelines available on website.
TIPS "Remember that your submission is a representation of who you are and how you work—if you send us a thoughtful, neat, and well-organized submission, we are likely to be intrigued."

JEWELRY AFFAIRE

22992 Mill Creek Dr., Laguna Hills CA 92653. E-mail: jewelryaffaire@stampington.com. Website: www.stampington.com/jewelry-affaire. "*Jewelry Affaire* celebrates the beauty that can be found in easy to make jewelry. These pieces are not only feasts for the eyes, but they can easily dress up and adorn any outfit and its wearer. This jewelry is precious in its own right."
HOW TO CONTACT "We prefer submissions of original art. If original art is not available, our next preference is high resolution digital images (300 dpi at 8½ × 10). If hi-res digital images are not available, we will very rarely consider professional-quality transparencies or color slides. Color-copy submissions are not accepted. All artwork must be identified with the artist's name, address, e-mail and phone number clearly printed on a label attached to each sample. Inscribe your name and address somewhere on each piece of art. If you desire acknowledgment of artwork receipt, please include a self-addressed stamped postcard. If the artwork is three-dimensional, please attach your identification with a removable string, or pack the sample in a plastic bag with your identification. If you have a unique artistic technique you'd like to share with others, please send samples of your artwork accompanied by a query letter outlining your article idea to the respective Managing Editor at: *Jewelry Affaire*, 22992 Mill Creek Drive, Laguna Hills, CA 92653. Managing editors also welcome brief e-mail inquiries."
NEEDS "Managing editors seek first-rate projects and encourage artists who have not published articles before to submit ideas, as editorial assistance will be provided."

TERMS Competitive editorial compensation is provided for all published articles. "We may hold your sample for an extended period of time—9 to 12 months is common. Due to the large volume of artwork we receive, Somerset Studio will return only those submissions accompanied by sufficient postage in the form of cash, check or money order made out to Stampington & Company. We can not offer delivery confirmation; however, we are happy to put insurance on the submission. If you wish to have your artwork insured for the return journey, please include sufficient funds and indicate your preference in a postcard or letter enclosed with your submission. Please do not attach postage to packaging, and do not send loose postage stamps. Contributors from outside the US, please send cash, check, or money order in US funds to Stampington & Company. For questions regarding your artwork, please send inquiries to artmanagement@stampington.com."

JEWELRY STRINGING

E-mail: stringingsubmissions@interweave.com. Website: www.beadingdaily.com/blogs/stringing/default.aspx. *Jewelry Stringing* magazine is published quarterly. "Each issue of *Jewelry Stringing* includes more than 70 fabulous necklaces, bracelets, and earrings, accompanied by clear step-by-step instructions and beautiful photography. The projects range from quick and easy to more complex, but all are made using basic stringing, wireworking, and knotting techniques."
HOW TO CONTACT Please send the following to stringingsubmissions@interweave.com: 2-3 photos and/or sketches of the project(s) you'd like to write about; a short outline of the project, including a materials list; a 100-word bio; and your full address and contact information, including blog, website, and social-media information.

JUST CROSSSTITCH

E-mail: editor@just-crossstitch.com. Website: www.just-crossstitch.com. Estab. 1983. Just CrossStitch is the first magazine devoted exclusively to counted cross stitch and the only cross-stitch title written for the intermediate to advanced-level hobbyist.

KIDS CRAFTS 1-2-3

E-mail: editors@kidscrafts1-2-3.com. Website: www.kidscrafts1-2-3.com. *Kids Crafts 1-2-3* is bi-monthly magazine. "Each issue of *Kids Crafts 1-2-3* is filled with over 30 fun DIY crafts for kids, tweens and everyone in-between. Projects range from crochet to collage. The magazine is geared towards kids, but crafty moms and dads will walk away from each inspired to make their own Day of the Dead birdhouse or felt owl ornament."

KNIT 1-2-3

E-mail: editors@knit1-2-3.com. Website: www.knit1-2-3.com. *Knit 1-2-3* is published bi-monthly and features over 20 fresh and exciting projects in every issue.

● KNIT NOW MAGAZINE

Practical Publishing, Suite G2, St. Christopher House, 217 Wellington Rd. S., Stockport SK2 6NG United Kingdom. Website: www.knitnowmag.co.uk. Estab. 2012. Four weekly (13 issues/year) consumer magazine. "*Knit Now Magazine* is the UK's best knitting magazine, focused on quick, simple, stylish knits. We are particularly committed to British wool, supporting independent designers and publishing new and interesting knits every issue." Circ. 25,000 (per issue). Submission guidelines available by request.
HOW TO CONTACT Request guidelines via e-mail. Accepts unsolicited submissions. Approached by 300 project/pattern designers/year. Buys 130 project/pattern designs/year from freelancers. Preferred subjects: knitting, crochet. Submission format: PDF. Include swatch, sketch and brief description.
TERMS Send PDF submission in response to a focused call for submission. Responds in 2 weeks. Pays $100 minimum, $320 maximum for project/pattern design. Credit line given. Pays on publication. Buys first rights. Finds freelancers through submissions, word-of-mouth. Undergoes technical edit before publication.
TIPS "See our blog post that offers advice for designers who want to work for us at www.knitnowmag.co.uk/item/193-submission-tips-for-designers. Be sure to include a clear swatch and sketch with submission."

KNITSCENE

E-mail: apalmer@interweave.com. Website: www. knittingdaily.com/blogs/knitscenemagazine. "In each issue, we feature up-and-coming designers, popular yarns, fun and concise tutorials, and fresh photography that invites the reader into a yarn-filled daydream. The projects are simple but intriguing, stylish but wearable, and designed for knitters of all ages and sizes."

KNIT SIMPLE

E-mail: helen.chrystie@thegmcgroup.com. Website: www.thegmcgroup.com. "*Knit Simple* with easy to use and well-organised instructions, this magazine offers exactly what it says in the title. Whatever your skill level, here is a great resource for casual creations and simple, easy-to-wear knits that accommodate all shapes and sizes."

KNITSTYLE

7 Waterloo Rd., Stanhope NJ 07874. (973)347-6900. Fax: (973)347-6909. E-mail: editors@knitstylemag. com. Website: www.knitstylemag.com. Contact: Cari Clement, editor. "*KNITstyle*, formally *Knit 'n Style*, is a bi-monthly magazine that inspires beginner to expert knitters with a wide range of 'knit me' projects, in styles ranging from classic to contemporary. Knitters are inspired by glossy, full-color photography and a project format that features the latest yarns and fibers from international fashion runways. Trendsetting knitwear projects are provided for women, men, and children."

❺ THE KNITTER

E-mail: theknitter@futurenet.com. Website: www. theknitter.co.uk. "*The Knitter* is the magazine for knitters seeking a creative challenge." Published 13 times a year.

KNITTER'S MAGAZINE

Knitter's Magazine Submissions, 1320 S. Minnesota Ave., Floor 2, Sioux Falls SD 57105. E-mail: managingeditor@xrx-inc.com. Website: www.knitting universe.com/K113. A quarterly publication featuring popular designers and the latest knitwear fashions, techniques and supplies.

HOW TO CONTACT All submissions should include a swatch, sketch or picture of the project, and description of the design and techniques it will use. A short biography is helpful.

❺ KNITTING

E-mail: helen.chrystie@thegmcgroup.com. Website: www.thegmcgroup.com. "*Knitting* is the UK's original and best magazine devoted to this popular craft. Bridging the divide between fashion and hand-Knitting, each issue offers at least 25 new and contemporary patterns, including knits for women, men, children and the home."

❺ KNIT TODAY

Website: www.knit-today.co.uk. "*Knit Today* magazine is for everyone who enjoys knitting. Whether you've just started knitting or an experienced knitter, you'll find lots to read and at least 20 great patterns in every single issue. All our patterns are brand new so you won't have seen them anywhere else before. We pride ourselves on having the most accurate, easy to follow pattern instructions so you can enjoy knitting to the very last stitch!" Published 13 times a year.

LAPIDARY JOURNAL JEWELRY ARTIST

E-mail: ljeditorial@interweave.com. Website: www.jewelrymakingdaily.com/blogs/jewelryartist magazine/default.aspx.

❺ LET'S GET CRAFTING

Website: www.letsgetcrafting.com. "*Let's Get Crafting Knitting & Crochet* contains everything you need to get started right away! Perfect for both beginners and experienced crafters, each issue comes with a high-value yarn pack, plus knitting needles and a crochet hook. We'll guide you step-by-step through gorgeous projects from some of the UK's leading designers, plus we have all the latest news and gossip from the UK crafting community as well as shopping guides and informative features."

LET'S KNIT

21-23 Phoenix Court, Hawkind Rd., Colchester Essex CO2 8JY, United Kingdom. E-mail: sarah.neal@aceville.co.uk. Website: www.letsknit.co.uk. Contact: Sarah Neal, editor. Estab. 2007. "Let's Knit is the UK's best knitting magazine! Every issue is packed with patterns for knitters of all ages and skill levels, with a fun and fashionable flavour that's perfect for today's knitter. It has all the practical help, informative features and shopping info you could possibly want, along with a fantastic high-value free gift with every issue."

LOVE CRAFTING

Website: www.cross-stitching.com/magazines/lovecrafting. "*Love Crafting* is a brand-new magazine full of inspiration for crafters of all abilities. Inside our sewing special you will find over 50 amazing makes with easy-to-follow instructions and templates, plus our top budget buys!"

LOVE CROCHET

Website: www.immediate.co.uk/brands/lovecrochet/. "*Love Crochet* is a quarterly magazine filled with over 30 beautiful crochet projects for clothes, accessories and the home. As well as an inspiring mix of on-trend makes, you'll find all the latest crochet news plus designer interviews, blogs, courses and kits. This is the perfect magazine for those who enjoy crochet or want to learn this exciting craft."

LOVE KNITTING FOR BABY

Website: www.immediate.co.uk/brands/love-knitting-for-baby. "*Love Knitting for Baby* is a bi-monthly must-knit collection of beautiful clothes and accessories for babies and toddlers. Each issue includes over 25 knitting patterns, plus best buys, expert advice, baby yarn reviews and interviews with top designers."

LOVE OF QUILTING

P.O. Box 171, Winterset IA 50273. (515) 462-1020. Fax: (515)462-5856. Website: www.fonsandporter.com. Contact: Diane Tomlinson, associate editor. Estab. 1996. Bimonthly consumer magazine. Also publishes special interest issues (*Easy Quilts, Quilting Quickly, Scrap Quilts & Patriotic Quilts*) quarterly and bi-annually. Focus is quilting projects. Circ. 350,000. Sample available by request

HOW TO CONTACT Guidelines available online. Accepts unsolicited submissions. Approached by 200 project/pattern designers/year. Busy 400 projects/pattern designs/year from freelancers. Has featured projects/patterns by Liz Porter, Marianne Fons, Nancy Mahoney. Preferred subjects: quilting. Submission format: PDF, JPEG and Illustrator files. Include detailed descriptions including measurements and fabric.

TERMS Send e-mail. Does not keep samples on file; samples not returned. Responds in 1 month. Pay varies by project. Pays on acceptance. Buys all rights (for contracted period of time). Finds freelancers through submissions, word-of-mouth, magazines, online. Edits as required.

TIPS "We are looking for traditional, easy and precut quilt ideas in all skill levels. Have good artwork and descriptions."

LOVE PATCHWORK & QUILTING

Website: www.lovepatchworkandquilting.com. "*Love Patchwork & Quilting* is a dedicated modern quilting magazine from the makers of *Mollie Makes* and *Simply Crochet*. We publish 13 times a year, featuring projects, techniques, interviews, news and reviews from the world of modern quilting. Every issue also comes with a FREE gift!"

MACHINE KNITTING MONTHLY

Website: www.machineknittingmonthly.net. "*Machine Knitting Monthly* magazine is packed with great new pattern ideas, features on different stitches, letters, club news, reviews on related books and products and much more."

MACHINE QUILTING UNLIMITED

P.O. Box 918, Fort Lupton CO 80621. E-mail: submissions@mqumag.com. Website: www.machinequilting.mqumag.com. "*Machine Quilting Unlimited* is for the machine-quilting enthusiast. We cover techniques and fundamentals, whether using a domestic sewing machine, a small frame system, a midarm machine, or a longarm machine. There will also be design inspiration, profiles of your favorite quilting stars, reviews of products, books, and DVDs, ideas for setting up your studio or workroom, help for beginners, and a calendar of quilt shows and events."

MAKE

E-mail: editor@makezine.com. Website: www.makezine.com. Bi-monthly magazine for DIY enthusiasts

● MAKE & SELL JEWELLERY

1 Phoenix Court, Hawkins Rd., Colchester Essex CO2 8JY, United Kingdom. E-mail: lorraine.luximon@aceville.co.uk; melissa@aceville.com. Website: www.makeselljewellery.com. Contact: Lorraine Luximon; Melissa Hyland. "*Make & Sell Jewellery* magazine is the UK's glossiest and most glamorous dedicated jewellery making magazine, aimed at hobbyists and those wanting to sell their creations alike. Each issue features a regular Make & Sell section packed with advice and tips from experts to start your business and boost sales, plus exclusive, copyright-free projects. Beginners and those making for themselves aren't forgotten with step-by-step guides to create designer-style jewellery, from simple bead stringing and wirework to more advanced techniques such as polymer and precious metal clay and resin. Whether making jewellery as a hobby or small business, *Make & Sell Jewellery* provides all the know-how needed to create accessories that are both original and on-trend. With beautiful and clear photography including jewellery showcased on models so you can see how to wear the designs too, it stands out from other jewellery magazines. And with a bounty of shopping pages to help you with your purchases, it really is the only jewellery magazine you need, whether a beginner or pro!"

● MAKING

E-mail: helen.chrystie@thegmcgroup.com. Website: www.thegmcgroup.com. "*Making* is the UK's first contemporary craft magazine, bringing its readers 25 bespoke projects every month. Filled with inspiration, beautiful projects and stunning photography, *Making* is essential reading for the discerning crafter. Covering a wide range of techniques and disciplines, clear how-to's and style advice along with regular fea-

tures and shopping pages, *Making* is the perfect combination of craft and lifestyle for a creative audience."

● MAKING JEWELLERY

E-mail: helen.chrystie@thegmcgroup.com. Website: www.thegmcgroup.com. "*Making Jewellery* is the UK's first and best-selling jewellery magazine. Each month we feature more than 45 projects to make stylish, fashionable and professional-looking jewellery. There are step-by step projects for ever skill level using a variety of techniques from simple stringing to metal clays, polymer, shrink plastic, wirework, silversmithing, resin, lampworking and more. *Making Jewellery* offers an innovative approach to jewellery making with instruction on basic techniques and insight into the creative minds of leading makers."

MARTHA STEWART LIVING

E-mail: living@marthastewart.com. Website: www.marthastewart.com. Monthly magazine for gardening, entertaining, renovating, cooking, collecting, and creating.

MCCALL'S QUICK QUILTS

E-mail: mcq@creativecraftsgroup.com. Website: www.mccallsquilting.com. Bi–monthly consumer publication, nationally distributed, and written for quilters of all skill levels.

MCCALL'S QUILTING

E-mail: mcq@creativecraftsgroup.com. Website: www.mccallsquilting.com. Bi–monthly consumer publication, nationally distributed, and written for quilters of all skill levels.

MINGLE

22992 Mill Creek Dr., Laguna Hills CA 92653. E-mail: mingle@stampington.com. Website: www.stampington.com/mingle. "*Mingle*, along with the uplifting stories behind uniquely creative get-togethers—from small and intimate 'girls' nights in' to larger scale art retreats. Discover creative ways for bringing friends and loved ones together—is complete with entertaining tips, one-of-a-kind invitations and party favor ideas, recipes, artful décor, creative inspiration, and an all around good time! Make your next get-together 'the talk of the town' with ideas from the pages of this photography-rich and engrossing magazine."

HOW TO CONTACT "We prefer submissions of original art. If original art is not available, our next preference is high resolution digital images (300 dpi at 8½ × 10). If hi-res digital images are not available, we will very rarely consider professional-quality transparencies or color slides. Color-copy submissions are not accepted. All artwork must be identified with the artist's name, address, e-mail and phone number clearly printed on a label attached to each sample. Inscribe your name and address somewhere on each piece of art. If you desire acknowledgment of artwork receipt, please include a self-addressed stamped postcard. If the artwork is three-dimensional, please attach your identification with a removable string, or pack the sample in a plastic bag with your identification. If you have a unique artistic technique you'd like to share with others, please send samples of your artwork accompanied by a query letter outlining your article idea to the respective Managing Editor at: *Mingle*, 22992 Mill Creek Drive, Laguna Hills, CA 92653. Managing editors also welcome brief e-mail inquiries."

NEEDS "Managing editors seek first-rate projects and encourage artists who have not published articles before to submit ideas, as editorial assistance will be provided."

TERMS Competitive editorial compensation is provided for all published articles. "We may hold your sample for an extended period of time—9 to 12 months is common. Due to the large volume of artwork we receive, Somerset Studio will return only those submissions accompanied by sufficient postage in the form of cash, check or money order made out to Stampington & Company. We can not offer delivery confirmation; however, we are happy to put insurance on the submission. If you wish to have your artwork insured for the return journey, please include sufficient funds and indicate your preference in a postcard or letter enclosed with your submission. Please do not attach postage to packaging, and do not send loose postage stamps. Contributors from outside the US, please send cash, check, or money order in US funds to Stampington & Company. For questions regarding your artwork, please send inquiries to artmanagement@stampington.com."

MODERN QUILTS UNLIMITED

P.O. Box 918, Fort Lupton CO 80621. E-mail: editor@mqumag.com. Website: www.modernquilts.mqumag.com. "*Modern Quilts Unlimited* is published quarterly and offers quilt, accessory and home decoration patterns by exciting new designers, interviews with the innovators in this field, machine quilting tips and quilts and projects made by those who find that this new genre of quilting fits their needs and lifestyles."

⬤ MOLLIE MAKES

Website: www.molliemakes.com. "*Mollie Makes* brings you the best of craft online, a look inside the homes of the world's most creative crafters, tutorials on inspiring makes, round ups of the most covetable stash and tours of the crafty capitals of the world."

⬤ NEW STITCHES

E-mail: janice@ccpuk.co.uk. Website: www.newstitches.co.uk. Published monthly, "*New Stitches* features designs for your favourite embroidery techniques such as cross stitch, hardanger, blackwork and much more."

ONLINE QUILT MAGAZINE

P.O. Box 57, Buxton NSW 2571, Australia. (61)2-4683-2912. E-mail: jody@onlinequiltmagazine.com. Website: www.onlinequiltmagazine.com. Contact: Jody Anderson, editor. Estab. 2010. Monthly online publication. "We publish a monthly online quilting magazine that has a large readership around the world. Our readers range from beginners to more experienced quilters, and as such we like to offer a variety of articles, how to's and patterns so there is something to appeal to everyone. There is a smaller free version each month and a super cheap twice-as-big paid issue as well." Circ. 20,000. Sample available by request

HOW TO CONTACT Request via e-mail. Accepts unsolicited submissions. Exchanges free publicity and ad space for project/pattern designs. Has featured projects/patterns by Pat Durbin, Jenny Bowker, Kathy McNeil, Frieda Anderson, Toby Lischko, Elaine Quehl. Preferred subjects: quilting. Submission format: DOC and JPEG files. E-mail with general idea before submitting materials/content. Responsible for submitting print-ready photos and step-by-step/assembly diagrams for completed project. Photo captions only required if needed to make photo clear. Accepts images in digital format only via e-mail as JPEG file.

TERMS Send e-mail with project concepts. Responds in 7 days. Offers free publicity and ad space in exchange for designs/articles. Credit line given. Buys one-time. Finds freelancers through word-of-mouth, online. Edits as required.

TIPS "We welcome everyone! We're always looking for new projects and quilting articles, and whilst we can't pay money for your submissions, we do offer great advertising promotion to our large reader base in exchange. It's a great way of attracting traffic to your site! Please just get in touch with me!"

PAINT-IT... TODAY

E-mail: editor@paint-it-today.com. Website: www. paint-it-today.com. *Paint-It...Today* is published bimonthly by Valu-Publishing, LLC.

PAINTWORKS

7 Waterloo Rd., Stanhope NJ 07874. (973)347-6900. Fax: (973)347-6909. E-mail: editors@paintworksmag. com. Website: www.paintworksmag.com. Contact: Linda R. Heller, editor. "*PaintWorks* looks to present quality painting projects in a straightforward, easily understandable style. As a how-to magazine, we aim to teach our readers principles and techniques for painting, lay foundations that encourage readers to develop their own ideas, inform readers of new ideas, products and trends within the industry, and present as wide a variety of projects as space, editorial focus, and audience interest allow."

HOW TO CONTACT Submissions should include introduction, complete list of materials, thorough step-by-step instructions, patterns, list of suppliers, high quality color photos. Submission format: send as Microsoft Word document or Rich Text.

TERMS Submit only original material that has not been published elsewhere nor is currently under consideration by another publisher. Provide an appropriate-sized pre-stamped envelope for the return of your materials.

☻ PAPERCRAFTER MAGAZINE

E-mail: ella.johnston@aceville.co.uk. Website: www. papercraftermagazine.co.uk. Contact: Ella Johnston, editor. "*PaperCrafter* is a must-buy mag for makers who adore all things paper, offering everything you need to create cards and papercraft projects in one package. It comes with beautiful kits and paper books that are designed by a different illustrator every issue, giving projects a fresh new look and providing inspiration with every purchase."

PAPERCRAFT ESSENTIALS

Website: www.papercraftmagazines.com/the-magazines/papercraft-essentials. "*Papercraft Essentials* is packed with fun cards you can make in an evening! With the emphasis on cute and traditional styles, the magazine combines quick makes for beginners with more in-depth projects for intermediate and advanced crafters."

PAPERCRAFT INSPIRATIONS

E-mail: papercraft@futurenet.com. Website: www. papercraftinspirationsmagazine.co.uk. "Britain's best-selling card making magazine—filled with help, advice, oodles of ideas and techniques for card makers of all levels of experience!"

PAPER CRAFTS & SCRAPBOOKING

E-mail: editor@papercraftsmag.com. Website: www. papercraftsmag.com. *Paper Crafts & Scrapbooking* is an enthusiast-based magazine with worldwide circulation.

PAPER CREATIONS

7 Waterloo Rd., Stanhope NJ 07874. (973)347-6900. Fax: (973)347-6909. E-mail: editors@scrapbookingandbeyondmag.com. Website: www.paper creationsmag.com. Contact: Jane Guthrie, editor. *Paper Creations* is a quarterly magazine that "offers creative projects and ideas that encompass the versatile world of paper. Geared toward both seasoned pros and newcomers, each issue includes an impressive assortment of paper projects, complete with step-by-step instructions, full-size patterns, and helpful tips. *Paper Creations* teaches readers how to make stunning

cards, stationery, table decorations, gift boxes, jewelry, and more using the most popular techniques (including embossing, stamping, stitching, and everything in between) and products."

HOW TO CONTACT Please provide photos, diagrams or other appropriate visuals to support the project or article you wish to submit.

TERMS Submit only original material that has not been published elsewhere (including websites, blogs, etc.) nor is currently under consideration by another publisher.

PIECEWORK

E-mail: piecework@interweave.com. Website: www.interweave.com/needle/piecework_magazine. *Piece-Work* is a bimonthly magazine with "high visual impact focusing on the historical aspects of needlework around the world. *PieceWork* readers are passionate about needlework; they value the role needlework has played, and plays, in the ongoing human story."

⦿ POPULAR PATCHWORK

E-mail: bridget.kenningham@myhobbystore.com. Website: www.popularpatchwork.com. Contact: Bridget Kenningham. "Bringing traditional and contemporary patchwork & quilting to the fabricaholics of the United Kingdom."

POTTERY MAKING ILLUSTRATED

600 N. Cleveland Ave., Suite 210, Westerville OH 43082. (614)895-4213. Fax: (614)891-8960. E-mail: editorial@potterymaking.org. Website: www.ceramic artsdaily.org/pottery-making-illustrated. *Pottery Making Illustrated* provides well-illustrated, practical, how-to instruction for all skill levels on all aspects of ceramic art.

HOW TO CONTACT "We require professional digital images for publication. Digital images should be delivered as uncompressed four-color (CMYK), 300 dpi image files with a minimum print size of 5 inches (preferably tiff or eps format). Image files should be burned to a CD and mailed to our editorial offices with your complete submission. Images can also be uploaded to our ftp site. Uploaded files must be stuffed or zipped. Include all captions on a separate sheet of paper. Each image or graphic element must have a

caption. Make sure image file names clearly match up with caption numbers. Captions for processes and techniques should describe the activity shown. Captions for finished ware should include: the title, dimensions, specific ceramic medium (earthenware, porcelain, etc.), forming/glazing techniques, cone number and firing process (pit fired, high fire, raku, etc.). Provide a brief one or two sentence biography about yourself and include an e-mail address, web address, fax number or postal address if you want direct reader feedback. Our authors have indicated that this has been a valuable tool. If images or illustrations were provided by a third party, include her/his name so proper credit may be published. It is your responsibility to obtain the rights for any photographs, illustrations or other third-party materials submitted."

TERMS "We ask for exclusive worldwide rights for the text (both print and electronic versions, including but not limited to publishing on demand, database online services, reprints or books), and nonexclusive rights for use of the photographic materials in print or electronic media. This nonexclusive agreement allows for the continued use of the photographic material in any way the artist chooses after the article has appeared in *Pottery Making Illustrated*. When your article is published, you'll be paid at the current rate of $0.10 per word for text and $25.00 per image or graphic illustration."

PRIMITIVE QUILTS & PROJECTS

E-mail: homespunmedia@aol.com. Website: www.primitivequiltsandprojects.com. "A premium quilting magazine dedicated to the primitive quilter, rug hooker, stitcher and more! Each issue features at least 15 projects from some of the most admired designers in the primitive fiber arts world."

PRIMS

22992 Mill Creek Dr., Laguna Hills CA 92653. E-mail: prims@stampington.com. Website: www.stampington.com/prims. "*Prims* exclusively features art inspired by a bygone era. You will find artwork of primitive, folk, historic, and early Americana style artists that will captivate the imagination and enchant with their simple beauty. The traditional beauty of handcrafted art making includes dolls, paintings and mixed-media artwork, along with teddy bears in Stampington & Company's unique publication."

HOW TO CONTACT "We prefer submissions of original art. If original art is not available, our next preference is high resolution digital images (300 dpi at 8½ × 10). If hi-res digital images are not available, we will very rarely consider professional-quality transparencies or color slides. Color-copy submissions are not accepted. All artwork must be identified with the artist's name, address, e-mail and phone number clearly printed on a label attached to each sample. Inscribe your name and address somewhere on each piece of art. If you desire acknowledgment of artwork receipt, please include a self-addressed stamped postcard. If the artwork is three-dimensional, please attach your identification with a removable string, or pack the sample in a plastic bag with your identification. If you have a unique artistic technique you'd like to share with others, please send samples of your artwork accompanied by a query letter outlining your article idea to the respective Managing Editor at: *Prims*, 22992 Mill Creek Drive, Laguna Hills, CA 92653. Managing editors also welcome brief e-mail inquiries."

NEEDS "Managing editors seek first-rate projects and encourage artists who have not published articles before to submit ideas, as editorial assistance will be provided."

TERMS Competitive editorial compensation is provided for all published articles. "We may hold your sample for an extended period of time—9 to 12 months is common. Due to the large volume of artwork we receive, Somerset Studio will return only those submissions accompanied by sufficient postage in the form of cash, check or money order made out to Stampington & Company. We can not offer delivery confirmation; however, we are happy to put insurance on the submission. If you wish to have your artwork insured for the return journey, please include sufficient funds and indicate your preference in a postcard or letter enclosed with your submission. Please do not attach postage to packaging, and do not send loose postage stamps. Contributors from outside the US, please send cash, check, or money order in US funds to Stampington & Company. For questions regarding your artwork, please send inquiries to artmanagement@stampington.com."

QUICK & EASY CROCHET

Website: www.quickandeasycrochetmagazine.com. "America's No. 1 crochet magazine. Filled with easy-to-follow instructions for crocheted fashions, pillows, potholders, afghans, coverlets, bridal gowns, dollies, and more."

❥ QUICK CARDS MADE EASY

Website: www.cardmakingandpapercraft.com/magazine/quickcards. *Quick Cards Made Easy* is packed with stylish card projects, for every occasion, each issue. Published 13 times a year.

QUILT

E-mail: quiltmag@epix.net. Website: www.quilt mag.com. "Published 6 times per year, *Quilt* will fulfill your every quilting need. Each issue is bursting with patterns in a variety of styles for all skill levels. Quilts are showcased in beautifully styled room settings, and clear directions and illustrations accompany each project. Our talented designers use current fabric collections, so you can create the exact quilt shown, and many projects include kit information for easy ordering."

QUILT ALMANAC

E-mail: quiltmag@epix.net. Website: www.quiltmag. com. "Published each January, *Quilt Almanac* features quilts for all seasons, from traditional to modern, and showcases a variety of techniques. This newsstand-only issue will provide you with inspiring projects to keep you busy all year long. Our designers create both quilts and small projects ideal for newer quilters or for experienced quilters looking for a quick and relaxing project."

THE QUILTER

7 Waterloo Rd., Stanhope NJ 07874. (973)347-6900. Fax: (973)347-6909. E-mail: editors@thequiltermag.com. Website: www.thequiltermag.com. Contact: Laurette Koserowski, editor. "*The Quilter* magazine provides quilters, beginner through advanced, with

a wide variety of step-by-step projects specially designed to use today's fabrics and innovative techniques with home decor in mind.

HOW TO CONTACT "It is recommended that you submit a query first. Manuscripts must be typewritten, double-spaced on one side of the paper and, if possible, submitted on CDs, saved in Microsoft Word (.DOC) or text (.TXT) format. Write simple, clear, and thorough directions, including a list of materials, finished sizes, seam allowances, assembly diagrams, appliqué patterns, etc. Be sure patterns are perfectly accurate, and marked clearly with cutting, sewing, and fabric grain directions. Articles about quilts and quilt exhibits must be accompanied by professional quality digital images. If you submit a query, attach a good photograph and description of your project. Include an SASE with sufficient postage for the return of your material. Submissions without an SASE will not be returned."

TERMS "*The Quilter* pays $150-250 per article for first North American Rights for original, hitherto unpublished, articles. For quilts, pillows, and other projects, payment is made at a flat rate of $175-$375 per project. Payment is made upon publication. We respond within approximately six (6) weeks on manuscripts and queries."

QUILTER'S NEWSLETTER MAGAZINE

E-mail: questions@qnm.com. Website: www.quilters newsletter.com. "*Quilters Newsletter* is a specialized publication for quilt lovers and quiltmakers. Its domestic and international readership of approximately 200,000 includes professional and nonprofessional quiltmakers, quilt collectors, historians, and teachers."

TERMS "Our rates depend on what rights we buy, how much editing or rewriting is required, if you can provide usable sewn samples, and whether we use your photos or do the photography in our studio.We reserve the right to use accepted material in any appropriate issue and for any editorial purpose. For general articles, as well as for each pattern that we develop from a submitted quilt, payment will be negotiated upon acceptance. We make no payment for material used in our News columns or for feature material sent by industry professionals or their representatives that promotes a person, event, or product. Payment for Top Tips used in Short Takes is $25.Payment for showcas-

ing a quilt on our cover andpresenting a pattern for a portion of or all of the quilt is $350 plus 10 copies of that issue. Paymen tfor Photo Finish and About Space is $50 and 10 copies of that issue."

QUILTER'S WORLD

E-mail: editor@quiltersworld.com. Website: www. quiltersworld.com. Estab. 1979. "*Quilter's World* features classic and current trends in quilt design.

QUILTING ARTS MAGAZINE

E-mail: submissions@quiltingarts.com. Website: www.quiltingdaily.com. "At *Quilting Arts*, we celebrate contemporary art quilting, surface design, mixed media, fiber art trends, and more. We are always looking for new techniques, innovative processes, and unique approaches to the art of quilting."

HOW TO CONTACT Guidelines available on website.

QUILT-IT...TODAY

E-mail: editors@quiltittoday.com. Website: www. quiltittoday.com. *Quilt-it...Today* magazine features quick, easy, and fun quilting projects and inspiring articles for all skill levels. Each bi-monthly issue of *Quilt-it...Today* magazine features a wide variety of easy to intermediate skill level quilting projects.

HOW TO CONTACT "It is recommended that you submit a query first by mail or e-mail with simple, clear, and thorough directions, including a list of materials, finished sizes, seam allowances, assembly diagrams, appliqué patterns, etc. Be sure patterns are perfectly accurate and marked clearly with cutting, sewing, and fabric grain directions. Articles about quilts, quilters, and quilt charities must be accompanied by professional-quality digital images. If you submit a query, attach a good photograph and description of your project. Include an SASE with sufficient postage for the return of your material if submitted by mail. Submissions without an SASE will not be returned."

NEEDS Articles relating to quilting, original quilting projects, and profiles of outstanding quilting instructors, designers, and charities.

TERMS "Valu-Publishing, LLC, pays $150-$250 per article for first North American rights for original, hitherto unpublished, articles. For quilts, pillows, and other projects, payment is made at a flat rate between

$100-$375 per project, depending on size and difficulty of project. Payment is made approximately 4-6 weeks after the publication appears on the newsstand. Send all designs and manuscripts to: Valu-Publishing, 46 Rock Creek Rd., Cumberland VA 23040 or e-mail dhearn@valu-publishing.com."

THE QUILT LIFE

P.O. Box 3290, Paducah KY 42002-3290. E-mail: submissions@thequiltlife.com; info@thequiltlife.com. Website: www.americanquilter.com. "*The Quilt Life* is the American Quilter's Society's newest publication. Published bi-monthly, it is a print community for all who have a passion for quilts and who let quilting inform the many facets of their lives."

HOW TO CONTACT Manuscripts and visuals should be submitted on a CD in .doc format with a hard copy printout accompanying the disk. Articles can range from 500 to 2,000 words. Slides or 4×5 transparencies may be submitted, but digital photos are preferred. For all photos in any format, sharp focus and even lighting are key to acceptance. While low-resolution photos may be sent with the submission, high-resolution photos are imperative for print publication and should be available should the material be accepted. Each digital photo file, transparency, or photograph should be labeled with the owner's name and a number for the visuals that go with the article (LAST NAME_1 of 3.jpg). Illustrations, charts, diagrams, and drawings should be neatly and carefully drawn on plain or graph paper. Manuscripts may be submitted electronically. E-mail the text in .doc format along with digital images to submissions@thequiltlife.com, making sure to include your full name, surface address, and contact information.

TERMS Because of a large volume of submissions and a lengthy review process, it may be several months before you receive a reply. A contract will be sent to you if an article is accepted for publication. Payment is made when the article is prepared for publication in a specific issue. Article ideas or inquiries may be submitted to info@thequiltlife.com.

QUILTMAKER

E-mail: editor@quiltmaker.com. Website: www.quiltmaker.com. "*Quiltmaker* publishes 6 regular issues per year, available by subscription (print and digital), at quilt shops and on newsstands.

☻ QUILTMANIA

Website: www.quiltmania.com/english/home.html. *Quiltmania*, is published every 2 months in 3 versions: French, Dutch and English.

QUILTS & MORE

E-mail: apq@meredith.com. Website: www.allpeoplequilt.com/magazines-more/quilts-and-more.

QUILT SAMPLER

Website: www.allpeoplequilt.com/magazines-more/quilt-sampler.

QUILT TRENDS

7 Waterloo Rd., Stanhope NJ 07874. (973)347-6900. Fax: (973)347-6909. E-mail: editors@quilttrendsmag.com. Website: www.quilttrendsmag.com. "*Quilt Trends* is a quarterly magazine that offers quilters a variety of quilting projects, ranging from quick weekend pieces to full-size bed quilts, all with a focus on the use of fresh, current fabric in classic and contemporary settings. The seasonally-inspired patterns are fresh; geared for all skill levels; and include gorgeous photography, clear instructions, and color diagrams. In-depth articles give readers insight into popular fabric and quilt designers and what inspires their work, quilting companies, industry shakers and movers, and quilting entrepreneurs. Each issue also includes clever decorating ideas, quick on-trend projects, previews of the latest quilt books and notions, and a gallery of new and upcoming fabric collections."

QUILTY

E-mail: contributors@qnntv.com. Website: www.heyquilty.com. Quilting magazine, focused on simple and beginner quilts.

☻ RELOVED

E-mail: sally.fitzgerald@anthem-publishing.com. Website: www.relovedmag.co.uk. Contact: Sallyl Fitzgerald, editor. "*Reloved* is the exciting new magazine at the heart of thrifting, shabby chic and upcycling. With an emphasis on breathing new life into old, forgotten objects, it brings a hands-on approach to this thriving pastime."

SAMPLER & ANTIQUE NEEDLEWORK QUARTERLY

E-mail: editor@sanqmagazine.com. Website: www.sanqmagazine.com. "*Sampler & Antique Needlework Quarterly* is the premiere magazine for those who look at the handwork from centuries past with a sense of awe, wonder, and inquisitiveness."

◗ SCRAP 365

Traplet Publications Ltd., Traplet House, Pendragon Close Malvern WR14 1GA, United Kingdom. E-mail: scrap365@traplet.com. Website: www.inspired tomake.com/zone/scrap-365/home. Contact: Alison Parris, editor. "Published 6 times a year, every issue is 90 pages stuffed with scrappy inspiration. As our strap line suggests, our magazine is aimed at keen scrapbookers who love and live their hobby."

SCRAPBOOKING & BEYOND

7 Waterloo Rd., Stanhope NJ 07874. (973)347-6900. Fax: (973)347-6909. E-mail: editors@scrapbookingandbeyondmag.com. Website: www.scrapbookingandbeyondmag.com. Contact: Jane Guthrie, editor. "*Scrapbooking & Beyond* is a quarterly magazine geared for both the archival and creative scrapbooker. Learn how to create and display treasured keepsakes. Discover how to preserve special memories in unique ways. Simple to elaborate page layouts, altered books, and other memory keepsakes are but a few of the exciting projects and articles featured in full color and presented with complete and easy instructions."
TERMS Submit only original material that has not been published elsewhere (including websites, blogs, etc.), nor is currently under consideration by another publisher.

◗ SCRAPBOOK MAGAZINE

Website: www.papercraftmagazines.com/the-magazines/scrapbook-magazine. "*Scrapbook Magazine* is Britain's biggest selling scrapbook magazine. Published every six weeks, each issue shows you the ins and outs for bringing your photos and memories to life through the wonderful world of scrapbooking, allowing you to create stunning and personalised mini works of art using your photos, papers, found objects and recycled elements.

◗ SEWING WORLD

Traplet Publications Ltd., Traplet House, Pendragon Close Malvern WR14 1GA, United Kingdom. Website: www.inspiredtomake.com/zone/sewing-world/home. "*Sewing World* is a monthly magazine packed full of delicious, contemporary sewing projects as well as fabrics, techniques, products, features and interviews."

SEW IT ALL

Website: www.sewitallmag.com. *Sew It All* is published once a year in December. It is a special newsstand issue brought to you by the editors of *Sew News*.

SEW-IT...TODAY

E-mail: editors@sewittoday.com. Website: www.sewittoday.com. *Sew-it...Today* magazine features quick, easy, and fun stitching/quilting projects and inspiring articles for all skill levels. Each bi-monthly issue of *Sew-it...Today* magazine features a wide variety of easy to intermediate skill level sewing and quilting projects.
HOW TO CONTACT "It is recommended that you submit a query first by mail or e-mail with simple, clear, and thorough directions, including a list of materials, finished sizes, seam allowances, assembly diagrams, appliqué patterns, etc. Be sure patterns are perfectly accurate and marked clearly with cutting, sewing, and fabric grain directions. Articles about quilts, quilters, and quilt charities must be accompanied by professional-quality digital images. If you submit a query, attach a good photograph and description of your project. Include an SASE with sufficient postage for the return of your material if submitted by mail. Submissions without an SASE will not be returned."
NEEDS Articles relating to quilting, original quilting projects, and profiles of outstanding quilting instructors, designers, and charities.

TERMS "Valu-Publishing, LLC, pays $150-$250 per article for first North American rights for original, hitherto unpublished, articles. For quilts, pillows, and other projects, payment is made at a flat rate between $100-$375 per project, depending on size and difficulty of project. Payment is made approximately 4-6 weeks after the publication appears on the newsstand. Send all designs and manuscripts to: Valu-Publishing, 46 Rock Creek Rd., Cumberland VA 23040 or e-mail dhearn@valu-publishing.com."

❥ SEW MAGAZINE

E-mail: lorraine.luximon@aceville.co.uk. Website: www.sewmag.co.uk. Contact: Lorraine Luximon, editor. "Inspiration for you, your home & the little ones—the UK's only sewing magazine that gives you a FREE full sized dressmaker's pattern every month!"

SEW NEWS

741 Corporate Circle, Suite A., Golden CO 80401. E-mail: sewnews@sewnews.com. Website: www.sewnews.com. "*Sew News* is the go-to guide for the most current and relevant information that the sewing world has to offer."

HOW TO CONTACT Query by letter or e-mail; do not send finished manuscripts. Query should consist of a brief outline of the article, a sketch or photo of the intended project, a list of the illustrations or photographs you envision with it, an explanation of why your proposed article would be of interest to the *Sew News* reader, and why you are qualified to write it.

NEEDS Articles should teach a specific technique, inspire the reader to try a project, introduce the reader to a new product or company related to sewing, or inform the reader about current fashion and sewing trends.

TERMS When an article is accepted, you'll be sent an assignment sheet detailing what is expected of you for the assignment and the intended payment (from $50 to $500, new writers generally $50 to $150, depending on the length and complexity of the subject, and the garment(s), samples, photography, illustrations or sources to be supplied). After you receive the assignment, please sign and return it within 10 days. If you're unable to meet a deadline for any reason, please inform *Sew News* immediately. Failure to do so will void assignment. All articles, including those specifically assigned, are written "on speculation." All payments will be made upon publication. To receive the full payment suggested in the assignment sheet, the article must be submitted by the specified deadline, include all elements detailed in the assignment sheet, and be of acceptable quality (to be determined by the *Sew News* editorial staff). Payment may be decreased for late arrival, missing elements or poor quality. *Sew News* reserves the right to return articles for rewriting or clarification of information, return samples for redo/corrections and, in extreme cases, to return them without payment.

SEW SOMERSET

22992 Mill Creek Dr., Laguna Hills CA 92653. E-mail: sewsomerset@stampington.com. Website: www.stampington.com/sew-somerset. "*Sew Somerset* represents a new way of looking at sewn art. More than ever before, artists are discovering the joy of combining sewing with mixed-media projects, showing the world that stitches are not just for fabric anymore! In this 144-page publication, readers will find gorgeous photographs, easy-to-understand techniques, and endless inspiration. *Sew Somerset* will help crafters and artists alike learn how to add stitches of varied lengths, sizes, colors, and dimensions into their next project to create a look that is 'So Somerset!'"

HOW TO CONTACT "We prefer submissions of original art. If original art is not available, our next preference is high resolution digital images (300 dpi at 8½ × 10). If hi-res digital images are not available, we will very rarely consider professional-quality transparencies or color slides. Color-copy submissions are not accepted. All artwork must be identified with the artist's name, address, e-mail and phone number clearly printed on a label attached to each sample. Inscribe your name and address somewhere on each piece of art. If you desire acknowledgment of artwork receipt, please include a self-addressed stamped postcard. If the artwork is three-dimensional, please attach your identification with a removable string, or pack the sample in a plastic bag with your identification. If you have a unique artistic technique you'd like to share with others, please send samples of your artwork accompanied by a query letter outlining your article idea to the respective Managing Editor at: *Sew Somerset*, 22992 Mill Creek Drive, Laguna Hills, CA

92653. Managing editors also welcome brief e-mail inquiries."

NEEDS "Managing editors seek first-rate projects and encourage artists who have not published articles before to submit ideas, as editorial assistance will be provided."

TERMS Competitive editorial compensation is provided for all published articles. "We may hold your sample for an extended period of time—9 to 12 months is common. Due to the large volume of artwork we receive, Somerset Studio will return only those submissions accompanied by sufficient postage in the form of cash, check or money order made out to Stampington & Company. We can not offer delivery confirmation; however, we are happy to put insurance on the submission. If you wish to have your artwork insured for the return journey, please include sufficient funds and indicate your preference in a postcard or letter enclosed with your submission. Please do not attach postage to packaging, and do not send loose postage stamps. Contributors from outside the US, please send cash, check, or money order in US funds to Stampington & Company. For questions regarding your artwork, please send inquiries to artmanagement@stampington.com."

SIMPLE QUILTS & SEWING

E-mail: quiltmag@epix.net. Website: www.quiltmag.com. Magazine about quilting and sewing.

● THE SIMPLE THINGS

E-mail: thesimplethings@futurenet.com. Website: www.thesimplethings.com. "*The Simple Things* is published thirteen times a year and celebrates the things that matter most."

● SIMPLY CARDS & PAPERCRAFTS

Website: www.papercraftmagazines.com/the-magazines/simply-cards-papercraft. "*Simply Cards & Papercraft* is the UK's most inspirational papercraft magazine full of inspiration for quality cards for every occasion. It's full of the newest techniques, products and up-to-the-minute ideas."

● SIMPLY CROCHET

E-mail: simplycrochet@futurenet.com. Website: www.simplycrochetmag.co.uk. "*Simply Crochet* is a dedicated crochet magazine from the makers of *Simply Knitting*, *The Knitter*, *Crochet Today!* and *Mollie Makes*. Featuring over 20 crochet patterns every month and technical advice, clear instructions and crochet inspiration, *Simply Crochet* will get you hooked on handmade!" Based in the United Kingdom.

● SIMPLY HOMEMADE

Website: www.simplyhomemademag.com. "*Simply Homemade* is a magazine designed specifically for those of us who love crafting and can't get enough of making things." Based in the United Kingdom.

● SIMPLY KNITTING

E-mail: simplyknitting@futurenet.com. Website: www.simplyknitting.co.uk. On sale 13 times a year, "*Simply Knitting* is packed with patterns, yarn reviews, knitting tips and knitting news."

SOMERSET APPRENTICE

22992 Mill Creek Dr., Laguna Hills CA 92653. E-mail: somersetapprentice@stampington.com. Website: www.stampington.com/somerset-apprentice. "*Somerset Apprentice* takes its readers by the hand to teach them the fundamentals of creating Somerset-style art—one basic step at a time. Successful artists share their favorite tips and techniques, including layered collage, mixed media, and assemblage art, which are presented through detailed, close-up photographs and clear, concise instructions. Join the pros on a step-by-step journey as they complete an entire work of art! This top selling magazine has everything you'll need to learn a new craft, fine-tune your technique, and gather inspiration for your creative adventure."

HOW TO CONTACT "We prefer submissions of original art. If original art is not available, our next preference is high resolution digital images (300 dpi at 8½ × 10). If hi-res digital images are not available, we will very rarely consider professional-quality transparencies or color slides. Color-copy submissions are not accepted. All artwork must be identified with the artist's name, address, e-mail and phone number clearly printed on a label attached to each sample. Inscribe your name and address somewhere on each piece of art. If you desire acknowledgment of artwork receipt, please include a self-addressed stamped postcard. If the artwork is three-dimensional, please attach your identification with a removable string, or pack the sample in a plastic bag with your identification. If you have a unique artistic technique you'd like to share with others, please send samples of your artwork accompanied by a query letter outlining your article idea to the respective Managing Editor at: *Somerset Apprentice*, 22992 Mill Creek Drive, Laguna Hills, CA 92653. Managing editors also welcome brief e-mail inquiries."

NEEDS "Managing editors seek first-rate projects and encourage artists who have not published articles before to submit ideas, as editorial assistance will be provided."

TERMS Competitive editorial compensation is provided for all published articles. "We may hold your sample for an extended period of time—9 to 12 months is common. Due to the large volume of artwork we receive, Somerset Studio will return only those submissions accompanied by sufficient postage in the form of cash, check or money order made out to Stampington & Company. We can not offer delivery confirmation; however, we are happy to put insurance on the submission. If you wish to have your artwork insured for the return journey, please include sufficient funds and indicate your preference in a postcard or letter enclosed with your submission. Please do not attach postage to packaging, and do not send loose postage stamps. Contributors from outside the US, please send cash, check, or money order in US funds to Stampington & Company. For questions regarding your artwork, please send inquiries to artmanagement@stampington.com."

SOMERSET DIGITAL STUDIO

22992 Mill Creek Dr., Laguna Hills CA 92653. E-mail: somersetdigitalstudio@stampington.com. Website: www.stampington.com/somerset-digital-studio. "*Somerset Digital Studio* showcases some of the best digitally created artwork around, and these breathtaking samples of scrapbook pages, ATCs, and collages will have readers joining in this growing trend of creating digitally altered artwork in no time. Each of the 144 lush, full color pages found in every issue contain captivating feature articles, a full gallery of digital eye candy, a digital dictionary, software comparison chart, digital tutorial, and more."

HOW TO CONTACT "We prefer submissions of original art. If original art is not available, our next preference is high resolution digital images (300 dpi at 8½ × 10). If hi-res digital images are not available, we will very rarely consider professional-quality transparencies or color slides. Color-copy submissions are not accepted. All artwork must be identified with the artist's name, address, e-mail and phone number clearly printed on a label attached to each sample. Inscribe your name and address somewhere on each piece of art. If you desire acknowledgment of artwork receipt, please include a self-addressed stamped postcard. If the artwork is three-dimensional, please attach your identification with a removable string, or pack the sample in a plastic bag with your identification. If you have a unique artistic technique you'd like to share with others, please send samples of your artwork accompanied by a query letter outlining your article idea to the respective Managing Editor at: *Somerset Digital Studio*, 22992 Mill Creek Drive, Laguna Hills, CA 92653. Managing editors also welcome brief e-mail inquiries."

NEEDS "Managing editors seek first-rate projects and encourage artists who have not published articles before to submit ideas, as editorial assistance will be provided."

TERMS Competitive editorial compensation is provided for all published articles. "We may hold your sample for an extended period of time—9 to 12 months is common. Due to the large volume of artwork we receive, *Somerset Studio* will return only those submissions accompanied by sufficient postage in the form of cash, check or money order made out to Stampington & Company. We can not offer delivery confirmation; however, we are happy to put insurance on the submission. If you wish to have your artwork insured for the return journey, please include sufficient funds and indicate your preference in a postcard or letter enclosed with your submission. Please do not attach postage to packaging, and do not send loose postage stamps. Contributors from outside the US, please send cash, check, or money order in US funds to Stampington & Company. For questions regarding your artwork, please send inquiries to artmanagement@stampington.com."

SOMERSET HOME

22992 Mill Creek Dr., Laguna Hills CA 92653. E-mail: somersethome@stampington.com. Website: www.stampington.com/somerset-home. "*Somerset Home* magazine beautifully blends 'Somerset-esque' art together with functional, everyday items to add an artful touch of décor. The result is a truly distinctive annual magazine that exemplifies creative living and showcases hundreds of tips, techniques, and charming accents designed to enlighten, organize, and beautify any dwelling place. When you wander through the inspiring pages of *Somerset Home*, you'll be enthralled by room after room of beautiful projects, and inside this inviting 160-page publication, you'll find unique and artistic creative ideas for every corner of your home."

HOW TO CONTACT "We prefer submissions of original art. If original art is not available, our next preference is high resolution digital images (300 dpi at 8½ × 10). If hi-res digital images are not available, we will very rarely consider professional-quality transparencies or color slides. Color-copy submissions are not accepted. All artwork must be identified with the artist's name, address, e-mail and phone number clearly printed on a label attached to each sample. Inscribe your name and address somewhere on each piece of art. If you desire acknowledgment of artwork receipt, please include a self-addressed stamped postcard. If the artwork is three-dimensional, please attach your identification with a removable string, or pack the sample in a plastic bag with your identification. If you have a unique artistic technique you'd like to share with others, please send samples of your artwork accompanied by a query letter outlining your article idea to the respective Managing Editor at: *Somerset Home*, 22992 Mill Creek Drive, Laguna Hills, CA 92653. Managing editors also welcome brief e-mail inquiries."

NEEDS "Managing editors seek first-rate projects and encourage artists who have not published articles before to submit ideas, as editorial assistance will be provided."

TERMS Competitive editorial compensation is provided for all published articles. "We may hold your sample for an extended period of time—9 to 12 months is common. Due to the large volume of artwork we receive, Somerset Studio will return only those submissions accompanied by sufficient postage in the form of cash, check or money order made out to

Stampington & Company. We can not offer delivery confirmation; however, we are happy to put insurance on the submission. If you wish to have your artwork insured for the return journey, please include sufficient funds and indicate your preference in a postcard or letter enclosed with your submission. Please do not attach postage to packaging, and do not send loose postage stamps. Contributors from outside the US, please send cash, check, or money order in US funds to Stampington & Company. For questions regarding your artwork, please send inquiries to artmanagement@stampington.com."

SOMERSET LIFE

22992 Mill Creek Dr., Laguna Hills CA 92653. E-mail: somersetlife@stampington.com. Website: www.stampington.com/somerset-life. "Each issue of *Somerset Life* provides an abundance of inspiring ideas to infuse our daily lives with simple pleasures, art, romance, creativity and beauty. Stunning photography and insightful and entertaining articles illustrate touching moments captured in poetry and artwork, unique ways to present gifts and treasured items, simple but beautiful remembrances, fresh ideas to elevate the art of letter writing, and many other imaginative ideas to enhance our lives with artful elements. *Somerset Life* will inspire you to make every day extraordinary!"

HOW TO CONTACT "We prefer submissions of original art. If original art is not available, our next preference is high resolution digital images (300 dpi at 8½ × 10). If hi-res digital images are not available, we will very rarely consider professional-quality transparencies or color slides. Color-copy submissions are not accepted. All artwork must be identified with the artist's name, address, e-mail and phone number clearly printed on a label attached to each sample. Inscribe your name and address somewhere on each piece of art. If you desire acknowledgment of artwork receipt, please include a self-addressed stamped postcard. If the artwork is three-dimensional, please attach your identification with a removable string, or pack the sample in a plastic bag with your identification. If you have a unique artistic technique you'd like to share with others, please send samples of your artwork accompanied by a query letter outlining your article idea to the respective Managing Editor at: *Somerset Life*, 22992 Mill Creek Drive, Laguna Hills, CA

92653. Managing editors also welcome brief e-mail inquiries."

NEEDS "Managing editors seek first-rate projects and encourage artists who have not published articles before to submit ideas, as editorial assistance will be provided."

TERMS Competitive editorial compensation is provided for all published articles. "We may hold your sample for an extended period of time—9 to 12 months is common. Due to the large volume of artwork we receive, Somerset Studio will return only those submissions accompanied by sufficient postage in the form of cash, check or money order made out to Stampington & Company. We can not offer delivery confirmation; however, we are happy to put insurance on the submission. If you wish to have your artwork insured for the return journey, please include sufficient funds and indicate your preference in a postcard or letter enclosed with your submission. Please do not attach postage to packaging, and do not send loose postage stamps. Contributors from outside the US, please send cash, check, or money order in US funds to Stampington & Company. For questions regarding your artwork, please send inquiries to artmanagement@stampington.com."

SOMERSET MEMORIES

22992 Mill Creek Dr., Laguna Hills CA 92653. E-mail: somersetmemories@stampington.com. Website: www.stampington.com/somerset-memories. "*Somerset Memories* provides a showcase for arts and crafts that feature family photographs and memorabilia. This unique semi-annual magazine presents sophisticated scrapbook and journal pages, plus a gorgeous array of paper crafts, fabric arts, memorabilia and mixed-media art made by our talented readers and contributors."

HOW TO CONTACT "We prefer submissions of original art. If original art is not available, our next preference is high resolution digital images (300 dpi at 8½ × 10). If hi-res digital images are not available, we will very rarely consider professional-quality transparencies or color slides. Color-copy submissions are not accepted. All artwork must be identified with the artist's name, address, e-mail and phone number clearly printed on a label attached to each sample. Inscribe your name and address somewhere on each piece of art. If you desire acknowledgment of artwork receipt,

please include a self-addressed stamped postcard. If the artwork is three-dimensional, please attach your identification with a removable string, or pack the sample in a plastic bag with your identification. If you have a unique artistic technique you'd like to share with others, please send samples of your artwork accompanied by a query letter outlining your article idea to the respective Managing Editor at: *Somerset Memories*, 22992 Mill Creek Drive, Laguna Hills, CA 92653. Managing editors also welcome brief e-mail inquiries."

NEEDS "Managing editors seek first-rate projects and encourage artists who have not published articles before to submit ideas, as editorial assistance will be provided."

TERMS Competitive editorial compensation is provided for all published articles. "We may hold your sample for an extended period of time—9 to 12 months is common. Due to the large volume of artwork we receive, Somerset Studio will return only those submissions accompanied by sufficient postage in the form of cash, check or money order made out to Stampington & Company. We can not offer delivery confirmation; however, we are happy to put insurance on the submission. If you wish to have your artwork insured for the return journey, please include sufficient funds and indicate your preference in a postcard or letter enclosed with your submission. Please do not attach postage to packaging, and do not send loose postage stamps. Contributors from outside the US, please send cash, check, or money order in US funds to Stampington & Company. For questions regarding your artwork, please send inquiries to artmanagement@stampington.com."

SOMERSET STUDIO

Somerset Studio, 22992 Mill Creek Dr., Laguna Hills CA 92653. E-mail: somersetstudio@stampington.com. Website: www.stampington.com/somerset-studio. "Paper crafting, art stamping and the lettering arts are elevated to an artistic level in *Somerset Studio*! Come join in the celebration of these popular handcrafting styles by exploring the industry's most trusted and innovative mixed-media magazine, as you learn from fellow artists working with exotic papers, intriguing art stamps, fine calligraphy, and a variety of mediums."

HOW TO CONTACT "We prefer submissions of original art. If original art is not available, our next preference is high resolution digital images (300 dpi at 8½ × 10). If hi-res digital images are not available, we will very rarely consider professional-quality transparencies or color slides. Color-copy submissions are not accepted. All artwork must be identified with the artist's name, address, e-mail and phone number clearly printed on a label attached to each sample. Inscribe your name and address somewhere on each piece of art. If you desire acknowledgment of artwork receipt, please include a self-addressed stamped postcard. If the artwork is three-dimensional, please attach your identification with a removable string, or pack the sample in a plastic bag with your identification. If you have a unique artistic technique you'd like to share with others, please send samples of your artwork accompanied by a query letter outlining your article idea to the respective Managing Editor at: *Somerset Studio*, 22992 Mill Creek Drive, Laguna Hills, CA 92653. Managing editors also welcome brief e-mail inquiries."

NEEDS "Managing editors seek first-rate projects and encourage artists who have not published articles before to submit ideas, as editorial assistance will be provided."

TERMS Competitive editorial compensation is provided for all published articles. "We may hold your sample for an extended period of time—9 to 12 months is common. Due to the large volume of artwork we receive, Somerset Studio will return only those submissions accompanied by sufficient postage in the form of cash, check or money order made out to Stampington & Company. We can not offer delivery confirmation; however, we are happy to put insurance on the submission. If you wish to have your artwork insured for the return journey, please include sufficient funds and indicate your preference in a postcard or letter enclosed with your submission. Please do not attach postage to packaging, and do not send loose postage stamps. Contributors from outside the US, please send cash, check, or money order in US funds to Stampington & Company. For questions regarding your artwork, please send inquiries to artmanagement@stampington.com."

SOMERSET GALLERY

22992 Mill Creek Dr., Laguna Hills CA 92653. E-mail: somersetstudiogallery@stampington.com. Website: www.stampington.com/somerset-gallery. "*Somerset Studio Gallery* is filled with hundreds of samples of extraordinary artwork presented up close and in detail. Whether your passion is rubber stamping, calligraphy or paper crafting, the newest Gallery features everything you love about Somerset Studio in 200 lush pages, including enlightening how-to-articles, beautifully photographed projects and hundreds of handmade creations by your favorite artists, as well as by you, our talented readers."

HOW TO CONTACT "We prefer submissions of original art. If original art is not available, our next preference is high resolution digital images (300 dpi at 8½ × 10). If hi-res digital images are not available, we will very rarely consider professional-quality transparencies or color slides. Color-copy submissions are not accepted. All artwork must be identified with the artist's name, address, e-mail and phone number clearly printed on a label attached to each sample. Inscribe your name and address somewhere on each piece of art. If you desire acknowledgment of artwork receipt, please include a self-addressed stamped postcard. If the artwork is three-dimensional, please attach your identification with a removable string, or pack the sample in a plastic bag with your identification. If you have a unique artistic technique you'd like to share with others, please send samples of your artwork accompanied by a query letter outlining your article idea to the respective Managing Editor at: *Somerset Studio Gallery*, 22992 Mill Creek Drive, Laguna Hills, CA 92653. Managing editors also welcome brief e-mail inquiries."

NEEDS "Managing editors seek first-rate projects and encourage artists who have not published articles before to submit ideas, as editorial assistance will be provided."

TERMS Competitive editorial compensation is provided for all published articles. "We may hold your sample for an extended period of time—9 to 12 months is common. Due to the large volume of artwork we receive, *Somerset Studio* will return only those submissions accompanied by sufficient postage in the form of cash, check or money order made out to Stampington & Company. We can not offer delivery confirmation; however, we are happy to put insurance on the submission. If you wish to have your artwork insured for the return journey, please include sufficient funds and indicate your preference in a postcard or letter enclosed with your submission. Please do not attach postage to packaging, and do not send loose postage stamps. Contributors from outside the US, please send cash, check, or money order in US funds to Stampington & Company. For questions regarding your artwork, please send inquiries to artmanagement@stampington.com."

SOMERSET WORKSHOP

22992 Mill Creek Dr., Laguna Hills CA 92653. E-mail: submissions@stampington.com. Website: www.stampington.com/somerset-workshop. "Learn fabulous techniques to help you make breathtaking projects that are illustrated from start to finish. All chapters in this 144-page book include simple stepped-out photographs with clear instructions to help you create exciting projects from some of the finest art and crafting instructors in our industry."

HOW TO CONTACT "We prefer submissions of original art. If original art is not available, our next preference is high resolution digital images (300 dpi at 8½ × 10). If hi-res digital images are not available, we will very rarely consider professional-quality transparencies or color slides. Color-copy submissions are not accepted. All artwork must be identified with the artist's name, address, e-mail and phone number clearly printed on a label attached to each sample. Inscribe your name and address somewhere on each piece of art. If you desire acknowledgment of artwork receipt, please include a self-addressed stamped postcard. If the artwork is three-dimensional, please attach your identification with a removable string, or pack the sample in a plastic bag with your identification. If you have a unique artistic technique you'd like to share with others, please send samples of your artwork accompanied by a query letter outlining your article idea to the respective Managing Editor at: *Somerset Workshop,* 22992 Mill Creek Drive, Laguna Hills, CA 92653. Managing editors also welcome brief e-mail inquiries."

NEEDS "Managing editors seek first-rate projects and encourage artists who have not published articles before to submit ideas, as editorial assistance will be provided."

TERMS Competitive editorial compensation is provided for all published articles. "We may hold your sample for an extended period of time—9 to 12 months is common. Due to the large volume of artwork we receive, *Somerset Studio* will return only those submissions accompanied by sufficient postage in the form of cash, check or money order made out to Stampington & Company. We can not offer delivery confirmation; however, we are happy to put insurance on the submission. If you wish to have your artwork insured for the return journey, please include sufficient funds and indicate your preference in a postcard or letter enclosed with your submission. Please do not attach postage to packaging, and do not send loose postage stamps. Contributors from outside the US, please send cash, check, or money order in US funds to Stampington & Company. For questions regarding your artwork, please send inquiries to artmanagement@stampington.com."

SPIN-OFF

Interweave Press, 201 E. 4th St., Loveland CO 80537. E-mail: spinoff@interweave.com. Website: www.spinningdaily.com. "*Spin-Off* is a quarterly magazine devoted to the interests of handspinners at all skill levels. Informative articles in each issue aim to encourage the novice, challenge the expert, and increase every spinner's working knowledge of this ancient and complex craft."

HOW TO CONTACT Guidelines available on website.

TIPS "*Spin-Off* is many things. As a contributor, think of it as a forum where you can share your experiences and knowledge with your community. Consider how your contribution will serve the reader."

THE STAMPER'S SAMPLER

22992 Mill Creek Dr., Laguna Hills CA 92653. E-mail: thestamperssampler@stampington.com. Website: www.stampington.com/the-stampers-sampler. "This delightful magazine provides over 200 cards and stamped project ideas—complete with detailed shots and step-by-step instructions to provide an added dose of paper crafting inspiration. The artwork contributed by our talented readers is published in full color on gorgeous, glossy paper stock. Newly revamped, this quarterly publication comes complete with a free bonus artist paper and almost 40 more pages of featured hand-stamped projects tucked inside. In every issue, readers will also find a free Tempting

Template and unique challenge results to help spark their creativity."

HOW TO CONTACT "We prefer submissions of original art. If original art is not available, our next preference is high resolution digital images (300 dpi at 8½ × 10). If hi-res digital images are not available, we will very rarely consider professional-quality transparencies or color slides. Color-copy submissions are not accepted. All artwork must be identified with the artist's name, address, e-mail and phone number clearly printed on a label attached to each sample. Inscribe your name and address somewhere on each piece of art. If you desire acknowledgment of artwork receipt, please include a self-addressed stamped postcard. If the artwork is three-dimensional, please attach your identification with a removable string, or pack the sample in a plastic bag with your identification. If you have a unique artistic technique you'd like to share with others, please send samples of your artwork accompanied by a query letter outlining your article idea to the respective Managing Editor at: *The Stamper's Sampler*, 22992 Mill Creek Drive, Laguna Hills, CA 92653. Managing editors also welcome brief e-mail inquiries."

NEEDS "Managing editors seek first-rate projects and encourage artists who have not published articles before to submit ideas, as editorial assistance will be provided."

TERMS Competitive editorial compensation is provided for all published articles. "We may hold your sample for an extended period of time—9 to 12 months is common. Due to the large volume of artwork we receive, Somerset Studio will return only those submissions accompanied by sufficient postage in the form of cash, check or money order made out to Stampington & Company. We can not offer delivery confirmation; however, we are happy to put insurance on the submission. If you wish to have your artwork insured for the return journey, please include sufficient funds and indicate your preference in a postcard or letter enclosed with your submission. Please do not attach postage to packaging, and do not send loose postage stamps. Contributors from outside the US, please send cash, check, or money order in US funds to Stampington & Company. For questions regarding your artwork, please send inquiries to artmanagement@stampington.com."

STEP BY STEP WIRE JEWELRY

630 Freedom Business Center Dr., 3rd Floor, King of Prussia PA 19406. E-mail: dpeck@interweave.com. Website: www.jewelrymakingdaily.com. Contact: Denise Peck. "*Step by Step Wire Jewelry* is published 6 times/year by Interweave Press. The magazine is project-oriented, with step-by-step instructions for creating wire jewelry, as well as tips, tools, and techniques. Articles range from beginner to expert level. Writers must be able to substantiate that material submitted is accurate and must make sure that all steps involved in the creation of the piece are feasible using the tools listed."

HOW TO CONTACT Guidelines available on website.

STITCH

E-mail: stitchsubmissions@interweave.com. Website: www.sewdaily.com. "*Stitch* is a special issue sewing magazine all about creating with fabric and thread. Yes, it's sewing, but oh so much more. It's loaded with clever projects and modern designs for your wardrobe and home, inspiring designer profiles, plus hot trends, news, and inspiration from the global community of sewing. Whether you're just learning to sew or have been sewing forever, *Stitch* will inspire you to make beautiful things that showcase your unique point of view."

HOW TO CONTACT Guidelines available on website.

STITCH-IT...TODAY

7 Waterloo Rd., Stanhope NJ 07874-2621. (973)347-6900. Fax: (973)347-6909. E-mail: editors@stitch-it-today.com. Website: www.stitch-it-today.com. Contact: Terrie Studer, editor. Estab. 2013. Bi-monthly consumer magazine. "*Stitch-it...today* is a how-to craft magazine featuring quick and easy hand-stitched projects. Our designs are fun and trendy and explore different ways thread can enhance everyday objects, embellish accessories, and personalize clothing. The projects are ideal for the beginner stitcher or for the advanced stitcher who wants to quickly work up multiple projects." Sample available for $3.99 + S/H.

HOW TO CONTACT Request guideleins via e-mail. Accepts unsolicited submissions. Approached by 12 project/pattern designers/year. Buys 120 project/pattern designs from freelancers/year. Has featured projects/patterns by Alice Okon, Cheryl Rezendes, Debra

Arch, Halley Philips. Preferred subjects: cross stitch, needlepoint, mixed media art, punch needle, embroidery, felt appliqué, plastic canvas. Submission format: DOC and PDF files. Include concept only with portfolio photos of previous projects. Model release preferred; property release required. Accepts images in digital format via e-mail as TIFF files at 300 dpi.

TERMS Send query e-mail with project concepts and photos of past work. Does not keep samples on file; returned only by SASE. Responds in 2 weeks. Pays $50 minimum, $150 maximum for project/pattern design. Credit line given. Pays 6 weeks from the magazine on sale date. Buys first rights and electronic rights; will negotiate with designers unwilling to sell all rights. Finds freelancers through submissions, word-of-mouth. Undergoes technical edit before publication.

TIPS "Projects must be quick and easy with more imagination than stitching. Designs should follow current interests and trends. Keep your name and contact information with every submission and e-mail!"

STUFFED

Stuffed, 22992 Mill Creek Dr., Laguna Hills CA 92653. E-mail: stuffed@stampington.com. Website: www.stampington.com/stuffed. *Stuffed* celebrates the loveable and huggable creatures known as "softies."

HOW TO CONTACT "We prefer submissions of original art. If original art is not available, our next preference is high resolution digital images (300 dpi at 8½ × 10). If hi-res digital images are not available, we will very rarely consider professional-quality transparencies or color slides. Color-copy submissions are not accepted. All artwork must be identified with the artist's name, address, e-mail and phone number clearly printed on a label attached to each sample. Inscribe your name and address somewhere on each piece of art. If you desire acknowledgment of artwork receipt, please include a self-addressed stamped postcard. If the artwork is three-dimensional, please attach your identification with a removable string, or pack the sample in a plastic bag with your identification. If you have a unique artistic technique you'd like to share with others, please send samples of your artwork accompanied by a query letter outlining your article idea to the respective Managing Editor at: *Stuffed*, 22992 Mill Creek Drive, Laguna Hills, CA 92653. Managing editors also welcome brief e-mail inquiries."

NEEDS "Managing editors seek first-rate projects and encourage artists who have not published articles before to submit ideas, as editorial assistance will be provided."

TERMS Competitive editorial compensation is provided for all published articles. "We may hold your sample for an extended period of time—9 to 12 months is common. Due to the large volume of artwork we receive, Somerset Studio will return only those submissions accompanied by sufficient postage in the form of cash, check or money order made out to Stampington & Company. We can not offer delivery confirmation; however, we are happy to put insurance on the submission. If you wish to have your artwork insured for the return journey, please include sufficient funds and indicate your preference in a postcard or letter enclosed with your submission. Please do not attach postage to packaging, and do not send loose postage stamps. Contributors from outside the US, please send cash, check, or money order in US funds to Stampington & Company. For questions regarding your artwork, please send inquiries to artmanagement@stampington.com."

TAKE TEN

22992 Mill Creek Dr., Laguna Hills CA 92653. E-mail: taketen@stampington.com. Website: www.stampington.com/take-ten. "From the publisher that brings you *The Stampers' Sampler* and *Somerset Studio* comes a 144-page special issue brimming with card ideas. Take Ten offers rubber stamp enthusiasts of all levels great ideas for creating quick and easy cards in 10 minutes or less. You'll find hundreds of full-color samples inside each volume of this unique publication."

HOW TO CONTACT "We prefer submissions of original art. If original art is not available, our next preference is high resolution digital images (300 dpi at 8½ × 10). If hi-res digital images are not available, we will very rarely consider professional-quality transparencies or color slides. Color-copy submissions are not accepted. All artwork must be identified with the artist's name, address, e-mail and phone number clearly printed on a label attached to each sample. Inscribe your name and address somewhere on each piece of art. If you desire acknowledgment of artwork receipt, please include a self-addressed stamped postcard. If the artwork is three-dimensional, please attach your identification with a removable string, or pack the sample in a plastic bag with your identification. If you have a unique artistic technique you'd like to share with others, please send samples of your artwork accompanied by a query letter outlining your article idea to the respective Managing Editor at: *Take Ten*, 22992 Mill Creek Drive, Laguna Hills, CA 92653. Managing editors also welcome brief e-mail inquiries."

NEEDS "Managing editors seek first-rate projects and encourage artists who have not published articles before to submit ideas, as editorial assistance will be provided."

TERMS Competitive editorial compensation is provided for all published articles. "We may hold your sample for an extended period of time—9 to 12 months is common. Due to the large volume of artwork we receive, Somerset Studio will return only those submissions accompanied by sufficient postage in the form of cash, check or money order made out to Stampington & Company. We can not offer delivery confirmation; however, we are happy to put insurance on the submission. If you wish to have your artwork insured for the return journey, please include sufficient funds and indicate your preference in a postcard or letter enclosed with your submission. Please do not attach postage to packaging, and do not send loose postage stamps. Contributors from outside the US, please send cash, check, or money order in US funds to Stampington & Company. For questions regarding your artwork, please send inquiries to artmanagement@stampington.com."

⦿ TEXTILE FIBRE FORUM MAGAZINE MAGAZINE

Website: www.artwearpublications.com.au/subscriptions/textile-fibre-forum-magazine.html. "*Textile Fibre Forum* has been in print since the 1980s. It has been under the ArtWear Publications banner since late 2011, with Janet De Boer and Marie-Therese Wisniowski as co-editors." Based in Australia.

THREADS

The Taunton Press, Inc., 63 South Main St., PO Box 5506, Newton CT 06470-5506. (800)309-9262. E-mail: th@taunton.com. Website: www.threadsmagazine.com. "*Threads* is the trusted resource for both long-time sewers continuing to perfect their sewing skills and new sewers learning the fundamentals."

⦿ VINTAGE MADE MAGAZINE

Website: www.artwearpublications.com.au/subscriptions/vintage-made-magazine.html. "This great title is all about the love of vintage. It contains feature articles on dresses, hats, handbags and shoes, designer profiles and items or places of historic interest. This is mixed with some handy tutorials, such as how to achieve that perfect vintage hair style, or make that essential accessory. The feature of each issue is the full size dress pattern! The dress range is from a 32-inch to 40-inch bust, with instructions and tips on where to make alterations. This has been multi-sized from a genuine vintage dress pattern." Based in Australia.

VOGUE KNITTING INTERNATIONAL

Website: www.vogueknitting.com. "*Vogue Knitting* is the hand-knitting world's style leader and the magazine knitters turn to on a regular basis for inspirational patterns, chic styling and compelling techniques."

WHERE WOMEN COOK

22992 Mill Creek Dr., Laguna Hills CA 92653. E-mail: wherewomencook@stampington.com. Website: www.stampington.com/where-women-cook. "*Where Women Cook*, is an exciting publication packed to the brim with stunning photographs and heartwarming stories. Creative storage ideas, eye-catching décor, delicious food and drink recipes, and inspirational narratives will keep you intrigued from cover to cover."

HOW TO CONTACT "We prefer submissions of original art. If original art is not available, our next preference is high resolution digital images (300 dpi at 8½ × 10). If hi-res digital images are not available, we will very rarely consider professional-quality transparencies or color slides. Color-copy submissions are not accepted. All artwork must be identified with the artist's name, address, e-mail and phone number clearly printed on a label attached to each sample. Inscribe your name and address somewhere on each piece of art. If you desire acknowledgment of artwork receipt, please include a self-addressed stamped postcard. If the artwork is three-dimensional, please attach your identification with a removable string, or pack the sample in a plastic bag with your identification. If you have a unique artistic technique you'd like to share with others, please send samples of your artwork accompanied by a query letter outlining your article idea to the respective Managing Editor at: *Where Women Cook*, 22992 Mill Creek Drive, Laguna Hills, CA 92653. Managing editors also welcome brief e-mail inquiries."

NEEDS "Managing editors seek first-rate projects and encourage artists who have not published articles before to submit ideas, as editorial assistance will be provided."

TERMS Competitive editorial compensation is provided for all published articles. "We may hold your sample for an extended period of time—9 to 12 months is common. Due to the large volume of artwork we receive, Somerset Studio will return only those submissions accompanied by sufficient postage in the form of cash, check or money order made out to Stampington & Company. We can not offer delivery confirmation; however, we are happy to put insurance on the submission. If you wish to have your artwork insured for the return journey, please include sufficient funds and indicate your preference in a postcard or letter enclosed with your submission. Please do not attach postage to packaging, and do not send loose postage stamps. Contributors from outside the US, please send cash, check, or money order in US funds to Stampington & Company. For questions regarding your artwork, please send inquiries to artmanagement@stampington.com."

WHERE WOMEN CREATE

22992 Mill Creek Dr., Laguna Hills CA 92653. E-mail: wherewomencreate@stampington.com. Website: www.stampington.com/where-women-create. "*Where Women Create* invites you into the creative spaces of the most extraordinary women of our time. Through stunning photography and inspirational stories, each issue of this quarterly magazine will nourish souls and motivate creative processes."

HOW TO CONTACT "We prefer submissions of original art. If original art is not available, our next preference is high resolution digital images (300 dpi at 8½ × 10). If hi-res digital images are not available, we will very rarely consider professional-quality transparencies or color slides. Color-copy submissions are not accepted. All artwork must be identified with the artist's name, address, e-mail and phone number clearly printed on a label attached to each sample. Inscribe your name and address somewhere on each piece of

art. If you desire acknowledgment of artwork receipt, please include a self-addressed stamped postcard. If the artwork is three-dimensional, please attach your identification with a removable string, or pack the sample in a plastic bag with your identification. If you have a unique artistic technique you'd like to share with others, please send samples of your artwork accompanied by a query letter outlining your article idea to the respective Managing Editor at: *Where Women Create*, 22992 Mill Creek Drive, Laguna Hills, CA 92653. Managing editors also welcome brief e-mail inquiries."

NEEDS "Managing editors seek first-rate projects and encourage artists who have not published articles before to submit ideas, as editorial assistance will be provided."

TERMS Competitive editorial compensation is provided for all published articles. "We may hold your sample for an extended period of time—9 to 12 months is common. Due to the large volume of artwork we receive, Somerset Studio will return only those submissions accompanied by sufficient postage in the form of cash, check or money order made out to Stampington & Company. We can not offer delivery confirmation; however, we are happy to put insurance on the submission. If you wish to have your artwork insured for the return journey, please include sufficient funds and indicate your preference in a postcard or letter enclosed with your submission. Please do not attach postage to packaging, and do not send loose postage stamps. Contributors from outside the US, please send cash, check, or money order in US funds to Stampington & Company. For questions regarding your artwork, please send inquiries to artmanagement@stampington.com."

WILLOW & SAGE

22992 Mill Creek Dr., Laguna Hills CA 92653. E-mail: willowandsage@stampington.com. Website: www.stampington.com/willow-and-sage. "This brand-new publication features stunning photography, alongside recipes for creating handmade items that soothe and replenish both body and soul. In addition to showcasing natural bath salts and soaks, soaps, face masks, sugar scrubs, how to use essential oils, and more, *Willow & Sage* magazine highlights the art of presentation —giving special attention to beautiful packaging—and reveals how to create fragrant spa kits and must-have gift bundles for any occasion."

HOW TO CONTACT "We prefer submissions of original art. If original art is not available, our next preference is high resolution digital images (300 dpi at 8½ × 10). If hi-res digital images are not available, we will very rarely consider professional-quality transparencies or color slides. Color-copy submissions are not accepted. All artwork must be identified with the artist's name, address, e-mail and phone number clearly printed on a label attached to each sample. Inscribe your name and address somewhere on each piece of art. If you desire acknowledgment of artwork receipt, please include a self-addressed stamped postcard. If the artwork is three-dimensional, please attach your identification with a removable string, or pack the sample in a plastic bag with your identification. If you have a unique artistic technique you'd like to share with others, please send samples of your artwork accompanied by a query letter outlining your article idea to the respective Managing Editor at: *Willow & Sage*, 22992 Mill Creek Drive, Laguna Hills, CA 92653. Managing editors also welcome brief e-mail inquiries."

NEEDS "Managing editors seek first-rate projects and encourage artists who have not published articles before to submit ideas, as editorial assistance will be provided."

TERMS Competitive editorial compensation is provided for all published articles. "We may hold your sample for an extended period of time—9 to 12 months is common. Due to the large volume of artwork we receive, Somerset Studio will return only those submissions accompanied by sufficient postage in the form of cash, check or money order made out to Stampington & Company. We can not offer delivery confirmation; however, we are happy to put insurance on the submission. If you wish to have your artwork insured for the return journey, please include sufficient funds and indicate your preference in a postcard or letter enclosed with your submission. Please do not attach postage to packaging, and do not send loose postage stamps. Contributors from outside the US, please send cash, check, or money order in US funds to Stampington & Company. For questions regarding your artwork, please send inquiries to artmanagement@stampington.com."

WOMAN'S DAY

300 W. 57th St., 28th flr., New York NY 10019. (212)649-2000. E-mail: womansday@hearst.com. Website: www.womansday.com. "*Woman's Day* is an indispensable resource to 20 million women. The brand speaks to our reader's values and focuses on what's important. We empower her with smart solutions for her core concerns—health, home, food, style and money, and celebrate the connection she cherishes with family, friends and community. Whether in-book, online, mobile or through social outlets, we provide inspiring insight and fresh ideas on how to get the most of everything."

HOW TO CONTACT "Our editors work almost exclusively with experienced writers who have clips from major national magazines. As a result, we accept unsolicited manuscripts only from writers with such credentials. There are no exceptions. If you do have significant national writing experience, and you have an idea or manuscript that you think might interest us, e-mail us at womansday@hearst.com, and please include some of your most recent clips."

⊚ WOODCARVING

E-mail: helen.chrystie@thegmcgroup.com. Website: www.thegmcgroup.com. "*Woodcarving*'s inspiring features, projects, technical articles and reviews have wide appeal—it is read in 57 countries worldwide. Featuring the work of top professionals and the most talented amateur carvers from around the world, it has a new, picture-led design which offers insight into the process of creating both great and humble carvings." Based in the United Kingdom.

WOODCARVING MAGAZINE

E-mail: editors@woodcarvingillustrated.com. Website: www.woodcarvingillustrated.com. Magazine about woodcarving.

WOODCRAFT MAGAZINE

P.O. Box 7020, Parkersburg WV 26102-7020. (304)865-5268. Fax: (304)420-9840. E-mail: kiah_harpool@woodcraftmagazine.com. Website: www.woodcraftmagazine.com.

CONTACT: Jim Harold, editor-in-chief. Estab. 2005. Bimonthly trade magazine. Circ. 115,662. Samples available on request.

HOW TO CONTACT Request via e-mail Accepts unsolicited submissions. Approached by 15 project/pattern designers/year. Has featured projects/patters by Andy Rae, Marlen Kemmet, Craig Bentzley. Preferred subjects: woodworking. Submission format: PDF or DOC files. Include brief description and photos. Submit print-ready photography and step-by-step/assembly diagrams for proposal. Model and property release required. Photo captions required. Submit color photos and illustrations via CD, zip, e-mail as TIFF or JPEG files.

TERMS Send e-mail with project text, concepts, samples, photographs and website. Keeps samples on file; send business card. Responds only if interested. Will negotiate rights with designers unwilling to sell. Finds freelancers by word-of-mouth.

TIPS "Read and understand the magazine."

WOODTURNING DESIGN

7 Waterloo Rd., Stanhope NJ 07874. (973)347-6900. Fax: (973)347-6909. E-mail: editors@woodturning-design.com. Website: www.woodturningdesign.com. **CONTACT:** Joseph Herrmann, editor. Estab. 2011. "In 2011, we began publishing six issues per year. Each issue features full color photos, step-by-step instructions, helpful hints, new techniques, product reviews and much, much more!"

HOW TO CONTACT Submissions should include introduction, complete list of materials, thorough step-by-step instructions, patterns, high quality photos, sidebar. Submission format: send on PC-formatted CD with the text in MS-Word or on 3.5" floppy disc. Photographs must be numbered and submitted separately along with a photo narration. Include a printed, hard copy of the text with the rest of your materials. 12 point, Times New Roman is the preferred type style.

TERMS Articles will be edited for grammar, spelling, length, style, and clarity. "Due to the number of articles we receive and the quality we require, we cannot guarantee that all will be published. If we choose your article, we will advise you of the issue number and date of publication—which is subject to change. And, we will need you to ship the ACTUAL finished project to be professionally photographed. Payment for the article will be made upon publication. If we

do not publish your article, your materials will be returned to you."

THE WORLD OF CROSS STITCHING

Immediate Media Co. Bristol, 9th Floor Tower House, Fairfax St., Bristol BS4 3DH United Kingdom. **CONTACT:** Ruth Southorn, editor. Estab. 1997. 4 weekly (13 issues/year) consumer magazine. "*The World of Cross Stitching* is a special interest magazine focusing on cross stitch projects with related cross stitch/needlework-based feature articles for an audience who are primarily women ranging in age from late 20s-early 50s." Circ. 39,457.

HOW TO CONTACT Request via e-mail. Accepts unsolicited submissions. Approached by 4 project/pattern designers/year. Buys 90 project/pattern designs per issue from freelancers. Has featured projects/patters by Joan Elliott, Maria Diaz, Jenny Barton, Susan Bates, Rhona Norrie, Margaret Sherry. Preferred subjects: cross stitch. Submission format: JPEG, computer generated cross stitch charts. Include concept, sketch, or computer designed chart. Model and property release preferred.

TERMS Send query letter or e-mail with résumé, project concepts, project samples and website. Keeps samples on file; provide self promotion piece to be kept for possible future assignment. Responds in 1 week. Pays $320 maximum for project/pattern design; $100 maximum for industry related articles; pay also varies based on experience, design complexity, size of design. Credit line given. Pays on publication. Buys publication (digital & print) and syndication rights only. Finds freelancers through agent/reps, submissions, word-of-mouth, magazines, online. Undergoes technical edit before publication.

TIPS "Definitely read our magazine for indication of current style/fresh feel required. I am interested in a wide variety of design subject themes and techniques (e.g. whole stitch only vs. factional stitch, blackwork/assisi, techniques using specialty threads/metallic thread accents/bead detailing for more complex designs). When contacting me, let me know some details of your typical design style/interests, details of any particular subject areas which you are specifically interested in, with my requirements in mind. It is imperative that I can rely on freelance designers to adhere to our strict deadlines. The majority of our projects are worked on 14-count white aida to suit our audience, however, evenweave/linen fabrics are regularly used too, along with hand dyed fabrics. Although it is not common for me to accept designs as a result of direct submission, it has occasionally happened. It is more common that I discover a new freelance designer as a result of them getting in touch. When submitting ideas please indicate: 1)a suggestion of the finished design size (stitch count) and suggestion(s) for fabric usage; 2)ideas of color palatte to be used, if a pencil sketch only and color submission is not supplied; 3)

indication of techniques involved, so that I might get an idea of what experience level of stitcher will enjoy this design; 4)any ideas for possible finishing."

⟲ YARN MAGAZINE

Website: www.artwearpublications.com.au/ subscriptions/yarn-magazine.html. "Features patterns covering a wide range of skill sets and techniques, from beginner to advanced." Based in Australia.

ONLINE COMMUNITIES

The actual act of crafting—working with our hands to create a unique item—can be, by its very nature, solitary. Most of the time, crafting is a one-person job, and working from a home studio can be isolating. That's why it's so important to become part of the craft community. Connecting with other people who understand what you do and the personal toll it can take is valuable for a myriad of reasons. Not only do communities of like-minded people help encourage and inspire one another, they can be a valuable resource when questions arise. It's likely that you are not the first person to have a certain question or run up against a certain problem, and a member of your community will almost always be willing to lend a helping hand or offer an opinion. Remember to give back as much as you take! If you can help out another member of your community, lending a helping hand makes for a stronger group.

In the same way, keep in mind that the very community you look to for advice and support may also be your primary sales demographic! Joining a community as a member first and a seller second (or last!) makes real relationships built on trust—not commerce—possible. Look through the following listings for national organizations and online groups that are applicable to you and your craft, but also look into your local community for small craft groups that can provide in-person interaction. Searching through Meetup.com is a good way to find local groups with similar interests, as well as asking at your favorite craft store. If no groups exist, consider starting your own. Join a guild or take a class at a local shop, and begin building relationships. Soon, you'll know enough people to form a mini group with the exact focus you had in mind.

Break out of your studio every so often and check in with your fellow crafters. They may turn into your biggest supporters and your most reliable market research.

KEY TO SYMBOLS & ABBREVIATIONS

☮	Canadian market
☀	market located outside of the U.S. and Canada
⌂	market prefers to work with local artists/designers
b&w	black & white (photo or illustration)
SASE	self-addressed, stamped envelope
SAE	self-addressed envelope
IRC	International Reply Coupon, for use when mailing to countries other than your own

COMPLAINT PROCEDURE

If you feel you have not been treated fairly by a company listed in *Crafter's Market*, we advise you to take the following steps:

- First, try to contact the company. Sometimes one e-mail or letter can quickly clear up the matter.
- Document all your correspondence with the company. If you write to us with a complaint, provide the details of your submission, the date of your first contact with the company, and the nature of your subsequent correspondence.
- We will enter your complaint into our files.
- The number and severity of complaints will be considered in our decision whether to delete the listing from the next edition.
- We reserve the right to not list any company for any reason.

ALLIANCE FOR SUSTAINABLE ARTS PROFESSIONAL PRACTICES

Website: www.arflock.org. Estab. 2008. The Alliance for Sustainable Arts Professional Practices is a coalition of not-for-profit arts institutions in the New York area that shares resources, methods and best practices with artists as they build and manage their professional lives. Membership cost: Annual dues are based upon the organization's current operating budge (see website for details). Membership restrictions: nonprofit organizations offering professional practices programs. Goal/mission: "to identify overlaps and gaps in offerings, assist in inter-organizational collaborations, and to strengthen each individual organization's visibility and outreach to the arts community." Who should join: not-for-profit arts organizations and arts-related businesses dedicated to sharing professional development opportunities and best practice resources with artists in the New York City area.

AMERICAN CRAFT COUNCIL

(612)206-3100. E-mail: council@craftcouncil.org. Website: www.craftcouncil.org. Estab. 1943. National/international guild, professional resource. Membership cost: standard, $40/yr ($55/yr outside U.S.); professional, $55/yr. Membership restrictions: standard, none; professional, craft artists. Goal/mission: "We champion craft." Who should join: students, collectors, scholars, enthusiasts, craft artists. Sells advertisement space on website, in magazine; contact Joanne Smith (jsmith@craftcouncil.org) for advertising rates.
TIPS "Know the best practices when woodworking. From safety to tool use, to finishes and types of wood. It's important to have a wide range of woodworking knowledge and be able to express it on camera or in writing. Our videos & articles are a great resource for all level of woodworkers. We have over 400 articles & 400 videos which have in-depth woodworking instructions. We encourage woodworkers to get back in the shop."

AMERICAN NEEDLEPOINT GUILD

(608)443-2476. Fax: (608)443-2474; (608)443-2478. E-mail: membership@needlepoint.org. Website: www. needlepoint.org. Estab. 1972. National/international guild, online community, online forum, professional resource. Membership cost: $40/yr; Canada/Mexico $52/yr; all other international $60/yr; lifetime $2,000; international lifetime $2,200. Membership restrictions: none. Goal/mission: "educational and cultural development through participation in and encouragement of interest in the art of needlepoint." Who should join: all stitchers.

AMERICAN QUILTER'S SOCIETY

(270)898-7903; (800)626-5420. Fax: (270)898-1173. Website: www.americanquilter.com. Estab. 1984. National/international guild, online community, online forum, professional resource. Membership cost: $25/yr. Membership restrictions: standard, none; professional, craft artists. Goal/mission: to provide a forum for quilters of all skill levels to expand their horizons in quilt making, design, self-expression, and quilt collecting. Who should join: quilters. Sells advertisement space on website, in magazine; see website for media kit and advertising specifics.

AMERICAN SEWING GUILD

(713)729-3000. Fax: (713)721-9230. Website: www.asg. org. Estab. 1984. National/international guild, online community, online forum, professional resource, professional networking tool. Membership cost: varies, see website. Membership restrictions: none. Goal/mission: to help members learn new sewing skills, network with others who share an interest in sewing and participate in community service sewing projects. Who should join: sewing enthusiasts. Sells advertisement space through magazine; e-mail (advertising@asg.org) for rates.

THE ART QUILT ASSOCIATION

Grand Junction CO. E-mail: info@theartquilt association.com. Website: www.theartquiltassociation.com. Estab. 1996. National/international guild, professional resource. Membership cost: $25/yr. Membership restrictions: none. Mission/goal: "to explore textile manipulation and diversity of mixed media as an art form." Who should join: those interested in art quilt.

ASSOCIATION OF SEWING AND DESIGN PROFESSIONALS

(877)755-0303. E-mail: admin@sewingprofessionals.org. Website: www.paccprofessionals.org. Estab. 1984. National/international guild, online community, online forum, professional resource, professional networking tool. Membership cost: varies, see website. Membership restrictions: none. Goal/mission: to support individuals engaged in sewing and design related businesses, in both commercial and home-based settings. Educating the general public about the unique and valuable services offered by sewing and design professionals. Who should join: sewing professionals. Sells advertisement space in newsletter; e-mail (advertising@sewingprofessionals.org.) for rates or see website.

BURDA STYLE

Website: www.burdastyle.com. Estab. 2007. Online community, online forum. Membership cost: none. Membership restrictions: none. Goal/mission: to bring the traditional craft of sewing to a new generation of fashion designers, sewing hobbyists, DIYers and anyone looking to sew something. Who should join: people passionate about sewing. Sells advertisement space; e-mail (maryeveholder@comcast.net) for rates or see website.

CERAMIC ARTS DAILY

(614)794-5843. Fax: (614)794-5842. Website: www.ceramicartsdaily.org. Online community, online forum. Membership cost: none. Membership restrictions: none. Goal/mission: "CeramicArtsDaily.org provides a wide array of tools for learning about and improving skills, and a place for artists to display their work and to share ideas and perspectives about how their art and life interact to shape each other." Who should join: active potters & ceramic artists; those interested in learning about ceramics. Sells advertisement space; e-mail (mbracht@ceramics.org) for rates or see website.

CLAYSTATION

Website: www.claystation.com. Online community, online forum. Membership cost: none. Membership restrictions: none. Goal/mission: "to be a social research network for the ceramic arts." Who should join: people with an interest in ceramic arts. Sells advertisement space; see website for rates.

CRAFT & HOBBY ASSOCIATION

319 E 54th St., Elmwood Park NJ 07407. (201)835-1200. E-mail: info@craftandhobby.org. Website: www.craftandhobby.org. Estab. 2004. National/international guild, online community, online forum, professional resource, virtual classroom, professional networking tool. Membership cost: varies. Membership restrictions: none. Goal/mission: "to create a vibrant industry with an exciting image, an expanding customer base and successful members." Who should join: suppliers, buyers, industry professionals in craft. Sells advertisement space; see website for rates.

CRAFT BANTER

Website: www.craftbanter.com. Online forum. Membership cost: none. Membership restrictions: none. Goal/mission: "to be a craft forum acting as a gateway to the finest craft related newsgroups." Who should join: people interested in crafts.

CRAFTSTER

Website: www.craftster.org. Online community. Membership cost: none. Membership restrictions: none. Goal/mission: provide a community for indie crafts. Who should join: people interested in crafts. Sells advertisement; see website for details.

CRAFT YARN COUNCIL OF AMERICA

(704)824-7838. Fax: (704)671-2366. Website: www.craftyarncouncil.com. Online community, online forum, professional resource. Membership cost: none. Membership restrictions: none. Goal/mission: "to provide educational resources." Who should join: yarn companies, accessory manufacturers, magazine, book publishers, and consultants in the yarn industry.

○ THE CROCHET CROWD

10 Mullen Drive, P.O. Box 473, Walkerton ON N0G 2V0, Canada. E-mail: MikeysHelpDesk@hotmail.com. Website: www.thecrochetcrowd.com. Estab. 2008. Online community, online forum. Membership

cost: none. Membership restrictions: none. Mission/ goal: "to educate the consumer which leads to confident feel good buying power from the consumer that benefits distributors & manufacturers." Who should join: those interested in crochet. Sells advertisement; see website for details.

CROCHET GUILD OF AMERICA

1100-H Brandywine Blvd., Zanesville OH 43701. (740)452-4541. Fax: (740)452-2552. Website: www. crochet.org. National/international guild, online forum. Membership cost: varies. Membership restrictions: none. Goal/mission: to educate the public about crochet, provide education and networking opportunities, and set a national standard for the quality, art and skill of crochet through creative endeavors. Who should join: all those who desire to perpetuate the art and skill of crochet.

CROCHET ME

Website: www.crochetme.com. Online community. Membership cost: free. Membership restrictions: none. Who should join: those interested in crochet. Sells advertisement; see website for information.

CROCHETVILLE

Website: www.crochetville.com. Estab. 2004. Online community. Membership cost: none. Membership restrictions: none. Who should join: those interested in crochet.

DEVIANTART

Website: www.deviantart.com. Online community. Preferred subjets: art. Membership cost: none. Membership restrictions: none. Goal/mission: "to entertain, inspire, and empower the artist in all of us." Who should join: artists & art enthusiasts. Sells advertisement on website.

EMBROIDERER'S GUILD OF AMERICA

1355 Bardstown Rd., Suite 157, Louisville KY 40204. (502)589-6956. Fax: (502)584-7900. Website: www. egausa.org. Estab. 1970. National/international guild. Membership cost: varies. Membership restrictions: none. Goal/mission: "to promote cooperation and the exchange of ideas among those who are engaged in needlework throughout the world." Who should join: anyone interested in embroidery.

GANOKSIN

E-mail: service@ganoksin.com. Website: www.ganoksin.com. Estab. 1970. Online community, online forum, professional resource. Preferred subjects: gem & jewelry. Membership cost: none. Membership restrictions: none. Goal/mission: "to educate, improve working conditions and facilitate sharing between goldsmiths globally." Who should join: jewelers, professionals, hobbyists. Sells advertisement on website, e-mail blasts, and online video network; see website for rates.

❥ THE GUILD OF JEWELLERY DESIGNERS

Hockley, Birmingham West Midlands , United Kingdom. E-mail: alan@guildofjewellerydesigners.co.uk. Website: www.guildofjewellerydesigners.co.uk. International guild, online community, online forum. Membership cost: free; various paid options. Membership restrictions: none. Mission/goal: "to help promote UK jewellery designers." Who should join: Jewelery designers based in the UK. Sells advertisement; see website for details.

HANDMADE ARTISTS

P.O. Box 530, Point Pleasant NJ 08742. E-mail: admin@handmadeartistsshop.com. Website: www. handmadeartists.com. Online community, online forum. Membership cost: none. Membership restrictions: none. Goal/mission: "community of people banded together in an effort to support each other and handmade." Who should join: creative people who work with their hands.

HOME SEWING ASSOCIATION

P.O. Box 369, Monroeville PA 15146. E-mail: admin@ handmadeartistsshop.com. Website: www.sewing. org. Online community, online forum. Membership cost: none. Membership restrictions: none. Sells advertisement; see website for rates.

INDIE BUSINESS NETWORK

206-B N. Hayne St., Monroe NC 28112. (908)444-6343. Website: www.indiebusinessnetwork.com. Online community, online forum, professional resource, professional networking tool. Membership cost: varies. Membership restrictions: none. Goal/mission: to empower and to encourage the success of creative entrepreneurs. Who should join: manufacturers of handmade soaps, cosmetics, candles, artisan perfumes, aromatherapy products, jewelry, baked goods, confections and other artisinal consumer products.

INSTRUCTABLES

E-mail: info@instructables.com. Website: www.instructables.com. Online community, online forum, virtual classroom. Membership cost: free; paid options also available. Membership restrictions: none. Goal/mission: to share projects, connect with others, and make an impact on the world. Who should join: creative people who make things. Sells advertisement; see website for details.

INTERNATIONAL POLYMER CLAY ASSOCIATION

162 Lake St., Haverhill MA 01832. Website: www.theipca.org. National/international guild, professional resource. Membership cost: varies. Membership restrictions: none. Goal/mission: to educate the public about polymer clay, and to study and promote an interest in the use of polymer clay as an artistic medium. Who should join: those interested in the art of polymer clay.

INTERNATIONAL QUILT ASSOCIATION

7660 Woodway, Suite 550, Houston TX 77063. (713)781-6882. Fax: (713)781-8182. E-mail: iqa@quilts.com. Website: www.quilts.org. Estab. 1979. Non-profit organization. Membership cost: varies. Membership restrictions: only open to individuals. Goal/mission: "dedicated to the preservation of the art of quilting, the attainment of public recognition for quilting as an art form, and the advancement of the state of the art throughout the world." Who should join: individuals interested in the art of quilting.

JEWELRY MAKING DAILY

Website: www.jewelrymakingdaily.com. Estab. 1979. Online community, online forum. Membership cost: free. Membership restrictions: none. Who should join: those interested in jewelry making. Sells advertisement; see website for details.

KNITTER'S REVIEW

Website: www.knittersreview.com. Online community, online forum. Membership cost: free. Membership restrictions: none. Goal/mission: "to provide quality product information to help knitters make informed purchasing decisions and, ultimately, have a more fulfilling lifelong knitting experience." Who should join: serious fiber enthusiasts of all skill levels.

✎ KNITTING & CROCHET GUILD

Unit 4, Lee Mills Industrial Estate, St Georges Road, Scholes Holmfirth HD9 1RT, United Kingdom. E-mail: secretary@kcguild.org.uk. Website: www.kcguild.org.uk. Estab. 1978. International guild. Membership cost: varies. Membership restrictions: none. Goal/mission: "to share and develop skills, knowledge and enthusiasm about hand knitting, machine knitting and crochet." Who should join: all levels of quilters.

KNITTING DAILY

Website: www.knittingdaily.com. Online community, online forum. Membership cost: free. Membership restrictions: none. Who should join: those interested in knitting. Sells advertisement; see website for details.

THE KNITTING GUILD ASSOCIATION

1100-H Brandywine Blvd., Zanesville OH 43701-7303. (740)452-4541. E-mail: TKGA@TKGA.com. Website: www.tkga.com. National/international guild, local guild, online community, online forum. Membership cost: varies. Membership restrictions: none. Mission/goal: "representing you and your stitching art to the world." Who should join: knitters. Sells advertisement in magazine; see website for details.

KNITTING HELP

P.O. Box 3306, Amherst CA 01004. E-mail: amy@knittinghelp.com. Website: www.knittinghelp.com. Estab. 2004. Online community, online forum, virtual classroom. Membership cost: free. Membership restrictions: none. Who should join: those interested in knitting. Sells advertisement; contact sheldon@knittinghelp.com for details.

KNITTING PARADISE

382 N.E. 191st St., #74906, Miami FL 33179. E-mail: info@knittingparadise.com. Website: www.knittingparadise.com. Online community, online forum. Membership cost: free. Membership restrictions: none. Who should join: those interested in knitting.

KNITTING UNIVERSE

P.O. Box 965, Sioux Falls SD 57101-0965. (800)232-5648. Fax: (605)338-2994. Website: www.knittinguniverse.com. Online community. Membership cost: none. Membership restrictions: none. Who should join: all levels of knitters.

THE MODERN QUILT GUILD

4470 W. Sunset Blvd., #226, Los Angeles CA 90027. (740)452-4541. E-mail: info@themodernquiltguild.com. Website: www.themodernquiltguild.com. Estab. 2009. National/international guild, local guild, online community, online forum. Membership cost: varies. Membership restrictions: none. Mission/goal: "to support and encourage the growth and development of modern quilting through art, education, and community." Who should join: modern quilters.

NATIONAL ACADEMY OF NEEDLE ARTS

E-mail: membership@needleart.org. Website: www.needleart.org. Estab. 1985. National/international guild, professional resource. Membership cost: varies. Membership restrictions: none. Mission/goal: "to educate and elevate needlework to NeedleART in the works of creative expression known as art." Who should join: those interested in needlework.

THE NATIONAL NEEDLE ARTS ASSOCIATION

1100-H Brandywine Blvd., Zanesville OH 43701-7303. (800)889-8662; (740)455-6773. E-mail: info@tnna.org. Website: www.tnna.org. Membership organization, professional resource, professional networking tool. Membership cost: varies. Membership restrictions: open only to verifiable businesses providing services and/or products for the needlearts industry. Mission/goal: "The National NeedleArts Association advances its community of professional businesses by encouraging the passion for needlearts through education, industry knowledge exchange and a strong marketplace." Who should join: businesses providing services and/or products for the needlearts industry.

THE NATIONAL QUILTING ASSOCIATION

P.O. Box 12190, Columbus OH 43212-0190. (614)488-8520. Fax: (614)488-8521. Website: www.nqaquilts.org. Estab. 1970. Nonprofit organization. Membership cost: varies. Membership restrictions: none. Mission/goal: "The National Quilting Association, Inc. promotes the art, craft, and legacy of quiltmaking, encouraging high standards through education, preservation, and philanthropic endeavors." Who should join: quilters.

OH MY! HANDMADE GOODNESS

Website: www.ohmyhandmade.com. Estab. 2010. Online community, professional resource. Membership cost: see website. Membership restrictions: none. Mission/goal: "gather makers & entrepreneurs to cooperatively share their knowledge, resources, peer support, and mentorship." Who should join: creative makers & entrepreneurs. Sells advertisement; see website for details.

PALMER/PLETSCH

1801 N.W., Upshur St., Suite 100, Portland OR 97209. Website: www.palmerpletsch.com. Professional resource, virtual classroom. Membership cost: see website for details. Membership restrictions: none. Who should join: those interested in sewing.

PINTEREST

Website: www.pinterest.com. Online community. Membership cost: free. Membership restrictions: none. Who should join: anyone.

PRECIOUS METAL CLAY GUILD

Website: www.pmcguild.com. National/international guild, local guild, online community, professional resource. Membership cost: free. Membership restrictions: none. Mission/goal: "to serve as the ambassador of Precious Metal Clay™." Who should join: those interested in working with precious metal clay.

QUILTERS CLUB OF AMERICA

(888)253-0203. E-mail: admin@quiltersclubof america.com. Website: www.quiltersclubofamerica. com. Affinity quilting club, online community. Membership cost: free; $29.95/yr. Membership restrictions: none. Mission/goal: "to help members enhance their knowledge, skill, and enjoyment of quilting." Who should join: enthusiastic quilters.

QUILTING BOARD

E-mail: info@quiltingboard.com. Website: www. quiltingboard.com. Online forum. Membership cost: free. Membership restrictions: none. Who should join: quilters.

QUILTING DAILY

Website: www.quiltingdaily.com. Online community, online forum. Membership cost: free. Membership restrictions: none. Who should join: those interested in quilting. Sells advertisement; see website for details.

RAVELRY

203 Washington St., #244, Salem MA 01970. Website: www.ravelry.com. Online community. Membership cost: free. Membership restrictions: none. Who should join: knitters & crocheters. Sells advertisement; see website for details.

SCRAPBOOKING SOCIETY

Website: www.scrapbookingsociety.com. Online community. Membership cost: free. Membership restrictions: none. Who should join: those interested in scrapbooking. Sells advertisement; see website for details.

SEAMS

4921-C Broad River Rd., Columbia SC 29212. (803)772-5861. Fax: (803)731-7709. E-mail: info@ seams.org. Website: www.seams.org. Non-profit organization, professional resource. Membership cost: varies. Membership restrictions: none. Mission/goal: "to support the resurging U.S. sewn products industry by using membership networking and collaboration, offering members benefit packages that help control overhead expenses, giving members access to educational programs to help improve the quality and productivity of their companies and the industry as a whole, and keeping members informed about legislation in Washington, D.C., that may impact the industry." Who should join: sewn products manufacturing and contract manufacturing companies and their suppliers.

STUDIO ART QUILT ASSOCIATES

P.O. Box 572, Storrs CT 06268-0572. (860)487-4199. E-mail: info@SAQA.com. Website: www.saqa.com. Estab. 1989. Non-profit organization, professional resource. Membership cost: varies. Membership restrictions: none. Mission/goal: "to promote the art quilt through education, exhibitions, professional development, documentation, and publications." Who should join: artists, teachers, collectors, gallery owners, museum curators and corporate sponsors.

THE SWITCHBOARDS

Website: www.theswitchboards.com. Online community, online forum, professional resource, professional networking tool. Membership cost: $12/month; $97/yr. Membership restrictions: none. Mission/goal: "TSB is an online hub that plays hostess to crafty and crafty service-related businesses." Who should join: crafters, bloggers, web designers, photographers, artists, coaches.

TEXTILE SOCIETY OF AMERICA

P.O. Box 5617, Berkeley CA 94705. (510)363-4541. E-mail: tsa@textilesociety.org. Website: www.textilesocietyofamerica.org. Estab. 1987. Non-profit organization, professional resource. Membership cost: varies. Membership restrictions: none. Mission/goal: "dedicated to promoting and exchanging knowledge about textiles." Who should join: those interested in textiles.

WEAVOLUTION

7 St. Paul St., Suite 1660, Baltimore MD 21202. Website: www.weavolution.com. Online community, online forum. Membership cost: none. Membership restrictions: none. Mission/goal: "to have a website exclusively for handweavers where members could post drafts, pictures, details about their projects and to share ideas and struggles with each other." Who should join: handweavers.

WOODWORKERS GUILD OF AMERICA

Website: www.wwgoa.com. Contact: George Vondriska, managing editor. National/international guild, online community, professional resource. Preferred subjects: woodworking. Membership cost: free or paid; premium membership $29.98/year. Membership restrictions: none. Goal/mission: "to provide our members with the best instructional woodworking videos, articles adn plans on the internet. As well as foster a community where woodworkers can join together to share ideas & experiences." Who should join: woodworkers of all levels. Hires crafters/artisans as speakers/lecturers, blog/online article writers, online video talent. Sells advertisement space on website, newsletter, e-mail blasts; contact Jim Kopp (jimk@wwgoa.com) for advertising rates & options. Site traffic: 10,000 visits per day; 5,500 unique visits per day; 41,495 Facebook fans.

TIPS "Know the best practices when woodworking. From safety to tool use, to finishes and types of wood. It's important to have a wide range of woodworking knowledge and be able to express it on camera or in writing. Our videos & articles are a great resource for all level of woodworkers. We have over 400 articles & 400 videos which have in-depth woodworking instructions. We encourage woodworkers to get back in the shop."

INDEX

REGIONAL CRAFT
SHOW INDEX

Colorado

Indiana

Iowa

Kansas

SUBJECT INDEX

CROCHET

HOLIDAY

JEWELRY

KNITTING

MIXED MEDIA

SEWING

OTHER

GENERAL INDEX

CRAFT A BETTER BUSINESS!

These and other F+W titles are available online, or from your favorite craft retailer or bookstore.